ACA Simplified

Strategic Business Management Exam Room Notes 2020

D0318342

ICAEW
PARTNER IN
LEARNING

Recognised as an ICAEW Partner in Learning, working with ICAEW in the professional development of students

ICAEW takes no responsibility for the content of any supplemental training materials supplied by the Partner in Learning.

Disclaimer

The text in this book does not amount to professional advice on any particular technical matter and should not be taken as such. No reliance should be placed on the content as the basis for any investment or other decision or in connection with any advice given to third parties.

ACA Simplified expressly disclaims all liability for any losses or other claims, whether direct, indirect, incidental, consequential or otherwise arising in relation to the use of these materials.

We have made every effort to ensure that the materials are accurate and free from error. Please inform us immediately if you believe that you have discovered any problems with the text.

Whilst we strongly believe that our learning materials are an effective method of preparing for your examinations, ACA Simplified does not accept any liability whatsoever for your ultimate performance in the examination as a result of using this text.

Other ACA Simplified Resources for CR and SBM (and a discount!)

In addition to this book, we provide a range of other study resources for CR and SBM.

On-Demand Video Tuition

Our popular on-demand video courses provide a convenient way to obtain expert tutor guidance for CR and SBM. Our courses can be viewed at any time and as often as you wish – perfect for revising the tricky technical areas of the syllabus!

Our courses contain advice on examination technique, planning methods and time management. We also provide a large number of Tutor Talkthroughs of past paper, Question Bank and ICAEW Mock questions, helping you to identify the patterns in terms of what is rewarded in the model answer each time a topic is tested. This method of reviewing model answers in "batches" of examples on the same topic can be very effective as it teaches you what the examiners are going to be looking for every time. We also review the mark allocation in past paper answers so that you can understand how to allocate your time effectively.

As a thank you for purchasing this book, we are delighted to offer you a **10% discount on the 2020 edition of our CR or SBM on-demand courses (or both!)**. Simply email us with your proof of purchase for this book and we will be in touch to explain how to obtain discounted access to the relevant course(s). For administrative and technical reasons, this offer is only available if you contact us **before** purchasing your on-demand course(s): **retrospective discounts will not be provided**. Your discount request must be received no later than 31 July 2020 (in respect of the rearranged July/August 2020 sitting) and no later than 15 October 2020 (in respect of the November 2020 sitting). This offer is limited to one discount per course per original purchaser of this book: no discount will be provided on any second-hand purchase of the book. No cash alternative will be provided. This offer is not available to students on our classroom CR or SBM tuition courses as access to our on-demand courses is already provided for free as part of our classroom course fee. We regret that we cannot make this offer available to any students whose access to our on-demand courses is paid for by their employer: our offer is only available to students who are purchasing in a personal capacity. Please allow 5 working days for access instructions to be sent by email. All other aspects of the discount are subject to our reasonable discretion and the offer may be withdrawn at any time without notice.

For further information on our on-demand courses, including a free video explanation of how the courses work, please see our website at **www.acasimplified.com**.

Further Study Books and Exam Room Notes

We produce interactive, self-test Q&A books for Advanced Level financial reporting and Advanced Level audit and assurance. We have condensed and simplified the syllabus content into hundreds of short-form questions that help you learn by testing yourself – much more effective than trying to learn simply by reading from the page or making notes. Our Q&As provide an ideal way to build your technical knowledge so that you can then attempt full exam-standard questions on the basis of a firmer foundation of understanding.

In addition to this set of Exam Room Notes for SBM, we provide sets of Exam Room Notes covering financial reporting and audit & assurance for the Advanced Level.

Other ACA Simplified Resources for CR and SBM (and a discount!)

The Advanced Level examiners are always highly critical of weaknesses in brought-forward knowledge and a very large proportion of financial reporting marks at the Advanced Level are actually available for FAR syllabus content so our *Advanced Level Financial Reporting Exam Room Notes 2020* provide reminder notes on all key areas. Our *Advanced Level Financial Reporting Exam Room Notes 2020* are useful for both the Corporate Reporting and Strategic Business Management papers.

Our *Audit & Assurance Exam Room Notes 2020* book covers not only audit risks & procedures but also provides quick reference notes on specialist assurance areas such as Corporate Governance, internal auditing, social and environmental auditing, and other areas. Our *Audit & Assurance Exam Room Notes 2020* therefore provide you with coverage for all types of audit and assurance question in both CR and SBM.

This set of *Strategic Business Management Exam Room Notes 2020* is the only set of Advanced Level Exam Room Notes which are specific to a particular Advanced Level paper – our other 2 sets of Advanced Level Exam Room Notes (*Advanced Level Audit & Assurance Exam Room Notes 2020* and *Advanced Level Financial Reporting Exam Room Notes 2020*) are useful for **both** CR and SBM.

For further information on these resources, please see our website at **www.acasimplified.com**.

Contents – Complete Alphabetical Listing

Fixed / Variable loan -> QB Pg. 473

Working Capital / operating Cycle -> QB Pg. ? Q 13

Things to consider for international expansions -> Q 8
Exchange rates also

Disposal of Sub -> QB Q 39

Parent controlling Sub -> QB Q 20

Share for Share exchange -> QB ~~Q 40~~ Q29

Key risks, due diligence for acquisitions -> QB ~~Q 40~~ Q29

Share buyback -> Pg 442

Bond risks -> Pg 577 QB

Directors Duties / Ethics -> Pg 578 QB

Contents – Listed by Topic Area

Acquisitions

Assurance (Specialist Audit & Assurance topics)

Risk and Risk Management

Valuations

Working Capital and Treasury Management

SBM Technique Issues

List of Formulae

Please also see our Ratios – Calculations section on page 356.

Exam tip – remember to take in your own set of annuity tables – these will not be provided!

CAPM

$k_e = r_f + \beta_e (r_m - r_f)$

Degearing and Regearing for CAPM

$\beta e = \beta a\ [(E + D(1 - T)) / E]$

Therefore, to de-gear: $\beta a = \beta e \times [E / (E + D(1 - T))]$ where βe is average equity beta for the market

Then to re-gear: $\beta e = \beta a\ [(E + D(1 - T)) / E]$ using the βa derived from the above de-gearing step

Perpetuity with no growth

$$\frac{earnings\ or\ cash\ flow}{discount\ rate}$$

Perpetuity with positive growth

$$\frac{earnings\ or\ cash\ flow\ x\ (1 + g)}{(discount\ rate - g)}$$

Perpetuity with negative growth

$$\frac{earnings\ or\ cash\ flow\ x\ (1 - g)}{(discount\ rate + g)}$$

WACC

$WACC = k_e \times (E / E + D) + k_d \times (D / E + D)$

How To Use This Book

Thank you for purchasing this set of *Strategic Business Management Exam Room Notes 2020*. This book provides you with notes on over 100 key SBM scenario areas, all summarised into condensed and alphabetically-organised sections for super-quick usage under time pressure.

The Strategic Business Management (SBM) examination is a very open assessment: this is indicated by the extremely long Study Manual and the fact that "strategic management" can include a wide range of topics. You will have to generate your business ideas very quickly under time pressure but with so many potential areas to have to learn about, we thought it would be helpful to produce a simple, clear and quick reference set of reminders of what to write to ensure that you are **sticking closely enough to the kinds of points that are going to score marks**, rather than just writing good general business ideas.

The Expected Mark Allocation in SBM

The examiners have confirmed that the standard weightings in a typical SBM examination will always be as follows:

Topic	Standard weighting
Strategy	35-45%
Finance, valuations & investment appraisal	30-40%
Financial reporting[1]	15-20%
Assurance	10%
Ethics	5-10%

From the above we can see that the areas covered in this set of Exam Room Notes (we cover all elements except financial reporting, although we do include **some** financial reporting notes: see below) should generally account for **80-85%** of the marks in SBM. It is thus absolutely vital that you get accustomed to how these Exam Room Notes work and where to find the information under time pressure.

At the SBM Workshops at the recent ICAEW Tutor Conferences, the examiners have stated that SBM draws heavily on brought-forward knowledge from Business Strategy and Financial Management for the strategy and finance elements above (65-85% of the marks) but the examiners have also reminded tutors that the following topics are entirely new at the SBM level:

- Strategic marketing and brand management
- Supply chain management

[1] The examiners generally use the term "corporate reporting" to refer to this topic but because we think this may lead to confusion with the separate Corporate Reporting ACA paper, we have adopted the term "financial reporting" instead. By "financial reporting" we do **not** just mean the lessons that you learned in the Financial Accounting & Reporting paper at the Professional Level but also the new IFRS corporate reporting rules that you learn at the Advanced Level.

- Operations management
- Corporate Governance (meaning the appropriate governance structure for a business rather than testing the detailed rules of the UK Corporate Governance Code or similar codes: an awareness of the general content of the UK Corporate Governance Code is, however, expected for SBM)
- Human Resource Management
- Information strategy
- Performance management
- Treasury and working capital management

We would expect the examiner team to have the above list in front of them when designing an SBM examination in order to distinguish SBM from the examinations that candidates will already have passed at the Professional Level so please do check any SBM syllabus content on the above areas very carefully.

Please note that for the purposes of these Exam Room Notes, we have not necessarily created sections which are named in a way which matches the above headings as this may not always be the best way of organising and splitting out our notes – instead, we have in some cases included relevant points from within the above list of headings under other topic areas, based on how we would prefer to organise the information. In other cases (such as Corporate Governance, Treasury Operations and Working Capital), the section names for our notes in these Exam Room Notes do map closely to the above list of new topic areas as we feel that this does represent an appropriate way of organising our notes but, again, we have not done this in relation to all topics.

Memory Joggers and See Also Reminders

Under examination pressure, it is quite normal to find it harder to think of ideas than when you are more relaxed … but unfortunately in an examination you only have a limited time to generate those ideas (and much less time than you would have in a real-world assignment).

Examination nerves can also lead to the ultimate examination nightmare of a **mind blank**, something that is highly unlikely ever to happen to you outside the examination hall.

We have produced this set of Exam Room Notes to help you avoid these problems and thus improve the quality of your answers. Our Exam Room Notes are designed to stimulate ideas and remind you of areas that you may not have otherwise considered: we hope that this will give you the required range and breadth of points, preventing you from overdeveloping just a few basic ideas (something that can happen when you only have 1 or 2 useful things to say). As set out in our sister book *Smashing SBM™ – How to Pass the ACA Strategic Business Management Examination*, the SBM examiners want to see a broad **range** of ideas and therefore lots of **different** ideas, rather than just 1 or 2 very detailed points. By providing you with many different options in any given scenario or topic, our Exam Room Notes will help you to develop the **range** that you need.

For this reason, please do make use of the "See also" reminders provided at the end of many sections of this book – we have taken quite a bit of time to carefully cross-reference certain topics so that you can spot the next logical link in the chain if you need more ideas. Our "See also" references also serve a very important purpose of reminding you of connected topic areas – sometimes the examination question will not specifically ask you to look at some of these areas: instead, you are just supposed to know that they are connected. So, again, do make use of these cross-references.

Methodology to Develop the Book

To ensure that you stick to points that will be rewarded, we have reviewed the following materials to develop this book:

1. **All available Strategic Business Management past papers, ICAEW Mock examinations and the Strategic Business Management Electronic Question Bank**
2. **TI Business Change Question Bank 2014-15**
3. **Corporate Reporting Study Manual 2020**
4. **Strategic Business Management Study Manual 2020**

We have used the Corporate Reporting Study Manual 2020 to create notes on what we call "Specialist Audit & Assurance" areas such as Internal Audit, auditing social and environmental statements and Agreed Upon Procedures: in other words, assurance types other than statutory audit. We know that non-statutory assurance is **very likely** to be tested in Strategic Business Management.

We have reviewed the TI Business Change Question Bank 2014-15 (old ACA syllabus) because the previous TI syllabus is very similar indeed to Strategic Business Management and the previous Business Change paper was set by the same examiner team that now writes the Strategic Business Management examinations. Also, business strategy ideas do not "date" in the same way as, for example, tax rules so it is entirely valid to use all these materials as part of the development of this book.

In developing these materials, we have also used the philosophy and methodology set out in our student-focused textbook *Smashing SBM™ – How to Pass the ACA Strategic Business Management Examination*. *Smashing SBM™* is really intended to be a "sister" publication to these *Exam Room Notes* in which we focus more on general examination technique for SBM and therefore on some of the things to consider before examination day when developing your examination strategy. On the other hand, this set of *Exam Room Notes* is more to do with the provision of quick reference reminders for use in the examination itself.

Many students successfully pass the examination by purchasing only these *Exam Room Notes* but we wanted to make you aware of our other popular SBM publication which focuses on a different aspect of preparing for the examination.

Organisation of the Notes

Our *Exam Room Notes* are organised alphabetically so that you can very quickly access the correct topic areas. We provide 2 listings of topics:

1. Complete Alphabetical Listing

This listing provides all topics in alphabetical order, regardless of to what topic area or discipline (strategy, financial management, assurance, Ethics etc) the notes relate. Use this method if you know which specific topic you are looking for. (Or just flick through the book using the alphabetically-organised headings to help you locate the section that you need.)

2. Listed By Topic Area

This listing provides all topics grouped into several key thematic areas, based on typical scenarios examined in SBM:

Acquisitions

Assurance (Specialist Audit & Assurance topics)

Change and Change Management

Ethics

Finance

Financial Reporting Issues

Growth and Business Development

Investment Appraisal

Overseas Business Activities

Performance Management

Risk and Risk Management

Valuations

Working Capital and Treasury Management

SBM Technique Issues

Use this listing if you know the basic general area at which the question is driving but you are not quite sure which specific topics to look for. In other words, this second listing also serves as a kind of "memory jogger" or "idea generator".

2020 Syllabus Update Process

We have carefully reviewed the model answers to the 2 past papers set in 2019 to add a few further relevant points to these *Exam Room Notes*: however, in our opinion, nothing radical or unexpected arose from the 2019 past papers. Unfortunately, the questions in the ICAEW 2019 SBM Mocks were repeats of ICAEW Mock questions set in earlier years so we were not able to add much from this source either.

Unlike the very extensive updates in the 2019 syllabus (to allow for IFRS 9 and IFRS 15 becoming the main examinable standards at the Advanced Level), the updates to the 2020 syllabus are relatively modest so this is good news if you already studied for the SBM examination in 2019. The most important technical change relates to the fact that IFRS 16 is now the main examinable standard on leases, replacing the previous IAS 17.

Please refer to Appendix 1a and Appendix 1b of this book for a detailed review of all changes in the 2020 editions of the Corporate Reporting and Strategic Business Management Study Manuals, respectively. Please note that in the interests of completeness, Appendix 1a and Appendix 1b review all 2020 syllabus changes, rather than just those changes relating to the subject matter of this book (SBM). We have taken the decision to include all syllabus changes in Appendix 1a and Appendix 1b to avoid any risk of unintentionally deleting changes relevant to SBM through an editing down of our complete list of changes and also because, as an Advanced Level candidate, you need to be aware of all syllabus changes.

We have fully updated the text of this 2020 edition of our Exam Room Notes to take account of the above changes to both the SBM and CR Study Manuals.

Please Practise Some Exam Papers Using this Book!

Our *Exam Room Notes* are not something that you need to try to memorise before the examination: this is because, in an open book examination, you can always refer quickly to the book if needed. However, **this does not mean that you should just take our *Exam Room Notes* into the examination without doing any prior practice using the book**: if you did so, you would not know which topics were contained in the book and you would not know your own best personal method of using the notes. We have tried to place our notes under the most appropriate heading and where possible we have **duplicated** key points in the appropriate different sections so that you do not miss these depending on which heading you refer to – however, we do not know what the examination will test and therefore we do not know what combination of topics from this book will be relevant so it is important that you invest some time looking through the book so that you know where to find particular sections or points. Please do feel free to add your own annotations and cross-referencing if you feel this is useful to you individually, in order to find sections quickly under time pressure.

We **strongly recommend** that you use the book in quite a few Mock examination attempts: this is the only way to get to know how to make **best** use of our notes. You are obviously welcome to purchase our own original SBM Mock exams written to full ICAEW standards as part of your practice attempts! Please see **www.acasimplified.com** for further details on our original SBM Mock exams.

How Not to Use this Book

Please do not treat these *Exam Room Notes* as **points that you just copy out in the examination**: you must firstly ensure that you only pick **relevant** points and, secondly, you must take the general reminder included here and connect it to the specific examination scenario **data** in order to gain the credit. You can make this connection quite simply by quoting specific figures or people or products from within the examination data but just ensure that you are not simply copying out the reminders that we have included here with no additional added value points. **As a general rule, we would want you to be <u>starting</u> most of your sentences/paragraphs in an SBM answer with a scenario-specific point taken from the exam paper Exhibit material rather than from this book – this will ensure you are not just copying out our notes.**

Our aim is really to provide you with a list of "**reminders**" or "**memory joggers**" to help you make the connections and comments that the examiner wants to see – our aim is not to provide you with fully formed "ready-made" answers and **you will quite simply not be given the marks if you just copy out this book**.

Smashing SBM™ – How to Pass the ACA Strategic Business Management Examination 2020

This set of *Exam Room Notes* is designed to pair up well with its sister publication, *Smashing SBM™*. *Smashing SBM™* contains over 400 pages of practical planning and revision tips, including our MAP planning strategy which is designed to ensure that you can correctly estimate the mark allocation of the different Tasks that you need to complete for each of the 2 questions, given that the examination will not break these down for you. *Smashing SBM™* also explains the correct writing style to succeed in SBM and revises some key technical areas and calculations.

Whilst we obviously believe that the principles and methods explained in *Smashing SBM™* are useful as part of your preparations, this set of *Exam Room Notes* does not in any way assume that you have purchased *Smashing SBM™* and we will not make any references to *Smashing SBM™* in the remainder of this book. We simply wanted to make you aware of *Smashing SBM™* as a way to revise examination technique as this is not something that we focus on specifically in this set of *Exam Room Notes*.

Specialist Audit & Assurance Areas

This set of *Exam Room Notes* includes detailed notes on the following specialist areas which are generally newly-introduced at the Advanced Level[2]:

- Agreed Upon Procedures
- Assurance Engagements on Greenhouse Gas Statements
- Assurance Reports on Controls at a Service Organisation (ISAE 3402)
- Compilation Engagements
- Corporate Governance
- Forensic Audits
- Integrated Reporting
- Internal Audit
- Prospective Information (ISAE 3400)
- Reporting on Information Contained in a Prospectus
- Review Engagements (ISRE 2400)
- Sustainability Reporting and Social Reporting (Social and Environmental Audit)

We give emphasis to these areas because we know that around 10% of the marks in any SBM examination will be for assurance areas which do not require any calculations and for which we expect the basic narrative structure or "skeleton" to remain the same every time.

[2] The topic of Prospective Information (ISAE 3400) is included in the Professional Level Audit and Assurance learning materials but as this standard does not tend to be examined very often at the Professional Level, we are aware that most SBM candidates do not really know ISAE 3400 very well. Based on our review of the available ICAEW SBM practice materials such as the SBM Question Bank and SBM Mocks, ISAE 3400 has one of the most formulaic narrative answering patterns of any SBM assurance topic so please capitalise on this by learning the required points and structure well as part of your preparations for SBM. Detailed reminder notes on ISAE 3400 are of course included in this set of *Exam Room Notes*.

Whilst the emphasis is likely to be on these "specialist" assurance areas rather than statutory audit, the examiners can do as they wish and **could** include statutory audit testing or assurance areas that use similar tests to statutory audit. Such tests and procedures are reasonable elements of brought-forward knowledge which you will need to know anyway for your Corporate Reporting examination. You may therefore wish to consider purchasing our *Advanced Level Audit & Assurance Exam Room Notes 2020* book: this book applies the same approach that we have used in these SBM *Exam Room Notes* but also covers the area of statutory audit (and therefore is also very useful in Corporate Reporting).

(Please note that the non-statutory assurance content of this set of Exam Room Notes and our *Advanced Level Audit & Assurance Exam Room Notes 2020* is identical: this is because non-statutory assurance is more likely to be tested in SBM so we want to ensure that SBM-only students who just purchase this set of *Strategic Business Management Exam Room Notes* have access to the relevant content. Likewise, we must then also allow for CR-only candidates who will only be purchasing our *Advanced Level Audit & Assurance Exam Room Notes 2020.*)

Financial Reporting Notes

Unfortunately, given that all the financial reporting rules examined in the Financial Accounting and Reporting Professional Level paper and the Corporate Reporting Advanced Level paper are examinable in SBM, it is not possible to provide notes on all such issues in this book as the book would then become too long and unusable. However, these *Exam Room Notes* **do** provide notes on **key** financial reporting topics for SBM. To determine whether the topic is "key", we have looked at what has been tested in SBM past papers and Mocks as certain financial reporting rules are obviously more likely to be tested in scenarios relating to substantial business change (the focus of SBM).

If you require a more detailed set of quick reference notes for financial reporting concepts (whether to be safer in SBM or because you are sitting the Corporate Reporting paper), please consider our *Advanced Level Financial Reporting Exam Room Notes 2020.* This publication contains alphabetically-organised, quick reference notes for all key financial reporting topics (including brought forward topics from the Professional Level paper in Financial Accounting and Reporting)

The Accountant in Business Concept

The SBM examiners have been keen to emphasise that SBM is designed to be a strategic accountancy examination which only an accountant (not a "pure" strategist) can pass. This is termed the "Accountant in Business" concept. In all your answers (and not just answers which specifically ask for it), you must consider the **financial reporting implications** of strategy: you will be rewarded whenever you provide appropriate advice that only a qualified Chartered Accountant could give.

Please see our book *Smashing SBM™ – How to Pass the ACA SBM Examination 2020* for more information on how to apply this concept. Our MAP planning sheets contained in *Smashing SBM™* also contain reminders of the Accountant in Business concept.

Disclaimer – We Cannot Cover Everything!

We have tried our best to produce a thorough yet useable summary of as many potentially examinable areas as possible. Unfortunately, SBM is a very wide-ranging examination and therefore it is impossible to cover all potential scenarios, particularly given the huge size of the Study Manual. We therefore cannot be sure that everything within your examination will be covered by these notes. We strongly recommend that you add to our notes based on your own studies if something important arises which we have not been able to cover. We would be grateful if you could let us know if you believe that there is a notable omission so that we can look at including this in future (but again repeating that it is never possible to include everything for an examination of this nature).

Despite these limitations, we strongly believe that this set of *SBM Exam Room Notes 2020* will benefit your studies and we wish you the very best for your examination!

A Reminder About Copyright

Please do not photocopy or otherwise distribute this book, either in whole or part. Copyright theft is a crime and we will pursue individuals who infringe our copyright. Copyright theft is a clear breach of professional ethics and may therefore be reported to ICAEW.

We have put a considerable amount of time and effort into developing innovative materials which we genuinely feel will give you an edge in the exams. We would be grateful if you would respect these efforts by not copying this text.

Errors

All content in this book has been carefully written and checked. We have made every effort to ensure that there are no errors.

If you believe you have discovered an error (other than formatting or spelling), please do notify us as soon as possible using the contact information provided on the ACA Simplified website. We will then investigate the matter for you. If something just does not seem to make sense, please do not suffer in silence – get in touch.

Feedback

We hope that you will find this set of *Strategic Business Management Exam Room Notes 2020* helps your revision, in particular by making it as time-efficient as possible.

We wish you all the best in the exam and would be very pleased to hear how you got on. We would also be grateful to hear your feedback on this book. We are keen to provide the best quality revision materials but can only do so with your feedback.

Please use the contact information provided on the ACA Simplified website if you would like to get in touch.

Thanks again for your purchase and good luck with your examinations!

Disclaimer – ICAEW Errata

We have made every effort to thoroughly check this text to ensure that it accurately reflects the content of the ICAEW Study Manual. However, the content of this book covers a number of complex technical areas and therefore it is your responsibility to check the content of this book for accuracy. Please note that it would not be reasonable to expect us to take into account any errata announced by ICAEW after the cut-off date for writing the technical content for this book (31 March 2020) so please ensure that you check the ICAEW website for any notifications of errata sheets issued after this date. Thank you for your understanding of our position in relation to our need to finalise the published version of this book at a specific point in time.

General Advice on SBM Answer Style

The mark allocation for Tasks and sub-Tasks within a question **will not be equal** – find a reasonable method to estimate the differences

Apply an MS² approach – **M**ake **S**cenario-**S**pecific points – avoid generic points

> Avoid copying out standards or lists of points: connect the point to the SBM business
>
> Define financial reporting points quickly and more briefly than in Corporate Reporting, using "inline definition" – refer to the financial reporting rule (e.g. IFRS rule) and a point from the exam Exhibits **in** the same sentence or **line** rather than listing out IFRS rules first as a separate section and then separately looking at the scenario Exhibit data as this will take a lot more time and is likely to result in too much detail on the financial reporting rules being copied out from your notes

Adopt the perspective of the "**Accountant in Business**" – explain both the practical business impact and the financial reporting impact

Apply professional scepticism

Offer conclusions and recommendations (even if not specifically stated to do so in the question)

The SBM examination is created based on the Case Study skills areas so follow these:

> **Assimilating & Using Information** – identifying the key information
>
> **Structuring Problems & Solutions** – processing the information to produce results
>
> **Applying Judgement** – deeper points including scepticism
>
> **Conclusions & Recommendations** – summarising main points and offering practical advice

Keep everything **as practical as possible** – the client needs advice on what to **do**, not just what to **report**

Short, succinct writing – "almost bullet point" and clinical style – avoid introductions, long section headings, linking between paragraphs, phrases like "Following on from the above discussion" or even just "Furthermore" or "Additionally"

Use lots of headings – easier for the marker and keeps you focused on the different things you need to do

Acquisitions – Benefits & Risks

Reasons to acquire

One of the major reasons for making an acquisition rather than growing organically is the speed of growth – acquisitions can be made to enter new product or geographical markets or to expand in existing markets much more quickly than via organic growth

- Synergies
- Marketing advantages
- Enhanced image
- Diversification
- Opportunity to share certain functions and rationalise
- Increase profits and RoCE
- Economies of scale
- Gain access to expertise
- Gain access to technology

Alternative could be **organic growth**

Risks

Strategic risks

- May not be close enough relationship to competences of target
- May result in overlap or duplication of resources/functions
- May require change in direction
- Management of acquiring company is reliant on information, honesty and ability of target management
- Will customer relationships continue?
- Earnings volatility
- Higher level of business risk
- Pricing – amount and/or form of consideration may be wrong
- Synergies may not occur
- Reputation risk if working with a company with the wrong image
- Reporting risk – impact on corporate reporting and group as a whole
- Strategic differences between the 2 entities – problems at Board level and waste of resources
- Becoming involved in an unfamiliar market
- Overpaying for an acquisition
- Failing to understand demand and supply
- Reliance on others for knowledge and skills
- Lack of strategic fit or direction
- Reputational damage
- Consider the size of issue – is it material to the whole business? If so, then a strategic issue
- Lack of managerial skills and experience
- Moving out of a core area
- Few common marketing activities
- Minimal level of integration
- Lack of gaining a competitive advantage over competitors

- Lack of strategic fit and brand confusion
- Lack of anything distinctive
- Few barriers to entry to prevent others entering the market (contestable market)

Operating risks

- Synergies failing to emerge
- Delays
- Cost overruns – who pays?
- Service quality could change
- Integration problems – culture, IT, pricing, support processes
- Management skills and time availability – unsuitable for new group?
- Hidden contractual or other legal obligations
- Hidden financial liabilities
- Debt financing → gearing
- Debt financing → security must be offered – possible loss of asset/control
- Dependent on individual(s) or individual product(s)?
- Operating gearing – share of fixed costs in total operating costs
- Exit costs high – specialist machinery or intangibles which cannot be sold on
- Target may have existing commitments which are expensive
- Overcapacity in the short term?
- Post-integration problems in an acquisition
- Administrative integration
- Problems in integrating cultures, accounting, HRM, IT, internal controls, supply chain management, deliveries and marketing
- Hidden contractual and other legal obligations (assuming that there are no indemnities)
- Hidden financial liabilities (assuming that there are no indemnities)
- Financing methods such as debt
- Dependence on key suppliers or individuals
- Limited amount of assets against which to raise future debts
- Uncertain sales of surplus assets
- Forecasts not achieved
- Sales uncertainty
- Cost overruns
- High level of fixed costs in cost structure → significant operational gearing and operating risk
- Significant up front sunk costs
- High exit costs
- Initial cash deficit
- Going concern issues
- Hidden liabilities

Financing risks

- Re-financing risk – problem if term of financing is short term or medium but the project cash inflows are long-term
- Interest rate risk – variable rates and costs of insurance/hedging
- Fair value risk – FV could change – FV and interest rates are inversely related
- Gearing – increased volatility and bankruptcy risks

- Cash flow and liquidity
- Covenant risk – risk of breaching covenants, resulting in lost of control
- Availability risk – poor takeup of shares/loans – cost of underwriting to insure against this

Acquisitions can be made without cash if share exchange transactions are acceptable to the company being acquired (this could be a cash flow advantage)

Governance risks

- Control environment
- Culture – entrepreneur v corporate
- Management style
- UK Corporate Governance Code applies? (exemptions for AIM and more limited exemptions for non-FTSE 350)
- Board size, balance and control – role and powers, rotation, changes after an acquisition
- Director pay and performance
- Non-Executive Directors – are there any NEDs? Independent? Quality?
- Committees (e.g. audit, remuneration or nomination)? Independent? Quality?

Other risks

- Overpaying
- Use consideration which is risky (e.g. shares, derivatives, performance target-based)
- Acquiring too much capacity
- Legal costs and problems
- Conflicts in interests of parties/control issues
- Financing considerations – cost, control, tax
- Cultural differences
- Staffing problems including redundancy costs
- Poor change management
- Poor integration plans
- High integration costs
- Unquoted target with uncertain value – normally a discount for lack of liquidity

Risk Mitigation

- Undertake thorough Due Diligence on feasibility
- Negotiate correct clauses into contract e.g. responsibility for cost overruns or delays or integration problems
- Ensure information fully disclosed – good quality Due Diligence procedures

Problems with acquisitions

Valuation issues – the management of the target company have all the best information and insight into the company's true value but they have an interest in demanding as high a price as possible so it is argued that the market is not efficient as frequently too high a price is paid due to information asymmetry between seller and purchaser

Post-acquisition costs – in addition to initial purchase costs, there could also be significant costs involved in integrating the acquired company's systems (production, IT etc) with those of the parent company

Lack of proper consideration of non-financial factors – most acquirers conduct financial audits of target companies but many do not conduct anything approaching a management audit

Human resources and personnel issues – morale, performance assessment and culture are all important – if key managers leave, the business will suffer – an organisation may look to streamline the workforce to make use of possible synergies from an acquisition but this could damage morale among the workforce (as well as leading to redundancy costs in the short term)

Post-acquisition phase is not properly managed – this can mean that the 2 component companies are never properly integrated so the potential benefits of the deal cannot be fully realised

Competitive policy issues – sometimes an acquisition cannot be pursued due to a refusal by a government on competition grounds

Issues to consider in acquisitions

Advantages of acquisitions

Speed of growth

Avoids barriers to entry

Acquisition of technical expertise and customer contacts

Disadvantages of acquisitions

Cost (and potential over-payment)

Potential negative customer reactions

Incompatibility and lack of cultural fit

Stakeholders in an acquisition process

Company's managers – some managers may want to make an acquisition and increase the size of the firm as a means of increasing their own status and power – other managers may view an acquisition as a means of preventing their own company being taken over, making their job safer

Corporate financiers and banks – these organisations can charge fees for advice and so have a vested interest in ensuring that the acquisition takes place (or at least reaches a fairly advanced state of negotiation!)

See also

Acquisitions – Debt-Funded

Consider the **current debt to equity (gearing) ratio** of the company and how this may be altered

Consider whether there are **fixed assets such as PPE to provide security** over the debt

Consider **interest cover** and how this may be affected by the acquisition

Consider the **potential earnings** of the target – adding these into the consolidated earnings will affect ratios such as interest cover and even gearing through increases in retained earnings over time

Consider the **impact on finance costs** if funding is hard to obtain or gearing changes to such an extent that providers of debt require a higher interest rate

Consider the **debt of the target** – how will this affect the consolidated SFP? How will any extra interest payments affect the consolidated IS and related ratios?

Cash may be used up in the acquisition, affecting the ability to meet obligations when due

The **growth prospects** of the target are particularly important if a risky strategy is being followed

Debt capacity

An advantage of degearing now is that if profitable investment opportunities were to present themselves in future, the entity would find it easier to raise debt in order to take advantage of the opportunity – reducing gearing preserves the entity's "debt capacity"

See also	Other Acquisitions topics	
	Bank loans	61
	Change – Definition & Models	101
	Change – Management & Implementation	103
	Marketing Strategies	314
	Overseas Operations topics	
	Prospective Information (ISAE 3400)	349
	Segmental Reporting (IFRS 8)	384
	Strategic Analysis Tools & Models	391
	Valuations topics	

Acquisitions – Due Diligence

Definition

Due Diligence is a term that describes a number of concepts involving the investigation of a company prior to signing a contractual agreement

This type of assurance engagement is typically carried out by an external firm appointed by the purchasers – the provider of the Due Diligence will assume a duty of care towards the party that appoints them

The term Due Diligence is fairly wide in its application and extends far beyond the review of the target company's financial statements – a specialist Due Diligence firm could be appointed to review the following areas:

information systems

legal status

marketing/brand issues

macro environmental factors

management capabilities

sustainability issues

production capabilities

plant and equipment

Mention that does not involve the level of detailed testing that would be carried out in a statutory audit – advisable to wait for a statutory audit to be completed if possible before doing the deal

Provides only limited assurance

Types of Acquisition Due Diligence

Financial	financial position, risks and projections, likely returns on investment
Commercial	markets and external economic environment, renewal of contracts?
Technical	new technologies
IT	nature and reliability and risks of IT systems and IT skills
Legal	legal rights and obligations on contracts, employment law
Human Resources	skills, contracts, redundancies
Tax	liabilities, losses available for relief, structuring

Note – certain types of DD will be more relevant depending on the type of company involved:

Services company	HR Due Diligence more important
Tech company	Technical and IT Due Diligence more important

Due Diligence Procedures for an Acquisition

identify legal title

confirm accuracy and assumptions of financial data and projections

commercial review – order book, contracts, realism of growth rates assumed and projected

identify and quantify areas of commercial and financial risk

identify possible areas of synergy

identify key personnel

give assurance to providers of finance if required

Due Diligence and Valuation Models

Clearly, some valuation models are very sensitive to changes in variables so these should always be part of the financial and commercial Due Diligence process

Ensure you make some points explaining or querying specific model variables

You may wish to note that the acquisition will change the risk profile of the combined company so previous cost of capital/discount rate figures may be out of date

Financial Due Diligence – some procedures

- Test forecasts against industry trends and recent sales patterns
- Test assumptions on production process and costs
- Verify projections of expenditure to suitable evidence e.g. independent evidence
- Assess costs and prices against plans
- Review marketing plans
- Determine capacity for further borrowing
- Test projected capital expenditure
- Discussions with management – reasons, alternatives, contingencies and Plan B

Income Statement Due Diligence

Note – these are simply examples taken from the SBM Question Bank – you must ensure that they are applicable to your exam scenario

Issue	Due Diligence Procedures
Revenue	Verify price and volume changes including timing of the price change Confirm that policy is consistent with IFRS 15
Cost of sales	Procedures to verify volume changes Verify reasons for changes
Depreciation	Confirm treatment fits with IAS 16 Confirm useful economic lives Confirm that depreciation policy reasonable Determine if assets incorrectly grouped
Impairment	Determine if impairment needed If impairment already proposed, determine if there are other assets that need writing off Confirm value in use and impairment methods used
Provisions	Professional scepticism if provision being reversed – why? Can relate to aggressive earnings management Consider causes and consequences Review the measurement of the original provision and the necessity of the reversal – has there been an intentional effort to distort profit?
Financing costs	Determine if changes are in line with other business changes such as loans and capital expenditure
PBT	Check for unusual movements such as increased PBT but falling GP or margins

SFP Due Diligence (Asset-based valuations)

Note – these are simply examples taken from the SBM Question Bank – you must ensure that they are applicable to your exam scenario

Issue	Due Diligence Procedures
PPE	Inspect any relevant valuer's reports Check whether depreciation rates are low Check FV of assets
Inventory	Physical inventory count at the acquisition date with attention to cut off Determine if any impairment is needed, especially if a technology company with high risk of obsolescence Determine inventory turnover rates
Receivables	Investigate returns and impairment Verify title to receivables
Cash	Probably low risk as an objective item but confirm whether cash is included as part of the deal
Loans	Determine carrying amount in accordance with IAS 38/IFRS 9 Review terms of the loan agreement
Pension obligation	Could be either over or understated Determine competence of actuary if used Assess discount rate – rate should be rate on AA corporate bonds Confirm that entries appear in IS, especially if errors made
Tax liability	Consider under and over provisions from last year and any tax payments needed Confirm whether a Deferred Tax balance is included and whether needed
Trade payables	Assess cut off issues Review whether trade payables days appear reasonable

Past paper example – SBM November 2018 past paper Q2

Note – the following points are taken from SBM November 2018 past paper Q2 which provided a useful and detailed model answer on Due Diligence procedures (9 marks were available on the markscheme) – note that although the question wording asked candidates to "identify and explain the Due Diligence procedures that should be performed", the model answer did not confine itself purely to referencing technical Due Diligence procedures and instead required the candidate to appreciate brand and strategic issues within an integrated style of response

The context of this question was that the client company had suffered a decline in performance and brand image and was therefore considering purchasing a supplier as part of efforts to revitalise its own brand

The brand of the target company could possibly be the **most significant asset recognised** in an acquisition deal

Carefully identifying intangibles being acquired and considering their fair value would then be a vital step in determining the consideration to be paid and ensuring that such consideration is a fair price

Brand valuation requires significant industry specific judgement and expertise

Due Diligence procedures should apply 1 or more of the 3 "approaches" to brand valuation (market approach, cost approach or income approach) based on the specific circumstances of the target

The company should either engage a valuation services team at a firm of accountants or could engage the experience of a specialist consultancy

The acquiring company will need to obtain assurance over any assumptions which have been made when determining fair value – for example, market assumptions and the impact that market conditions could have on future income generated by the brand

However, Due Diligence relating to brands should not be confined to narrow issues around valuation – the scope of commercial Due Diligence needs to cover a number of areas which are important in strategic marketing (see points below)

Legal Due Diligence to establish rights over the brand are important – there should be investigation of any existing use of those rights such as through existing licensing arrangements which may reduce their value

Consideration should be given as to how the brand will contribute to the group post-acquisition and how it fits with the group's overall brand strategy – how will the brand affect the company's ability to achieve its long-term objectives? What impact will the brand have on shareholder value in the future?

If the strategic level issues are not considered in advance, then the acquirer risks overpaying for assets that are not used or which have little value to it – therefore, **some** Due Diligence should **always** take place before the final decision to acquire a brand is taken

See also

Acquisitions – Financing

Useful mnemonic: CSL – **c**ash, **s**hares, **l**oans

Impact on cost of capital

Cost of equity should rise if the company increases its gearing by borrowing and should fall if you raises new capital with the share issue

This will affect the valuation of the company by affecting the WACC and therefore discounted value of future earnings/cash

Therefore the financing method is important

Cash financing – advantages

Shareholders of target company receive a certain amount (compared to contingent consideration)

Could be good use of surplus cash

No dilution of control

No issue costs

Cash financing – disadvantages

Acquiring company may need to find additional cash

May be tax issues for shareholders of target company

Shareholders of the target may not be happy to lose their interest in the business

Director-shareholders in the target are given cash but no shareholding – incentives for good performance reduced or removed?

Summary comparison of loans versus shares

Issue	**Loan**	**Shares**
Liquidity	Uncertain Capital repayable and interest payable	Certain No repayment Dividends optional
Gearing	Increased **!Calculate where possible**	Reduced **!Calculate where possible**
Transaction costs	Low	High
Draw down	When needed	All received up front
Tax	Interest tax deductible	Dividends not deductible

SAF -> compare for buyer

Share issue (including share for share exchange) – advantages

Preserves cash and liquidity – dividends only need to be paid at the discretion of the directors

Shareholders of the target company retain an equity interest

No immediate tax issues

Group has control over dividend policy – not obliged to pay every year

Reduces gearing as additional equity is issued with no extra debt – consider **recalculating** your gearing ratios to show the impact (if using the debt/equity equation then only the bottom half of the fraction will change)

If a substantial amount is issued to a particular entity, that entity will have a strong motivation to promote and demand improvements in the company's performance to improve the share price

Share issue (including share for share exchange) – disadvantages

Issue costs can be high – up to 15% of finance issued

Shareholders of the target receive an uncertain amount

Shareholders of the acquiring company have their shareholdings diluted

May not be possible to maintain a similar dividend per share to the previous year if the number of shares has increased substantially

Could impact on the market price of shares, affecting shareholder wealth

Share for share exchange – considerations for directors

Are shares received quoted? If not, may be hard to dispose of and illiquid

If shares received are quoted, can these be disposed of without overloading the market?

What % is retained? What profit flow and control does this yield?

What are the growth prospects of the new group?

Has a subsidiary now become only an associate with a lower control premium/value?

Debt/Loan financing – advantages

Shareholders of the acquiring company can keep control

Shareholders of target company get a certain return so may accept a lower price for the acquisition

Tax deductible and value of the tax debt shield

Minimal issue costs

Debt/Loan financing – disadvantages

Obligation to pay interest – cash implications

Shareholders of target company may want equity

Increased gearing* and risk

Refinancing risk – look at the term involved

Adds to financial risk

Loan covenants may exist

(*Could be an advantage if the increased gearing brings the company nearer to its optimum level)

Why are retained earnings not a source of financing?

Retained earnings are the cumulative profit since the company started training

Profits are not the same thing as cash so there may not be cash available for acquisitions purposes

Retained earnings are represented by an increase in net assets (not just cash)

Debt capacity

An advantage of degearing now is that if profitable investment opportunities were to present themselves in future, the entity would find it easier to raise debt in order to take advantage of the opportunity – reducing gearing preserves the entity's "debt capacity"

See also

Other Acquisitions topics	
Bank loans	61
Change – Definition & Models	101
Change – Management & Implementation	103
Loan Decision by a Bank	313
Marketing Strategies	314
Overseas Operations topics	
Prospective Information (ISAE 3400)	349
Segmental Reporting (IFRS 8)	384
Strategic Analysis Tools & Models	391
Valuations topics	

Acquisitions – Impact on Financial Statements

Areas to Consider

Earnings per Share – a key ratio considered by the financial markets

Gearing – a key indicator of risks of bankruptcy and could affect ability to secure more financing but also leads to tax savings compared to issue of equity – impact on covenants?

Non-current asset turnover – revenue earned per investment into fixed assets (ideally a high figure)

Interest cover – impact on covenants?

Note – compare the size of the changes in the above to the investment amount – Is it worth it?

Types of structure

Subsidiary, Associate, Joint venture, Investment

Intangible assets (IAS 38)

For many companies (particularly services companies), the value of the company exceeds the book value of its net tangible assets

On acquisition, there may be recognition of assets such as customer lists, software, internet domains, databases and so on at fair value. The remaining balance of the purchase price over the fair value of all net assets is treated as goodwill

It must be possible to establish the fair value of the intangible assets reliably – the assets must be identifiable and under the control of the acquirer and there must be probable future economic benefits from the assets

Once recognised, intangible assets should be amortised on a systematic basis over their expected useful lives

Goodwill is not amortised but is subject instead to annual impairment reviews – any impairments in value are written off to profit or loss

The acquisition of substantial amounts of intangible assets could lead to high charges to profit or loss for amortisation costs, potentially reducing earnings – this would be increased further if there is impairment of an intangible, including goodwill – there would be a substantial increase in intangible assets on the consolidated SFP, affecting ratios based on assets

An intangible asset with a finite useful life should be amortised over its expected useful life, commencing when the asset is available for use in the manner intended by management – a 2017 amendment to IAS 38 clarified that revenue-based methods of amortisation are not appropriate

Intangible software asset in the context of an acquisition – individual financial statements versus consolidated group financial statements

Individual financial statements

The asset is likely to be an internally-developed intangible asset and so would not be recognised in the individual financial statements of the target company

Any proceeds on sale would therefore be recognised in full in profit or loss

Group financial statements

Under IFRS 3, on acquisition the asset would need to be recognised in the group accounts as an intangible asset

The asset should be measured at its fair value on the acquisition date, assuming that this value can be ascertained reliably

IAS 38 allows 2 methods of measuring intangible assets – the cost model (cost less amortisation) and the revaluation model – the revaluation model is likely to be inappropriate as there is often no active market given the uniqueness of the asset

An impairment test should be carried out prior to any sale

If the asset is eventually sold, any excess net disposal proceeds above the initially-recognised fair value (after allowing for impairment) would be deemed to be a profit on disposal

Acquiring a 50%+ Subsidiary – Specific Considerations

Provides full control

Must follow the requirements of IFRS 3 *Business Combinations*

Consolidate in all revenue and expenses (and allow for NCI share) – could boost EPS but depends on whether profitable **and whether shares issued as part of the acquisition** (likely in SBM)

Eliminates intra-group trading and unrealised profits

Various items must be measured at fair value

Consolidate in all assets and liabilities – impact on gearing and SFP ratios?

If applicable, assets/liabilities should be initially translated at the historic/acquisition date exchange rate

Goodwill may arise an acquisition and is recognised as an intangible asset in the group financial statements – this could affect certain ratios – as this is treated as an asset of the subsidiary, if the subsidiary uses a different currency the goodwill is retranslated at the year-end using the closing rate

Controls company so has full access to information and ability to dictate changes based on that information

Can replace management team – no one else to depend on (or blame!) for performance outcomes

Acquiring a <50% Associate or Investment – Specific Considerations

Does not provide control – unknown control aspect – does not provide access to all information and shareholding of less than 25% lacks power

Share of profit from associate may boost EPS

No consolidating in of assets and liabilities – just an asset line for Investment in associate – less impact on gearing than a full subsidiary?

Subject to quality of management team and does not have full influence over this

See also

Acquisitions – Post-Acquisition Integration

Possible problems/differences

Scale and size

Marketing positioning – top end quality versus lower end price considerations

Location of operations – different locations but alternatively may be too close and "cannibalise" each other's sales, resulting in little net improvement

Product range

Customer perception and brand awareness

Change in brand style and nature of merging low and high quality

Ensuring synergies

Management challenges if continue to be operated separately

See also

Acquisitions – Struggling Company

Assurance

The most recent financial statements may not yet have been audited

The nature of the assurance review will be determined by contractual agreement

The contractual agreement will consider whether an assurance opinion is required, the timescale available to do the work and access to information made available by the administrator

Areas to cover in assurance

Goodwill	enquire whether impairment proposed
Non-current assets	IFRS 13 issues, verify title to assets, analyse charges
Inventories	review age, investigate nature, causes and value of slow moving items, check assets to registration documents, check valuations against trade guides, establish items of consignment inventories
Receivables	review age analysis of receivables, check for normal recovery, use of debt factors in the past
Brand	assess the terms and conditions, have there been other offers?, has the administrator made any attempt to sell the brand name? Incremental cash flows?

Projections and statement of profit or loss

Procedures on projections and statement of profit or loss

Examine year end cut off for revenue enhancement issues

Examine assumptions on which projections are made

Analytical procedures on financial statements to ascertain consistency

Review basis of assumptions for revenue and other changes

Challenge assumptions

Review transactions close to year end and up to date of possible transfer to ensure that ownership and condition of the assets is maintained

Commercial assurance

This process will establish if there are rights, obligations and liabilities that impact on asset value or the future operating of assets

Legal review of the terms of contracts

Checking of covenants, preferential interest rates and repayment terms

Ascertain any litigation, contingencies or contractual obligations or penalties

Consider tax issues outstanding

Review market conditions and competitors

Assess viability of different sites/revenue streams

See also

Other Acquisitions topics	
Bank loans	61
Change – Definition & Models	101
Change – Management & Implementation	103
Marketing Strategies	314
Overseas Operations topics	
Prospective Information (ISAE 3400)	349
Segmental Reporting (IFRS 8)	384
Strategic Analysis Tools & Models	391
Valuations topics	

Acquisitions – Synergies and Challenges

Synergies

Main justification for many acquisitions – but check that will actually happen – if not, shareholder value harmed

Revenue synergies

Benefits
- Higher revenues for acquirer
- Higher return on equity
- Longer periods of growth

Sources
- Increased market power
- Marketing synergies – two parties can combine advertising resources and cross-advertise
- Strategic synergies
- Locational synergies

Dangers
- Revenue synergies are harder to quantify than other synergies
- Hard to know how customers will react – will they actually buy?

Cost synergies

- Normally considered to be substantial – but will they happen and will they outweigh integration/redundancy costs?
- Primary source – economies of scale

Financial synergies
- Diversification – gain to shareholders if not already diversified themselves
- Uses surplus cash that otherwise not being used ("cash slack")

Human resources synergies
- Sharing of skills and expertise
- May be able to buy in access to information, techniques and networks

Accounting impact of an acquisition

Subsidiary – consolidate in debts – affects gearing but could increase profits (100% of subsidiary)

Associate – debts not consolidated in but profits boosted (by lower amount than a subsidiary: lower % owned)

Challenges – Integrating a Small Business with a Listed Company

Small business

May be owned by small group of shareholders or even a family

May have significant amount invested

May be important to self-esteem/pride of family members – primary objective not purely financial

May not be interested in maximum short term returns

Listed business

Needs to ensure high returns for shareholders immediately (stock market oversight)

Primary objective likely to be wealth maximisation – purely financial aims

See also

Other Acquisitions topics	
Bank loans	61
Change – Definition & Models	101
Change – Management & Implementation	103
Marketing Strategies	314
Overseas Operations topics	
Prospective Information (ISAE 3400)	349
Segmental Reporting (IFRS 8)	384
Strategic Analysis Tools & Models	391
Valuations topics	

Q31, Page 485

Agreed Upon Procedures

Examination example points

For a good example, see **SBM July 2016 past paper Q1** (model answer page 14) (worth **14 marks**)

In an AUP engagement, the practitioner provides a report on factual findings from procedures agreed in advance with the relevant party or parties.

Procedures and tests should be sufficiently detailed so as to be clear and unambiguous and discussed in advance to ensure that they are useful for the purposes.

The practitioner is required to comply at a minimum with ISRS 4400 *Engagements to Perform Agreed Upon Procedures on Financial Information*

The AUP report does not express a conclusion and is therefore not an assurance engagement – it will not provide recommendations based on the findings – the relevant parties are instead requested to review the procedures and findings and to use the information to draw their own conclusions

The value of the AUP process is in providing objective testing by a practitioner with relevant expertise – testing is independent and also protects confidentiality (practitioner is bound by the Code of Ethics for Professional Accountants under ISRS 4400) – saves one of the parties carrying out the procedures themselves (time and money saving)

Example of AUP performed on a licensing agreement (SBM July 2016 past paper)

Procedures on the contractual terms such as number of bags sold, number of customer complaints about product quality and the number of customer complaints about service quality

Benefit is that the engagement provides evidence of compliance with the terms of the licensing contract: ensures correct royalty payments and monitoring of quality control issues

The confidential nature of AUP might be the only way to give the parties enough confidence to allow the procedures to be carried out at all

General notes

Agreed upon procedures are procedures of a standard audit nature but which have been **specifically agreed upon by the auditor, entity and any appropriate third parties for a purpose other than preparation of a statutory audit**.

A difference with statutory audit is therefore that there must be **agreement on the procedures to be applied** (hence the name "agreed upon" procedures) whereas in a statutory audit it is the auditor who determines which procedures to use.

A second difference is that the recipients of the report containing the "agreed upon" procedures are **left to form their own conclusions – the auditor/practitioner does not offer a conclusion**, unlike in a statutory audit (or other types of assurance).

Agreed upon procedures are governed by **ISRS 4400**. Note that ISRSs have not been adopted in the UK.

In setting up the agreed upon procedures, agreement should be reached on the following matters:

- Nature of the arrangement as not constituting an audit or review i.e. no assurance is expressed at all
- Purpose of the engagement
- Identification of the financial information to which the agreed upon procedures will be applied
- Nature, timing and extent of the specific procedures to be applied
- Anticipated form of the report
- Limitations on distribution of the report

The report of factual findings should contain:

- Identification of specific financial or non-financial information to which the agreed-upon procedures have been applied
- Statement that the procedures performed were those agreed upon with the recipient
- Statement that the engagement was performed in accordance with the ISRSs applicable to agreed upon procedure engagements or with relevant national standards or practices
- If the auditor is performing the agreed upon procedures, a statement that the auditor is not independent of the entity
- Identification of the purpose for which the agreed upon procedures were performed
- A listing of the specific procedures performed
- A description of the auditor's factual findings including sufficient details of errors and exceptions found
- A statement that the procedures performed do not constitute either an audit or a review, and, as such, **no assurance is expressed**
- A statement that had the auditor performing additional procedures or an audit/review then other matters may have been arisen and reported
- A restriction on use of the report to only those parties that have agreed to the procedures which have been performed

- A statement that the report relates only to the elements, accounts, items or financial and non-financial information specified and does not extend to the entity's financial statements taken as a whole

Again, **no assurance or opinion is offered** – there is only a reporting of **factual findings**

See also Acquisitions – Due Diligence 33

Share based payments assurance Q3//

Assurance – General Points (ISAE 3000)

ISAE 3000 distinguishes between 2 types of assurance engagement:

reasonable assurance engagements – these engagements aim to reduce engagement risk to an **acceptably low level** – the **conclusion** is expressed in a form that conveys the practitioner's **opinion** on the outcome of the measurement or evaluation of the underlying subject matter against criteria

limited assurance engagements – these engagements give a **lower level of** assurance than reasonable assurance engagements – the nature, timing and extent of procedures carried out would be **limited** – even so, the level of assurance should still be **meaningful** in the judgement of the practitioner, meaning that it is likely to **enhance** the **intended user's confidence** about the subject matter information

Assurance	Level of risk	Conclusion	Procedures	Example
Reasonable	Low	Positive expression – an opinion **is** expressed	High	"The management has operated an effective system of internal controls"
Limited	Acceptable	Negative expression – no opinion is offered, conclusion only notes whether matters have come to attention indicating material misstatement	Limited but still meaningful	"Nothing has come to our attention indicating significant deficiencies in internal control"

Elements of an assurance engagement

- a 3-party relationship involving a practitioner, a responsible party (the client entity) and an intended user
- subject matter
- suitable criteria
- evidence
- an assurance report – written report containing the practitioner's assurance conclusion which is issued to the intended user in a form appropriate to the engagement (reasonable assurance or limited assurance)

Process at the end of an assurance engagement

The practitioner must express a conclusion **in writing** in an assurance report – the report should include the following elements:

1. description of the **level of assurance** obtained
2. subject matter information evaluated against **criteria** (for example, "The company's internal controls operated effectively in terms of criteria X in the period")
3. **identification** of the applicable criteria
4. description of **significant inherent limitations** (for example, noting that a historical review of internal controls does not provide assurance that the same controls will continue to operate effectively in the future)
5. if the applicable criteria are designed for a **specific purpose**, there should be a **statement** alerting readers to this fact – this statement should indicate that the subject matter information may **not** be suitable for another purpose
6. **responsible** parties and their **responsibilities** as well as the **responsibilities** of the **practitioner**
7. statement that the work was performed in accordance with a **relevant specific ISAE** or in accordance with **ISAE 3000 for general assurance work**
8. an **informative summary** of the work performed

Level of assurance possible

Absolute assurance is generally **not** attainable as a result of factors such as:

- use of **selective testing**
- the **inherent limitations** of control systems
- the fact that much of the evidence available to the practitioner is **persuasive** rather than **conclusive**
- the use of **judgement** in gathering evidence and drawing conclusions based on the evidence
- in some cases, the **characteristics of the subject matter**

Types of conclusion

An **unmodified opinion** is possible where the practitioner concludes:

in the case of a **reasonable** assurance engagement, the subject matter information is prepared, in all material respects, in accordance with the applicable criteria

in the case of a **limited assurance** engagement, that, based on the procedures performed and the evidence obtained, no matter has come to the attention of the practitioner that causes them to believe that there may be a material misstatement of the subject matter information as compared with the applicable criteria

A **modified conclusion** will be issued when the above **does not apply**.

Assurance Engagements on Greenhouse Gas Statements

Regulated by ISAE 3410 *Assurance Engagements on Greenhouse Gas Statements*

All businesses emit greenhouse gases, either directly or indirectly.

As the public has been seeking greater confidence in greenhouse gas emissions, ISAE 3410 has been created to enhance this confidence.

Reasons for preparing a greenhouse gas statement include:

- may be required under a regulatory disclosure regime
- may be required as part of an emissions trading scheme
- company may wish to make voluntary disclosures

An engagement performed in accordance with ISAE 3410 must also comply with the requirements of ISAE 3000.

An engagement under ISAE 3410 can provide either limited assurance or reasonable assurance, based on the circumstances (such as the requirements of law or regulation). ISAE 3410 does not itself specifically require the level of assurance to be limited or reasonable.

The key stages are the same as for any assurance assignment and include planning, obtaining an understanding of the entity, identifying and assessing the risks of material misstatement, obtaining written representations and forming an assurance conclusion.

The understanding required to perform a limited assurance engagement will be less than that required for a reasonable assurance engagement – in particular, for a limited assurance engagement there is no requirement to obtain an understanding of control activities relevant to the engagement or to evaluate the design of controls and determine whether they have been implemented.

Similarly, risk assessment procedures will be less extensive in a limited assurance engagement – assessment of the risks of material misstatement would not need to be performed at the assertion level in such an engagement.

Reporting will be similar to other assurance reports and should include a title, addressee, identification and description of the level of assurance, description of the entity's responsibility, identification of the applicable criteria, a description of the practitioner's responsibility and an overall assurance conclusion.

In relation to reporting, the following points must be included:

- a statement that the quantification of greenhouse gases is subject to inherent uncertainty
- a statement that the firm applies ISQC 1

a statement that the practitioner complies with the IESBA Code or other professional requirements

a statement that the engagement was performed in accordance with ISA 3410

if the practitioner expresses a conclusion that is modified, the report must include a section that provides a description of the matter giving rise to the modification and a section containing the modified opinion

Appendix 2 of ISAE 3410 includes illustrative examples of reports for both reasonable and limited assurance engagements.

See also Sustainability Reporting and Social Reporting 399

Assurance Reports on Controls at a Service Organisation

Definition of a service organisation – a third party organisation that provides services to user entities that are part of those entities' information systems relevant to financial reporting

Regulated by ISAE 3402 *Assurance Reports on Controls at a Service Organisation*, which expands on how ISAE 3400 is to be applied in a reasonable assurance engagement to report on controls at a service organisation

ISAE 3402 is to be applied in a reasonable assurance engagement to provide a report to user entities and their auditors on the controls at a service organization.

ISAE 3402 rules only apply where the service organisation is responsible for, or otherwise able to make a statement about, the **suitable design of controls**.

This means that ISAE 3402 does not apply where the assurance engagement is to:

report only on whether controls at the service organisation operated as described, or

report on controls at a service organisation other than those related to a service that is likely to be relevant to user entities' internal control as it relates to financial reporting

The 2 types of reports – Type 1 and Type 2

A Type 1 report is a report on the description and design of controls at a service organization.

In a Type 1 report, the service auditor will express his opinion as to whether the description fairly presents the service organisation system and that the controls related to the control objectives stated in the description were suitably designed.

A Type 2 report is a report on the description, design **and operating effectiveness** of controls at a service organization.

In a Type 2 report, in addition to the points reported on for a Type 1 report, the service auditor will **also** express an opinion as to whether the controls tested **operated effectively** throughout the specified period.

Where the auditor cannot agree with the details of the report or is unable to obtain sufficient appropriate evidence, a modified report must be issued.

ISAE 3402 states that the objectives of the service auditor are to obtain reasonable assurance about, and report on, whether, in all material respects, based on suitable criteria:

the service organisation's description of its system fairly presents the system as designed and implemented throughout the specified period or as at a specified date

the controls related to the control objectives stated in the service organisation's description of that system were suitably designed throughout the specified period where included in the scope of the engagement, the controls operated effectively to provide reasonable assurance that the control objectives stated in the service organisation's description of its system were achieved throughout the period

The following procedures are **required** under ISAE 3402:

consider acceptance and continuance issues

assess the suitability of the criteria used by the service organisation

consider materiality with respect to the presentation of the description, the suitability of the design of controls and, in the case of a Type 2 report, the operating effectiveness of controls

obtain an understanding of the service organisation's system

obtain evidence regarding the service organisation's description of its system, whether controls implemented to achieve the control objectives are suitably designed and the operating effectiveness of controls (when providing a Type 2 report)

determine whether, and to what extent, to use the work of internal auditors (where there is an internal audit function)

The service auditor must request the service organisation to provide written representations addressed to the service auditor. Written representations must include:

reaffirmation of the statement accompanying the description of the system

that it has provided the service auditor with access to all relevant information access

that it has disclosed to the service auditor (to the extent that it is aware) any non-compliance with laws and regulations, fraud or uncorrected deviations, design deficiencies in controls, instances where controls have not operated as described and subsequent events

The content of a report under ISAE 3402 is similar to that for any other assurance report and it will include a title, addressee, identification of the service organisation's description of its system, identification of the applicable criteria, responsibilities of the service organisation, a statement that the firm applies ISQC 1, a statement that the practitioner complies with the IESBA Code or other professional requirements, summary of the practitioner's procedures and statements on the limitations of controls.

The report must also contain the practitioner's opinion, expressed in a **positive** form.

See also Internal Controls 267
ISAE 3402 – example answer points 274

Automation and Intelligent systems

Automation

Automation is the creation and application of technology to monitor and control the production and delivery of products and services

Note that this definition means that automation is not solely restricted to manufacturing (where robots have long been used as a form of automation) – services and processes can also be automated because robotic process automation can be used as a way to automate repetitive and rules-based processes such as occur in a shared service centre or another part of the back office

Multiple software-based “robots” can effectively work as a back office processing centre without any human resources

Automation is particularly useful in rules-based, repetitive processes so the organisation must assess if they have low value, rules-based, repetitive processes which are currently performed by people but which could be automated – examples include billings or collections

Benefits of robotic process automation

Faster handling time so higher volumes of transactions can be processed

Reduced errors as no longer subject to human error – this can improve accuracy and customer service

Reduced costs – reduced need for human staff and an alternative to offshoring as the cost savings can be greater than those achieved by relocating processes off-shore

Improved productivity – humans can focus on more complex processes once rules-based ones have been automated

Efficiency of staff time – could reduce the amount of staff required to deal with rules-based processes, leaving staff to focus on more complex processes instead

Drawbacks of robotic process automation

There would be a need for more specialist staff in new roles such as AI specialists, Big Data specialists, process automation experts, information security analysts and human-machine instruction designers

An important issue for HRM in an organisation will be identifying the skills that it needs to be successful and take advantage of new opportunities, ensuring that its workforce is equipped with these skills, either by re-training and upskilling existing staff or by recruiting new workers

Intelligent systems

An intelligent system is "a computer-based system that can represent, reason about, and interpret data. In doing so it can learn about the structure of data, analyse the data to extract patterns and meaning, derive new information and identify strategies and behaviours to act on the results of its analysis" (University College London, 2018)

An alternative definition is "technologically-advanced machines that perceive and respond to the world around them" (University of Nevada, 2018)

Intelligent machines therefore have the functionality to interpret some form of stimulus and are then capable of responding in some fashion

Intelligent machines are closely associated with the concepts of Artificial Intelligence (AI) and Machine Learning

AI is concerned with creating computer systems which have the ability to think for themselves whereas Machine Learning is focused on the science associated with getting computer systems to learn how to act without being programmed to do so

See also Big Data topics

Balanced Scorecard

The 4 perspectives in the Balanced Scorecard

1. **Customer** – targets based on issues that matter to customers such as cost, quality and delivery, customer satisfaction

2. **Internal business** – improving internal process and decision making

3. **Innovation and learning** – ability to maintain competitive position through the acquisition of new skills and the development of new products

4. **Financial** – growth, profitability, market share and shareholder value

Problems with the Balanced Scorecard approach

Managers may not **understand** the measures used (especially if they are not financial specialists)

May be difficult to gain an **overall impression** of the results provided – hence hard to use the results for control action or as a means of determining the levels of bonus

Measures such as production development and cost reduction will **conflict** – may be difficult to determine the balance that will achieve the best results

Care must be taken in **selecting the correct measures** and ensuring that these do not lead to the wrong outcomes

Interpretation is still needed so there will be some **subjectivity**

Managers must be **genuinely committed** to the scorecard or it will not work

Does not provide a single aggregate summary performance measure (unlike ROI or ROCE)

No direct link to creation of shareholder value (unlike EVA®)

Does not necessarily cause the cultural change needed

Requires the organisation to start thinking in a more long term manner, which may be difficult but also risks distracting the business from day to day operational issues

See also

Change – Definition & Models	101
Change – Management & Implementation	103
Critical Success Factors	140
Key Performance Indicators	284

Bank Loans

Why use loans rather than other financing methods such as sale of assets, leases or equity?

Advantages

Certain amount received (compared to sale of assets or issue of equity)

Fixed and known repayment schedule (less so if a variable rate of interest applied), which is helpful for planning (compared to an overdraft)

Allows terms of financing and expenditure to be matched to avoid any problems

Disadvantages

Increases gearing (could lead to impact on valuation)

Covenants may need to be offered (loss of control)

Debt capacity

An advantage of degearing now is that if profitable investment opportunities were to present themselves in future, the entity would find it easier to raise debt in order to take advantage of the opportunity – reducing gearing preserves the entity's "debt capacity"

See also

Acquisitions – Financing	38
Bonds (Loan Notes) v Bank Loans – Comparisons	85
Loan Decision by a Bank	313
Overseas Operations – Financing	337

Big Data – Artificial Intelligence and machine learning

Artificial intelligence (AI) relates to machines' ability to identify patterns and make decisions – it can be contrasted with automation and robotic processes which are appropriate for repetitive, rules-based tasks

Artificial intelligence can be defined as the ability of a machine or system to perform cognitive functions we associate with human minds, such as perceiving, reasoning, learning and problem-solving, and acting in a way that we would consider to be "smart".

Machine learning can be defined as the use of algorithms to detect patterns and learn how to make predictions and recommendations by processing data and experiences, rather than by receiving explicit instructions

Algorithms adapt and respond to new data and experiences to improve efficacy over time

One of the key aspects of machine learning is that it is iteractive – as models are exposed to new data, they are able to adapt independently, learning from previous computations to produce reliable, repeatable decisions and results

This allows machines to make decisions without human intervention removing the risk of human error or bias in the decision-making process

Machine learning depends on 2 types of analytics:

> **Prediction** – anticipating what will happen, based on data and patterns in the data
>
> **Prescription** – providing recommendations for what to do in order to achieve goals or objectives such as personalised recommendations

Concerns regarding use of Artificial Intelligence

Security – technology could cause significant damage if used maliciously, reinforcing the importance of cybersecurity and systems which rely on AI or machine learning

Mistakes – the training phase required to allow the machine to learn how to detect the right patterns in data cannot cover all the potential situations a system may need to deal with in the real world – the system could also be "fooled" in ways that humans would not be

The problem of potential mistakes raises 2 important questions:

> How can organisations guard against mistakes (or unintended consequences) when using AI or machine learning? For example, one way of eradicating cancer in the world would be to kill everyone on the planet but this is clearly not what the human operator would want to achieve – nevertheless, if only instructed on a goal without inclusion of reasonable constraints, the AI solution would achieve its goal in a way which is not acceptable to humans
>
> Who is responsible for errors caused by an AI system? Is it the organisation **using** the system or the organisation which **created** the system?

These questions highlight the potential Ethical issues involved in the use of AI by organisations and society more generally

Applications of machine learning

Marketing and sales – websites can recommend items based on analysis of previous purchases and buying history – algorithms can be used to help encourage shoppers to complete a purchase by adjusting pricing, offering coupons or providing other incentives in real time

Transportation – routes can be made more efficient and potential problems can be identified ahead of time

Healthcare – wearable devices and sensors can use data to assess a patient's health in real time to potentially foresee dangerous health events in advance – Artificial intelligence tools can be used to diagnose illness by reviewing X-rays – machines can learn a patient's history and background more easily and quickly than can be done by a human doctor

Financial services

Fraud detection – detecting anomalies in patterns of payments or receipts and flagging these to security teams – fraud detection is one of the most important potential applications of machine learning in financial services

Loan applications – helping to identify the risk profile of potential clients

Portfolio management – robo-advisors use algorithms to calibrate a financial portfolio to the goals and risk tolerance of the investor and adjust to changes in investors' goals and real-time changes in the market, to ensure the best fit between investors' portfolios and their investment goals

Quick and accurate analysis of large and complex datasets and the insights gained from unique algorithms can allow organisations to gain a competitive advantage over others

Risks of machine learning

Machines can only learn from the data that they have been given – if there are gaps or bias in such "training" data then the models which the machines learn could be incomplete or inaccurate

In other words, machine learning is only as effective as the data that it learns from

Data accuracy – organisations need to ensure that the AI systems that they use produce correct, precise and reliable results – in many cases, machine learning involves "supervised learning" in which the machine "learns" a process or task from labelled training data – in order for the machine to learn accurately the training data needs to be free from bias and systematic error

Interpretability – as AI algorithms become more complex, it becomes increasingly difficult for humans to make sense of how they work – in some cases, AI applications are a "black box" where not even engineers can decipher why a machine made certain decision but this could make it difficult not only to identify when things go wrong but also to determine who is responsible in the event that they do

Accountability – accountability is a central element of corporate governance and implies that there should be a line of responsibility for business actions but as the point in relation to interpretability above identifies, allocation of responsibility can become difficult in the case of AI processes – if an algorithm goes wrong is it the designer or the company which is using it that is responsible? And if it is the company then whom within the company is accountable?

Institute of Business Ethics briefing paper *Business Ethics and Artificial Intelligence*

The Institute of Business Ethics notes in this briefing paper that people tend to trust those institutions that operate with openness and take account of the public interest so working with regulators and policymakers, businesses have the opportunity to make a significant contribution to agree on a framework of ethics and norms in which AI can thrive and innovate safely

Using AI to help improve an organisation's performance

Predictive maintenance – machine learning can use data from sensors throughout an operating system to identify performance issues in the system and can then take action to prevent and reduce downtime and operating costs

Real-time forecasts – real-time optimisation of delivery routes for logistics companies – this can help not only to reduce delivery times but also improve fuel efficiency

Product recommendations – combining customer demographic and past transaction data with social media monitoring can help generate individualised product recommendations which help to increase the conversion rate between the number of "hits" on a website and the number of sales generated

Personalised marketing – for example, data about an individual driver's driving patterns and distances driven can be used by insurance companies to customise premiums – in the retail sector, using customer data to personalise promotions can help retailers increase sales

Supply chain – forecasting inventory requirements based on causal drivers of demand rather than relying on prior outcomes or historic trends, can improve forecasting accuracy – this could help companies reduce their inventory costs and lead to a reduction in out of stock or overstock situations

Anomaly detection – machine learning can be valuable in analysing current (real-time) datasets to highlight unexpected patterns or outliers (anomalies) in them – this can be helpful to reduce repair and maintenance costs but also to identify fraudulent transactions or to identify potential malicious attacks on a website

Big Data – audit and data analytics

Data analytics does not relate only to "Big Data"

Data analytics is the process of collecting and examining data in order to extract meaningful business insights, which can be used to inform decision-making and improve performance – can be applied to internal data and external data

Data such as sales or purchases data (part of a company's traditional accounting records) could not really be described as "Big Data"

Data analytics should help both internal and statutory auditors to perform their work by monitoring large, complete data sets rather than testing samples as they may historically have done

Audit data analytics could be used to help the auditor identify trends, correlations and deviations from expected outcomes and/or potential risks in a client's data or control systems

Dashboards and graphics can be used to highlight unusual results – the current year figures could be compared with prior years to gain a deeper understanding of any outliers, variations or trends and to help an auditor determine what further audit tests might be needed to gain assurance over the figures

Big Data, data analytics and cloud computing

Artificial intelligence can be used as part of Big Data analytics to perform auditing of entire populations, not just samples, thus reducing human error and expanding the amount of data reviewed

Artificial intelligence can handle large data volumes without getting tired or making mistakes

Artificial intelligence and machine learning techniques can provide greater analysis of data to differentiate between "rogue" and "normal" activity

Problems with use of Artificial intelligence

Artificial intelligence may struggle with new and unusual situations which have little previous data to use for machine learning to occur

Artificial intelligence is currently not capable of exercising professional scepticism without human intervention

See also

Big Data topics	
Cloud computing and cloud accounting	104
Cyber security	145
Digital Strategies	176
Digital Transformation	184

Big Data – Blockchain

Blockchain is a type of distributed ledger (a form of collective bookkeeping)

Transactions are recorded between all the participants using a network which operates via the internet

All records are publicly-available and distributed across everyone connected to the network

All transactions between participants are recorded in identical records (ledgers) held by each user throughout the network

When a transaction occurs, the details are logged in all of the blockchain ledgers simultaneously – there will be recording of the time, date, value and participants involved

Blockchain records are only updated when all parties in the network have reviewed and verified that the transaction details are correct – the verification process is carried out by the computers that make up the network

Benefits of blockchain

The central benefit offered by blockchain is that all participants in the network have access to updated records in which each individual transaction has effectively been audited by the computers in the network

This should in theory protect against any attempt to fraudulently interfere with a transaction – incorrect details will be rejected by the network parties assigned to verify the transaction

Risks of blockchain

Blockchains are not themselves immune from being hacked so organisations should not assume that blockchains can automatically secure their data without fail

Distributed ledger technology

In a traditional ledger system, records are stored in a single, fixed location and processed and validated by a single party – for example, a company maintains its own accounting records, using its own accounting systems

On the other hand, a distributed ledger is a database that exists across several locations and with multiple participants

Instead of having a single “owner” to process, validate and authenticate transactions, records are spread out among all their uses but records are only stored once consensus is reached among all the parties involved, meaning that the ledger provides a single, agreed-upon record of transactions

2 potential applications of distributed ledger technology are blockchain and cryptocurrencies

Big Data – Chatbots

A chatbot is a service powered by rules and artificial intelligence that people interact with via a chat interface – this chat interface can either be written or verbal

Amazon's Alexa, Apple's Siri and Google Assistant are voice-activated virtual assistants which respond to instructions a user gives to them or a question a user asks them

Virtual assistants which communicate with customers are also increasingly used on organisations' websites and apps – the virtual assistant is aiming to mirror the type of experience a customer would receive when they go into a "physical" retail store

Organisations across various business sectors now use chatbots to answer questions and increase customer engagement

Benefits of chatbots

Always accessible – chatbots can operate 24 hours a day without getting tired so they are always available to answer a customer's query

Scalability – chatbots can have conversations with large numbers of people at any time so there is no need for customers to "wait to speak to the next available operator"

Cost effective – chatbots can reduce the number of employees an organisation needs to handle customer queries, reducing salary costs (although some human operators may still need to be retained to answer questions that cannot be dealt with by chatbots)

Customer satisfaction – chatbots will not react in any way if a customer appears to be rude or offensive

Disadvantages of chatbots

Virtual assistants run the risk of becoming intrusive

Chatbots may not be able to build a relationship or provide deeper benefits to customers

Big Data – ethics

Key Ethics issues in relation to Big Data:

-are organisations keeping data secure?

-do organisations have appropriate measures in place to deal with cyber attacks?

-are organisations complying with data protection regulations in their use of personal data?

-are organisations acting fairly and without bias (i.e. not discriminating against particular groups)?

Tailoring products could in effect equate to the exclusion of other customers (due to pricing or features not being suitable for them)

Organisations need to be accountable in their use of Big Data and ensure that customers are treated fairly

Algorithms and code written by humans could reflect their biases

Some algorithms and code could be so complicated that programmers/analysts cannot explain how they work to line managers, raising the question of whether a company can meet its fiduciary duty to clients (e.g. BlackRock suspended some AI-based liquidity-risk models)

The ICAEW White Paper *AI in Corporate Advisory* highlights that deep questions about transparency, monitoring and auditing of algorithm decision-making remain

A 2019 survey by Deloitte found that fewer than half of survey respondents had a policy in place for the safe and ethical use of AI

Significant ethical and privacy issues – individuals have a right not have their information shared

Collecting and selling data has become a business with some entities such as data brokers collecting massive amounts of data about individuals – this is likely to be unethical if it is not gathered with their consent

Must ensure compliance with data protection legislation and rules

Likely to be an ethical duty to prevent breach of security and therefore loss of data on customers

Should ensure that data is cleansed and anonymous wherever possible

Increase governance issues within the business to police the correct use of data within the organisation, including respect of legal rules

Overall there is a definite trade-off between privacy and utility of data

General Data Protection Regulation (GDPR)

In the context of Big Data, companies are collecting and storing increasingly large amounts of data

It is important that organisations remember their legal responsibilities in relation to personal data – for example, data regarding customers, account holders and staff

Personal data is any data or information that can be used to identify a person, including their name, address, date of birth or email address

The EU General Data Protection Regulations (GDPR) and the Data Protection Act (2018) in the UK control how personal data is used by organisations and requires them to ensure that data is kept secure, accurate and up-to-date

The Act notes that everyone responsible for using personal data has to follow strict data protection principles and must ensure that the information is:

- used fairly, lawfully and transparently
- used for specified, explicit purposes
- used in a way that is adequate, relevant and limited to only what is necessary
- accurate and, where necessary, kept up-to-date
- kept for no longer than is necessary
- handled in a way that ensures appropriate security, including protection against unlawful or unauthorised processing, access, loss, destruction or damage

The final point regarding security could be particularly significant in the context of cyber security

See also

Big Data topics	
Cloud computing and cloud accounting	104
Cyber security	145
Digital Strategies	176
Digital Transformation	184
GDPR	217

Big Data – general

High-volume, high-velocity and high-variety information assets that demand cost-effective innovative forms of information processes for enhanced insight and decision-making (Gartner)

Also defined as "datasets whose size is beyond the ability of typical database software to capture, store, manage and analyse" (McKinsey) or "the practices and technologies that close the gap between the data available and the ability to turn that data into insight" (Forrester Research)

Exploiting Big Data properly requires skills in computing and manipulation of data, statistical skills to build models and knowledge of business areas to ask the right questions and enable interpretation of the results

This requires teamwork between specialists in IT, data science and different business functions – if organisations do not currently have sufficient staff with the necessary skills, they will either need to recruit additional staff or train existing staff before they are able to take advantage of Big Data

The 4 Vs of Big Data (plus Veracity!)

Volume – the bigger the data the more potential insights it can give in terms of identifying trends and patterns, and in terms of getting a deeper understanding of customer requirements

However, the "volume" aspect of Big Data also presents the most obvious challenge to conventional IT structures, due to the volume of storage space required for the data

Velocity – the rate at which data flows into an organisation, and with which it is processed to provide useable results – the velocity concept applies to **both** these aspects (i.e. to both the speed with which data flows into an organisation and then also the speed with which it is processed)

Variety – variety of sources and a variety of formats (numerical, narrative, structured, unstructured)

Value – uncertainty regarding reliability so value can vary

Veracity – this fifth "V" relates to the truthfulness of the information – the value of any insights gained from Big Data depend on the quality and accuracy of the data – unreliable data could lead to the wrong decisions being made

Hidden biases in the data could present significant risks to an organisation

Poor data quality can often be the main barrier to executives integrating more data and analytics into their decision-making

Using Big Data

Not just for larger organisations – now much easier for small organisations to use the information due cloud software and lower cost hardware

Confers competitive advantage by providing insights that would otherwise not have been recognised

Ensures that the organisation can keep up with other organisations who are using the same processes

Drives innovation

Allows faster and deeper insights into customers

Analyses information from as many sources as possible

Online retailers are able to compile records of each click and interaction a customer makes whilst visiting their website rather than simply recording the final sale – this can be used to generate competitive advantage by recommending additional purchases

When thinking about the ways they can use data and analytics, it is important for organisations to consider whether they have sufficient, appropriately skilled staff to perform worthwhile Big Data analytics that adds value to the business

Social media analysis – as well as providing a means for organisations to communicate with customers and potential customers, the internet and social media can also provide a valuable source of customer insight and analysis – for example, by analysing the comments and feedback customers are giving about a company on social media, an organisation can identify areas it is performing well and ones where it needs to improve its performance

Recency-Frequency-Monetary (RFM) Analysis

RFM analysis can be a useful way of extracting insights from Big Data (see SBM November 2018 past paper Q2 for an example)

Recency of the latest purchase – useful for evaluating whether the customer is a "live" target

Frequency of purchases – useful for distinguishing regular customers from one-off purchasers

Monetary value of purchases – useful in targeting efforts upon customers who appear likely to spend the most

Benefits of Big Data according to McKinsey

Creating transparency

Performance improvement

Market segmentation and customisation

Decision-making

New products and services

Competitive Benefits of Big Data

Software and hardware advances have led to improvements in processing and storage capability which mean that it is economically viable for businesses to collect and process data from many sources:

Clickstream data such as searches, sites visited, goods viewed and actual transactions

Social media data such as status updates, comments and likes, photos and videos

Mobile technology is providing more opportunity to create social media and internet data and generates new data about the location of individuals

Open data such as geospatial data or transport data

The internet of things, resulting from computer chips and sensors being embedded in physical assets such as machines or domestic appliances

Current technology means that small companies can also benefit from Big Data analytics

For example, a business could use pattern recognition software to review CCTV footage (used primarily for crime prevention purposes) to understand customer footfall and which areas of the shop people go to, what products they look at and the conversion rates from looking at a product to buying it

The company could also use tools such as "Social Mention" which allow it to track comments made about it on social media and even to provide analysis of those comments

Better quality data should improve managers' ability to monitor and control business activities – it should lead to more accurate reporting, particularly when supported by dashboards that enable continuous monitoring and real-time insight into operations

Having a more detailed understanding of customer behaviour can also be useful in relation to strategic decisions – understanding the customer base of a target business could be an important element in an investment decision: customer loyalty rates could give a valuable insight into the value a business can generate from its customers

To benefit from data, businesses need to move from simply "having it" to getting insight from it and doing something differently as a result

The automation of use of Big Data could help organisations to automate non-routine decision-marking

Computers can hold far more information than humans and can quickly and accurately work through the possible scenarios without making mistakes or suffering from fatigue

Potential Limitations of Big Data

Correlation and not causation – Big Data analysis is good at spotting linkages but does not focus on explaining the cause of any trends and patterns

Sample population may not be representative

More data does not necessarily mean more benefit

Data silos – different parts of the business may not share data sufficiently or efficiently

Increased automation of analysis could lead to risks:

How will the business know if something has gone wrong?

How will the business correct potential errors?

Will computers actually be better decision-makers than humans? In some scenarios, human knowledge remains vital

When thinking about the ways they can use data and analytics, it is important for organisations to consider whether they have sufficient, appropriately skilled staff to perform worthwhile Big Data analytics that adds value to the business

Big Data and professional scepticism

Comparisons about the performance of 2 rival companies may be difficult because the data may not be entirely reliable if it has been collected in different ways, is based on different assumptions or is presented differently, under different headings, between the 2 relevant companies

These issues highlight the importance of professional scepticism when analysing data

Professional scepticism is a key SBM skill and some of the ways in which candidates can demonstrate it are: recognising bias or varying quality in data and evidence; identifying gaps in evidence; or identifying inconsistencies and contradictory information

Other questions to ask in relation to professional scepticism include: are there any gaps in the data you have been provided with? Are there any inconsistencies between that data and other sources? How does the data you have been given interact with data and information from other sources?

Importance of Data Cleansing

Data cleansing may be required if there is a risk that data may be inaccurate, inconsistent or out of date

The risks here are greater for Big Data as the new sources of data could be unreliable or become outdated very quickly

Blind analysis of large scale data sets is likely to lead to significant mistakes

High quality data is achieved by removing inaccurate records before analysis is carried out – this process is called data cleansing

In situations where data is being used to identify more general trends, accuracy may be less important – the data will still correctly identify general trends, even if some of the individual data items are unreliable

Example of use of Big Data to help forecast weekly demand

(Based on SBM November 2019 past paper Q1)

Data to be captured

Information needs to be at the level of each different product because it will not be useful to attempt to forecast the correct overall weekly demand if predictions for each type of product are not correct as the products are not likely to be substitutable for each other

Particular emphasis needs to be on items that may perish so daily forecasts within the 2 week period may be appropriate for these types of items so that they reach customers with a significant remaining "use by" date

A geographical spread of sales over the week may be important as lead times for items further away from the company's factory will need longer to deliver

Seasonality may need to be taken into account if demand follows predictable patterns

Granular information is needed for each type of product and for each geographical area

Information is needed about demand from both customers and end consumers

Customers

Information about customers is essential in predicting sales and as part of Customer Relationship Management

Customers will better understand local market conditions and how their own customers (end consumers) behave

Knowledge of how customers price the business's products to end consumers would be useful in predicting demand, particularly for future price changes

End consumers

There is pull demand from consumers which, if predictable, could be communicated to customers to encourage them to order the business's products on a more timely and efficient basis

Collection of data from the company's website may enable better prediction of pull demand from consumers (here you should try to provide some specific types of information that might be obtained from the company's website using the question Exhibit material – for example, the model answer to SBM November 2019 past paper Q1 which focused on a food company referred to downloads of recipes and discount vouchers)

Data analytics

Historic data could be collected for all customers to establish a large dataset to which data analytics could be applied to analyse point-of-sale information on the business's products (timing, amounts purchased, price charged)

More indirectly, data relating to the usage by customers of the company's website and social media could be usefully analysed – increased activity in terms of the number of hits may be a lead indicator for a forthcoming increase in future sales

More specifically, the hits on the web page for each type of product may indicate increased sales for that product in the near future

There need to be predictable patterns in the link between the number of hits and future sales and the lag between them – algorithms applied to this Big Data may be able to discern such patterns to provide better forecasts of sales

Internal data could be combined with external data to help predict demand

The number of hits on the company's website from individual end consumers may give some clues – intermediate retailer customers could be informed if demand predictions are related to a specific geographical area – for example, the downloading of discount vouchers may be a particular feature as retailers near where the end consumers live could be warned of an increase in expected demand based on the number of vouchers downloaded in the local area

The company could more actively use social media to predict consumer behaviour – for example, their use of blogs, vlogs, Twitter feeds etc – social media analytics allows companies to measure quantitative metrics such as the number of times its Facebook account has been "liked" but can also capture qualitative data such as keywords posted by customers about the company's products which can be used to perform "sentiment analysis" which would allow the company to respond to recent activity and trends

More general external data could also be used such as weather predictions if there is an established link between types of weather and demand for the company's products

See also

	Big Data topics	
	Cloud computing and cloud accounting	104
	Cyber security	145
	Digital Assets and Digital Asset Management	173
	Digital Strategies	176
	Digital Transformation	184

Big Data – impact on business models

Big Data can be described in relation to the 4 "V" characteristics:

volume – the bigger the amount of data, the more potential insights it can give in terms of identifying trends and patterns

velocity – the rate at which data flows into an organisation and with which it is processed to provide usable results

variety – the range of data types and sources from which to draw insights – in particular, Big Data combines structured and unstructured data (unstructured data means content such as conversations on social media, photographs or online video postings, and can be contrasted with structured data, which is more traditionally associated with computer storage such as database or spreadsheet information)

Volume and variety present challenges – large data sets are impossible to **capture**, **store** and **process** with standard technology: the sheer **volume** of data can end up **slowing down** a company's **systems** – it can also be a complex challenge to **turn the data into useful information**

value – uncertainty regarding reliability so value can vary

There is also a fifth V (**veracity**) – this fifth "V" relates to the truthfulness of the information – the value of any insights gained from Big Data depend on the quality and accuracy of the data – unreliable data could lead to the wrong decisions being made

Recency-Frequency-Monetary (RFM) Analysis

RFM analysis can be a useful way of extracting insights from Big Data (see SBM November 2018 past paper Q2 for an example)

Recency of the latest purchase – useful for evaluating whether the customer is a "live" target

Frequency of purchases – useful for distinguishing regular customers from one-off purchasers

Monetary value of purchases – useful in targeting efforts upon customers who appear likely to spend the most

Benefits of Big Data (according to the consultancy firm AT Kearney)

faster decisions – Big Data can provide more frequent, and more accurate, analysis which helps speed up strategic decision-making

better decisions – Big Data can estimate the impact of decisions using cross-organisational analysis and can help to quantify the impact of decisions

proactive decisions – use of predictive analytics to forecast customer market dynamics can help shape decisions

Big Data and competitive advantage (according to the consultancy firm AT Kearney)

Customer insight – Big Data puts the customer at the **heart** of corporate strategy by allowing the company to optimise product offerings in response to changing patterns of consumer demand

Big Data allows retailers, for example, to analyse data points regarding individual products at a **particular time and location** rather than at a more **generalised** store level or product group level as in the past

Insights from the analysis can be used to optimise product assortments by location, time and profitability

Product innovation – an increased level of feedback on how machines are operating through a new breed of connected, intelligent monitoring machines can be used to optimise performance and to forecast maintenance needs

Integration of the data generated by these intelligent monitoring machines could be a source of **competitive advantage** for a company which generates the data: customers may switch to such a company if it can **demonstrate improved performance and better management of maintenance** of its own products

Collecting data – the collection of data itself could generate revenues if that data can then be sold onto client companies, subject to Data Protection laws

Similarly, data, and the related analytics, are a **product in their own right** – technology and analytics firms have emerged to provide insights from the data

Simulations – Big Data sets could be valuable in helping companies to run experiments or test hypotheses regarding new products

Operations – detailed, **real-time information** from sensors or radio-frequency identification (RFID) can improve supply chain performance – processes, materials and asset movements can be monitored in real-time – retailers will be able to **monitor stock levels of all products** rather than focusing attention on, for example, the top 100 products which tend to be over- or under-stocked – companies can make use of pricing, promotion and loyalty card data to create deeper insights into what customers buy, and when, allowing retailers to build a **predictive model of distribution** to limit overstocking

It should be noted that Big Data and data analytics are simply a **means to an end** – they are tools which help organisations identify, and then implement, solutions which generate value, or **competitive advantage** – but **only if the data is used in the right way**

When thinking about the ways they can use data and analytics, it is important for organisations to consider whether they have sufficient, appropriately skilled staff to perform worthwhile Big Data analytics that adds value to the business

Big Data and professional scepticism

Comparisons about the performance of 2 rival companies may be difficult because the data may not be entirely reliable if it has been collected in different ways, is based on different assumptions or is presented differently, under different headings, between the 2 relevant companies

These issues highlight the importance of professional scepticism when analysing data

Professional scepticism is a key SBM skill and some of the ways in which candidates can demonstrate it are: recognising bias or varying quality in data and evidence; identifying gaps in evidence; or identifying inconsistencies and contradictory information

Other questions to ask in relation to professional scepticism include: are there any gaps in the data you have been provided with? Are there any inconsistencies between that data and other sources? How does the data you have been given interact with data and information from other sources?

Points from SBM November 2017 Mock 2 (Q1 – 7 marks)

Examples of the impact of Data Analytics on a restaurant chain

Demand and pricing

Demand at **individual** restaurants can be **forecast more accurately** – demand could be monitored by menu category at individual restaurants to enable **better planning**

Performance of **individual** restaurants can then be **monitored** more carefully to detect variations – underperforming restaurants can be **targeted for improvement** to ensure that targets are met

Data can then be **aggregated** to enable local and regional management to detect sales trends over time

Comparisons can be made to **rival** restaurants and pricing – potential customers are likely to perform this comparison themselves so such external data will be very useful when entering a new market or region

Operational management

Data analytics will allow managers to **monitor demand for different products in detail** and make informed decisions as a result

Detailed data in **real time** (or near to real time) will help managers to identify which product lines are selling better than others and to respond to this by **changing the mix of products** they offer – it will also allow managers to increase the amount of popular product lines **ordered from suppliers**

Demand on **different** days and at **different** times can be **predicted more accurately** – this will help with staff planning and the ordering of items from suppliers

Customer relationship management

Using data analytics to gather insights from **unstructured data** on social media sites may provide more reliable and informative results than traditional methods such as formal customer surveys – **recurring themes in social media comments** could help to highlight **specific areas for**

improvement or allow the company to obtain a **better understanding of customer requirements** – areas of outstanding performance might also be highlighted, allowing the company to take action to **maintain** such performance

Comments will provide information on **what is important to customers** – people are more likely to comment upon something which is important to them

Customer segmentation

Data analytics could be used to identify **different groups of customers – targeted** marketing strategies can then be developed and tailored for different customer types, increasing the effectiveness of marketing promotions

Segmentation of customers may also help **increase customer loyalty and retention**

Points from Business Strategy (Professional Level) March 2017 past paper (Q3 – 9 marks)

Big Data encompasses information from multiple internal and external sources – examples from the question Exhibit were then given

Companies can analyse the data and use it to adapt their products to meet customer needs and to find new sources of revenue

The 4 Vs were then defined and applied to the scenario

Use of Big Data can provide a competitive advantage in **marketing & sales**, **inventory & pricing** and **customer service**

> **Marketing & sales** – can establish a customer loyalty scheme to collect data on needs and buying habits – this could be analysed by Data analytics software – social media can be used to gain insights – marketing can be more targeted and can promote related/similar products to those purchased or based on recommendations
>
> **Inventory & pricing** – can provide a tailored experience and help predict inventory requirements – could help negotiate favourable rates with suppliers as a result – trends can be identified in real time to improve inventory and pricing decisions e.g. automatically offering a price reduction if something is not selling well – discounts could be sent to customers who have not purchased for some time – competitor pricing can be monitored
>
> **Customer service** – feedback can be left and made public via social media – this can help the company to proactively deal with potential issues and respond quickly to any complaints

Practical considerations include connections to IT strategy, cost, skills required, time, impact on customers through any disruption to website code and data protection and security

> Data protection and security was given most emphasis in the question – collecting and holding personal data has legal and security implications – the Board must ensure that appropriate controls are in place to prevent customer information falling into the wrong hands and to ensure compliance with the Data Protection Act – accountancy firms and legal advisers can assist here

Big Data – Internet of things

The internet of things refers to the connection of devices to the internet which would not normally be expected to have such a connection (such as traffic lights or smart heating systems)

Sensors which collect and transmit data can be used to automate systems, gather information, analyse information and create an action to perform a task or to learn from a process

Applications of the internet of things include:

Sensors on products or components to monitor if failure is likely to occur

Sensors can track location in real time to make supply chains more efficient

Sensors monitoring traffic flows can provide information about the best routes for delivery drivers to take

Sensors in smart buildings can adjust temperatures automatically

Data gathered by manufacturers can be just as useful as the data used by the customer – manufacturers can gather data about where consumers live, usage patterns and how often products are used and this can be analysed to amend advertising strategies to boost sales

However, everything that is connected to the internet can potentially be **hacked** so manufacturers and users need to ensure that all connected devices are **secure** – hacking into some kinds of sensors could lead to catastrophic events such as the overheating of power stations

See also Big Data topics

Big Data – Support Systems

Management information systems (MISs)

MISs provide middle managers with reports on an organisation's current and historical performance

MISs summarise data from transaction processing systems and enable it to be presented in reports which can be used to monitor and control the business

MISs provide answers to routine questions which have been specified in advance and which have a predefined procedure for answering them – for example, MIS reports could be used to compare monthly sales figures for different products to plan targets

MISs have the following characteristics:

- support structured decisions at operational and management control levels
- designed to report on existing operations
- have little analytical capability
- relatively inflexible
- have an internal focus

Decision support systems (DSSes)

DSSs can be used for less routine decision-making than MISs

DSSs focus on problems which are unique or rapidly change and which may not have a predefined procedure for finding their solution – for example, DSSs might be used to assess the impact on production schedules if sales were to double for a month

DSSs use internal information from transaction processing systems and MISs but also often incorporate information from external sources, such as competitors' product prices

DSSs have more analytical power than other systems, enabling them to analyse and condense large volumes of data into a form that helps managers make decisions – the objective is to allow the manager to consider a number of alternatives and evaluate them under a variety of potential conditions

Executive support systems (ESSs)

ESSs help senior managers make strategic and long-term decisions

ESSs incorporate external data (about industry trends, forecasts or external events such as tax changes or the emergence of new competitors) as well as summarise internal information from MISs and DSSs

An ESS is likely to have the following features:

- flexibility

quick response time

sophisticated data analysis and modelling tools

The outputs from ESSs are often presented as graphs or charts and are increasingly presented in the form of digital dashboards

See also Big Data topics

Bonuses – Audit Procedures

Verify managers' bonuses paid to salary records

Recalculate managers' bonuses

Examine the basis for allocating assets and other key variables to see if accounting policies have been correctly applied

Ascertain whether the level of bonuses is dependent on any other factors and verify these elements by recalculation or inspection of documentation

Ascertain whether managers' bonuses have been authorised by the board

Perform work on the income statement to include checks over cut-off expenditure for the year and also ascertaining whether any significant sales near the year end have influenced the bonus

Examine refunds and credits to customers after the year end to see if there have been any issues

Compare levels of key variables with the previous year and obtain explanations for significant changes

See also Remuneration Strategies 362

Bonds (Loan Notes) v Bank Loans – Comparisons

Elements of a comparison – look for **differences** between the 2 instruments relating to:

Interest rates

Fixed or variable interest rate? (Plus interaction with expectations of future rates – if future rates are expected to rise, then beneficial to have a fixed rate ... and vice versa)

Issue costs (tend to be higher for bonds)

Time period of the instrument and refinancing risk – shorter time may need renewing

Cash flow/liquidity benefits in paying later (e.g. zero coupon bond) – but will there be a large payment at the end rather than gradual payments over time as with a bank loan?

Interest rate risk

Fair value risk

Gearing – both types increase gearing, but how much and how volatile will interest rates be?

Covenant risk

Availability risk – bonds may not be taken up or not taken up in full (use underwriting) and bank loans may not always be offered

Do not forget to give a reasoned conclusion and recommendations about which option is best, making scenario-specific points

Financial reporting

IS – effective rate of interest

SFP – liability based on opening amount plus interest less cash paid – assess whether a current or non-current liability

SCF – cash actually paid

Bonds – Standard Narrative Points

Discuss cash flow and immediate business impact versus Effective Interest Rate and financial reporting impact

Consider timing – a zero coupon bond has no payments until the final day but then has a large single cash flow including the premium amount

Consider impact of exchange rate if applicable

Risk versus cost – perhaps one bond has a cheaper financing costs but is there more risk from a covenant, for example?

Risks in investing in a corporate bond

The return may be lower than the WACC of the company (although this could be balanced out by a lower level of risk than undertaking a new project)

The fair value of the bond is subject to variation as a result of changes in interest rates

Credit default risk – the risk of the issuer defaulting on its obligations to pay coupons and repay the principal – ratings issued by commercial rating companies could be used to assess this risk

Liquidity and marketability risk – the ease with which an issue can be sold in the market

Issue-specific risk such as risk of call – if the company has the right to redeem the bond early then it will only be logical for it to do so if it can refinance at a lower cost meaning that market interest rates would have to be lower than at the time that the company invested into the bond so it may now not be possible to find an alternative high-yielding investment if the bond is redeemed by the issuer – what is good for the issuer will be bad for an investor and thus the yield will have to be higher to compensate

Fiscal risk – the risk that taxes will be increased

Currency risk – for foreign currency bonds, there would also be the risk of currency fluctuation, meaning that the sterling equivalent of interest and principal may vary over time, creating uncertainty

BBB credit rating, above investment grade //
investment in corp bonds.
Pg 576 //

See also

Licensing Brand
QB 31, Page 483

QB 21

Branding and Rebranding (IFRS 13)

What is needed to create a strong brand?

Genuine commitment by key stakeholders and Board support

Detailed research to understand the position and market

Time – needs to be established for some time (NB SBM Question Bank question suggests less than 5 years not enough) – a brand can only be developed over time

Product quality

Reputation for good customer service

Ethical business practices including concerns for health and safety and relevant legislation

Avoid reputation risks – identify these in advance and take action

Marketing including advertising

Should a strong brand be built or should we wait? (According to SBM Question Bank)

If a fairly new company and a relatively small competitor in the market, brand strategy may be a longer term issue

May be important to build quality, service and reputation just to keep the business going rather than specifically to create a strong brand image

Brand Valuation under IFRS 13

Internally generated brands are not recognised as intangible assets under IAS 38 and so will not be recorded on the SFP but there may be a need to value before an acquisition or disposal (to help management determine a suitable price to pay/receive) and then if the acquisition/disposal takes place that value may be needed for financial reporting purposes as well

IFRS 13, paragraph 9: fair value is "the price that would be received to sell an asset or paid to transfer a liability in an orderly transaction between market participants at the measurement date"

IFRS 13 requires us to determine FV based on "highest and best use" from a market participant's perspective – acquirer permitted to assume that current use is highest and best use without searching for alternatives unless market or other factors suggest otherwise

Level 1 inputs – quoted prices in an active market – not normally relevant as a brand is unique

Level 2 inputs – other observable prices e.g. in non-active markets such as a recent bid

Level 3 inputs – unobservable inputs, including internal company data

Methods set out in IFRS 13:

Market basis – market price and other market transactions – difficult if brand is unique

Income basis – present value of **incremental** income generated by the brand, considering value including any possible price premium effect and additional sales

Cost basis – current replacement cost of the brand, which might be estimated as the present value of the advertising and other expenditure needed to set up an equivalent brand, including an allowance for risk and how expenditure could replicate the brand in varying market conditions (this requires a large amount of judgement and estimation, hence apply **professional scepticism** – see page **347** of these Exam Room Notes)

Determining brand value

One of the key aspects of branding is that branding and reputation are linked – a brand is something which exists in the minds of customers based on how they perceive the business

There is normally no active market for brands because, by definition, one brand should be differentiated from another brand and thus the 2 brands are not comparable – various techniques have therefore been developed to help with brand valuation:

Research-based approaches – these use consumer research into consumer behaviour and attitudes to assess the relative performance of brands – however, such methods do not put a financial value on a brand so, unless they are integrated with other approaches, they are insufficient for assessing the economic value of brands

Cost-based approaches – these methods define the value of a brand as the aggregation of all historical costs incurred to bring the brand to its current state – for example, development costs, marketing costs, advertising and other communication costs – however, there is not necessarily any direct correlation between cost incurred and the value added by the brand – analysis of financial investment needs to go beyond obvious costs such as advertising and promotion to include R&D, product packaging and design, retail design and employee training

Premium price – here the value of the brand is calculated as the NPV of the price premiums that branded products could command over an unbranded or generic equivalent – however, a difficulty with this method comes from finding an "unbranded" product to compare to as in today's markets, the majority of products are branded

Economic use approach – this approach combines marketing and financial principles – under the marketing principle, brands help to generate customer demand which translates into revenue through purchase volume, price and frequency and brands also help to retain customer demand in the longer term through repurchase and loyalty – under the financial principle, the brand's future earnings are identified and then discounted to an NPV using a discount rate which reflects the risk of the earnings being realised

FR implications of rebranding via an acquisition

IFRS 3 *Business Combinations* applies

May give rise to 2 different types of intangible asset: trade names and goodwill

Trade names

Acquiring other brand names means that future economic benefits are attributable

The trade names are also separable and identifiable

So prior to rebranding, there may be right to carry as separate intangible assets under IAS 38

An intangible asset with a finite useful life should be amortised over its expected useful life, commencing when the asset is available for use in the manner intended by management – a 2017 amendment to IAS 38 clarified that revenue-based methods of amortisation are not appropriate

Following the rebranding it is unlikely that the trade names will continue to have any separate value

Any remaining amounts will have to be written off and charge to profit or loss

Goodwill

An asset which is initially measured at cost (being the excess of consideration over fair value of all identifiable assets, liabilities and contingent liabilities)

These assets would include the trade names of the acquired chains of retail outlets

Measured at cost less impairment losses and is not amortised but tested annually for impairment

Rebranding should not affect goodwill as this is an historic amount and is not remeasured just because of a change in business activities

However there may be impairment considerations in the case of those acquired businesses which have already been identified as underperforming

Impairment tests should be carried out under IAS 36 by allocating the goodwill to cash generating units and testing these by comparing the carrying amount of the unit, including the goodwill, with the recoverable amount

Look out for a possible **gain on a bargain purchase** – this occurs if the purchaser pays less than the FV of the net assets acquired – this has been quite common in SBM Mocks and was also common under the previous Business Change syllabus

If a gain on a bargain purchase occurs, IFRS 3 requires the entity to reassess the identification and measurement of assets and liabilities acquired and, if a gain on a bargain purchase still occurs after this reassessment, to recognise immediately in profit or loss any gain on a bargain purchase (negative goodwill) remaining after the reassessment

FR implications of rebranding with significant business changes

IAS 16 PPE issues? Cost of refits and changed signage for the new brand should be capitalised as non-current assets in line with IAS 16 – depreciate over a reasonable number of years (e.g. the standard refit period of the company) and charge to profit or loss

Disposal issues? Write off capital assets no longer used under IAS 16 rules or perhaps profit or loss on disposal if can be sold? Charged to profit or loss

Marketing costs should be expensed as incurred and charged to profit or loss

Development costs – consider whether these can be capitalised or not

The post-acquisition strategy of the acquiring company may **affect the subsequent value** of the brand – if the brand name becomes **tarnished post-acquisition** then its commercial value will fall and this should be dealt with as **impairment** under the rules of IAS 36

Exam tip – Do not forget the obvious points on how something is treated in the IS or SFP – the client still needs to know this

Social Media and Brand Value

With the advent of social media and its ability to influence public opinion, a brand's value/company reputation can be affected very rapidly by adverse comments about it

Acquisitions and Brand Value

If an acquiring company does not research a brand properly, it could risk overpaying for assets which have lost their value or which may not translate effectively into the business environment facing the post-acquisition group – this is particularly important in marketplaces facing the threat of new entrants or the disruption of business models

Therefore Due Diligence should take place before the final decision to acquire a brand is taken

See also	Acquisitions topics	
	Cash Flow Forecasts – Evaluation	100
	Marketing Strategies	314
	Valuation topics	

Brexit

Exam tip – whilst you may gain some credit for mentioning Brexit, we do not recommend that you write more than a couple of sentences maximum unless the question strongly indicates that it is a major issue in the specific question being asked – also ensure that your own personal political views do not influence your points!

Could have an impact on various elements of the PESTEL framework

Could affect the attractiveness of the UK as a business location

On 23 June 2016 the British electorate voted to leave the European Union

The "Leave" campaign highlighted concerns about levels of immigration and excessive bureaucracy

The "Remain" campaign pointed out the benefits of EU membership such as the easier selling of goods and services to other EU countries and economic benefits provided by a migrant workforce – "Remainers" also claimed that Britain's status would be damaged by leaving and that being forced to "go it alone" would only cause economic harm

Arguments of those who voted to leave the EU

High levels of immigration

Excessive bureaucracy

Desire for the UK to negotiate its own way in the world

Decline in the value of the pound could drive higher exports

Arguments of those who voted to remain in the EU

Easier selling of goods and services to other EU countries

Economic benefits provided by a migrant workforce

Easier for UK businesses to send money, people, products and services around the world

Could cause economic harm as the UK may lose access to markets and trade deals

Decline in the pound and stockmarkets – the UK lost its AAA credit rating

Decline in the value of the pound to the lowest levels against the dollar since 1985, increasing costs

Strong sense of uncertainty created

Impact of Brexit vote on the UK economy

Immediately following the Brexit vote, there was a fall in the value of the pound against the dollar and in share prices

Britain lost its AAA credit rating

However, since the initial decline, share prices in the UK have recovered with the FTSE 100 trading higher than before the referendum

The biggest effect of Brexit has probably been a strong sense of uncertainty about the economic future of Britain and the future of the European Union itself, if more member states seek to leave

Following the decline in sterling, some companies have pointed out that certain goods have become more expensive but UK exporters may see increased orders because of the fall in the value of the pound

Invoking of Article 50

The UK government invoked Article 15 of the Treaty on European Union on 29 March 2017

While the focus so far has been on the implementation of Brexit with the setting up and starting of new departments, some of the practical steps that will need to be taken will depend upon the deal that is secured – however, the prospect of a "No Deal" Brexit is being discussed in the media

The demands of other member countries will determine what Brexit finally looks like and it is probable that the 2 years allowed under Article 50 will not be enough time to get all the new arrangements in place as there will be a requirement to unravel 43 years of treaties and agreements

Some UK government departments will be significantly affected (such as the Home Office, as it deals with immigration)

In the meantime, EU law still applies in the UK for as long as it remains a member state

Business ecosystems

In recent times, technology (especially digitisation) has changed the way products and services are produced and delivered

This has led to increased collaboration between organisations within business ecosystems, which can be defined as "dynamic networks of entities interacting with each other to create and exchange sustainable value for participants" (Gartner)

Rather than trying to meet customers' needs by themselves, organisations are looking to become part of ecosystems which leverage the skills and capabilities of different entities within the network to deliver products and services that would be too difficult (or too costly) for an individual organisation to deliver on its own

An important implication of a business ecosystems approach is that companies need to rethink how their business environment operates, how they partner with other organisations and how they interact with customers – for example, taking part in a successful ecosystem could provide sellers with an extremely large pool of customers of a type that they are not used to working with through opportunities created by operating other than on their own

Business ecosystems tend to be platform-based with the platform provider such as Uber providing the ecosystem which allows buyers and sellers to interact

Business partnering

Business partnering is about contributing to organisational performance

The involvement of finance professionals in business decision-making, strategy development and driving performance is not something that is new

However, involving the finance function as a business partner looks at whether finance professionals can make a valuable contribution to decision-making and successfully contribute to organisational performance outside of core work such as financial reporting

In smaller organisations, it is almost impossible for the most senior finance professional not to be a business partner – they will be directly involved in making sound finance, investment and dividend decisions with the focus of increasing shareholder wealth

In larger organisations, finance professionals are more likely to be centralised at headquarters and are often regarded as collators of reports and restrictors of innovation by imposing controls on capital spending and setting budgets – decentralising the finance function and locating accountants close to operational managers can increase the acceptance of the finance function as a business partner

Embedding finance in all functions will lead to accountants taking a more active role in becoming involved in decision-making and strategy development

Finance business partners are better positioned to support businesses when they report to local managers and are located alongside them – they will bring an expert financial perspective which may challenge other perspectives

Finance business partners will need to understand the organisation's strategy, competitive environment, commercial drivers, systems and culture

Labelling the finance function as a business partner can help to break down the stereotypes of what accountants and the finance department do – finance business partners will then be able to work with the business to find ways of increasing the return and keeping an organisation focused on its strategy

The finance function as a business partner will consider the key problems facing an organisation and use financial knowledge and techniques to suggest solutions – for example, Activity Based Costing and customer profitability analysis to look for cost efficiencies, target costing to make products more competitive and consideration of all available sources of finance to overcome financial constraints

To be successful, finance business partners will need to constantly adapt to the needs of the organisation and consistently demonstrate a positive impact on organisational performance

Business Plans

Elements

Statutory data

Executive summary

Marketing

Product/service details

Management team

Plant & equipment

Start-up costs

Business plan

Summary

Appendices

Constructing a business plan

Cash flows really are key here

Cash inflows

Cash sales
Cash from receivables
Interest receipts
New finance issues

Cash outflows

Payments to payables
Capital expenditure
Loan repayments
Interest payments
Tax payments
Dividend payments

Check for timing differences and the impact on the business

Evaluating a Business Plan

Are the sales and revenue forecasts reasonable and achievable? Compare to external data and estimates, looking at capacity and consideration of any limiting factors

Are costs understated and has account been taken of inflation (meaning specific inflation rates for the different elements of cost, and not just the general overall rate)? Do the costs reflect expansion possibilities?

Are market share projections realistic? This could be assessed again external market research data

See also

	Change – Definition & Models	101
	Change – Management & Implementation	103
	Professional Scepticism	347
	Prospective Information (ISAE 3400)	349

CAPM

$k_e = r_f + \beta_e (r_m - r_f)$

Based on the principle that risks and rewards of investment need to be appropriately balanced

The model calculates the reward expected from a given security, considering the risk of that security – this indicates the market price required

Total risk is made up of systematic and unsystematic risk

Unsystematic risk is unique to the security and therefore not to the economic system/market (hence **un**systematic risk) – this may relate to the nature of the company and its activities

Systematic risk is based on the risk associated with general market and economic factors

The average risk of all securities is measured by a beta value of 1

If the beta is more than 1, then the security is more risky than average and vice versa

Risk works in both directions – if the market were to rise by 10% overall, then an asset with a beta of 1.5 would rise by 15% because its risk is 1.5 times the average market value

Unsystematic risk is unique to the particular company being considered – this can be diversified away by investing in a greater range of companies

Systematic risk cannot be diversified away – the economic system is inherently risky and this cannot be avoided

Worked Example

Example plc has a beta of 1.8. The risk-free rate of return is 4% and the average market return is 8%.

Explain what each of these figures means and calculate Example's cost of capital using CAPM. Explain what CAPM is doing.

Beta of 1.8 – this means that the required return on Example plc's shares will change by 1.8 times the change in the return required for the market in general (increase or decrease). This suggests that Example plc has relatively volatile and high risk shares.

Risk-free rate of return of 4% – this means that investors can get a return of 4% by investing in the safest asset class available (probably government bonds). This is therefore the minimum rate of return an investor can achieve at no risk – shares, which involve higher risk, must therefore offer more.

Average market return of 8% – this means that the market is generally paying 8% on the cost of shares.

Cost of capital = 4% + (1.8 x (8% - 4%)) = 11.2%

The 4% at the start of the equation sets the minimum possible cost of capital (the minimum an investor will demand, given that they can get 4% on risk free government bonds).

By finding 8% - 4% in the brackets we are saying that the premium for investing in the market in general is a further 4%. We then multiply this by 1.8, which is the specific beta of Example plc, to adjust this risk premium up for the specific case. This means that investors should require 7.2% for investing in Example plc, on top of the 4% risk free element.

Degearing and Regearing Example

Apply the formula

$\beta e = \beta a \, [(E + D(1 - T)) / E]$

Example

A company is considering a new business venture: the company has equity with a market value of £84,770k and debt with a market value of £8,944k which will remain in place after the new project starts. A typical company in the prospective area has an equity beta of 1.9 and an equity:debt ratio of 83:17. The tax rate is 21%.

We have all the figures except βa, the asset beta for a company in the new market sector (i.e. the pure beta which is not affected by the financing structure used). So we first extract this and then run the formula again with our company's data

De-gear to find βa for the market sector

$1.9 = \beta a \, [(83 + 17(1 - 0.21)) / 83]$

$\beta a = 1.9 / [(83 + 17(1 - 0.21)) / 83]$ which is the same thing as 1.9 x the inverse of the brackets, so:

$\beta a = 1.9 \times [83 / (83 + 17(1 - 0.21))]$

$\beta a = 1.63$

Regear to find βe for our company

$\beta e = 1.63 \times [(84.770 + 8.944(1 - 0.21)) / 84.770]$

$\beta e = 1.77$

Tip – be very careful with your brackets and the order in which you perform the calculation – you may find it easier to deal with the tax element first as a **separate** calculation and insert the relevant result into the remaining calculations so that you do not then have quite so many brackets floating around e.g. in the first calculation for de-gearing above you would first deal with 17(1 - 0.21) to get a figure of **13.43**: you can then just use **13.43** throughout the rest of the de-gearing calculation rather than having to write in and deal with 17(1 - 0.21) every time.

Limitations of CAPM

Forecast figures should really be used to look at future excess return but in practice historical returns are used

Need to determine a risk-free rate – in practice interest rates vary with the term of the lending so this is harder to do than it may seem

Errors in statistical analysis used to calculate beta values

Historical betas may be a poor basis

Beta values change over time

Model is unable to forecast accurately returns for companies with low price/earnings ratio or to take account of seasonality month of the year or day of the week effects

Financial managers should use betas for industrial sectors rather than individual company betas as then measurement errors will tend to cancel each other out

CAPM fails to take into account the ways in which returns are paid – investors may prefer dividends or capital gains and will invest in the relevant companies accordingly

See also Valuations topics

Cash Flow Forecasts – Evaluation

Check for any **material omitted figures**

Check for any **material underestimates**

Consider whether the **forecast is full enough** – does it extend beyond gross profit activities or operating activities to include all relevant cash flows (e.g. CAPEX and taxation)?

Have any **finance costs** been omitted? (e.g. if there is not enough cash to make necessary purchases, credit will be needed but has this been allowed for in the model?) Consider an appropriate interest rate, taking into account the changes being considered (e.g. a higher gearing rate may increase the interest rate charged)

Has **enough been allocated to key categories** such as the advertising spend, administrative costs, new staff costs and CAPEX, etc?

Do **cost savings and synergies appear unrealistic**?

Do **variable costs change in line with activity** (e.g. staff costs, material costs, taxation figures)?

Use your professional scepticism – are there any reasons to think that the forecast could be biased (intentionally or otherwise)? Has the forecast been prepared by a manager who is keen to retain his or her job, for example, and has it therefore been estimated too generously?

See also

	Business Plans	95
	Prospective Information (ISAE 3400)	349
	Valuations – Free Cash Flow Model	432

Change – Definition & Models

CAMPS – change affects:

Costs
Accounting treatment
Markets
People
Systems

Factors promoting change

External – competitor behaviour, buyer behaviour, technology, economic events

Internal – changes in leadership style, individuals, groups, stakeholders, response to external events

Levels of change

- Strategic
- Process/operational

Types of change

- Predictable v unpredictable
- Adaptive/minor v fundamental/major
- Incremental v transformational

Barriers to change

- Groups and group thinking
- Culture
- Individuals, especially powerful or important individuals
- Personnel
- Stakeholders, including groups of stakeholders

Lewis & Schein

Unfreeze	create motive for change to remove individual and group barriers
Move	identify new behaviour and communicate and/or create new culture
Refreeze	consolidation and reinforcement of new behaviour

Types of reinforcement

Positive – praise and reward

Negative – sanctions and punishment for those who deviate

Gemini 4 Rs

Reframe

Restructure

Revitalise

Renewal

See also	Big Data topics	
	Change – Management & Implementation	103

Change – Management & Implementation

General overview of change process

Determine need or desire for a particular change

Prepare a tentative plan which considers alternatives (brainstorming)

Analyse probable reactions

Take a decision from alternative options

Establish a timetable

Communicate the plan

Implement the change

Review the change, via continuous evaluation

Communication of the plan – possible stakeholders and their concerns

Shareholders	share price, profits, dividends
Staff	job security and earnings
Management	involvement, impact on power and control
Customers	availability of product, quality, price, reliability including delivery
Financial press/analysts	how and why decision has been made, impact on share price and profits

Project life cycle model

Define – identify the need served

Design – find an approach that leads to maximum added value

Deliver – develop a clear and feasible timetable

Develop – post-implementation review to determine whether the change in processes was as efficient as it could be and that expected value is being obtained

See also

Big Data topics	
Change – Definition & Models	101
Flexible workforce management	208
Organisational Structures	324

Cloud computing and cloud accounting

Cloud computing can be defined as "a model for enabling ubiquitous, convenient, on demand access to a shared pool of configurable computing resources that can be rapidly provisioned and released with minimal management effort or service provider interaction"

Alternatively, cloud computing can be defined as "The delivery of on-demand computing resources – everything from applications to data centres – over the internet on a pay-for-use basis" (IBM)

In effect, cloud computing is access to business services through the internet – this includes **software as a service**, **a platform as a service** or **infrastructure as a service** (for example, data storage and backup).

Benefits of cloud computing

cost effectiveness – removes the **capital cost** required for buying hardware and replaces this expenditure with revenue costs for the services that an organisation uses

flexibility – allows companies the capacity to **scale up or down** as required, which could be ideal for businesses with growing or fluctuating demand

speed – establishing a cloud-based approach to data storage and management can be done **faster** than establishing the same technology in-house

accessibility – data is accessible **anywhere around the world** where there is internet connectivity – this can promote more effective collaboration between teams at different locations, including by improved document control through **central storage of a single version of files** (reducing the risk of conflicting versions, formats and so on if colleagues send multiple documents by email rather than using a centrally-stored, single document cloud approach)

availability – cloud computing is available **both** to **larger** organisations and **very small** entities alike – **small companies** can then adopt the latest cutting-edge technology **without the need for significant capital investment**

automatic software updates – these are rolled out on a **regular and automatic basis** by the cloud service provider so organisations **do not have to worry about updating** system software or systems themselves

Risks of cloud computing

entrustment of data – company data must be entrusted to the cloud so it is essential that the service provider's infrastructure is **secure** – there is an **increased risk** that the data held by the service provider may be **stolen**, **lost** or **corrupted** (not only by hackers but also by the service provider's own staff)

outages – even the best cloud service providers can suffer **technical issues** or there could be more serious **connectivity** issues preventing an organisation from connecting to the cloud so it will be important to have a **plan** to deal with such **disruption**

lack of diminishing marginal cost – if a company invests in its own capital infrastructure and significantly increases demand, it will be able to **spread the initial fixed cost over a larger and larger volume of output** whereas if it uses a cloud computing service then it could be **locked into** increasing costs as it grows because the service provider may not necessarily provide any **discount** for very large volumes of activity

Cloud accounting

Cloud accounting software changes the way organisations store and manage financial data

Instead of sorting and processing data on the organisation's internal servers alone, data is now sent "to the cloud", meaning that it is stored and can be accessed remotely

Cloud computing can be defined as "a model for enabling ubiquitous, convenient, on-demand access to a shared pool of configurable computing resources (e.g. networks, servers, storage, applications and services) that can be rapidly provisioned and released with minimal management effort or service provider interaction"

Cloud accounting can address several of the common problems which organisations can experience with traditional accounting software:

- it only works on one computer or a small number of computers – data has to be manually transferred which is not a secure or reliable process
- only one person, or a small number of people, have access to data – key stakeholders cannot access financial or customer information on a timely basis
- cloud accounting software can be used by any key stakeholder with an internet connection so it is easier for managers and an organisation's accountants to stay connected to relevant data
- as in any instance of effectively outsourcing a service, the service provider (cloud accounting software company) can take care of routine tasks (maintaining data, updating software) so that the organisation itself can concentrate on high value tasks
- ensuring that an organisation's technology team has capacity to focus on high value tasks could be particularly important in relation to designing and implementing a digital strategy

Issues to consider before transferring information to a public cloud (ICAEW paper *Security and Assurance in the Cloud)*

Data privacy, risk and security – if the information is **critical** to the business, or an organisation **cannot be reassured** that information will be adequately **protected**, then information should probably **not** be moved to the cloud – the organisation should also consider if there is a practical way to **encrypt** sensitive information before it is **uploaded** to the cloud

Access and identity – the potential cloud service provider should be asked about how it **controls** access to data – in particular, the organisation will need to know how staff and customers are **identified** and **given access** – if data is held in an environment alongside data from other clients, there must be effective **access separation** and **confidentiality protection**

Resilience and business continuity – the organisation should ask how the service provider deals with **outages** and **backups** of data

Regulatory compliance – the organisation should consider any **regulatory** or **legal** restrictions which could affect a move to the cloud: for example, are there any restrictions which require the organisation to process (or not process) information in a specific jurisdiction or country?

Assurance – the organisation should consider seeking **assurance** from potential service providers around key aspects of the service they provide in relation to their plans for data security, service outage, recovery and other key issues before entering into any contract with them – **the organisation should work through a comparative evaluation of the different providers on the market**, identifying the provider which best fits its needs, rather than simply engaging the first provider that it finds – the organisation may wish to request that an assurance report on the service provider's systems be carried out under ISAE 3402

Cloud computing versus owned technology

The **balance** between **benefits** and **risks** (see above) becomes critical for senior management

Organisations with IT staff that possess the levels of **expertise** required to manage an IT system may prefer to **retain** data storage and data management **in-house**

Complex data **compliance** requirements or a **risk-averse** attitude will make **in-house** management more likely

For organisations (particularly **smaller** and **medium-sized** entities) that need a multi-national or global presence but **lack the necessary IT expertise and resources** to manage their data and infrastructure in-house, a **cloud-based** approach may be appropriate

A related question is: **what data** will be stored in the cloud? Will **personal data** be part of the data accessed or stored in a cloud computing service? An organisation must **still comply** with data protection laws even if it uses external providers – the **organisation** is likely to be considered to be the "**data controller**" for legal purposes, with the **cloud service provider** simply being the "**data processor**"

Assurance over cloud services

ISAE 3402 provides guidance regarding any assurance work over the services provided by another organisation – see our notes on **ISAE 3402 – example answer points** starting on page **274** of these Exam Room Notes.

Under this standard, the objectives of the service auditor are to obtain **reasonable assurance** about whether, in all **material** respects, and based on suitable **criteria**:

- the service organisation's **description** of its system **fairly presents** the system as designed and implemented throughout the specified period or as at a specified date
- the **controls** related to the control objectives stated in the service organisation's description of its system were **suitably designed** throughout the specified period
- where included in the scope of the engagement ("**Type 2 report**"), the controls **in fact operated effectively** to provide reasonable assurance that the control objectives stated in the service organisation's description of its system were achieved **throughout the period analysed**

Security and the cloud (ICAEW document "Cloud adoption – Understanding the risk of cloud services")

It is **impossible** to **guarantee** that data can be **totally secure** – the level of security deemed necessary will depend on the value of the data in the users' eyes

The following questions should be asked as best practice:

-is the platform regularly tested by third-party "**penetration testers**" for potential vulnerabilities? Do such testers vigorously test the platform to determine whether an attacker could gain unauthorised access?

-what is the process in the event of a **security breach** being determined?

-is data held on the platform stored in an **encrypted** format?

-is **payment data** held on a platform which complies with the payment card industry's data security standard (**PCI DSS**)?

-is the platform protected against "**denial of service**" attacks, where attackers could prevent access to the service indefinitely by flooding the platform with erroneous traffic or requests for information?

See also

Compilation Engagements

Collection, classification and compilation of financial information. In this type of engagement, the accountant is using his or her **accounting** expertise rather than **auditing** expertise. The process is governed by **ISRS 4410**.

Example outputs from this process include historical financial information, pro forma financial information and prospective financial information including financial budgets and forecasts.

There should be agreement on:

- the intended use and distribution of the financial information and any restrictions on its use or distribution
- identification of the applicable financial reporting framework
- the objective and scope of the engagement
- the responsibilities of the practitioner, including the requirement to comply with relevant ethical requirements
- the responsibilities of management for the accuracy and completeness of the information and records and documents
- the expected form and content of the practitioner's report

The practitioner works to **obtain an understanding of the entity's business and operations**, including the accounting system and records and the applicable financial reporting framework. **The specific nature of the work varies considerably, depending on the nature of the engagement.**

If the practitioner becomes aware that the information provided by management is incomplete, inaccurate or otherwise unsatisfactory then the practitioner must bring this to the attention of management and request additional or corrected information. The practitioner must withdraw from the engagement and inform management/those charged with governance if management fail to provide this information and the engagement cannot be completed or if management refuse to make the amendments proposed by the practitioner.

The practitioner obtains an acknowledgement from management/those charged with governance that they take responsibility for the information in its final form. The practitioner's report should contain the following elements:

- a statement that the practitioner has used the information provided by management
- a description of the responsibilities of management or those charged with governance

- identification of the applicable financial reporting framework and any special purpose financial reporting framework

- identification of the financial information, including the titles of each element of the financial information

- a description of the practitioner's responsibilities in compiling the financial information

- a **description** of what a compilation engagement entails

- explanation that the compilation engagement is **not an assurance engagement** and therefore the practitioner is not required to verify the accuracy or completeness of the information provided by management

- explanation that the practitioner does not express an audit opinion or a review conclusion on whether the financial information is prepared in accordance with a financial reporting framework

- an explanatory paragraph which describes the purpose of the financial information and which draws the attention of readers to the fact that the information may not be suitable for other purposes, if it is the case that a special purpose framework has been used

Suspected non-compliance with laws and regulations

Under ISRS 4410, the practitioner should always consult internally, obtain legal advice and consult with the regulator or professional body in order to understand the implications of different courses of action

Convertible Bonds

Split into equity and liability elements

Comment on need to unwind the liability element (look out for time apportionment here) and consider whether it is a current or non-current liability

Use round thousands to make the calculation quicker – the examiner just wants to see the principle

Worked Example

Show the split accounting of the following compound instrument:

Issue of 10,000 6% convertible bonds at par of £100

Each bond is redeemable at par or convertible into 4 shares in 2 years

The market rate of interest for similar debt without the conversion option is 8%

The value of the bonds is £100 x 10,000 = £1m

Annual interest is based on the **nominal or coupon** amount of 6%, so £60,000 per year

Always discount at the market rate of interest EXCLUDING the conversion option

So discount the cash flows at 8%

In this case, there will be three cash flows: £60,000 interest in year 1, £60,000 interest in year 2, and £1,000,000 redemption in year 2

The PV of these flows gives us the liability element

The balancing figure is the equity element

	Cash flow @ 6%	DF @ 8%	PV
Year 1	60,000	1/1.08	55,556
Year 2	1,060,000	1/1.08/1.08	908,779
Liability element			964,335
Equity element Balancing figure			35,665 (B)
Total proceeds			1,000,000

There will be impacts on the financial statements in the intervening period before conversion

profitability/income statement
finance cost on the unwinding of the liability element (check for time appointment issues)

statement of financial position
liability element will increase due to unwinding, increasing gearing

Narrative points

Likely take up in the market – are the terms attractive?

Investors are generally willing to accept a lower interest yield

Unusual instruments – not many real world issues

Advise client to take advice from an investment bank

See also

Corporate Governance – Aims of Corporate Governance reports

Ensuring integrity – stressing the role of directors in influencing the culture, tone and core values of the company

Promotion of strategic objectives – explanation of how strategic decision-making activities will enhance performance

Control of companies – creation of a framework for the control of multinational companies

Enhancing risk management – requirement for compliance with accepted good practice and ensuring appropriate systems of control are in place

Protection of shareholders – corporate governance reports aim to protect shareholders in the same way that investors are protected by any other financial investment products

Involvement of shareholders – provides more details about company activities and improves proceedings at AGMs by recommending votes on remuneration policy and the Directors' report and accounts

Protection of stakeholders – minimising potential conflicts of interest between the owners, managers and wider stakeholder community

Establishment of accountability – addresses the problem of an over mighty managing director by emphasising the need for a clear division of responsibilities and the involvement of non-executive directors

Maintenance of effective scrutiny – ensures the independence of those with primary responsibility for scrutinising company activities – prescribing what constitutes, or what might jeopardise, the independence of non-executive directors – enhancing the position of non-executive directors by prescribing that a certain number of directors be non-executive

Provision of accurate and timely information – emphasising the need for the accounts to present a true and balanced picture of what is happening in the organisation – also emphasises the importance of timely information as an aid, enabling directors to supervise company activities better

See also Other Corporate Governance topics

Corporate Governance – Board, directors and NEDs

The Role of the Board

- **decisions on fundamental matters** to the business such as mergers and takeovers, acquisitions, investments, capital projects, bank borrowing facilities and loans

- monitoring the **Chief Executive Officer**

- overseeing **strategy**

- monitoring **risks and control systems**

- monitoring the **human capital aspects** of the company regarding succession, morale, training and remuneration

- ensuring that there is **effective communication of its strategic plans**, both internally and externally

The Principles of the UK Corporate Governance Code identify the role of the Board as:

> to provide effective and entrepreneurial leadership for the company, and to promote its long-term, sustainable success, generating value for shareholders and contributing to wider society
>
> to establish the company's purpose, value and strategy and to satisfy itself that these are aligned with the company's culture
>
> to ensure that the necessary resources are in place for the company to meet its objectives and to measure performance against them
>
> the Board should also establish a framework of prudent and effective controls which enable risk to be assessed and managed

One of the Board's key responsibilities is to measure a company's performance against its objectives

Drew, Kelley and Kendrick (2005) suggest that the company's ability to engage in effective Corporate Governance is underpinned by 5 elements: culture, leadership, alignment, systems and structure

Importantly, these elements do not operate in isolation – each element is linked to, and supports, the others

Board effectiveness

The UK Financial Reporting Council (FRC) published a document entitled "Guidance on Board Effectiveness" in 2018 to accompany the updated UK Corporate Governance Code

The "Guidance on Board Effectiveness" stresses that an effective Board "defines the company's purpose and then sets a strategy to deliver it, underpinned by the values and behaviours that shape its culture and the way it conducts its business"

An effective Board will also be able to explain the main trends and factors affecting the company's long-term success such as technological change and how these and the company's principal risks and uncertainties have been addressed

One of the most important characteristics of an effective Board is that it makes well-informed and high-quality decisions – factors that contribute to this include:

robust debate in the boardroom, reflecting the diversity of skills and perspectives of the directors and avoiding "group think"

allowing sufficient time for debate and discussion of all issues within the Board's remit

obtaining input from key stakeholders

obtaining expert opinions when necessary

The FRC guidance document also stresses that Boards need to be aware of factors that can limit effective decision-making (and should try to avoid them):

a dominant personality or group of directors on the Board, inhibiting contribution from others

insufficient diversity of perspective on the Board, contributing to "group think"

excess focus on risk mitigation, or insufficient attention to risk

treating risk as a compliance issue rather than as part of the decision-making process

insufficient knowledge and ability to test underlying assumptions

failure to listen to, and act upon, concerns that are raised

failing to recognise the consequences of running the business on the basis of self-interest and other poor ethical standards

a lack of openness by management, reluctance to involve non-executive directors or a tendency to bring matters to the Board to sign off, rather than to debate

complacent or intransigent attitudes

inadequate information or analysis and poor-quality Board papers

lack of time for debate and truncated debate

undue focus on short-term time horizons (rather than longer term issues)

Board diversity

The UK Corporate Governance Code states that "appointments to the Board should be subject to a formal, rigorous and transparent procedure"

The Code also highlights that appointments "should be based on merit and objective criteria (i.e. avoiding discrimination) and, within this context, should promote diversity of gender, social and ethnic backgrounds, cognitive and personal strengths"

Diversity can have a positive effect on the quality of decision-making by directors by reducing the risk of "group think"

Directors will be more likely to make good decisions and maximise the opportunities for the company's success if the right skill sets and an appropriate breadth of perspectives are present in the boardroom

Role of the Board chairperson

The Board chairperson has responsibilities for ensuring that the composition of the Board meets the requirements of the company

In the UK, it is common in listed companies for the Board chairperson also to be the chairperson of the Nomination Committee although the chair of the Board must not chair the Nomination Committee if it is dealing with the appointment of their successor

Role of the Remuneration Committee

The UK Corporate Governance Code highlights that "Remuneration policies and practices should support strategy and promote long-term sustainable success. Excessive remuneration should be aligned to company purpose and values, and be clearly linked to the successful delivery of the company's long-term strategy"

When setting remuneration, it is important to ensure that incentives and rewards are aligned with an organisation's culture

Non-Executive Directors – Roles, Advantages and Disadvantages

NEDs have the same legal duties, responsibilities and potential liabilities as executive directors, even though they are not expected to give the same continuous attention to the company's business

However, as the UK Corporate Governance Code notes, NEDs have a key role in scrutinising and holding to account the performance of management and individual executive directors against their performance objectives

NEDs on the Remuneration Committee are responsible for deciding the appropriate levels of remuneration for executive directors whilst NEDs on the Audit Committee are responsible for monitoring the integrity of the company's financial statements and reviewing its internal financial controls as well as its internal control and risk management systems

NEDs also have a prime role in succession planning and in the appointment and removal of executive directors

Appointment period

Under the 2016 edition of the UK Corporate Governance Code, NEDs should ideally not be appointed for a period exceeding 6 years

Under the 2018 edition of the UK Corporate Governance Code, all directors (including NEDs) should be subject to annual re-election

Remuneration policy

Under the 2016 edition of the UK Corporate Governance Code, controls are required to limit the use of options for remuneration NEDs and for remuneration policies for NEDs where shareholders are involved

Under the 2018 edition, NEDs' fees should either be set by the Board or set out in the company's Articles of Association, with no share options or performance-related elements allowed

The **roles** of NEDs are:

- **Strategic** – NEDs contribute to, and challenge, strategy
- **Performance** – NEDs scrutinise performance of management in meeting goals and objectives
- **Risk** – NEDs should ensure that financial information is accurate and that controls are robust
- **Remuneration and succession** – NEDs should be responsible for determining appropriate levels of remuneration for executives and should be key figures in the appointment and removal of senior managers and in succession planning

Some **advantages** of having NEDs on the Board include[3]:

- possess **external experience and knowledge** which executive directors do not have
- can provide a **wider perspective**
- **provide comfort to third parties** such as investors or creditors
- can play **certain important roles** such as father-confessor (being a confidant for the chairman and other directors), an oil-can (making the Board run more effectively) and acting as high sheriff (removing the chairman or chief executive if necessary).
- **dual role** as full Board members but also having a strong, independent element

Some **problems** with having NEDs on the Board include:

- may **lack independence**

---

[3] If the client company discussed in the question wording is relatively small and perhaps family-owned, then the client will be missing out on these advantages so this should give you something to discuss.

- may not include people **other than those proposed by the Board**
- the **best candidates for an NED role might naturally work at the best-run companies** anyway i.e. companies that do not need any input from good NEDs
- may have **difficulty in imposing their views** on the Board
- may not **pay enough attention** to preventing trouble or advising on the early warning signs of a problem
- **limited amount of time** to devote to the role

Independence of NEDs

When assessing the independence of NEDs, consider:

- whether the NED has been an **employee of the company in the last 5 years**
- whether the NED has had a **material business relationship** with his or her company as a result of serving in a senior role with another company
- whether the NED receives **additional remuneration** apart from a director's fee or participates in share options or pension schemes
- whether the NED has any **close family ties** with the company's advisers, directors or senior employees
- whether the NED holds **cross-directorships** or has significant links with other directors or through involvement in other companies or bodies
- whether the NED has a **significant shareholder**
- whether the NED has **served on the Board for a substantial period of time**

Establishing an effective Group Control Framework

Ensure that each subsidiary has both responsibility for performance and the ability to control that performance – e.g. if the subsidiary will be monitored based on ROCE then the subsidiary should have control over its capital base and have the ability to borrow funds

Consider the alternatives of centralised control on a divisionalised basis or giving more autonomy to the management of the subsidiary for local decisions (while maintaining accountability to the parent Board for overall performance)

A more localised decision-making should lead to more rapid decisions being made

A more localised decision-making could also incentivise managers to improve performance as their actions can now impact on that performance

The main Board should set clear objectives and monitor achievement of these objectives – the subsidiary should have control over the means required to achieve objectives

See also Other Corporate Governance topics

Corporate Governance – Definition, concepts and problems

Auditor Responsibilities – ISA 720 *The Auditor's Responsibilities Relating to Other Information*

In the UK, statutory other information includes the directors' report, strategic report and the separate governance statement.

The auditor must include a separate section in the auditor's report headed up as "Other Information".

The auditor should identify any material misstatement of the other information, arising from an inconsistency between the "other information" and the financial statements.

Corporate Governance – Definition and Concepts

Corporate governance can be defined as "the system by which organisations are directed and controlled".

The OECD definition is that "Corporate Governance involves a set of relationships between a company's management, its Board, its shareholders and other stakeholders. Corporate Governance also provides the structure through which the objectives of the company are set, and the means of attaining those objectives and monitoring performance are determined … providing shareholders, Board members and executives as well as financial intermediaries and service providers with the right incentives to perform their roles within a framework of checks and balances" (OECD, 2015)

We would advise you to start your answer with a definition, before applying the definition to the scenario given.

High standards of corporate governance should be based on a number of fundamental principles:

responsibility – the leaders of the company should accept responsibility for acting in the best interests of the company so as to achieve the company's objectives

accountability – the board of directors should be fully accountable to the company's shareholders (and other stakeholders) within the company, executive management should be properly accountable to the board of directors

integrity and honesty – the company should operate in a way that displays fairness and honesty in its dealings – good corporate governance has a strong ethical element

transparency – through reporting or other methods of communication, the company should be open and transparent about their policies and objectives, as well as past performance

CG is used to:

- reduce risk
- specify distribution rights and responsibilities between different stakeholders

- specify rules and procedures for corporate decisions
- provide a structure through which objectives are set
- provide a framework for ethical and other safeguards
- promote new investment and confidence in companies

Fundamentally, as a matter of good governance the Board should have clear strategic objectives.

The Board should also establish its risk appetite and framework for considering risks.

Regulation and Corporate Governance

Regulation is important for corporate governance because the company should have an effective internal control system to ensure compliance with key regulatory requirements

There are also some regulations that apply to the conduct of corporate governance including criminal laws that apply to activities such as money laundering, insider dealing and bribery, statutory duties of directors, some of the listing rules and disclosures and transparency rules that are applied to listed companies by stock market regulators and requirements for listed companies either to comply with the provisions of the corporate governance code (such as the UK Corporate Governance Code) or explain any non-compliance in their annual report

The "comply or explain" approach is an aspect of corporate governance in the UK which has been widely copied elsewhere in the world

Indicators of Corporate Governance problems

- domination by a single individual
- lack of involvement of the Board
- lack of an adequate control function, including internal audit
- lack of supervision due to systems deficiencies or a lack of segregation of key roles
- lack of independent scrutiny by the external auditors
- lack of contact with shareholders
- emphasis on short-term profitability rather than long term investment
- misleading accounts and information
- persistent Board disagreements between Executive Directors and NEDs

Evaluation of Corporate Governance Mechanisms

- **reviewing minutes** of the meetings of the Board of directors
- **reviewing supporting documents** prepared for the Board of directors
- **making inquiries of certain directors** and the company secretary
- **attending meetings of the audit committee** at which the annual report and accounts are considered and approved
- **making appropriate enquiries** and reviewing the statements made by the Board
- **reporting by exception** if problems arise such as the Board summary not reflecting the auditors' understanding of that process or there has been a failure to disclose or conduct an annual review

See also Other Corporate Governance topics

Corporate Governance – Disclosure and other requirements

Areas on which the Board should report

How the company has applied the core principles of the Code (including satisfaction of the more detailed provisions)

Board leadership and company purpose

Division of responsibilities

Composition, succession and evaluation

Audit, risk and internal control

Remuneration

Disclosure requirements in relation to "Board leadership and company purpose"

The opportunities and risks that the company faces, the corresponding sustainability of the current business model and how the current system of governance adopted by the company helps to achieve each of these

An overview of the company's culture and how the company manages the workforce

Details of any significant disagreements between the Board and shareholders when voting on a resolution

An overview of how the company has engaged with the company's key stakeholders

Disclosure requirements in relation to "Division of responsibilities"

The independence of NEDs and the company's rationale for reaching this assessment

The number of meetings of the Board and its committees and individual attendance by all directors

Disclosure requirements in relation to "Composition, success and evaluation"

Transparency over the identity and independence of any external recruiters used as part of any Board recruitment and any external evaluators used when assessing Board performance

An overview of the work of the Nomination Committee, including processes, policies and its commitment to diversity

Disclosure requirements in relation to "Audit, risk and internal control"

Disclosure of the work of the Audit Committee including:

reasons for the absence of an Internal Audit function where there is none

significant issues that are considered in relation to the financial statements, and how these issues were addressed

an explanation of how it has assessed the effect of the external audit process and the approach taken to the appointment or reappointment of the external auditor, including the length of tenure of the current audit firm and when the tender was last conducted

explanation of why the Board did not accept any of the Audit Committee's recommendations regarding the external auditor

if the external auditor provides non-audit services, an explanation of how auditor objectivity and independence is safeguarded

An explanation from the directors of their responsibility for preparing the financial statements and how they believe these statements support shareholders in holding them to account

The processes used by directors for identifying and managing the company's principal risks

A report on the Board's review of the effectiveness of the company's risk management and internal controls systems

Confirmation that the company will continue to be a viable going concern and any material uncertainty that might place this under some form of jeopardy

An assessment of the company's future prospects and ability to meet future liabilities

Disclosure requirements in relation to "Remuneration"

Where remuneration consultants have been appointed, whether they have any other connection with the company

A description of the work of the Remuneration Committee, including the rationale behind the processes used and how the company has engaged with shareholders and the workforce

Corporate Governance – requirements other than disclosure

Note – the following list of 12 requirements is based on a list of additional requirements which do not relate to disclosure but which "could appear in exam questions" and are therefore points which candidates "should be familiar" with, according to the 2020 edition of the Corporate Reporting Study Manual (see page 146 of the 2020 edition of the Corporate Reporting Study Manual)

Requirements other than disclosure requirements which could appear in exam questions

1. The need for an independent Chair, separate from the Chief Executive, and Chief Executive who should not go on to chair the same company

2. Length of service limits of no more than 9 years for the Chair and any NEDs
3. NEDs (preferably independent, excluding the Chair) to make up the majority of the Board
4. The crucial roles that both the senior independent director and NEDs can play in supporting the Board and shareholders
5. Nominations Committees consisting of a majority of NEDs
6. All directors (including NEDs) to be subject to annual re-election
7. Audit Committees should consist entirely of at least 3 independent NEDs with at least 1 member possessing suitable financial experience
8. Audit Committees should review the financial statements, internal control and risk management systems, as well as the effectiveness of internal audits and all matters related to the appointment of the external auditor, terms of reference, independence, effectiveness and any non-audit work carried out
9. Remuneration Committees should consist entirely of at least 3 independent NEDs
10. NED fees should either be set by the Board or set out in the company's Articles of Association, with no share options or performance-related elements allowed
11. Executive remuneration schemes where share options are used should use a vesting period of at least 5 years
12. Executive remuneration schemes should allow for awards to be reclaimed from directors for a specified reason

See also Other Corporate Governance topics

Corporate Governance – G20/OECD and ICGN principles

The details of codes of Corporate Governance vary by country and there is no single model of "good governance"

However, underlying any governance models or codes is the logic that good governance is required to create an environment of market confidence in business integrity – this will help reassure shareholders and other stakeholders

G20/OECD Principles of Corporate Governance (2015)

This document provides an international benchmark

The Principles are based on the underlying logic that a high level of transparency, accountability, Board oversight and respect for the rights of shareholders and the role of key stakeholders are key parts of a well-functioning Corporate Governance system

OECD Principles of Corporate Governance

The Principles are not intended to be detailed prescriptions but instead aim to provide a reference which policymakers can use to develop their own Corporate Governance framework

1. **Transparency and fairness** – the Corporate Governance framework should promote transparent and fair markets and the efficient allocation of resources – it should be consistent with the rule of law and support effective supervision and enforcement

2. **Shareholders' rights** – the Corporate Governance framework should protect and facilitate the exercise of shareholders' rights and ensure the equitable treatment of all shareholders, including minority and foreign shareholders

3. **Investors and stock markets** – the Corporate Governance framework should provide sound incentives throughout the investment chain and provide for stock markets to function in a way that contributes to good Corporate Governance

4. **The role of stakeholders in Corporate Governance** – the Corporate Governance framework should recognise the rights of stakeholders established by law or through mutual agreements and encourage active cooperation between companies and stakeholders in creating wealth, jobs and the sustainability of financially-sound enterprises

5. **Disclosure and transparency** – timely and accurate disclosure should be made on all material matters regarding the company, including its financial situation, performance, ownership and governance

6. **Board responsibilities** – the Corporate Governance framework should ensure strategic guidance of the company, effective monitoring of management by the Board and the Board's accountability to the company and shareholders

International Corporate Governance Network (ICGN) Global Governance Principles

The ICGN also offers a supranational perspective on Corporate Governance and its Global Governance Principles highlight 8 key principles of effective governance

1. **Board role and responsibility** – the Board should act on an informed basis with good faith, care and diligence in the best long-term interests of the company, for the benefit of shareholders but with regard to the interests of other relevant stakeholders

2. **Leadership and independence** – Board leadership requires clarity and balance in Board and executive roles, and an integrity of process to promote the success of the company as a whole, as well as the interests of minority investors

3. **Composition and appointment** – there should be a sufficient mix of directors with relevant knowledge, independence, competence, industry experience and diversity of perspectives to generate effective challenge, discussion and objective decision-making

4. **Corporate culture** – the Board shall adopt high standards of business Ethics, ensuring that the company's vision, mission and objectives are sound and reflect its values – codes of conduct should be communicated effectively and integrated into the company's strategy and operations, including its risk management systems and remuneration structures

5. **Risk oversight** – the Board should proactively oversee, review and approve the approach to risk management, and should satisfy itself that the approach is functioning effectively

6. **Remuneration** – remuneration should be designed to align the interests of the CEO and executive directors with those of the company and its shareholders to help ensure long-term performance and sustainable value creation – aggregate remuneration should be appropriately balanced with the need to pay dividends to shareholders and retain capital for future investment

7. **Reporting and audit** – the Board should oversee timely and high-quality disclosures for investors and other stakeholders relating to financial statements, strategic and operational performance, Corporate Governance and significant environmental and social factors – a robust audit practice is critical for necessary quality standards

8. **Shareholder rights** – the rights of all shareholders should be equal and must be protected – shareholder voting rights must be directly linked to the shareholder's economic stake in the company – minority shareholders must have voting rights on key decisions or transactions which affect their interest in the company

See also Other Corporate Governance topics

Corporate Governance – past paper points

Summary of Key Corporate Governance Points

- Ensure that you can offer a **brief definition of CG** and **explain why it is necessary**
- Ensure that you can spot the **warning signs** or "**red flags**" which could indicate a **CG problem**
- Consider mentioning the **basic aspects of the UK Corporate Governance Code** but check whether this will apply in the scenario (if not (for example, an AIM-listed company), then just apply the same concepts but state that the Code would be "best practice", so many stakeholders may wish to see the Code followed anyway)
- Indicate the **roles of the Board and NEDs** (including **advantages and disadvantages of NEDs**)
- Indicate **procedures** relating to the **testing of CG at the Board level**
- Consider **stakeholders and their interests**, applying **scepticism to any proposed changes**
- Look at the **existing and potential balance of power**, always considering the **key cut off points of 75% and 50% shareholdings**
- Discuss some possible ways of **improving CG** and the **operation of Boards**
- **Identify different stakeholder groups** and try to provide some **different points for each group**, perhaps under headings, to show the impact of a CG change

See also Other Corporate Governance topics

Corporate Governance – Stewardship Code

The UK Stewardship Code

"Stewardship" is defined as the responsible allocation and management of capital across the institutional investment community to create sustainable value for beneficiaries, the economy and society

The UK Stewardship Code was originally issued in July 2010 and then revised in September 2012

The UK Stewardship Code aims to enhance the quality of engagement between investors and companies to help improve long-term returns to shareholders and to enhance the efficient exercise of governance responsibilities

The FRC views the relationship between the UK Stewardship Code and the UK Corporate Governance Code as being a complementary relationship – the Stewardship Code sets out good practice to which institutional investors should aspire

The UK Stewardship Code should be applied on a "comply or explain" basis

The UK Corporate Governance Code states that, in line with their responsibilities under the UK Stewardship Code, investors should engage constructively with companies and discuss with them any departures from recommended practice

The FRC published a consultation paper in 2019 with a view to strengthening the Stewardship Code in the future

The draft 2019 Stewardship Code

At the time of writing of the 2020 edition of the Corporate Reporting Study Manual, the FRC was consulting on a new 2019 version of the UK Stewardship Code

The 6 categories stated in the draft 2019 Stewardship Code are:

- Purpose, objectives and governance
- Investment approach
- Active monitoring
- Constructive engagement and clear communication
- Exercise rights and responsibilities
- Service providers

The 5 key changes that are expected to be seen in the 2019 version of the UK Stewardship Code are:

1. clarification of an investor's purpose in order to assess whether it meets the objectives and governance responsibilities expected by those typically displaying effective stewardship qualities

2. recognising that capital used may include asset types other than UK-listed equity

3. inclusion of environmental, social and governance (ESG) factors including climate change when assessing stewardship roles

4. recognising that the Stewardship Code will apply to different roles in the investment community and tailoring the advice given accordingly

5. using a 2-stage reporting approach (effectively once signing up to the Stewardship Code and then an annual disclosure of investment activities and outcomes)

See also Other Corporate Governance topics

Corporate Governance – UK Corporate Governance Code 2018

Key Points in the April 2016 update to the UK Corporate Governance Code

The audit committee is required to have "competence relevant to the sector in which the company operates"

The audit committee report within the annual report must provide "advance notice of any retendering plans"

The provision that FTSE 350 companies are expected to put the audit out to tender at least every 10 years has been removed – but note that this has been replaced with the EU Audit Regulation and Directive requirements for mandatory tendering and rotation of the audit firm.

Corporate Governance Code 2018

The latest version of the UK Corporate Governance Code came into effect in July 2018 – 4 main changes were made:

> Workforce and stakeholders – there is a new provision to enable greater Board engagement with the workforce and the Board is required to describe how they have considered the interests of stakeholders when performing their duty under Section 172 of the 2006 Companies Act
>
> Culture – Boards are asked to create a culture which aligns company values with strategy and to assess how they preserve value over the long term
>
> Succession and diversity – the new Code emphasises the need to refresh Boards and undertake succession planning to ensure the right mix of skills and experience and to promote constructive challenge – Boards should consider the length of term that Chairs remain in post beyond 9 years – the role of the Nomination Committee is strengthened
>
> Remuneration – to address public concern over executive remuneration, the new Code emphasises that Remuneration Committees should take into account workforce remuneration and related policies when setting director remuneration – formulaic calculations of performance-related pay should be rejected – Remuneration Committees should apply discretion when the resulting outcome is not justified

The 2018 edition of the UK Corporate Governance Code contains 18 core principles and a further 41 more detailed provisions

Points in the 2016 edition of the UK Corporate Governance Code which were not carried forward into the 2018 edition

The need to arrange insurance cover in respect of legal action against directors

Boards should be of sufficient size to accommodate business needs

NEDs should be appointed for a fixed period, ideally not exceeding 6 years

Benchmarking remuneration against other companies, leading to policies that risk the upward ratchet of remuneration levels with no corresponding improvement in performance

Remuneration disclosures for executives who leave the company to take up a non-executive position at another company

Controls to limit the use of options for remunerating NEDs and remuneration policies for NEDs where shareholders are involved

Shareholders should be involved in approving long-term incentive schemes

Various miscellaneous rules about AGMs and proxy votes

"Comply or explain" approach

Reporting should be meaningful when explaining how the Code has been applied, avoiding what is sometimes referred to as "boilerplate" reporting

Non-compliance may be justified when factors such as the size, complexity, history or ownership structure of the company demand that an alternative approach is reported
Temporary departures from any of the Code's provisions should indicate a timescale for conformance

Explanations should be seen as an opportunity not an obligation

Governance disclosures should complement all other forms of reporting to present a coherent view of the company and how it has been run

5 main categories of the 2018 edition of the UK Corporate Governance Code

Board leadership and company purpose

Division of responsibilities

Composition, succession and evaluation

Audit, risk and internal control

Remuneration

Summary of key points made regarding the 2018 edition of the UK Corporate Governance Code in the 2020 edition of the Corporate Reporting Study Manual

In the UK, companies with a premium listing should be guided by the UK Corporate Governance Code as revised in July 2018

The Code emphasises the value of good Corporate Governance as a contributing factor to long-term sustainable success and identifies a set of key Principles which help to define good governance

The Listing Rules require companies to explain how they have applied the Principles so that, in turn, shareholders can evaluate how effectively the Principles have been applied

In this respect, the quality of a company's reporting is important in order to allow shareholders to evaluate how the Principles have been applied and the company's governance practices

However, the UK Corporate Governance Code sets out Principles rather than a rigid set of rules so that it offers Boards and companies flexibility by allowing them to "comply or explain" with the Principles

This also means that shareholders and investors need to assess a company's approach thoughtfully and (particularly if the company has not complied with a Principle) to determine whether or not they are satisfied that the company's governance practices are contributing to its sustainable success and helping it achieve its strategic objectives

As such, investors as well as directors have an important role in governance – investors should engage constructively with companies and discuss with them any departures from recommended practice and the company's rationale for these

Principles of the UK Corporate Governance Code

Board Leadership and Company Purpose

A	A successful company is led by an effective and entrepreneurial Board, whose role is to promote the long-term sustainable success of the company, generating value for shareholders and contributing to wider society
B	The Board should establish the company's purpose, values and strategy and satisfy itself that these and its culture are aligned – all directors must act with integrity, lead by example, and promote the desired culture
C	The Board should ensure that the necessary resources are in place for the company to meet its objectives and measure performance against them – the Board should also establish a framework of prudent and effective controls which enable risk to be assessed and managed
D	In order for the company to meet its responsibilities to shareholders and stakeholders, the Board should ensure effective engagement with, and encourage participation from, these parties
E	The Board should ensure that workforce policies and practices are consistent with the company's values and support its long-term sustainable success – the workforce should be able to raise any matters of concern

Division of Responsibilities

F	The Chair leads the Board and is responsible for its overall effectiveness in directing the company – the Chair should demonstrate objective judgement throughout their tenure and promote a culture of openness and debate – the Chair facilitates constructive Board relations and the effective contribution of all NEDs and ensures that directors receive accurate, timely and clear information
G	The Board should include an appropriate combination of executive and non-executive (and, in particular, independent non-executive) directors such that no one individual or small group of individuals dominates the Board's decision-making – there should be a clear division of responsibilities between the leadership of the Board and executive leadership of the company's business
H	NEDs should have sufficient time to meet their Board responsibilities – they should provide constructive challenge, strategic guidance, offer specialist advice and hold management to account
I	The Board, supported by the company secretary, should ensure that it has the policies, processes, information, time and resources it needs in order to function effectively and efficiently

Composition, Succession and Evaluation

J	Appointments to the Board should be subject to a formal, rigorous and transparent procedure, and an effective succession plan should be maintained for Board and senior management – both appointments and succession plans should be based on merit and objective criteria and, within this context, should promote diversity of gender, social and ethnic backgrounds, cognitive and personal strengths
K	The Board and its committees should have a combination of skills, experience and knowledge – consideration should be given to the length of service of the Board as a whole and membership regularly refreshed
L	Annual evaluation of the Board should consider its composition, diversity and how effectively members work together to achieve objectives – individual evaluation should demonstrate whether each director continues to contribute effectively

Audit, Risk and Internal Control

M	The Board should establish formal and transparent policies and procedures to ensure the independence and effectiveness of internal and external audit functions and satisfy itself of the integrity of financial and narrative statements
N	The Board should present a fair, balanced and understandable assessment of the company's position and prospects
O	The Board should establish procedures to manage risk, oversee the internal control framework and determine the nature and extent of the principal risks the company is willing to take in order to achieve its long-term strategic objectives

Remuneration

P	Remuneration policies and practices should be designed to support strategy and promote long-term sustainable success – executive remuneration should be aligned to company purpose and values and be clearly linked to the successful delivery of the company's long-term strategy

Q	A formal and transparent procedure for developing policy on executive remuneration and determining director and senior management remuneration should be established – no director should be involved in deciding their own remuneration outcome
R	Directors should exercise independent judgement and discretion when authorising remuneration outcomes, taking account of company and individual performance and wider circumstances

Engagement with stakeholders

The UK Corporate Governance Code notes that in order for a company to meet its responsibilities to its stakeholders, the Board needs to "ensure effective engagement with, and encourage participation from" stakeholders

Stakeholders can be internal (within the company such as the directors and employees) or external to the company (such as most shareholders in a public company, lenders, customers, suppliers, regulators, pressure groups and the general public)

Engagement with the workforce

The UK Corporate Governance Code emphasises the importance of companies understanding the views of key stakeholders and considering them in decision-making

In order to understand the views of stakeholders, it is important that company Boards engage with stakeholders effectively

A company's workforce is likely to play a key role in its ongoing success so it is important that directors engage with staff – this will be necessary not only to listen to their issues and concerns but also to benefit from suggestions and ideas that they may have

The UK Corporate Governance Code also suggests that in order to facilitate engagement with the workforce, companies should use the following method:

- appointment of a director from the workforce to give the workforce a "voice" in the boardroom
- formal workforce advisory panel
- designated non-executive director who spends more time in the business, getting an insight into the concerns of employees across the business

Going concern – listed companies

The UK Listing Rules require premium listed companies to include in the annual report a statement that the company is a going concern

The UK Corporate Governance Code requires directors to state whether they consider it appropriate to adopt the going concern basis of accounting – any material uncertainty should be disclosed

A company's strategic report must include a description of the principal risks and uncertainties facing the company – there should be a statement about how these are being managed or mitigated and a statement about the longer-term viability of the business

Listing Rules

At the time of writing of the 2020 edition of the Corporate Reporting Study Manual, the Listing Rules had not been updated for the 2018 edition of the UK Corporate Governance Code

Reporting by AIM companies

With effect from 28 September 2018, all AIM companies need to report on their application of a recognised corporate governance code

AIM companies will be required to include:

details of the recognised corporate governance code that the board of directors of the company decides to apply

how the company complies with that code, and

where it departs from its chosen code, an explanation of the reasons for doing so ("comply or explain")

This information should be reviewed annually

While the AIM Rules themselves do not specify what a "recognised corporate governance code" is, AIM Notice 50 (issued by the London Stock Exchange) indicates that an AIM company should comply or explain against a code of corporate governance that is "appropriate for a company admitted to a public market" – AIM Notice 50 includes examples of existing codes such as the FRC UK Corporate Governance Code

Overseas companies with an AIM listing or companies with a second listing on an overseas market may consider it more appropriate to report using an appropriate code from a foreign jurisdiction

See also Other Corporate Governance topics

Corporate Social Responsibility (CSR)

Why apply CSR?

Ethically correct approach

Could have strategic value – promoting image of the company to customers

Analysis Frameworks for the Examination

Stakeholders – always consider a **range** of affected stakeholders – for example:

Employees
Shareholders
Customers
Government
Local residents
Supply chain

Risks – consider the potential risks from not following CSR – for example:

Legal risks – costs, fines
Reporting risks if CSR is reported (e.g. quoted) – will breach reported commitments
Reputation risk – poor reputation will mean stakeholders do not want to deal with the company

Other Exam Tips

A business is a business – it is not a charity and it is not the government – it is not responsible for making everyone happy at all times – **consider the limits of CSR**: is the company always responsible to all stakeholders or are there limits?[4] This consideration will add valuable **nuance** to your answer.

Environmental decision-making

Firms will face increasing scrutiny over their environmental decisions as public interest in sustainability increases

Firms will have to make decisions with financial implications such as investing in more energy-efficient technologies and water-reducing processes or recognising the environmental costs (emissions, pollution) of their strategic initiatives

Corporate Social Responsibility versus Sustainability

Correct to distinguish the terms as they are different but related

Sustainability can refer both to protecting resources such that future generations can enjoy a prosperous existence and also to how a business can ensure that it develops and succeeds commercially

---

[4] Example from an SBM past paper: a commitment to provide employment to a specific group of employees 10 years ago arguably no longer has implications for the same business today.

Corporate Social Responsibility focuses more on ethical responsibilities – the first meaning of sustainability (environmental) may be one of these but there will be further CSR responsibilities in addition such as responsibilities to its work force, helping local communities and promoting the interests of society more generally – CSR is about the company being a good citizen in its society

See also

Corporate Governance topics
Ethics topics
Stakeholders and Stakeholder Management 390

Costs of Quality

The costs of quality can be analysed into 4 categories:

Prevention costs – costs incurred to prevent the production of products that do not conform to the specification being produced – examples: staff training, extra costs of acquiring high quality raw materials

Appraisal costs – costs incurred in order to ensure that outputs produced meet required quality standards – examples: costs of inspection

Costs of internal failure – costs incurred as a result of outputs not meeting required quality standards but where these deficiencies are identified before a product is transferred to the customer – examples: costs of repair and re-inspection, work stoppages caused by defects

Costs of external failure – costs resulting from products or services failing to meet requirements or to satisfy customer needs but where these deficiencies are only identified after the products or services have been delivered to the customer – examples: costs of handling customer complaints, costs of repairing/replacing products returned from customers

Problems with using a Costs of Quality approach

Really it is external costs that matter – these are what will lose future business so the other costs are actually just ways of minimising external costs so there will be a trade off between the costs of the other 3 areas and the impact on external costs

There are also trade offs between the other 3 types of cost – e.g. spending more to prevent problems (prevention costs) is likely to leave a lower budget available for appraisal and internal failure costs

Must evaluate the benefits and costs of the quality control costs rather than assuming that it is always sensible to spend more to get a quality improvement … but the negative impact on customer goodwill is hard to measure

See also Supply Chain Improvements 397
Working Capital 446

Cost reduction strategy

Example of methods of reducing R&D costs

(Based on SBM July 2019 past paper Q1)

In cutting R&D costs, there is a reduction in investment meaning that there is likely to be a sacrifice in future returns

The factors to consider in deciding where to reduce these costs include:

- **wastage and efficiency savings** – if they can be identified, these are the most appropriate cost to reduce as a reduction in such expenditure would not impact on return
- **identify** the elements of R&D expenditure which are expected to yield the **lowest return**
- **short-term gain** – there may be a temptation to reduce R&D expenditure on new projects as there is a short-term gain in cost savings without an immediate impact on revenue but new projects may be strategically the most important in the long run when entering new markets
- **reduction in R&D expenditure on newer projects** – there may be a temptation to reduce R&D expenditure on newer projects as these are more likely to be research expenditure (rather than development costs which can be capitalised) and so would result in a short-term increase in accounting profit as compared to development costs which are capitalised
- **risk reduction** – R&D activity is, by its nature, risky as not all projects are likely to be successful so in identifying cost savings, the highest risk projects may be selected

Overall, the choice will depend on the extent to which different types of R&D project fit into the business's strategic plan and whether expenditure falls into the above categories

If it is determined that a particular project is strategically essential then cuts will need to be found elsewhere

If the business is not able to make the necessary cuts purely through waste and efficiency savings, there is a risk that in making more broad-based cuts the business could simply end up delaying the completion of the project by spreading costs over more years and hence would not in fact reduce the overall cost of the project over its lifetime – additionally any delay in the launch could enable rivals to gain competitive advantage

Critical Success Factors

"Key goals/issues vital to the success of an organisation (sometimes associated with product features, but can be applied more broadly)"

Some example CSFs

Note – ensure these are relevant to the scenario as CSFs will vary widely depending on what industry we are looking at – the below are just some suggestions

High levels of customer service

Wide product range

Speed of product delivery

Quality products

Staff training and development

Use of CSFs

Identification of CSFs helps alert management to things that need controlling

CSFs can be turned into Key Performance Indicators for periodic reporting

CSFs can guide the development of information systems

Can be used for benchmarking organisational performance internally

See also	Balanced Scorecard	60
	Key Performance Indicators	284

Cryptocurrency

Cryptocurrency is a form of decentralised, digital currency, designed to serve as a medium of exchange, and which uses cryptography to secure and verify transactions

Cryptocurrency allows users to pay for items purchased online and to receive payments with anonymity

Cryptocurrencies are not controlled by a central banking mechanism so there can be dramatic fluctuations in value due to the market forces of demand and supply affecting the currency

Transactions using cryptocurrencies are recorded using blockchain technology

Coins are held in digital wallets, secured using cryptographic techniques – payments are collected into "blocks" which are recorded in blockchain but, once appended to the ledger, transactions cannot be changed

"Miners" are rewarded with cryptocurrency for their work in using software to add records of new transactions to the blockchain

Cryptocurrencies can also be purchased online from brokers

Central banks and regulators remain sceptical of cryptocurrencies: in particular, they are concerned that such currencies are not regulated in the way that traditional currencies are

Benefits of cryptocurrencies

Frictionless transactions – can be used anywhere in the world to transact in almost real-time – this removes the time and cost of making cross border payments

Removes intermediaries – it can take several days for transactions to be processed and transaction fees have to be paid

Reduces risks – speed of settlement reduces cash flow risk – credit risk can be eliminated as there can be a requirement for funds to be present in the purchaser's wallet at the time a payment is made

Currency management – if a business purchases and sells entirely in a particular cryptocurrency then this eliminates the need to manage multiple currency accounts and removes the risk of any sudden adverse movements in exchange rates

Disadvantages of cryptocurrencies

Multiple currencies – in practice, customers and suppliers may use different cryptocurrencies so there would still be a need to manage different currencies

Acceptability – some countries may not permit certain (or any) cryptocurrencies to be used – some customers and suppliers may prefer to continue to use traditional currencies so there will probably still be a need to maintain existing arrangements for these currencies as well – employees may wish to continue to be paid in the normal way

Volatility – if a company cannot work in a single cryptocurrency then there will remain exchange rate risk because the value of the different currencies used by a business (whether cryptocurrencies or traditional currencies) will continue to fluctuate amongst one another

Borrowing – banks do not lend in cryptocurrency so if a company needs to obtain trade finance then it may still need to borrow in traditional currency and then convert it to the relevant digital currency

Accounting for cryptocurrencies (reflections from ICAEW experts)

There may be no specific requirements in either IFRS or local GAAP so organisations may need to work by analogy to comparable standards and refer to the conceptual frameworks for financial reporting

It is generally accepted that cryptocurrencies cannot be classified as cash nor as a financial asset as they do not involve any contractual right to receive cash or another financial asset – they do not appear to qualify as inventory as they are not held for sale in the ordinary course of business

So it would seem that the default classification would be as an intangible

This then leads to complications regarding measurement – the most appropriate method would appear to be at fair value through profit or loss but a cost-based measurement model is normally used for intangibles

A fair value or revaluation approach can be used for intangibles if an active market exists but this model normally puts value changes through OCI rather than profit

It is certain that clear disclosures will need to be made whenever cryptocurrency transactions are material to an entity

Further considerations in the accounting of cryptocurrencies

It will be essential that the organisation records its cryptocurrency transactions in its management information so it will need to decide the accounting treatment it is going to apply, and then apply it consistently, even though there are currently no specific accounting requirements for cryptocurrencies

There is potential volatility in the value of the cryptocurrencies themselves so the use of cryptocurrency could increase an organisation's balance sheet exposure, depending on the process of converting between cryptocurrency and fiat currency (£, $, Euros etc) – this volatility could increase the importance of disclosing information about an organisation's cryptocurrency transactions and balances, particularly if the organisation makes a significant number of cryptocurrency transactions

Currency Risks

Mnemonic	**TET**
Transaction risk	adverse short term movements during ordinary progress of business
Economic risk	effect of exchange rates over the longer term on international competitiveness of a company
Translation risk	risk of exchange losses when translating foreign branches/subsidiaries into home currency

Commercial impact of a change in exchange rates

A significant decline in sterling will make imports of raw materials and commodities (often priced in non-sterling currencies such as the US dollar) more expensive

Manufacturers in the UK then face a choice – either try to pass on the higher costs to consumers by increasing their prices or keep prices unchanged and absorb the higher costs themselves through lower profit margins

But a decline in sterling could benefit UK exporters – if sterling declines in value then other currencies must be rising in value so each time we earn a unit of foreign currency then this will translate into more units of sterling than previously – alternatively if we are happy to continue to earn the same number of units of sterling, we can cut our foreign currency price to do so at the new lower exchange rate: cutting prices will help to penetrate the market

See also Hedging topics
Overseas operations topics

Customer Relationship Management (CRM)

CRM involves the use of database technology and IT systems to help an organisation develop long-term and mutually valuable relationships with its customers

An effective CRM system involves a comprehensive database which can be accessed whenever the customer interacts with the company

This could include website transactions, contact with sales teams, queries and other order processing functions

All employees in customer facing processes should coordinate their efforts so that the customer receives a consistent and suitable service such as targeted marketing – this means that employees in sales, customer service and marketing will need to work well together

Benefits of CRM

Specialised software and hardware can be used to help the company provide the products its customers want, provide better customer service, help the marketing team to cross sell products, to attract new customers and to understand its existing customers better

Ability to track a customer's account history to help personalise products and services for that customer

Ability to measure marketing campaigns, analysing customer clicks and subsequent sales

Provides an ability to "mine" data to identify purchasing and other trends

Allows transaction information to be aggregated to provide KPIs for the business

Helps with forecasting by using sales history to generate sales projections

Could help to promote sales growth

See also Big Data topics
Digital Transformation 184

Q17 -> Concerns about recent attacks

Cyber security

Controls relating to cyber security need to incorporate **external** factors and so must move beyond traditional approaches based on **internal controls** to maintain the confidentiality, integrity and availability of data:

Potential threats can now come from **around the world** (organised criminals, corporate spies, disgruntled or careless employees)

Security weaknesses can be found **throughout a supply chain** rather than just within a single business – the disparate nature of data storage across servers, cloud storage and mobile devices provides a range of access points for attackers to exploit

The impact of security failures could affect **every aspect** of a business: disruption of operations and customer service, interference with production, damage to brand and reputation, theft of intellectual property or commercially-sensitive information and regulatory fines

The "four flags" which should be considered in relation to cyber security (ICAEW report *Audit insights: cyber security* (2013 version))

1. Businesses should consider "cyber" in all their activities

Businesses need to **manage risks** to ensure that they can **exploit the opportunities** of technology in a **secure** and **sustainable** way – therefore, businesses should treat **cyber security as a business risk** rather than as a technical risk, considering the implications for cyber security of **all** their **strategies** and **operations**

This approach could be particularly relevant to organisations considering a **change in supply chain arrangements** or considering an **acquisition**

Having a plan in place to deal with cyber security issues could provide the organisation with a **competitive advantage** against competitors in the market – the organisation could be seen to be a trusted partner for suppliers and strong security capabilities could be a way of improving its **reputation** with customers

2. Businesses need to accept that security will be compromised

Businesses must concentrate on **intelligence and monitoring**, **detection** and **response**

1. **Intelligence and monitoring** – intelligence on threats can be gathered from a **variety of sources** such as social media or information-sharing schemes with trusted partners or the government
2. **Detection** – hackers can sometimes breach systems for **weeks or months before detection** – data analytics can be important in this respect by identifying **abnormal activity** such as high levels of data downloading or access from unusual places
3. **Response** – an organisation may need to manage a **variety of stakeholder concerns** to limit the impact of the breach – this could include **communicating** with customers who may have been affected and ensuring **compliance** with any **regulatory** requirements – **investors** may also need to be kept informed

Given the growth in social media, a business which does not respond effectively is likely to face **substantial public criticism which could damage its reputation**

3. Businesses should focus on their critical information assets

Instead of trying to do **too much** by protecting **everything**, businesses should **prioritise** their information assets – organisations should identify **where** breaches would have a **substantial** impact on the competitiveness and sustainability of their business and **focus** their security on these areas

4. Most businesses don't get the basics right

According to the ICAEW report, up to **80%** of security breaches could be prevented by implementing **basic good practices**

Complex IT environments, and **lack of expertise**, are both reasons that basic good practices are not implemented in practice

However, **people** are always the **weakest link** in implementing effective security – human failings are being exploited by attackers to gain access to confidential information

Measures to implement in relation to cyber security (ICAEW report *Audit insights: cyber security* (2018 version))

ICAEW's 2018 report *Audit insights: cyber security* recommends that businesses should instigate the following measures:

Embed a greater awareness of cyber risk throughout their strategy and operations – ultimately, it is the Board's responsibility to ensure that management responds to the risks identified and takes appropriate steps to mitigate them

Build a security focused culture – this should be based on continuous improvement and integrated thinking around cyber security, rather than seeing it as a series of one-off tactical activities

Improve cyber risk reporting – make cyber risk reporting more transparent, qualitative and focused on the impact of security investments – for example, threat analysis and the extent to which investments have reduced cyber risk

Reduce the complexity of the IT environment – systems should be standardised where possible and risks should be mitigated through effective controls between legacy and modern environments – having a variety of complex and disparate bespoke systems makes effective cyber security (such as patch management) more difficult so businesses should be encouraged to simplify and standardise the IT environment as far as possible

This point could also be an important issue in the context of an acquisition and integrating legacy systems in the company being acquired

Manage talent – develop talent management strategies at all levels of the organisation to cope with skill shortages in relation to managing cyber security in order to reduce reliance on contractors and consultants

Apply discipline – focus on applying strong discipline around security and consistently complying with good practice

In addition, management can also help to improve cyber security by:

Learning from past security breaches – following a security breach, senior management should use this as an opportunity to promote the importance of cyber security throughout the organisation and should look to put in place measures to address the weaknesses that allowed the security breaches to occur in the past

Determining the organisation's tolerance to cyber risks – this is an important step in designing management strategies – such an exercise may lead to the conclusion that additional funding is required to enhance the cyber security features of the organisation's IT/IS infrastructure

Ensure that NEDs play an active role in promoting cyber security during their interactions with the Board – this may involve keeping their knowledge about the evolving nature of cyber risks up-to-date and challenging executive directors about the need to follow best practice in cyber security

ISO 27001

The International Organisation for Standardisation standard **ISO 27001** establishes **best practice** for an information security management system and **identifies** the **requirements** for **establishing**, **implementing**, **maintaining** and **continually improving** such a system

Complying with **ISO 27001** should help an organisation **improve** its **defences** against cyber attacks and increase the **confidence** that **customers** and **other interested parties** have in the organisation's systems

ICAEW 10 steps to cyber security

1. **Allocate responsibilities** – responsibility should rest with a senior manager who has a broad view of all the risks and how to tackle them – other individuals can then be assigned specific roles
2. **Protect your computers and your network** – firewalls should be used to protect against both outside attacks from hackers and to manage the internet activity of staff by blocking access to sites which could cause risks
3. **Keep your computers up-to-date** – the latest patches from software providers should always be applied – a single vulnerable computer network puts all other computers at risk
4. **Control employee access to computers and documents** – use specific user accounts and passwords with a unique username in each case to regulate access
5. **Protect against viruses** – ensure that up-to-date antivirus software is installed and that it regularly scans computers for threats
6. **Extend security beyond the office** – ensure that laptops, phones or tablets used outside the office are also covered by antivirus software, password protection and firewalls – ensure that sensitive data is kept encrypted – ensure that employees are reminded of the dangers of connecting to unencrypted public wifi
7. **Don't forget disks and drives** – removable disks and drives such as USB sticks can introduce malware into computers and could also be lost when containing sensitive information – antivirus and anti-malware software should be applied to such disks and drives and not just to computers
8. **Plan for the worst** – consider whether external help would be required and whether key customers or suppliers would need to be contacted – consider whether some functions can

continue to operate using other computers while systems are repaired – ensure there is a clear plan identifying who is responsible for doing what in an emergency

9. **Educate your team** – ensure everyone in the business is aware of the importance of security matters and how to ensure that security can be upheld – for example, by keeping passwords safe and changing them regularly – staff should be reminded not to click on web links or email attachments from unfamiliar sources – employees should be trained to watch out for social engineering or "phishing" where hackers try to trick staff into revealing details

10. **Keep records – and test your security** – keep a record of the hardware and software an organisation uses to help build up a picture of the organisation's security status and to spot potential weak points – apply good record-keeping to effectively test systems on a regular basis

The importance of the weakest link

Ultimately, any organisation is only as secure as its **weakest link** – regular testing will help ensure that no weaknesses get overlooked

Responsibilities of senior management regarding cyber security

Senior management now has to do more than in the past to promote an awareness of cyber security – this may involve:

1. **employing** a **Chief Information Security Officer** to help communicate the threats posed by cyber risks

2. **reorganising roles and responsibilities** to ensure there is **accountability** for cyber security matters within the organisation

3. **learning** from **past** security **breaches**

4. **determining** the organisation's **tolerance** to cyber risks

5. ensuring that **Non-Executive Directors** play an active role in promoting cyber security – this may involve **keeping their knowledge** about the evolving nature of cyber risks **up-to-date** and **challenging the Executive Directors** about whether best practice in cyber security is being followed

See also

Big Data topics	
Cloud computing and cloud accounting	104
Digital Strategies	176
Digital Transformation	184
Internal Audit – cyber security	256

Debt Factoring

In a **factoring** transaction, one party transfers the **right to cash to be collected from its receivables** to another party in return for **immediate cash** payment

This allows an organisation with a receivables balance to **receive cash quickly** rather than **waiting** the 30 to 60 days that it can take a customer to pay

The factor advances a percentage of the invoice value and retains the rest of the amount as security against any bad debts – the factor will then also deduct its own fee from the amount paid from the invoice when the invoice is paid by the customer

The **cash advance** rate will typically range from **80%** to **95%** of the invoice value

For financial reporting purposes, the entity will need to determine how to treat its receivables if factoring is in operation

Factoring with recourse

Here the transferor fully or partially **guarantees** the performance of receivables: if the receivables are ultimately not paid then **the factor will not lose out** because the transferor will **pay any shortfall** – the transferor is therefore **not fully transferring the credit risk** to another party

In most factoring with recourse, the transferor **does not allow the transferee to sell the receivables**, in which case the **transferor still retains control** over the asset

In this case, the **criteria for derecognition are not satisfied** and the asset should **not be derecognised**

Instead, the amount advanced by the factoring company should be treated as a **financial liability** in the accounts – effectively a **loan** from the factor

Factoring without recourse

Here the transferor **does not provide any guarantees** about the ultimate performance of the receivables so the **factoring company will bear the loss of any bad debts**

In this case, the entity **has transferred the risks and rewards of the ownership** of the receivables and should **derecognise** them accordingly

Because **risk has been transferred**, this type of factoring is **significantly more expensive** than factoring with recourse

Costs of factoring to a business

Interest – typical interest charges range from **1.5%** to **3%** over base rate

Fees – these fees cover the costs of administration and credit control, and typically amount to between **0.75%** and **2.5%** of turnover

Cost of bad debt risk – in factoring without recourse, there will also be a charge for the cost of bearing the risk of bad debts

See also		
	Bank Loans	61
	Bonds (Loan Notes) v Bank Loans – Comparisons	85
	Finance – Sources for SMEs	199

Derivatives Calculations – Currency Forward

Reminders

ADDIS – always ADD a discount (and therefore deduct a premium) to the relevant spot rate

Choosing the spot rate to adjust

Spot rates will be quoted on a bid/offer basis such as 1.65 – 1.75

Foreign currency will be received by the company

If the company wishes to exchange foreign currency received **into** sterling, then use the **right hand/higher** spot rate – dividing by the **higher** alternative figure will **minimise** the sterling amount that the bank pays to the company in return for the foreign currency

Foreign currency is required by the company

If the company needs to purchase foreign currency by **paying** sterling, then use the **left hand/lower** spot rate – dividing by the **lower** alternative figure will **maximise** the sterling amount that the customer needs to pay to buy the foreign currency needed

Standard narrative points

Tailored specifically for the needs of the client (value, timing, exchange rate) (contrast with futures and options)

No secondary market exists so hard to get out of the contract if not wanted (contrast with futures and options)

Does not give any flexibility (unlike an option) – what if the foreign customer never pays? We would still have to sell the agreed number of foreign currency units to the bank under the contract – these would need to be purchased in the market at the spot rate, which may be unfavourable

Removes upside risk – we cannot use the spot market at the future date if that is preferable (unlike an option)

Option forward contracts

An option forward contract is a forward exchange contract where the customer can decide precisely **when** to invoke the contract

Performance **must** take place at some time and **cannot be avoided** altogether.

Option forward contracts are normally used to cover whole months which **straddle** the likely payment date where the **customer is not sure the exact date** on which they will want to buy or sell currency.

The purpose of an option forward contract is to **avoid having to renew** a forward exchange contract and **extend it by a few days** because this can be **expensive**.

Example option forward contract

A UK company must pay $1m in approximately 2.5 months' time.

The bank will offer a contract which allows the company to choose when, between 2 and 3 months' time, the currency is needed.

The rate applied to the contract will be **either** the **2** or **3-month** rate, **whichever is more beneficial** to the bank.

Derivatives Calculations – Currency Futures

Reminders

Use the futures quote rate when deciding the number of contracts – do NOT use the spot rate at this stage

Only use the spot rate right at the end of the calculation, after you have done everything else in relation to the futures trade

To work out whether the company needs to buy or sell futures, look at the position with different exchange rates, using easy to work with numbers

e.g. company is going to receive US$2m

at an exchange rate of $1:£1 this would be £2m

at an exchange rate of $2:£1 this would be £1m

Therefore, the company will lose money if the exchange rate number rises (appreciation of the £) – so enter into a futures hedge which will make a gain in that situation – therefore BUY futures now and sell futures if the exchange rate number rises (buying low and selling high generates a profit)

Calculation steps

1. Calculate net amount payment or receivable in the foreign currency

2. Divide the amount from step 1 by the futures quote rate and the contract size (often, £62,500 but check)

e.g. US$ 1.5m / 1.564 / 62,500 = 16 contracts (rounded up)

Do NOT use the spot rate at this stage

Round the number of contracts to a whole figure – if you round up then you will overhedge, if you round down then you will underhedge

3. Work out whether the futures were sold or bought (see rule above)

4. Calculate the movement in the futures quote from the initial position to the final position (should be given in the question as an estimated future figure) – then multiply this by the number of contracts and contract size

e.g. (1.564 – 1.582) x 16 contracts x £62,500 (assuming contract size of £62,500)

The gain or loss here will be in the foreign currency

5. Re-calculate the net amount payable or receivable in the foreign currency, allowing for the gain or loss from step 4

e.g. if the company has to purchase dollars and has made a gain on the hedge then deduct the hedging gain from the underlying dollar purchase as the bank will give the company that amount of dollars under the hedging contract and so the company does not need to purchase that amount any more

Use the forecast future spot rate at this stage – for advice on selecting the correct spot rate, see below.

Choosing the spot rate

Spot rates will be quoted on a bid/offer basis such as 1.65 – 1.75

Foreign currency will be received by the company

If the company wishes to exchange foreign currency received **into** sterling, then use the **right hand/higher** spot rate – dividing by the **higher** alternative figure will **minimise** the sterling amount that the bank pays to the company in return for the foreign currency

Foreign currency is required by the company

If the company needs to purchase foreign currency by **paying** sterling, then use the **left hand/lower** spot rate – dividing by the **lower** alternative figure will **maximise** the sterling amount that the customer needs to pay to buy the foreign currency needed

Standard narrative points

Not tailored so could lead to under- or overhedging

Requires a margin to be deposited at the futures exchange when the deal is set up (as collateral)

May create liquidity pressure if a margin call is made by the exchange (i.e. the company's hedging position worsens – the exchange may demand further collateral as assurance that the company will be able to pay if the hedging position remains negative from the company's perspective)

Secondary market exists so the company can get out of the deal if not needed (e.g. if the counterparty is going to default) – not possible with a forward

Basis risk exists as the futures quote is at a different rate to the spot rate and will usually move by a different percentage compared to the spot market – therefore unlikely that a perfect hedge is possible

Main elements of futures transactions

The contract size	The **contract size** as the fixed quantity which can be bought or sold with one futures contract Dealing on futures markets must be in a whole number of contracts – the implication of this is that the amount of exposure and the amount covered by a futures hedge may not match exactly

The contract price	The **contract price** is the price at which the futures contract is bought or sold Prices for futures change continually so the gain or loss in a position is the difference between the original buying or selling price to open the position and the price obtained to close it at a later date
The settlement date	The **settlement date** (or delivery date or expiry date) is the date when trading on a particular futures contract stops and all accounts are settled For example, the settlement dates for all currency futures are at the end of March, June, September and December
The initial margin	When futures contracts are bought and sold, a **deposit** known as the **initial margin** must be paid to the futures exchange This will typically amount to about 5% of the value of contracts dealt in – this deposit is refunded when the contract is closed out The objective of the initial margin is to cover any possible losses made from the first day's trading – thereafter, any variations in the contract price are covered by a **variation** margin Profits are advanced to the trader's account but losses must be covered by advancing further margin – this process is known as **marking to market**
Basis	The price of the futures contract will normally be different from the spot price on any given date – this difference is called the **basis** The exception is on the settlement date when the basis is zero because the exchange settlement price and the spot market price are the same on this date The effect of basis is to **prevent** hedges from being 100% efficient and the change in the spot over a period is not matched exactly by the change in the futures price – this means that there is basis risk for anyone hedging a position with futures Candidates will not be asked to calculate basis in the examination but must recognise that it causes hedges to be less than 100% efficient
Hedge efficiency	The only risk to hedgers is that the futures market does not provide a perfect hedge: -the value of the commodity being hedged must be rounded to a whole number of contracts, causing inaccuracies -basis risk exists as noted above A measure of hedge efficiency compares the profit made on the futures market with the loss made on the cash or commodity market, or vice versa

Derivatives Calculations – Currency Options

Reminders

A put option means an option to sell – a call option means an option to purchase

But check the wording regarding traded options carefully – just because the option price is $1.65 does not necessarily mean that the option is over dollars – the option could be a **sterling** option with a $1.65 exercise price so in this case the put and call terminology is from the point of view of **sterling**

Calculation steps

Note – there are 2 types of option to understand: OTC options and traded options

An OTC or over the counter option is an option over a direct purchase/sale of a specific amount of currency – a traded option is an option to engage in a currency futures trade

OTC options – calculation steps

1. Calculate option premium cost – generally you will multiply the foreign currency amount by the given figure to find the premium cost in sterling – check when this is payable: if it is payable now, add on an interest cost (as the company will lose the opportunity cost of interest income if it has to pay the premium now) – this is likely to require some kind of time-apportionment

2. Apply the exchange rate agreed in the contract to the relevant foreign currency sum

3. Compare this to the spot rate to determine if the option gives a better result – if so, exercise the option – if not, let the option lapse (but state this in your answer)

For advice on selecting the correct spot rate, refer to our instructions on the next page

4. Remember to deduct the premium cost from the final calculation – this must be paid even if the option is not actually exercised

Traded options – calculation steps

1. Calculate option premium cost – divide* foreign currency amount by the exchange rate agreed in the option (**not** the spot rate) and then divide again by the contract size – round the number of contracts – then calculate premium as number of contracts x premium x contract size – if this is a foreign currency amount and payable now, then divide by the relevant **spot rate** (not the exchange rate agreed in the option)

(*Assumes that the exchange rate is quoted as “foreign currency units to £1”)

For advice on selecting the correct spot rate, refer to our instructions on the next page

2. Apply the exchange rate agreed in the contract to the relevant foreign currency sum

3. Compare this to the spot rate to determine if the option gives a better result – if so, exercise the option and engage in a futures trade – if not, let the option lapse (but state this in your answer)

For advice on selecting the correct spot rate, refer to our instructions on the next page

4. Remember to deduct the premium cost from the final calculation – this must be paid even if the option is not actually exercised

Choosing the spot rate

Spot rates will be quoted on a bid/offer basis such as 1.65 – 1.75

Foreign currency will be received by the company

If the company wishes to exchange foreign currency received **into** sterling, then use the **right hand/higher** spot rate – dividing by the **higher** alternative figure will **minimise** the sterling amount that the bank pays to the company in return for the foreign currency

Foreign currency is required by the company

If the company needs to purchase foreign currency by **paying** sterling, then use the **left hand/lower** spot rate – dividing by the **lower** alternative figure will **maximise** the sterling amount that the customer needs to pay to buy the foreign currency needed

Standard narrative points

Offers flexibility – if the counterparty does not pay or the currency is not needed, or if the spot market at the future date is favourable, then the option can simply be left to lapse – "allows the company to protect itself from downside risk whilst preserving the upside potential of [add whether a depreciation or appreciation of sterling is beneficial in the particular case]"

Can be expensive – premium has to be paid even if the option is not used – additional interest cost to consider if the premium is payable up-front

Traded options are not tailored to the specific needs of the client (contract size, maturity date) so can lead to over- or underhedging

However, OTC options are tailored so these points can be reversed in your answer

Traded options have a secondary market so easy to unwind the hedge if no longer needed – however, the options may be worth less when sold back into the market

However, OTC options are tailored so there is no secondary market

Basis risk applies if the rate in the option contract differs from today's spot rate (quite likely to be the case) – could lead to under- or overhedging in relation to the movement between today's spot rate and the rate at which the option contract could kick in if exercised

Derivatives Calculations – Summary of Currency Hedging Methods

	Forward	Money Market	Futures
Tailored?	Yes	Yes	No
Secondary market to "unwind"?	No	Yes	Yes
Transaction cost	Via spread	Via spread on interest and spot rate	Brokerage fees
Complexity	Low	Medium	High
Management costs	Low	Medium	High
Application	Small and medium companies	Banks	Companies with large currency exposures

Derivatives Calculations – Forward Rate Agreements (FRAs)

Reminders

Some questions may have a single FRA interest rate specified – other questions will have 2 alternative rates as a spread such as 3.5% - 2.5%

If a spread is offered, choose the rate that is in the bank's interests i.e. which minimises the amount the bank might have to pay out and maximises the amount the bank might receive

> If the company has taken on borrowing and so wishes to hedge an **increase** in interest rates, then use the higher figure or lefthand side – then if interest rates do rise, the bank will have to pay a lower amount (in our example, only the difference between the market rate and 3.5%, which is better for the bank than the difference between the market rate and 2.5% if interest rates are relatively high)
>
> If the company is going to start saving and so wishes to hedge a decrease in interest rates, then use the lower figure or righthand side – then if interest rates do **fall**, the bank will have to pay a lower amount (in our example, only the difference between the market rate and 2.5%, which is better for the bank than the difference between the market rate and 3.5% if interest rates are relatively low)

Terminology

The FRA rate may be specified as "4 v 7"

The first figure (lefthand side) states when the FRA will start (so starting in 4 months from now in this example)

The second figure (righthand side) states when the FRA will end (so ending in 7 months from now in this example)

Therefore the time period of the FRA itself is the difference between the righthand figure and the lefthand figure – this will often be 3 months

Remember to pro-rate any annual interest rates for the time period (the difference between the lefthand and righthand side above)

Calculation steps

1. Calculate the amount the company has to pay based on the market rate

2. Calculate the payment to or receipt from the bank – remember to pick the correct rate (see above) and to allow for time-apportionment (often at 3/12)

If the calculation is correct, the net position from steps 1 and 2 should be equal to the FRA rate agreed

Make sure you end by specifying the net amount payment in cash terms i.e. not just the % but the amount of cash that this amounts to (this should be equal to the FRA rate multiplied by the relevant total amount of the loan/saving)

Example FRA calculation

A company intends to take out a £1m fixed rate loan in 4 months for a period of 3 months.

This company is therefore worried about a rise in interest rates and so the bank will offer the lefthand side of the quoted spread (so that the difference between the market rate and the bank's offered rate is minimised if the bank does have to pay anything out)

The following quotes are available:

4 v 6	3.55 - 2.50%
4 v 7	3.58 – 2.52%
4 v 8	3.63 – 2.56%

Illustrate the position if the company has to pay (1) 3% and (2) 4% on the loan.

Solution

The numbers in the "v" quoting system refer to "start month v end month" so if we are starting in 4 months and borrowing for 3 months then our end month is in 7 months so we use a 4 v 7 instrument, using the lefthand side quote.

(1) loan rate is 3%

In this case, the rate is below the rate in the FRA so the company will pay money to the bank – this is the price of protecting itself against high interest rates

Company pays (3.58 – 3.00) x £1m x 3/12 = £1,450 to the bank under the FRA

Company pays 3% x £1m x 3/12 = £7,500 on the underlying loan

Total cost of £1,450 + £7,000 = £8,950 or (£8,950/£1m) x 4 quarters = 3.58% per annum

(2) loan rate is 4%

In this case, the rate is above the rate in the FRA so the company will receive money from the bank under the FRA – this helps the company protect its interest rate against any increase

Company receives (4.00 – 3.58) x £1m x 3/12 = £1,050 from the bank under the FRA

Company pays 4% x £1m x 3/12 = £10,500 on the underlying loan

Total cost of £10,000 - £1,050 = £8,950 or (£8,950/£1m) x 4 quarters = 3.58% per annum

Conclusion

Under either option, the net interest cost is 3.58%, the rate agreed under the FRA.

Standard narrative points

An FRA eliminates downside risk but prevents the company benefiting from upside risk if interest rates in the market move favourably

Derivatives Calculations – FTSE Hedging

Reminders

In most questions, the company will have an existing holding of FTSE shares and will be worried about a decline in value – so it will use a PUT option or SELL futures

> This allows the company to enter into an agreement to sell FTSE shares/FTSE futures at a pre-agreed price – the company will then make a profit if share prices fall because it can purchase the relevant shares in the market at a lower price (sell high, buy low)

Calculation steps – options

1. Calculate the number of contracts – divide the company's portfolio value by (option exercise price x £10)

> For example, £7.5m / (6,454 x £10)

Round the number of contracts – if you round up then you will overhedge, if you round down then you will underhedge

2. Calculate premium cost as number of contracts x £10 x relevant premium from table in the question

3. Calculate gain or loss if options exercised as (option exercise price – FTSE value) x £10 x number of contracts

4. Calculate net position as portfolio value plus gain on options (if applicable) less premium

> As the option should not be exercised if a loss is caused you should never have a loss on the options (just a zero gain after the options are left to lapse as a result of share prices rising i.e. no loss in value on the portfolio to protect against)

Calculation steps – futures

1. Calculate the number of contracts – divide the company's portfolio value by (futures price x £10)

> For example, £7.5m / (6,454 x £10)

Round the number of contracts – if you round up then you will overhedge, if you round down then you will underhedge

2. Calculate gain or loss as (futures price – FTSE value) x £10 x number of contracts

3. Calculate net position as portfolio value plus/minus any gain or loss on the futures

Standard narrative points

May not lead to a 100% efficient hedge due to rounding of contracts

Basis risk may lead to the hedge not being 100% efficient due to the fact that the initial value of the FTSE index may differ from the options/futures exercise price so there will not be exactly the same movement in the FTSE index and the hedging instrument

Futures do not allow the company to benefit from upside risk if the market moves favourably – an option can be left to lapse if the market moves favourably

Futures require a margin to be deposited at the exchange as security and margin calls may subsequently be required if the company's hedge moves significantly out of the money – this may not be good for liquidity

Index futures

Index futures are futures contracts on a portfolio of shares represented by a stock market index – these can be used to protect investors against future falls in the value of a portfolio of shares

Index futures can be of real importance to organisations with significant investments such as pension funds

Futures can also be used for speculative purposes

The transaction costs of investing in index futures are much less than the cost of actually selling and buying the underlying shares – buying or selling futures is an alternative to adjusting the share portfolio, which may not be appealing because of the time and cost involved

FTSE 100 index futures

Each FTSE 100 index futures contract is for a notional value of the futures price multiplied by £10

Therefore, if the FTSE index futures price stands at 6,700 then the notional value of the contract is £67,000

The gain or loss on the futures in terms of index points must also be multiplied by £10 to derive the gain or loss per contract – you will then need to multiply the gain or loss per contract by the number of contracts employed to determine the overall gain or loss on the index futures trade

Use of futures for speculative purposes

Index futures are used by speculators because it is possible to take a very large position in share prices for a relatively small cost – with futures, there is a deposit to pay (the margin) for having an open or closed position but the cost is much less than buying the underlying shares themselves

The speculator hopes to make a big profit from a favourable movement in the stock market index for a relatively small investment

Qb 474//

Derivatives Calculations – Interest Rate Futures

Reminders

If the company is worried that interest rates will rise, it should SELL futures – if rates rise from, say, 2% to 4% then the futures quote would fall from 98 to 96 – so profit is obtained by selling high and buying low

If the company is worried that interest rates will fall, it should BUY futures – if rates fall from, say, 4% to 2% then the futures quote would increase from 96 to 98 – so profit is obtained by buying low and selling high

Remember that the gain or loss must be calculated using a 3/12 fraction even if the hedge is not for 3 months – this is because futures are based on a 3 month quoting basis so we always apply 3/12 to the quoted annual rates – we adjust for the hedging periods that are longer than 3 months by buying more futures so the additional length is factored into the calculation already when determining the number of contracts – therefore it would be double counting to also apply a fraction other than 3/12 when calculating the gain or loss

Calculation steps

1. Calculate the number of contracts – divide the amount to be hedged by the contract size and then pro-rate for time if the period is not 3 months

   e.g. (£20m / £0.5m) x 7/3 if we are hedging for 7 months

Round the number of contracts to a whole figure – if you round up then you will overhedge, if you round down then you will underhedge

2. Work out whether the futures would have been bought or sold (see rule above)

3. Determine the gain on the futures as the difference in the final rate versus the futures rate, multiplied by the contract size, number of contracts and **by 3/12 regardless of the time period to pro-rate the annual premium % down to the 3 month rate involved in 3 month futures**

6. Determine the interest cost/income on the underlying loan/savings and then adjust for the gain or loss on the futures to determine the effective rate

   Remember to time apportion upwards to allow for annual rate e.g. multiply by 12/7 if hedging for 7 months

Standard narrative points

Not tailored so could lead to under- or overhedging

Requires a margin to be deposited at the futures exchange when the deal is set up (as collateral)

May create liquidity pressure if a margin call is made by the exchange (i.e. the company's hedging position worsens – the exchange may demand further collateral as assurance that the company will be able to pay if the hedging position remains negative from the company's perspective)

Secondary market exists so the company can get out of the deal if not needed – not possible with a forward

Basis risk exists as the futures quote is at a different rate to the spot rate and will usually move by a different percentage compared to the spot market – therefore unlikely that a perfect hedge is possible

Main elements of futures transactions

The contract size	The **contract size** is the fixed quantity which can be bought or sold with one futures contract Dealing on futures markets must be in a whole number of contracts – the implication of this is that the amount of exposure and the amount covered by a futures hedge may not match exactly
The contract price	The **contract price** is the price at which the futures contract is bought or sold Prices for futures change continually so the gain or loss in a position is the difference between the original buying or selling price to open the position and the price obtained to close it at a later date
The settlement date	The **settlement date** (or delivery date or expiry date) is the date when trading on a particular futures contract stops and all accounts are settled For example, the settlement dates for all currency futures are at the end of March, June, September and December
The initial margin	When futures contracts are bought and sold, a **deposit** known as the **initial margin** must be paid to the futures exchange This will typically amount to about 5% of the value of contracts dealt in – this deposit is refunded when the contract is closed out The objective of the initial margin is to cover any possible losses made from the first day's trading – thereafter, any variations in the contract price are covered by a **variation** margin Profits are advanced to the trader's account but losses must be covered by advancing further margin – this process is known as **marking to market**

Basis	The price of the futures contract will normally be different from the spot price on any given date – this difference is called the **basis** The exception is on the settlement date when the basis is zero because the exchange settlement price and the spot market price are the same on this date The effect of basis is to **prevent** hedges from being 100% efficient and the change in the spot over a period is not matched exactly by the change in the futures price – this means that there is basis risk for anyone hedging a position with futures Candidates will not be asked to calculate basis in the examination but must recognise that it causes hedges to be less than 100% efficient
Hedge efficiency	The only risk to hedgers is that the futures market does not provide a perfect hedge: -the value of the commodity being hedged must be rounded to a whole number of contracts, causing inaccuracies -basis risk exists as noted above A measure of hedge efficiency compares the profit made on the futures market with the loss made on the cash or commodity market, or vice versa

Derivatives Calculations – Interest Rate Options

Reminders

If the company is worried that interest rates will rise, it should purchase PUT options – if rates rise from, say, 2% to 4% then the futures quote would fall from 98 to 96 – so profit is obtained by selling high and buying low – a put option allows the company to engage in a futures SELL trade, which is advantageous

If the company is worried that interest rates will fall, it should purchase CALL options – if rates fall from, say, 4% to 2% then the futures quote would increase from 96 to 98 – so profit is obtained by buying low and selling high – a call option allows the company to engage in a futures BUY trade, which is advantageous

Remember that the gain or loss and option premium must be calculated using a 3/12 fraction **even if the hedge is not for 3 months** – this is because the option is an option to engage in a futures trade – futures are based on a 3 month quoting basis so we always apply 3/12 to the quoted annual rates – we adjust for the hedging periods that are longer than 3 months by buying more futures so the additional length is factored into the calculation already when determining the number of contracts – therefore it would be double counting to also apply a fraction other than 3/12 when calculating the gain or loss, or option premium

Calculation steps

1. Calculate the number of contracts – divide the amount to be hedged by the contract size and then pro-rate for time if the period is not 3 months

    e.g. (£20m / £0.5m) x 7/3 if we are hedging for 7 months

Round the number of contracts to a whole figure – if you round up then you will overhedge, if you round down then you will underhedge

2. Calculate the premium payable by multiplying the number of contracts by the premium % and by the contract size – **finally multiply by 3/12 regardless of the time period to pro-rate the annual premium % down to the 3 month rate involved in 3 month futures**

    e.g. 93 x 0.52% x 0.5m x 3/12

3. Work out whether the futures would have been bought or sold (see rule above)

4. Determine if the option is worth exercising – have interest rates moved in the direction feared by the company?

5. Determine the gain on the futures as the difference in the final rate versus the futures rate, multiplied by the contract size, number of contracts and **by 3/12 regardless of the time period to pro-rate the annual premium % down to the 3 month rate involved in 3 month futures**

6. Determine the interest cost/income on the underlying loan/savings and then adjust for the gain or loss on the futures to determine the effective rate

    Remember to time apportion upwards to allow for annual rate e.g. multiply by 12/7 if hedging for 7 months

Standard narrative points

Options can hedge downside risk whilst allowing the company to take advantage of upside potential – FRAs and interest rates will lock the company into a particular rate

However, options can be expensive due to the premium cost

Can be traded on the secondary market

Requires a margin to be deposited at the futures exchange when the deal is set up (as collateral)

May create liquidity pressure if a margin call is made by the exchange (i.e. the company's hedging position worsens – the exchange may demand further collateral as assurance that the company will be able to pay if the hedging position remains negative from the company's perspective)

Interest Rate Collars

Consists of a pair of interest rates options – a cap and a floor

A borrower would buy a cap giving the right to borrow at the exercise price for the relevant period – this option is used if the market interest rate increases and therefore cancels out the increased cost of borrowing on the underlying asset

A borrower would sell a floor obligating it to lend at the exercise price for the relevant period – the borrower may have to lend at this rate if the market interest rate falls but the cost of servicing the underlying loan would also be falling, cancelling out the cost

The cost of cap is intended to be offset to some extent or completely by the revenue from selling the floor

The net effect is to create a fixed rate at zero or low cost

Derivatives Calculations – Interest Rate Parity Concept

The interest rate parity equation predicts the forward exchange rate based on today's spot rate, adjusted for interest differentials between countries

The IRP equation assumes that a country with a relatively high interest rate will experience a depreciation in the forward exchange rate to cancel out the benefit of saving at the high interest rate

> If it were possible to lock in a forward rate which did not allow for the relatively high interest rate then everyone would invest in that country at the high interest rate, take out a forward contract and therefore benefit from a risk-free deal to increase interest earnings
>
> Therefore market forces will lead to the foreign exchange rate depreciating for that country (if there is very high demand for forwards from investors looking to lock in their high interest rate returns then banks will be able to offer less favourable terms)

The IRP equation is calculated as

spot rate x (interest rate in foreign country / interest rate in UK)

Use the average of the bid:offer spread to find the spot rate and the average of the lending and borrowing interest rates to find the interest rate

Example

Spot rate (EUR / £)	EUR 1.19985
Average of lending and borrowing rates in the Eurozone	7.5%
Average of lending and borrowing rates in the UK	9.25%

Forward contract rate per IRP equation = 1.19985 x (1.0075 / 1.00925) = EUR 1.1977

IRP predicts that sterling will weaken from being worth EUR 1.19985 to EUR 1.1977 due to interest rates in the UK being relatively **higher** than in the Eurozone

Question Application

You can use IRP to estimate the expected future exchange rate if you are given interest rate information – this can be used to determine whether exchange rates will move for or against your client (and therefore whether hedging is necessary in the first place)

You can also use IRP as a sense check on the quoted forward discount or premium if this is given in the question

Derivatives Calculations – Interest Rate Swaps

Reminders

You should first calculate the split "difference in differences" to determine what each party to the swap should end up paying on a net basis – this is then entered into the bottom of the Interest Rate Swap pro-forma (see below)

> In other words, in a way, you work backwards when applying the Interest Rate Swap pro-forma

Calculation steps

1. Find the "difference in differences" – find the difference between the fixed rates possible for each party – find the difference between the variable rates possible for each party – find the difference between these 2 figures

> For example, if party 1 can borrow fixed at 5.2% and party 2 can borrow fixed at 6.4% then the difference in fixed rates is 1.2%
>
> If party 1 can borrow variable at LIBOR + 1.2% and party 2 can borrow variable at LIBOR + 1.6% then the difference in variable rates is 0.4%
>
> Therefore the difference in differences is 1.2% - 0.4% = 0.8%

2. Split the differences in differences from step 1 equally between the 2 parties (divide the gain by 2)

3. Complete the bottom of the Interest Rate Swap pro-forma working with the party's desired type of borrowing but at a rate equal to the current offer less the split gain from step 2

> For example, if the party can borrow fixed at 6.4% but the difference in differences is 0.4% then we know that this party should, in the end, obtain fixed borrowing at 6.0% if the swap is set up correctly

4. Complete the other sections of the Interest Rate Swap pro-forma working (see below) with the current rate being paid and then swap rates to ensure that the final result calculated in step 3 is obtained

> **Tip** – it is often convenient to make one party pay a rate of LIBOR under the swap to cancel the LIBOR element and just leave an easier to work with percentage available – for example, if the company is paying LIBOR + 1.6% already and receives LIBOR under the Interest Rate Swap then this nets to just + 1.6% through the cancellation of LIBOR payment and receipt

Example Interest Rate Swap Calculation

Fortitude plc borrowed at 5.2% last year and can obtain a variable rate of LIBOR + 1.2%

Fortitude plc would like to move to a variable rate form of borrowing.

Veracity plc borrowed at LIBOR + 1.6% last year and can obtain a fixed rate of 6.4%.

Veracity plc would like to move to a fixed rate form of borrowing.

The 2 companies are considering an Interest Rate Swap to allow them to move onto the type of borrowing that they prefer.

Solution

Difference in fixed rates is 6.4 - 5.2 = 1.2

Difference in variable rates is 0.4

Difference in differences is 1.2 - 0.4 = 0.8

Split equally, this means that each company should be able to obtain is preferred type of borrowing at 0.4% less than it can otherwise obtain.

So Fortitude plc should end up with a rate of LIBOR + 0.8% and Veracity plc should end up with a fixed rate of 6.0%

We can therefore enter these amounts into the bottom of the Interest Rate Swap pro-forma first (see below) – the payment in the third row from Veracity to Fortitude is a balancing figure to achieve the target amounts identified above

	Fortitude	**Veracity**
Paying now	(5.2%)	(LIBOR + 1.6%)
Fortitude pays Veracity	(LIBOR)	LIBOR
Veracity pays Fortitude	4.4%	(4.4%)
Net payment	(LIBOR + 0.8%)	(6.0%)

Remember that the net payment row is actually filled in first, once we know what the correct "target" is i.e. the company's desired type of borrowing, adjusted for the equally split "difference in differences"

Standard narrative points

An Interest Rate Swap costs significantly less than terminating an existing loan and taking out a new one

Interest rate savings are possible by using the principle of comparative advantage

Interest Rate Swaps are available for longer periods than short-term methods such as FRAs, futures and options

Flexible since they can be arranged for tailor-made amounts and periods – can be reversed if not needed

Allows the company to obtain the type of interest (fixed or floating) that the company wants

Can help with cashflow planning e.g. if switching from a variable rate to a fixed rate, where cash payments then become known and fixed in advance

Compare the effective interest rate before and after the swap – clearly state the better deal and quantify the savings obtained

Risk of counterparty default – this should also be considered when evaluating the rate

Are there better alternatives? See our notes on the **Hedging topics**

See also

Derivatives Calculations – Money Market Hedging

Reminders

If we are going to receive foreign currency in future, then we can take on an initial foreign currency debt now, allow the debt to grow slightly over time up to the same value as our receivable and then clear the debt when the customer pays

> We therefore take on a foreign currency debt now, convert to sterling at today's spot rate and **save in sterling**
>
> Foreign currency receivable → borrow in foreign currency, save in sterling

If we are going to have to pay foreign currency in future, then we need to start saving in foreign currency now, benefiting from interest income to grow the relevant amount up to the same value as our payable, allowing us to make payment at the future date

> To pay for saving in the foreign currency, we take on a sterling debt now, convert to foreign currency at today's spot rate and **save in the foreign currency**
>
> Foreign currency payable → borrowing sterling, save in foreign currency

Check the terminology – the interest rates are likely to be quoted as "lending" and "borrowing" – this means from the point of view of the **company** so "lending" means that the company lends to the bank (i.e. saves)

Calculation steps

1. Work out whether the first step is to save or borrow – see Reminders above

2. Divide the amount from step 1 by the applicable time-apportioned interest rate to reduce the figure from step 1 slightly – the debt/saving will then grow slightly over time up to the full receivable/payable

Remember to time apportion the quoted annual interest rates (probably by 3/12, 4/12 or 6/12 – check the question)

3. Apply the correct spot rate to the slighted reduced figure created in step 2

4. Apply the applicable time-apportioned interest rate to the figure from step 3

If you used a borrowing rate in step 2, then you must be using a lending/savings rate in step 4

If you used a lending/savings rate in step 2, then you must be using a borrowing rate in step 4

The result from step 4 is the overall cost of the Money Market Hedge

You may wish to compare the sterling cost from step 4 to the foreign currency figure to calculate the equivalent "synthetic" exchange rate that you have created from the Money Market Hedge – then compare with the exchange rates involved in alternative hedging arrangements (if applicable)

Example of Money Market Hedging calculation (foreign currency payable)

Company needs to pay CU145.6m (a foreign currency) in 3 months

Spot rate today	78.81 – 90.62
Sterling borrowing interest rate	3.6% pa
CU borrowing interest rate	6.6% pa
Sterling lending interest rate	2.9% pa
CU lending interest rate	5.6% pa

Solution

Company needs to have CU145.6m available in 3 months so start saving an amount just less than this (to allow for savings income)

CU savings rate, time-apportioned is 1 + (5.6% x 3/12) = 1.014

CU145.6m / 1.014 = CU143,589,744

To fund this at the spot rate, we need to borrow sterling at 78.81 (lower or lefthand spot rate as bank will want to maximise the cost of the borrowing by dividing by the lower figure)

CU143,589,744 / 78.81 = £1,821,974

Sterling borrowing rate, time-apportioned is 1 + (3.6% x 3/12) = 1.009

£1,821,974 x 1.009 = £1,838,372

(or you can present the sterling interest cost separately as £1,821,974 x 0.009 = £16,398)

Equivalent synthetic rate = 145.6m / 1,838,372 = 79.2

Standard narrative points

Creates a fixed exchange rate – eliminates downside risk but also removes upside risk of just using the future spot rate if the market has moved in a beneficial direction

If the counterparty fails to pay a receivable then the company would still need to repay the foreign currency debt that it took on as the first part of the money market hedge – this could expose the company to a foreign currency loss (equally, a foreign currency gain could occur)

If the company no longer needs the foreign currency then it would still need a way to repay its sterling debt so it would need to liquidate its foreign currency savings taken on as the first part of the money market hedge – this could expose the company to a foreign currency loss (equally, a foreign currency gain could occur)

Money market hedge can be customised to company's requirements – not a standardised or market product

Digital Assets and Digital Asset Management

Digital assets are assets held in a digital form (not in a physical form)

Examples include electronic documents such as PDFs, presentations, images, logos, audio and video files

Most organisations now hold at least some of their assets in digital form – these can be strategically important resources so many organisations now use Digital Asset Management (DAM) software (a business process management solution which enables organisations to create, manage, share, track and find digital assets)

Most DAMs are effectively a centralised, easy-to-use, repository in which different types of digital asset can be stored

DAMs are required because of the sheer volume of digital assets in existence

Features of DAMs

Digital assets are saved centrally to avoid the need for multiple network locations

Access rights can be set so that only individuals with appropriate authorisation can access and amend digital content

Digital assets can be saved according to their file type which is designed to support ease of use

A search function which allows users to search for digital assets in the event that the asset name cannot be recalled

Integration with cloud-based technologies so that the organisation's digital assets can be securely-stored and accessed around the world

Benefits of DAMs for marketing

Digital asset management can be very important in relation to marketing and brand management, enabling the marketing team to find the files they need to produce inspiring on-brand content quickly and easily

Streamlining file creation and repurposing – this allows marketers to create an asset once or edit an existing asset and distribute it quickly via multiple channels

Ensure brand consistency – improve the quality of published assets by preventing accidental use of assets that are outdated or off-brand

Reduce time taken searching for files – use of tags and metadata enables users to find what they need more quickly and removes the need to recreate the assets when they cannot be found

Implementing a digital asset management strategy

Infrastructure capabilities and storage needs – management need to assess the organisation's current approach to the storage of digital assets in order to best configure and structure their digital asset management system to ensure it meets the needs of users

Management support – introduction requires senior management support especially given the extensive upheaval to existing work patterns which may be required during the implementation stage

Selection of supplier – it will be important to take care to ensure that the supplier of the system is appropriate for the organisation's needs

Project team – implementation should be overseen by a dedicated project team to ensure that any disruption caused by implementation of the system is minimised

Problems with digital assets

Difficulties in finding the correct asset on the network especially when required for use by more than one individual or department

Digital assets getting lost

Issues around version control of digital assets saved on the network

Impact of problems with digital assets

Hinders workforce productivity and ultimately the ability of organisations to utilise their digital assets in the realisation of their overall strategy

Importance of data quality and data security

The fact that companies are collecting and analysing increasing amounts of data reinforces 2 key points:

> data quality – as the volume and variety of data increases, companies need processes in place to ensure they have good quality data – to be valuable to an organisation, data needs to be accurate, consistent and complete
>
> data security – organisations need an effective strategy to keep data secure, particularly that data which is perceived to be most important to the company – this point is central to the issue of cyber security

McKinsey 5 step approach to protecting critical digital assets (from the McKinsey article Protecting your critical digital assets)

Step 1 – identify and map digital assets, including data, systems and applications across the business value chain

Step 2 – assess the risks for each asset, and its importance to the business (in order to identify the key assets of the business – its "crown jewel" assets)

Step 3 – identify potential attackers, the availability of assets to users, and current controls and security measures protecting the systems through which access to the assets can be gained

Step 4 – locate where security is weakest around "crown jewel" assets and identify controls that should be in place to protect them

Step 5 – create, and implement, a set of initiatives to address the high priority risks and control gaps – this list of initiatives should be regularly refreshed to reflect new data, systems, applications and risks

Digital Strategies

Digital strategy can be defined as "the use of digital technology and digital assets to challenge existing ways of doing things and to restructure accordingly, in particular in relation to the way businesses interact with their customers"

Types of digitisation

Digitisation can affect **products and services** – for example, turning a DVD into a digitally streamed experience

Digitisation can transform the **way** a product or service is **delivered** to the customer – for example, through online commerce rather than a retail store

Digitisation of the **supply chain** – for example, introduction of an inventory management system which connects all retailers, distribution centres, manufacturers and suppliers such that orders placed are fulfilled automatically, smoothing out gluts and shortages

Digitisation of the **wider business environment** – for example, enabling customers to be linked via crowdsourcing platforms, eliminating the need for business intermediaries

The **internet** has changed the nature of the supply chain and channel structure

Customers can book flights and hotel rooms directly rather than using travel agents

Customers can choose from a vast range of products through single retail platforms such as Amazon

Impact of digital disruption – general points from SBM Study Manual

Customers develop expectations about speed, convenience and ease of use from companies which are leaders in customer experience and increasingly expect similar quality of experience across all products and services, regardless of industry

Increasing internet and smartphone use means consumers are increasingly becoming used to a world where they can have access to products and services at any time on-demand

Companies increasingly use digital techniques to differentiate their offering since quality is no longer necessarily a differentiator – examples include smart sensors. Experience is now key

Customers no longer need to own a product to benefit from it – instead they access products or services when they want to e.g. Netflix

This change from ownership (buying) to access (sharing) can have a significant impact e.g. on-demand transportation rather than owning a car

Impact of digital disruption (according to the consultancy firm McKinsey)

unconstrained supply – digital technology has reduced transaction costs and therefore sources of supply which were previously not economic are now possible

removal of distortions in demand – customers have more complete information about products – products and services are becoming unbundled in ways that were previously combined by necessity or convenience (for example, customers can now buy individual tracks rather than whole music albums)

making of new markets – supply and demand can be connected in ways which were impossible before (for example, Airbnb has not constructed new buildings but has simply brought people into contact with each other)

creation of new and enhanced value propositions – as markets evolve, the expectations of customers increase (for example, customers now expect instant or at least quicker delivery than in the past) so companies must meet those heightened expectations through digital features, digital automated delivery and distribution models

reimagined business systems – new entrants can surprise incumbents by introducing completely different ways to make money

hyperscale platforms – companies like Amazon span many product categories and customer segments due to their very large scale – this allows such companies to offer customers a unified value proposition across products and services and to gather large amounts of information about customers – this information can be used to identify opportunities to move into new sectors

best-in-class user experience – customers no longer compare a company's online offerings with those of their direct rivals but with, for example, best-in-class operators such as Apple or Amazon – therefore, a firm must offer improved search filter tools, streamlined and user-friendly order processes, smart recommendation engines and customised bundling of products or services in order to compete

Digitisation as a source of competitive advantage

According to the consultancy McKinsey, **to date**, digital strategies have primarily focused on **digital distribution** and **marketing** – in most cases companies have merely been trying to **keep pace** with their competitors rather than using digitisation as a source of competitive advantage (in other words, digital distribution and marketing has become a **threshold competence** rather than a **unique competence**)

To gain **competitive advantage**, digitisation would need to differentiate a business from competitors through investment in other dimensions of digitisation that have seen less adoption such as digitisation of the supply chain – companies must invest in creating a **competitive premium** based on doing things in ways that other companies cannot

Digitisation must be grounded in **broader corporate strategy** rather than being an aim in itself

Digitisation should **not** be seen as a **purely IT strategy** – successful digital transformation involves fundamental changes in **capabilities**, **business processes**, **governance** and **culture**, as well as having purely technological aspects

Mass customisation is one example of a business model which has evolved to take advantage of digitisation: for example, the appliance manufacturer Haier makes its washing machines and refrigerators in China to order – customers specify features they want on their computer and those specifications are transmitted directly to the assembly line

Developing a digital strategy

The company will need to decide whether to **attack** or **defend** in the face of digital disruption

A company operating in a high margin business may not see the need to set up a low-cost innovative proposition but this could lead to problems in the longer term if attackers prove sufficiently attractive to customers to capture market share

New channels/methods and new low-cost entry options are promoted by digitisation

The strategy must **differentiate** the company from competitors

Big Data and marketing

Big Data can be used to **personalise** marketing messages and offers – marketing can be **targeted** more precisely than ever before

Real-time data **visualisation** technologies such as **dashboards** enable managers to **adjust tactics** based on live data feeds – for example, sales managers are able to adjust pricing based on online sales, and inventory, data

Big Data increases the **volume** and **variety** of customer **data available to marketers** – for example, online purchase data, click-through rates and browsing behaviour on websites as well as social media interactions

Simply **having** Big Data **does not automatically** give an organisation a marketing advantage, or competitive advantage – it is the **insights** organisations gain from the data and the **quality** of decisions that they make based on that data, which make the difference

If Big Data is used well, it should benefit the organisation in 3 key areas:

1. **customer engagement** – Big Data can provide insight into not only who an organisation's customers are but where they are, what they want, how they want to be contacted and when

2. **customer retention and loyalty** – Big Data can help organisations identify what factors influence customer loyalty, and what encourages them (or discourages them) to continue to purchase from an organisation

3. **marketing optimisation** – Big Data can help organisations determine the optimal marketing spend across different channels because analytics can help organisations measure, in detail, the impact of different forms of marketing

Recency-Frequency-Monetary (RFM) Analysis

RFM analysis can be a useful way of extracting insights from Big Data (see SBM November 2018 past paper Q2 for an example)

Recency of the latest purchase – useful for evaluating whether the customer is a "live" target

Frequency of purchases – useful for distinguishing regular customers from one-off purchasers

Monetary value of purchases – useful in targeting efforts upon customers who appear likely to spend the most

See also

Digital Strategies – past paper example

Note – our notes provided in this section are based on SBM November 2018 past paper Q2 which provided a very detailed model answer on various elements of Digital Strategies and Marketing (including Big Data analytics) for a total of **10 marks** on the markscheme – we have included plenty of notes from this past paper example on the basis that it is probably the best existing example within the SBM past papers of the testing of these "trendy" areas regarding which the SBM examiners have added a lot of Study Manual content over the last few years – however, as with all SBM past paper model answers, the content is more than can be included in the time available so please select the most appropriate points from our review below and ensure that your remarks are **appropriately tailored** to the position of the company involved in your own examination question

The context of this question was that the client company had suffered a weakening of performance and therefore damage to its brand image – candidates were asked to "explain how a new digital marketing strategy, used in combination with data analytics, could increase revenue and improve the long-term value and effectiveness" of the client company's brand – we would remind you that 10 marks were available for this answer

Examples of insight gained from a customer database

Percentage of customers who are recorded as buying more than one category of item – if this percentage is low, the company will then know that its digital marketing can largely focus on at least 2 separate groups of people to segment the market

Percentage of total sales accounted for by 20% of customers – focusing marketing spend and effort on the customers identified as larger spenders may obtain greater impact in terms of improved sales and less resistance to price increases if they are in higher income groups

Percentage of total sales from existing customers (i.e. customers who have made previous purchases before from the company) – this will inform the company regarding the benefits of relationship marketing and increases the value of the current database which has details of all historic customers

Use of database information regarding existing customers

The company can use individually-addressable marketing media and channels to contact such customers further in relation to promotional messages, help and support or any other relationship building activities

Data on existing customers can be interrogated and manipulated in various ways through Big Data analytics

Data can be used for a range of relationship-marketing projects including identifying the most profitable customers using RFM analysis (**R**ecency of the latest purchase, **F**requency of purchases and **M**onetary value of all purchases)

The company can tailor messages and offerings based on customer purchase profiles

Data allows personalisation of customer service by providing service staff with relevant customer details

Data can be used to eliminate conflicting or confusing communications, presenting a coherent image over time to individual customers – in this respect, it will be important to differentiate the message to different customer groups

Use of database information regarding new customers

The company can use database marketing to build models of its target demographic/income group

These models can then allow it to focus advertising budgets on these target groups in the hope of realising and improving the return on investment (ROI) on its advertising spend

Big Data and marketing (including CRM)

A CRM system involves a comprehensive database that can be accessed from any of the points of contact with the customer including website contacts, stores and order processing functions

Information can be accessed and updated from any point so that participants in customer-facing processes such as sales, customer service and marketing can coordinate their efforts and give consistent, coherent messages to the customer

Information can also be analysed through Big Data analytics to determine profitability, purchasing trends and web-browsing patterns

Use of techniques such as analysis of loyalty card data can be used to personalise marketing messages and offers sent to customers

Target marketing and the insights the company can gain will enable the company to focus its marketing strategies more precisely – Big Data can therefore influence the success of digital marketing

Customer relationship management (CRM) can help an organisation develop, maintain and optimise long-term, mutually valuable relationships between the organisation and its customers

In particular, CRM can be used to:

- Enable the company's marketing department to better predict and manage customer behaviour by allowing the company to learn and analyse what customers value (e.g. about products, services, customer service and web experiences)
- Segment customers based on their relative profitability or lifetime value to the company
- Enhance customer satisfaction and retention by facilitating seamless, coherent and consistent customer service across the full range of communication channels and multiple points of contact between the customer and company staff

Specific benefits of digital marketing

Global reach – a website can reach anyone in the world who has internet access – this could allow the company to find new markets and compete with only a small investment required

Lower cost – a properly-planned and effectively-targeted digital marketing campaign can reach the right customers at a much lower cost than traditional marketing methods

Ability to track and measure results – marketing by email or banner advertising makes it easier for companies to establish how effective their campaigns have been

24-hour marketing – using a website, customers can find out about the company's products even when its physical shops or offices are closed

Personalisation – if the customer database is connected with the company's website then whenever someone visits the website they can be greeted with targeted offers – the more they buy from the company, the more the company can refine the customer profile and market effectively to them

One-to-one marketing – digital marketing helps to reach people who want to know about products and services instantly

More interesting campaigns – digital marketing helps to create interactive campaigns using music, graphics and videos, based on their individual preferences

Better conversion rates – customers are only ever a few clicks away from completing a purchase

In order for digital marketing to be effective, it is important that the company is consistent regarding its overall marketing goals so that its digital marketing links in appropriately with its existing marketing mix and marketing communications

The key strategic decisions for digital marketing are similar to the strategic decisions required for traditional marketing – these involve identifying target customer groups and deciding how to deliver value to those groups – segmentation, targeting, differentiation and positioning are all key elements in effective digital marketing

Brands and digital marketing

Digital marketing can be used to support the branding message by contributing to the wider marketing of products and supporting services

Digital marketing enables online customer support through 24-hour services to make customers feel supported and valued

In developing a relationship with customers, the use of social media interaction allows brands to be supported by receiving both positive and negative feedback from customers

Customers can potentially post feedback online regarding their experience with a product or brand through social media sources, blogs and websites – the company can encourage these conversations through newly-developed social media channels to have direct contact with customers and manage the feedback they receive appropriately

Setting up a social media page would further increase relationship quality between new consumers and existing consumers as well as consistent brand reinforcement, thereby improving brand awareness

Effective use of digital marketing can result in a relatively lower cost compared with traditional means of marketing – this includes low external service costs, advertising costs, promotion costs, processing costs, interface design costs and control costs

Digital Transformation

Digital disruption relates to the impact that new digital technologies have on business as usual

Digital transformation refers to the way in which the impact of digital disruption can be proactively managed

Digital transformation involves understanding the existing information and dataflows in a business and then reshaping business processes and systems to maximise the use of digital technologies

New, underlying and enabling technologies include

Ever-increasing processing power

Ever-increasing data storage

Improved operating systems and networking infrastructure

The internet as a platform

Increasing reach and bandwidth of broadband

Emergence of open source software

Miniaturisation and the rise of the mobile

Benefits of digital transformation

Can help a business to improve its existing business model and also create new opportunities

Can help add value through increased customer engagement and retention, personalisation of products and services, integration of systems and collaboration with suppliers to speed up fulfilment, and improved quality control processes

The ICAEW (2016) publication Digital transformation – the next steps: a business guide to digital change management suggests that some key areas to consider in relation to the evaluation of a business's current position and its priority areas for change include:

Knowledge management

How well is knowledge managed in the business?

Is there an intranet?

Can information such as business performance information be shared easily?

Efficiency and productivity

Does the business use ERP or manufacturing resource planning systems?

Does the business use cloud technology to be more efficient, flexible and mobile?

Payment and finance

Can the business accept telephone, mobile and online payments?

Does the business use online banking?

Do managers have access to accounts and finance at any time, anywhere?

Is the business' e-commerce system integrated with back office functions?

Customers and marketing

Does the company's website engage customers and add value?

Does the website work with tablets and mobile devices?

Does the business delivery products/services online?

Does the business have a search engine optimised website?

Do you regularly evaluate competitors' products, websites and social media?

Do you have a CRM system?

Do you regularly send out e-communications to customers?

Does the business offer personalised products or services?

How responsive do customers think the business is?

Does the business use social media? Does it have a good online interaction with its customers?

Does the business check all online channels for customer feedback and any issues which could affect brand reputation?

Does the business use information gathered from websites and social media to identify potential new ways of working or potential new products/services?

IT systems

How does the business manage its computer network?

Has it implemented cloud technologies for its infrastructure?

Does the business use technology to collaborate with other businesses?

Governance

Does the business have an IT policy covering use of hardware and software, data protection and Internet usage?

Does the business have a disaster recovery plan? Is the plan updated regularly?

Are the business's systems secure and protected from viruses/malware and hackers?

Does the business have measures in place to enable staff to use their own devices securely when accessing organisational data?

See also

See also	Big Data topics	
	Cloud computing and cloud accounting	104
	Cyber security	145
	Digital Assets and Digital Asset Management	173
	Digital Strategies	176

Disposals and Assets Held for Sale (IFRS 5)

Consider IFRS 5 rules on disposal groups: a group of assets to be disposed of, by sale or otherwise, together as a group in a single transaction – consider IFRS 5 held for sale criteria:

1. Available for immediate sale in its present condition

2. Sale highly probable (**significantly** more likely than not):

    - Management committed to a plan to sell
    - Active programme to locate a buyer
    - Marketed at a price that is reasonable in relation to its current fair value
    - Sale should be expected to take place within one year from date of classification
    - Unlikely that significant changes to the plan will be made or that the plan will be withdrawn

Remember to apply the above criteria by using the scenario – always consider if impairment applies

If there are Assets Held for Sale then very often there may also be a discontinued operation – see below.

Is a division available for immediate sale?

If the company has an ongoing requirement for a specific component made by the division which will be categorised as held for sale, it is questionable whether the division is genuinely available for immediate sale

If the board states that it would be willing to use a short-term supplier as an alternative then this may be relevant but professional scepticism regarding intent and realisation should be exercised

Immediately before reclassification as held for sale (IFRS 5, IAS 36)

Review the carrying amounts of assets per IFRS 5 – assess the evidence of **each individual** asset or CGU immediately prior to the held for sale date

Determine if depreciation correctly treated (ceases at the correct time and yearly charge reflects this)

After classification as held for sale (IFRS 5, IAS 36)

Measure at the lower of carrying amount and FV less costs to sell

Impair if the carrying amount is greater than the FV less costs to sell

Test for impairment based on the disposal group as a whole (notice the difference with reclassification as held for sale)

Allocated impairment under IAS 36 in the following order: goodwill and then pro rata over the other assets

No asset shall be reduced below its recoverable amount nor below zero

Non-monetary items should be retranslated at the exchange rate at the date of impairment

Remember to look out for any further impairment during the year after the date of classification as an asset held for sale – this should be recognised as a further impairment in the P&L for the year

Discontinued operation (IFRS 5)?

If there is disposal of a cash-generating unit (CGU) which relates to a separate line of business then the entity must provide an analysis of the contribution of the discontinued element separately presented from profit from ongoing operations to help the user assess possible future profitability, cash flows, financial position and earnings-generating capacity

A CGU generates revenue, is material and is operationally distinguishable from the rest of the company.

You should also consider whether it represents a separate major line of business

Shareholding in a subsidiary in the context of a disposal – individual financial statements versus consolidated group financial statements

Individual financial statements

The shares in the owned company would be initially recognised as a financial asset (i.e. an investment) at their original cost

Where there is an indication of impairment then the financial asset should be impaired at its recoverable amount

If the asset is eventually sold, any excess net disposal proceeds above the current book value (cost less impairment) would be deemed to be a profit on disposal

Group financial statements

The shares in the owned company would be treated as a shareholding in a subsidiary and so the results and assets of the subsidiary would be fully consolidated into the group statements with goodwill being recognised as appropriate

The profit or loss on disposal in the group financial statements will be the difference between the sale proceeds and the parent's total investment in the subsidiary i.e. the net assets of the subsidiary as they would appear in the group SFP immediately prior to disposal plus any remaining value for goodwill relating to the subsidiary

As a subsidiary, the disposed-of company is likely to constitute a reportable segment and therefore meet the definition of the discontinued activity in accordance with IFRS 5 – appropriate disclosures will therefore be required

Enterprise Risk Management (ERM) and the COSO Framework

ERM can be defined as:

"The culture, capabilities, and practices that organisations integrate with strategy-setting and apply when they carry out that strategy, with the purpose of managing risk in creating, preserving and realising value" (COSO (2017))

The Committee of Sponsoring Organisations of the Treadway Commission (COSO) is one of the global leaders in developing guidance on risk management and internal controls, designed to improve organisational performance and governance

In 2017, COSO published a revised guidance document *Enterprise Risk Management – Integrating with Strategy and Performance* which provides greater insight into the links between strategy, risk and performance

In particular, the revised guidance highlights the need for organisations to consider risk in the strategy setting process, as well as considering the ways risks could affect an organisation's ability to deliver a strategy successfully

Traditionally, organisations have viewed ERM as a way of identifying, assessing and managing risks and threats to their existing strategies – this approach focuses primarily on managing downside risk

However, COSO highlights that ERM potentially has greater value to organisations through the way it can enhance strategy selection

ERM can play a very important role in helping organisations deliver value to their stakeholders by ensuring that management evaluates alternative strategies properly before choosing a particular option

COSO's ERM Framework

The COSO ERM framework is a set of 20 principles which represent the things an organisation should do as part of its ERM practices – these principles are organised into 5 groups ("components"):

Governance and culture

Strategy and objective setting

Performance

Review and revision

Information, communication and reporting

Governance and culture

Governance and culture together form the basis of all the other components of ERM

Governance sets the organisation's tone, including reinforcing the importance of ERM and establishing oversight responsibility for it

Culture encompasses an organisation's ethical values and desired behaviours as well as an organisation's understanding of risk – an organisation's culture is typically reflected in its decision-making

1	**Exercises Board risk oversight** – the Board of directors provides oversight of the strategy – for example, reviewing management's proposed strategies and risk appetite to ensure that they align with the organisation's mission and core values
2	**Establishes operating structures** – the organisation establishes appropriate operating structures in the pursuit of its strategy and business objectives
3	**Defines desired culture** – the organisation defines the desired behaviours that characterise its desired culture
4	**Demonstrates commitment to core values** – where the organisation demonstrates a commitment to its core values then this will generally pervade throughout all decision-making, improving ethical values and risk management
5	**Attracts, develops and retains capable individuals** – the organisation is committed to building human capital, in alignment with its strategy and business objectives

Strategy and objective setting

ERM is integrated into an organisation's strategic plans through the process of setting its strategy and business objectives

By gaining an understanding of business context, an organisation can gain insight into internal and external factors such as strengths, weaknesses, opportunities and threats, together with their impact on risk

An organisation sets its risk appetite in conjunction with setting its strategy – business objectives allow strategy to be put into practice, and to shape the organisation's day-to-day operations and priorities

6	**Analyses business context** – the organisation considers the potential effects of the internal and external environment on its risk profile
7	**Defines risk appetite** – the organisation defines risk appetite in the context of creating, preserving and realising value
8	**Evaluates alternative strategies** – the organisation evaluates alternative strategies and their potential impact on its risk profile – the suitability of potential strategies could be influenced by the organisation's risk appetite
9	**Formulates business objectives** – the organisation considers risk while establishing the business objectives, at various levels, that align and support strategy

Performance

An organisation needs to identify and assess the risks that may affect its ability to achieve its strategy and business objectives – risks should be prioritised according to their severity and considering the organisation's risk appetite

The organisation then needs to select appropriate risk responses

In this way, the organisation develops a portfolio view of the amount of risk it has assumed in the pursuit of its strategy and business objectives – the results of this process are reported to key risk stakeholders

10	**Identifies risk** – the organisation identifies risk that affects the performance of strategy and business objectives
11	**Assesses severity of risk** – an assessment of the severity of each risk will help define a suitable response to each risk
12	**Prioritises risks** – the organisation prioritises risks as a basis for selecting responses to risks
13	**Implements risk responses** – the organisation identifies and selects appropriate risk responses
14	**Develops portfolio view** – the organisation develops and maintains a comprehensive view of all risks and how they could collectively impact across the business

Review and revision

An organisation needs to review its performance in order to consider how well its ERM components are functioning over time and in the light of substantial changes – for example, changes in the business environment

The organisation also needs to consider what revisions may be needed to its strategy and business objectives as a result of the changes – for example, investing in new business areas or scaling back its operations in other areas

15	**Assesses substantial change** – the organisation identifies and assesses changes that may substantially affect its strategy and business objectives
16	**Reviews risk and performance** – the organisation understands the relationship between risk and future performance so it can take preventative steps to avoid specific scenarios
17	**Pursues improvement in Enterprise Risk Management** – an objective of continuous improvement to ERM improves the organisation's agility to respond to risk events

Information, communication and reporting

ERM requires a continual process of obtaining and sharing necessary information from internal and external sources which flows up, down and across the organisation

18	**Leverages information and technology** – the organisation leverages its information systems and technology to capture, process and manage data and information to support ERM
19	**Communicates risk information** – the organisation uses communication channels to support ERM by sharing information
20	**Reports on risk, culture and performance** – the organisation reports on risk, culture and performance at multiple levels and across the entity

Benefits of ERM

COSO's ERM Framework document (2017) highlights a number of benefits that organisations can gain from integrating ERM across their entities

These benefits highlight the fact that risk should not be viewed solely as a constraint or challenge to setting and carrying out a strategy – instead, the way an organisation responds to challenges could be a source of strategic opportunities and ways for it to differentiate itself from its competitors and achieve competitive advantage over them

1. Increase the range of opportunities – by considering all reasonable possibilities (both positive and negative aspects of risk) management can identify new opportunities, as well as challenges associated with current opportunities

2. Identify and manage risk entity-wide – every organisation faces a number of risks which can affect different parts of the organisation – sometimes, a risk can emanate from one part of an organisation but have an effect on another part but by looking across the organisation as a whole, management can identify and manage these risks to help sustain and improve performance

3. Increase positive outcomes and advantage while reducing negative surprises – ERM helps an organisation to improve its ability to identify risks and establish appropriate responses, thereby reducing negative surprises and their related costs or losses and allowing the organisation to benefit from advantageous developments

Having discussions about alternatives and possibilities does not mean that an organisation will not face challenges and threats but it should mean that the organisation is less surprised by them

4. Reduce performance variability – the challenge for some companies has less to do with surprises and more to do with variability in performance – performing significantly ahead of schedule beyond expectations can cause problems just as performing below expectations does – ERM allows organisations to anticipate risks of over- or underperformance and to take action to minimise disruption

5. Improve resource deployment – having information about risks (and which risks are most important) allows an organisation to assess resource needs and enhance resource allocation – having a greater focus on resources should mean an organisation uses its resources (money, people, time) more efficiently and in turn this should improve its ability to generate value for its stakeholders

6. Enhance resource resilience – an organisation's medium and long-term viability depends on its ability to anticipate and respond to change, not only to survive but also to evolve and thrive – this ability to respond effectively to change becomes increasingly important as the pace of change accelerates and business complexity increases

See also

Key Risk Indicators	286
Risks – Governance	376
Risks – Horizontal Acquisition	378
Risks – Types and Examples	379
Risks – Risk Reviews	383

Ethics – Independence

Potentially very examinable in SBM – you are likely to be working at an advisory firm and will be asked to assist the client further – is this permissible?

Advisory Manager joining a client

Raises independence, self-interest and familiarity threats

Procedures should be in place such that the advisory firm is notified as soon as possible

Consider safeguards such as not having further involvement in the work

Consider discussing with Ethics Partner/Director of the advisory firm

Note – restrictions and safeguards will not be as strong if your firm in the examination is not an audit firm (and normally it will not be)

See also Ethics – Frameworks and Problems 193

QB 486 ↓ favourable conditions/terms to supplier://

Ethics – Frameworks and Problems

Note – although the IESBA published a revised Code of Ethics in 2018 (and students should therefore be aware of this for their working lives), the revised Code is not examinable in SBM until 2021

In SBM you are supposed to adopt a nuanced or careful approach – not everything is a disaster and not everything is necessarily an ethical problem

You should always start your answer by stating that it is necessary to **first establish the facts before doing anything further**

Framework 1 – Case Study Approach: IIR Framework[5]

Issue – clearly explain why there is a potential ethical problem, using moral language such as "breach of confidentiality", "breach of distrust", "lack of integrity" and so on

Impact – clearly explain how significant the issue is, considering the different stakeholder groups (and considering that there will likely be differential impact on different groups)

Recommendations – clearly explain how the client should deal with the issue

Framework 2 – Institute of Business Ethics: TEF Framework

Transparency – is the client being open, honest and upfront with affected parties or is information being unethically withheld for self-interested reasons?

Effect – who is impacted by the issue and how serious is the impact? (Consider different stakeholders and recognise the likelihood of differential impact/effect on each group of stakeholders.)

Fairness – would a reasonable, informed but independent third party view the action as fair to all parties?

Framework 3 – ICAEW Ethical Conflict Resolution: The 6 Steps

Establish the:

1. Relevant **facts**
2. Relevant **parties**
3. Ethical **issues** involved
4. Fundamental **principles** related to the matter
5. Established **internal procedures**
6. **Alternative** courses of action

---

[5] There is not really any choice over framework in Case Study – IIR is what you **must** use so this is why we have termed the IIR Framework as the "Case Study Approach". You can therefore "kill 2 birds with 1 stone" by learning this approach for SBM using the notes that we have provided here and then re-using the same ideas when you attempt the Case Study examination.

Framework 4 – ICAEW Code Principles: The 5 Core Principles

1. Integrity
2. Objectivity
3. Professional competence and due care
4. Confidentiality
5. Professional behaviour

Framework 5 – Threats and Safeguards

- **Self-interest** threat (very common)
- **Self-review** threat
- **Advocacy** threat
- **Familiarity** or **trust** threat
- **Intimidation** threat

Be careful of giving too much of an "auditor approach" to your answer: generally the SBM paper will indicate that the **advisory firm is not the auditor of the client** so **conflicts and threats** will be of a different nature.

Past paper problems and ethical issues raised

Example	Ethical issues	Recommendations
Not informing staff of information	Lack of integrity, unfair, dishonest, broken promises	Inform staff fully, consider using a change agent, use change management models
Appraisal systems	Fairness, lack of objectivity if some managers have more say in decisions, self-interest threat if decide own bonuses	Inform staff fully, prevent individuals deciding own remuneration
Reduction in training costs after making promises	Lack of integrity, lack of professional competence and due care, compromises commitments to customers, broken promises	Implement improved training, discuss with staff
Termination of apprenticeship scheme without notice	Lack of integrity, lack of corporate responsibility	Discuss with staff immediately, legal advice
Possible bribery or inducement	Could fall under the Bribery Act, could be fraud, self-interest threat, failure of fiduciary duty to shareholders	Confirm all facts immediately, seek legal advice, check whether inducement has occurred or is rather a future possibility, speak to the Board,

Example	Ethical issues	Recommendations
		consider disclosing to Police (after taking legal advice), if any doubt, do not act
Transactions on unusual terms	Confidentiality, self-interest threat, deals below market value, lack of integrity	Investigate further to obtain more facts, transparency so the Board is aware of all arrangements, investigate possible inducements or self-interest threats for directors, legal advice to determine if the Bribery Act is relevant
Use of low quality raw materials	Could lead to health and safety concerns, might breach contractual agreement, might breach the spirit of a contract (even if it is legally permissible) damaging business trust, could result in deceptive behaviour if the final product is advertised in a way that suggests that all raw materials used are high quality	Check terms of contract, determine the appropriate disclosure of any change in materials used, ensure customer has appropriate quality assurance procedures in place, provide transparency in any cases of doubt or concern Compliance with the contractual terms could be an appropriate defence provided that the contract terms are clear and there is a common understanding
Directors voting in their own self-interest	Self-interest and fiduciary duty – directors have a legal fiduciary duty to act in the interests of the company and shareholders Intimidation threat if the directors involved try to apply pressure to other directors Intimidation threat to the adviser firm if the directors involved try to apply pressure to the firm	Establish the full facts, especially if based merely on an overheard conversation Disclose the issue to the full board Suggest that the company takes legal advice regarding criminal actions and breach of fiduciary duties Consider ceasing to act as adviser to the company if the matter is not resolved appropriately by the board If continuing to act, make clear to the company that any advice or report will be an objective assessment and will be unaffected by the self-interest of any particular stakeholder

Example	Ethical issues	Recommendations
Recording a conversation	Confidentiality – overhearing and recording a conversation could be a breach of confidentiality even though the overhearing may be inadvertent Recording a conversation may be illegal and requires a deliberate act so cannot be explained away as being inadvertent or accidental	Take legal advice Consider destroying or deleting the recording permanently Adviser firm may need to disclose its knowledge of the issue
Senior staff member using company's data analytics software for personal use The staff member in question was the original author of the code used in the software	Conflict of interest between private interests and interests of the company Use of company assets for personal reasons is potentially fraudulent, raising legality issues Breach of fiduciary duty by any director using assets for their own use Breach of fiduciary duty by any director who refuses to take action regarding alleged personal use	Establish the facts, particularly if the staff member is asserting that only software (not customer or supplier data) was used for personal purposes – confirm whether this defence is true Establish that no sensitive data was accessed, used or transferred Raise the issue with the board to facilitate a proper review of the matter Apply a degree of professional scepticism to any remarks made by the senior staff member in question Take legal advice on any potentially fraudulent use but taking into account the fact that the staff member in question was the original designer of the software involved (she may retain some form of right of use) Inform the informer that they have a duty to disclose the facts to the board – otherwise, the professional adviser has a legal duty to make disclosure to the board or to NCA
Known fault in software provided to a customer	Client has asked for a confidential discussion but could be a duty for the firm to	Establish the facts and exercise professional scepticism – evidence is

Example	Ethical issues	Recommendations
	make disclosure if there is a possibility of illegal behaviour Breach of honesty and integrity in knowingly selling a faulty product which could cause problems for the customer and consumers at a later date – this could amount to deception Transparency – would the client mind if other people knew that the software was sold with a fault? An opportunity was available to correct the fault before sale	currently only from a single individual Take legal advice Obtain advice from the ICAEW helpline if it is believed that a transaction is illegal – should not speak to the individual or client Board as this may amount to tipping off Even if the transaction is legal, it appears to be unethical so the advisory firm should raise the issue formally with the client Board and ask for a full explanation – the response should be recorded The ICAEW Chartered Accountant at the advisory firm should consider reporting the matter to the Ethics Partner of the advisory firm Even though the advisory firm is not the auditor of the client, the firm should not continue to act for the client if there has been an illegal act
Possible bribery or inducement	Provision of "free" samples worth £1,800 could be an inducement This could be illegal under the Bribery Act 2010 Conflict of interest from making a decision based on a friendship rather than what is in the interests of his employer Transparency – matter was not disclosed to other members of the Board and so was not open Independence – influencing decisions through the provision of private gifts or personal friendships means	Inform the Board of the full facts surrounding her actions – supporting evidence should be provided where appropriate – any responses should be recorded Obtain legal advice if there is a belief that the transaction is illegal – care should be taken to avoid any tipping off If the value of the goods seems to be beyond any reasonable level of personal use then it should be established what has happened to them as evidence of motivation (e.g. were they subsequently sold on?)

Example	Ethical issues	Recommendations
	that the individual is not taking an objective decision	Should disclose whether any further and more significant inducements have been made

See also Ethics – Independence 192

Finance – Sources for SMEs

Owner financing

Equity finance

Business angel financing

Venture capital

Leasing

Factoring

Bank loans

Microfinance

SMEs experience problems in obtaining financing because of the problem of uncertainty and lack of data – they do not have the business history or track record that larger organisations possess

They are also less subject to scrutiny by law so there is less trust

Banks use scoring systems to control exposure to SMEs – these systems may not always identify the correct results

See also

Bank Loans	61
Bonds (Loan Notes) v Bank Loans – Comparisons	85
Loan Decision by a Bank	313

Financial Performance Review in SBM – Some Advice

- Use tables of figures, particularly if comparing different years or different business streams, and present such tables at the **start of your answer before the narrative**: the examiners really seem to like this and it also automatically gives you an overview of the position and a range of points to look out for.

- Look out for **exceptionals** – are there any unusual events in only one of the years considered or only one of the business streams considered? If you do not have time to make the adjustments numerically then at least still comment on the issue to get some partial credit.

- **Do not forget the obvious** – mention that revenue declined by X% and mention that profit increased by Y% – just because this is one of your last few examinations, do not assume that every point has to be rocket-science.

- Suggest **causes** – look for reasons for the changes: you do not have to be certain here as anything sensible, based on the scenario date, should score some credit.

- **Margin anomalies** – are the margin movements strange given the revenue changes? Are the margins moving in different directions (GPM up but OPM down)? Why?

- **Revenue versus the market** – does the change outpace the market/industry or is it weaker? Why?

- Compare **volume versus price changes** (if the data allows) – still on the theme of causes, try to assess whether it is a change in price or the change in sales volumes which is driving the overall change (note that this may not always be possible if you do not have price information but you could look at margins)

- If **price has changed**, look at the "**elasticity**" or responsiveness of demand to the changes – was the price change a good decision?

- Consider the **product mix** and any changes

- **Look for any missing figures/provisions etc – but do not go too crazy as there will always be plenty of factors not considered!** Try to stick to **MS^2** points – if there has been a legal dispute in the year but there is no provision then this is relevant but mentioning a missing deferred tax balance is probably not material (unless the scenario mentions tax). If CAPEX has increased funded by loans then a lack of change in finance charges is significant but only if the scenario puts some emphasis on CAPEX spend.

- Comment on **margins** but ensure that you add narrative – do not just say that the margin has gone up or down, give some reasons why.

- Look for **patterns** – are all costs up? Was there only one business stream which suffered a loss? Recognising these patterns will help you to understand the big picture.

- **Exceptions** – is there only one revenue stream that is growing? Is operating profit down, even though gross profit is up?

- **Scenario-specific indicators** – make sure you include plenty of points on these, moving beyond the typical accountant's figures such as gross profit margin and operating profit margin to consider the unique forms of data that are specific to the company in the scenario[6] (for example, revenue per passenger, profit per staff member etc)

- Try to identify the **major drivers of the changes** and also specifically comment that these are the main drivers

- Look for **interdependencies** between streams

- Comment on **particularly high and low margins**

- **Compare changes in monetary figures with absolute underlying numbers** e.g. revenue changes versus changes in passenger numbers

- Consider **fixed costs**, **operating gearing** and **marginal costs**

- Analyse **different cost categories** (but only if there are **material** changes)

- Consider **cash flows versus financial reporting treatment** (providing the perspective of the "Accountant in Business")

See also Q1 – Technique Reminders 354

[6] In the July 2014 paper, company-specific "operating data" was provided below the P&L: weaker candidates concentrated too much on the P&L as this was more familiar territory. Familiar/typical information is of course at the other end of the spectrum to scenario-specific points so you will not be getting as much credit for generic points.

Financial Performance Review in SBM – Audit Procedures

Obtain a split of overheads into fixed and variable overheads and investigate changes

Ascertain whether sales revenue changes are due to volume or price, based on production records and pricing lists

Ascertain reasons for changes in variables and confirm changes to documentation

Review the assumptions on which budgets were prepared

Seek explanations from management for changes in figures that cannot be verified independently: consider additional audit procedures

See also Q1 – Technique Reminders 354

Financial Reconstruction

Key impact is on cost of capital, as a result of changes in the cost of equity and cost of debt

Impact is hard to judge and will depend on scenario-specific factors – may also not be possible to assess given the figures provided

Change in debt profile (amount, interest rate, period) will have an impact e.g. on gearing and earnings

Consider existing versus new debenture holders: value, amount held, covenants, effective amount of interest they receive, rights to conversion if any, reduction in income

Financial Reconstruction – possible calculation pro-forma

The funds generated may need to be calculated based on the following pro forma, probably involving PPE, inventories and trade receivables. The liquidator's fee should then be deducted, together with any **fixed** charge due.

Once the remaining net amount after the liquidator's fee and fixed charge(s) ("Remaining funds") is known then we can estimate what we can potentially repay to any creditors with a **floating** charge – this is found by dividing the Remaining funds by the floating charges due to find how much per £1 of floating charge will actually be repaid (it will probably be less than £1 due to the difficulties the company is facing).

(A fixed charge is a charge over a specified asset of the entity: the entity loses the freedom to dispose of this asset without the permission of the owner – a floating charge is a charge over the assets in general of the entity: the entity retains the freedom to dispose of assets unless a default has occurred as the charge is not in connection with any specified asset.)

Overall the proforma might look like that below:

Funds generated	
PPE	
Inventories	
Trade receivables	
Total proceeds	
Less liquidator's fee	
Less paid to holder's of a fixed charge	
Remaining funds	R
Floating charges	
Loans	
Overdraft	
	F

Amount paid to holders of a floating charge (per £1 of floating charge) = R/F

For example, if the company has been lent amounts subject to floating charges of £10m but the R figure is only £5m then holders of floating charges will only receive back 50% (5/10) of their original investment.

After this, you should make some standard narrative points (see below).

Note that if the result of the fraction R/F is less than 1, then this means that floating chargeholders will not receive back the full amount of their investment – it follows that unsecured creditors and shareholders (neither of whom have any charges at all) will not receive anything back at all.

The calculation steps to follow again are:

Step 1 Calculate proceeds received based on assets

Step 2 Deduct liquidator's fee and fixed charges

Step 3 Arrive at Remaining funds I

Step 4 Calculate Floating charges (F)

Step 5 Find amount repayable per £1 of Floating charge (R/F) (probably to a bank)

Step 6 Make standard narrative points (see below)

Based on SBM November 2014 past paper Q1, you can ignore the "prescribed part" in your calculation but should comment that this would be reserved for unsecured creditors by law: effectively, this preserves a small amount for the unsecured creditors.

Will the reconstruction succeed?

Generally the equity holders should suffer a greater loss – this is the nature of equity

If the proposal puts most of the loss onto providers of debt capital then the debt holders are more likely to benefit from a liquidation of the company's assets or take over by an asset stripper, rather than from the reconstruction (particularly if they have covenants in place)

Such a loss would prevent new debenture holders apply to fund the capital – alternatively equity holders will have to suffer dilution by offering an equity element to attract debenture holders

Consider information on likely turnaround and amounts – earnings and dividends need to be considered

Exercise scepticism of what the board of directors say

Estimate the amount by which the reconstruction will leave the company short of capital (or, less likely in an exam question, have an excess of capital)

Debentures

Consider lifetime and coupon rate – distinguish cash payments from effective interest rate for accounting purposes

Consider difference from the coupon rate and the market rate (i.e. the running yield: if a 5% coupon bond is sold at a price that has a running yield of 10% (i.e. a bond with a face value of £100 costs £50) then consider why this may be

Will the issue achieve the funds needed, based on the issue price estimated (see below)?

Expected market issue price of debentures

Perform an IRR calculation using the required return as the discount rate i.e. discount the coupon amounts and redemption amount in a tabular form (as done in FM or for the liability element of a convertible bond)

The PV which results will be the estimated market price

Use this to determine whether the issue will raise the funds needed

Equity

State the increase in number of shares (physical number of shares) and increase in net assets (£)

Discuss any differences compared to issue/cancellation of debentures

Calculate net asset value per share before and after the equity issue

The share price should move based on perceptions by the market/shareholders of the impact of the financial reconstruction

Issue of shares will increase the number of shares and decrease the price per share in most cases (unless there is another impact on expectations)

Consider how EPS may be affected – remember that if the equity is used to redeem debentures then there will be an impact on interest costs and therefore earnings

Corporate Governance issues

Consider if investor engagement by the board of directors is satisfactory – need to be informed and given information about the impact if there is no reconstruction and if there is a reconstruction

Ending in a position where a reconstruction is needed raises questions about the board's position and approach to risk – has it been taking excessive risk?

Is the board showing enough concern for all stakeholders? Is the board promoting a fair approach or is it favouring one set of stakeholders (such as equity stakeholders) over another?

Has the board failed in terms of providing leadership for the company? Perhaps investors should seek a significant change to the senior executive team and composition of the board.

Essential requirement for a successful restructuring deal must be the ability to improve operational performance – important that the right stakeholders (e.g. a purchaser) have control over this

Consider whether there is a stakeholder that should insist on appointment of an NED to represent its interests (e.g. a purchaser investing for a minority stake may insist on board representation)

Share schemes – amendments

Consider the terms of the agreement to establish the altered entitlements that scheme holders may have

May consider buying out existing options and cancelling these – offer a price based on expected future increase in value

Tougher approach – insist that cancelled for the reconstruction to take place – either go through with this or use it as a negotiating tactic

Estimate the likely impact on annual profits

Financial reconstruction and liquidation: Narrative points

Unsecured creditors and shareholders will receive nothing if the ratio of R/F (remaining funds to floating charges) is less than 1 – if the ratio is less than one, then we are saying that floating chargeholders are not receiving all of their money back so there is clearly nothing further available to those without any charges recorded at all (unsecured creditors and shareholders).

In some cases, it may be that you need to **compare a liquidation against an alternative option** (such as keeping the business going, but on revised terms – this would be a financial reconstruction). Again, try to consider the matter from the perspective of different **stakeholders** such as the funding bank, shareholders and creditors.

Points to consider could include:

Bank

The bank receives **certain cash back under a liquidation** but could be subject to **further risk if the money is left invested under a financial reconstruction**.

Consider the **interest rates** under the financial reconstruction – these will probably be higher than before in order to give the bank an incentive to continue to invest.

Consider **whether other stakeholders would invest** under the financial reconstruction or **will the bank remain the main funder** and therefore subject to the most risk?

Consider the **potential return** under the financial reconstruction – is this probable and/or attractive to the bank?

Shareholders

The shareholders **may get nothing back under a liquidation** but at least have some **voting power** to determine what happens.

You may wish to comment on what **shareholders are being asked to do** under the financial reconstruction option.

The amount invested in the original shares could be considered to be a sunk cost if liquidation is an active option: in other words, if the financial reconstruction does not happen then that money is lost anyway so the cost of the original investment is not a relevant or incremental cost – only the new capital injected under the financial reconstruction is a relevant cost.

Use the **forecast returns** for calculation purposes but **apply professional scepticism** as the projections may be optimistic in order to keep the company going (look at the position of the Board of Directors here).

Suppliers

Suppliers **may get nothing back under a liquidation** and, unlike shareholders, have no **voting power** to determine what happens.

Unsecured creditors would only get a small "**prescribed part**" back in a liquidation whereas if a financial reconstruction works then, over time, they may receive the **full** amount back.

As **suppliers are in a weak position**, it may be possible for the client company to negotiate hard and improve its position.

Resorting to court action would be a waste of time if there are other creditors which rank ahead of the suppliers (fixed and floating charge holders).

Financial reporting points

Although it remains outside the scope of this book to discuss financial reporting issues in detail, any discussion of liquidation and financial reconstruction is likely to be paired up with some financial reporting marks for points such as:

- IAS 1 and going concern presentation (valuation and also classification of liabilities and assets as current or non-current)
- ISA 570 *Going Concern* issues and the position of the auditor
- IAS 10 *Events after the reporting period*

See also

Flexible workforce management

Long-range, detailed people planning is a necessary form of risk management, preparing businesses for foreseeable contingencies

However, organisations also need to take action to reduce costs and increase productivity

Traditional staffing models based around full-time employees working a standard number of hours each week are proving inefficient in terms of matching demand and supply – at times, there is too much work while employees are underutilised in less busy periods

Flexible working can also be attractive to employees – for example, by helping them to manage their worklife balance or by combining responsibilities as a parent of young children with their careers

Elements of workforce flexibility: where, when, how much

Where: flexibility in where someone works

This could involve working from home for some or all of the time, working in several different offices or on several different sites within the same organisation or working remotely from a number of different sites

If data is stored in the cloud, employees can access it from anywhere there is an internet connection so cloud-based systems help to support the flexibility around where people can work

When: flexibility when someone works

This could involve flexible start or finish times, compressed work (e.g. working 4 days of 9 hours each and then having 3 days off rather than working 5 days of 7 hours each and then having 2 days off) or shift work

An important consideration here will be to flex when someone works to try to match availability with workload peaks and troughs – doing this could be more cost-effective than having to hire additional temporary staff or having to pay large amounts of overtime to meet workload demands in busy periods

How much: flexibility in how much someone works

This could involve working part-time or job sharing

Multi-skilling

If employees are multiskilled, the organisation has the flexibility to arrange them in the way which best fits its needs at any given time, helping to deal with capacity matters

This can also help reduce costs because the business may be able to operate with fewer employees than a business whose employees are not multiskilled – workers who are only skilled in a single area may have periods of idle time, waiting for work to become available – multiskilled workers may be able to move to different areas, reducing the amount of idle time, and meaning the overall level of work can be carried out by fewer people

Multi-skilling can also increase job satisfaction among employees by increasing the variety in their work and giving them the opportunity to learn and apply new skills

Perils of homeworking

Some research articles have indicated that homeworking can take a heavy psychological toll where workers are encouraged to adopt an "always on" mentality where the lines between work and home life are increasingly blurred

Working away from the office can isolate employees from social networks and career opportunities

Working away from the office can foster a "grazing" instinct that keeps dangerous stress hormones at persistently high levels – "grazing" is the term used to describe the compulsion to work outside of normal office hours, leading to ever longer days, increased stress and depression and poor diet and sleep among home workers

Work has, for some people, become more intense as new technology enables, and even forces, people to work faster, do more and multitask

This can in turn lead to "presenteeism" where people continue to work even when they are off ill

According to some reports, on average adults in the UK spend more time using technology than sleeping each day

Contract workers and freelancers

The increased use of freelance or contract workers in place of permanently employed staff can form part of an HRM strategy which ensures that the appropriate people are brought together to complete a specific project or task

Such a model fundamentally changes the nature of job vacancies, compared to a model in which organisations employ staff on a full-time basis

Advantages of the freelancing model for organisations

For organisations, particularly ones involved in project work, the use of short-term contracts enables particular skills to be brought in as and when required

This means that organisations only incur employee costs when work is required rather than having to pay regular salaries (and associated costs) for full-time members of staff

Advantages of the freelancing model for workers

Workers can be selective about the work they undertake, based on the opportunities they are most interested in (subject to there being sufficient work available to provide them with an income to live on)

The "gig economy"

They "gig economy" is a labour market characterised by the prevalence of short-term contracts or freelance work instead of permanent jobs

Workers get paid for the specific tasks or "gigs" that they perform

The gig economy offers flexibility to companies and workers – companies only pay when work is available and do not incur staff costs at times when there is no demand

Workers can benefit from flexible hours and can control how much time they work – they can also manage how they juggle work around other priorities in their lives

The gig economy has proved contentious because workers are classed as independent contractors, rather than employees – this means they have no right to receive the minimum wage, paid holiday, or sickness pay and they have no protection against unfair dismissal

A number of labour disputes have arisen regarding the economy with people who work for large companies fighting to have their status upgraded to that of a worker or employee

See also

	Change – Definition & Models	101
	Change – Management & Implementation	103
	Organisational Structures	324

Forensic Audits

Defined as "the process of gathering, analysing and reporting on data for the purpose of finding facts and evidence in the context of financial or legal disputes and giving preventative advice in this area".

A key aspect of forensic auditing is therefore that the issue must arise in the context of a financial or legal **dispute**.

Applications of forensic auditing include:

- Fraud
- Negligence
- Insurance claims
- Shareholder and partnership disputes
- Contract disputes
- Business sales and purchase disputes
- Matrimonial disputes
- Investigation of terrorist financing
- Expert witness services

When providing expert witness services, the duties of the witness are set out in the Civil Procedure Rules (CPR):

- experts owe a duty to exercise reasonable skill and care to those instructing them but their overriding duty is to the court to help the court judge the matter justly
- experts should provide opinions which are independent
- experts should confine their opinions to matters which are material to the dispute between the parties
- experts should only offer opinions on matters which lie within their expertise

Planning a Forensic Audit

As with a statutory audit, there should be a planning stage, an evidence-gathering stage, a review process and a report to the client provided at the final stage. There are some differences to a statutory audit:

- there will be no materiality threshold
- the timing of the report will be more variable – there will not be a standardised reporting date
- documentation needs to be reviewed more critically than on a standard audit
- interviews may be required, and these will need a high level of experience and skill
- there may be greater use of sophisticated data mining techniques
- the environment could be one defined by conflict such as in a fraud of matrimonial dispute

Example procedures for a Fraud investigation could include[7]:

- developing a profile of the entity/individual under investigation
- identifying weaknesses in internal control procedures and record-keeping
- performing trend analysis and analytical procedures to identify significant transactions and variations
- identifying changes in patterns of purchases/sales
- identifying significant variations in consumption of raw materials and consumables
- identifying unusual accounts and account balances
- reviewing transaction documentation for discrepancies and inconsistencies
- tracing the individual responsible for fraudulent transactions
- obtaining information regarding all responsibilities of the individual involved
- inspecting and reviewing other transactions of a similar nature conducted by the individual

[7] As forensic audits/investigations vary considerably in nature, always ensure that you include points which are relevant to the scenario set.

- considering all other aspects of the business which the individual is involved with and performing further analytical procedures

See also Internal Audit topics

Qb://

Franchising

Risks

Limited control over the actions of franchisees – could damage brand quality

Financial failure of franchisee may lead to non-payment of the franchise fees (unless collected up front) – impact on cash and profits

Risk of understatement of franchise fees through understatement of sales by franchisee

Insufficient franchisees to grow the business

Risk that franchisees will not renew their agreements if they are unsuccessful

Operational and contractual disputes with franchisees

Increased monitoring costs

Franchisees may request a lower fee to allow prices to be cut but will volume respond?

Controls over understatement of fees by franchisees

Establish clear link between goods purchased and sales

Link sales with purchases within systems

Regular reconciliations of till control totals with amounts banked

Banking of all cash receipts intact (do not allow payments being made in cash from cash receipts)

Review bank reconciliations as regularly as is feasible and include a requirement for regular reconciliation in franchise agreements

Reconcile revenues reported with the financial statements and tax returns of franchisees

Require franchisees to provide management accounting records on a regular basis

Review management accounting information comparing monthly sales over time and between outlets for evidence of understatement – for example, an unusual fall in sales or unusual movements in gross profit margins

Review of staff physically in the branches against payroll records

Random unannounced visits and cash accounts

Overall, ensure that the franchise agreement reflects the above points so that both parties understand the controls and requirements

See also	Joint Arrangements – Assurance	279
	Organic Growth	322
	Outsourcing	333

FRC Risk Guidance

The FRC publication *Guidance on Risk Management, Internal Control and Related Financial and Business Reporting* was published in September 2014 – this is known as the Risk Guidance

It revises, integrates and replaces existing FRC guidance on internal control and going concern and reflects changes made to the UK Corporate Governance Code

Objectives

To encourage companies to adopt a risk-based approach to establishing a system of internal control i.e. to manage and control risk appropriately rather than eliminate it – the company must:

Establish business objectives

Identify the key risks associated with these objectives

Agree the controls to address the risks

Set up a system to implement the decision, including regular feedback

Responsibilities of Directors

Ensure the design and implementation of appropriate risk management and internal control systems

Determine the nature and extent of the principal risks faced and the organisation's risk appetite

Ensure that appropriate culture and reward systems have been embedded throughout the organisation

Agree how the principal risks should be managed or mitigated

Monitor and review the risk management and internal control systems and the management's process of monitoring and reviewing

Ensure sound internal and external information and communication processes are in place and communicate with external stakeholders on risk management and internal control

Determine the company's going concern status as part of assessing how risks affect longer term sustainability

The 2014 UK Corporate Governance Code contains a new provision requiring a "viability statement" – directors should explain how they have assessed the prospects of the company, over what period they have done so and why they consider that period to be appropriate – except in rare circumstances the period covered should be significantly longer than 12 months but the longer the period considered the lower the level of certainty possible

The guidance emphasises the importance of identifying those risks that might threaten business sustainability and suggests the use of stress testing and sensitivity analysis as useful techniques for assessing both the company's overall resilience and the appropriateness of the going concern assessment

Responsibilities of management

Implement board policies on risk and control

Provide the board with timely information

Establish clear internal responsibilities and accountabilities at all levels of the organisation

Responsibilities of employees

Acquire the necessary knowledge, skills and authority to establish, operate and monitor the system of internal controls

GDPR

Reminder – the SBM examiners have included a note to candidates that GDPR is European Union legislation so the detailed points of the legislation may not apply to companies outside the European Union – therefore, rather than focusing on detailed points of the legislation, the examiners may be inviting candidates to think about the principles the legislation is designed to uphold

GDPR was introduced in May 2018

The General Data Protection Regulation (GDPR) requires organisations to have appropriate security measures in place to protect any personal data they hold

GDPR requires organisations to be able to prove that any personal data they collect is relevant, fit for a specific purpose, accurate and up-to-date

Definition of personal data under GDPR

Any data related to a person such as a name, address, date of birth, bank details, medical records, photo, email address or posts on social networking websites

Principles of GDPR

It is important that organisations handle personal data responsibly and securely and this has been emphasised by data protection legislation such as GDPR

GDPR requires all organisations to follow strict data protection principles in relation to collecting and using personal data

GDPR is designed to give individuals more power over their data and to restrict the ability of organisations to collect and use data for monetary gain such as by selling individuals' data to third parties

GDPR gives customers greater rights about how their data is used and requires organisations to adhere to the following principles:

- Consent must be given – organisations may not process personal data unless they have been given specific consent to do so by the individual whose data is being processed
- The right to be informed – individuals must be informed before data is gathered – customers must give consent for their data to be gathered and consents must be specifically given rather than implied
- The right to be forgotten – if an individual stops being a customer of an organisation, or withdraws their consent, they have the right to have their data deleted
- The right to access – individuals have the right to request access to their personal data and to how it is being used – the company must provide a copy of the data, free of charge, if requested

The right to have information corrected – individuals can have their data updated if it is out of date, or incorrect in any way

The right to object – individuals have a right to stop their data being processed and used for direct marketing – there are no exemptions to this rule and any processing must stop as soon as the request is received

The right to be notified – if an organisation suffers a data breach which compromises an individual's personal data, the individual should be informed directly and without undue delay, at most within the first 72 hours of the organisation becoming aware of the breach

When notifying a data subject about a breach, an organisation needs to describe clearly the nature of the breach, and the likely consequences of it – this helps people whose data is potentially affected to protect themselves from the potential effects of the breach

Notification of a data breach

If a breach occurs, the organisation must also notify the relevant supervisory authority without undue delay and within 72 hours of becoming aware of the breach

In the UK, the relevant supervisory authority with respect to GDPR and the UK's own data protection legislation is the Information Commissioner's Office (ICO)

Business implications of GDPR

Scope – GDPR is very wide-ranging as it applies to all businesses and organisations established in the European Union – even if the organisation is not based in the European Union, if it offers goods or services to European Union citizens, it is subject to GDPR

Penalties – there are tough financial penalties for non-compliance – companies and organisations who do not comply with GDPR could face fines of up to 4% of annual global revenue or EUR 20m, whichever is greater

Controlling data – an important implication of GDPR is that it forces organisations to get a better understanding of the personal data they hold – questions an organisation needs to consider are:

What data does it hold? (Does it need this data or should it be erased?)

Where is the data stored?

Who can access the data?

Are there any risks to the data?

Data security – organisations need to develop and implement safeguards to help prevent data breaches and to contain any breaches which do occur – organisations need to have a communication plan in case a data breach occurs so that they can rapidly notify affected individuals and the relevant authorities

Companies that process a lot of sensitive personal data have to employ a Data Protection Officer (DPO) – this officer has to report to senior members of staff, monitor compliance with GDPR and be a point of contact for employees and customers

Compliance and accountability – one of the principal aims of GDPR is to make organisations (accountable) with regard to how data is collected, used and processed

An organisation must have an "appropriate level of security" over the personal data it holds – this "appropriate" level of security can depend on the specific risks an organisation faces but some general measures which could help to demonstrate compliance include:

- measures to protect the confidentiality of personal data e.g. encrypting it
- measures to strengthen the resilience of data processing systems e.g. firewalls, antivirus software
- checking that consents obtained meet GDPR requirements, and re-obtaining them where necessary
- data minimisation – safeguards to minimise the amount of data collected and the period for which it is stored
- HR-based measures, including staff training about data handling
- internal audits of data-processing activities
- regularly testing, assessing and evaluating the effectiveness of technical and organisational measures for ensuring the security of data-processing

The ICAEW report *The essential guide to GDPR* also highlights that "accountability" means not only that an organisation complies with the regulation but also that it must show how it complies – for example, by documenting the security measures it has in place

Data Protection Impact Assessment (DPIA)

GDPR encourages a risk-based approach to data protection

In the UK, the Information Commissioner's Office (ICO) recommends conducting a Data Protection Impact Assessment (DPIA) to help document the decision to collect data, as well as related usage and processing and the reasons for them

A DPIA is a process designed to help organisations systematically analyse, identify and minimise the data protection risks of a project or plan

Conducting a DPIA can also help an organisation ensure that it is only using the minimum of personal data necessary for any given purpose

By taking a risk-based approach and documenting how personal data is being used in a process, an organisation will also be able to demonstrate their approach to data protection if the need arises

Use of encryption

The Data Protection Act 2018 and GDPR do not impose an obligation on organisations to use encryption – however, if encryption is not being used, then an organisation will be expected to demonstrate what other technical and organisational security measures it is using to protect personal data

GDPR and acquisitions

Companies should also be aware of the potential data protection implications in an acquisition or other business transactions

Purchasers need to review a target business's data protection compliance in their Due Diligence investigations

Purchasers also need to consider how they will integrate acquired businesses with their own and how this integration process could affect the holding and use of personal data

However, data protection is not only an issue for purchasers – sellers also need to prepare for a possible sale by reviewing their operational processes to ensure they will not breach any data protection laws when providing data to a potential purchaser

For example, the seller needs to check whether they have a right to share any personal data about employees or customers to potential purchasers in the course of the deal – it is possible that such data may have to be anonymised

Equally, sellers need to ensure that access to personal data is only given to those who need it – for example, by using virtual data rooms, with restricted access, as a means of providing data to potential purchasers

Globalisation

Globalisation can be defined as "the procurement, production, distribution and selling of products and services of a homogenous type and quality on a worldwide basis" – key aspects include:

- consumers having the same needs and attitudes and using the same products
- extended supply chains – different parts of the product (or service) originate in different countries
- global human resource management – pan-national recruitment and development of human resources

Requires an effective IT infrastructure to allow work and collaboration anywhere in the world – needs to allowing sharing of ideas and best practice and create and maintain relationships with supply chain partners

Improved digital technologies have made it easier for entrepreneurs and start-ups to enter markets – equally, competition from foreign competitors is likely to become more pervasive

There should be greater opportunity for small businesses who specialise in one activity to collaborate with other best-in-class organisations to compete internationally or globally

Impact on business management

Managers will need to change the way they think about their industry because of the fast pace of innovation and change

Managers will need to change the way they think about their firms and management tasks

Significant diversity in enterprise structures and management styles is expected

Multinational companies and taxation

Transfer pricing is likely to be very important here – high profile media stories have emerged suggesting that some large companies have used transfer pricing to reduce the amount of tax that they pay in the UK

The OECD Base erosion and profit shifting (BEPS) programme addresses tax planning strategies and exploits gaps and mismatches in tax rules to artificially shift profits – developing countries are particularly dependent on corporate income tax from multinational companies

The UK government has begun to offer low corporation tax rates with a proposal to reduce rates to 18% to bring the UK into competition with the statutory rates in Switzerland, Singapore and Hong Kong – this could be helpful in attracting overseas business in the UK and dissuading businesses from relocating operations away from the UK

Hedging – Audit and Financial Reporting Points

Audit Points

Exam tip – always check whether these are really needed – is there an assurance aspect to the question? If not, just leave out the below and do something else

Check whether the following documentation is available:

- Details of the risk management objectives and strategy for undertaking the hedge – confirmation of the economic relationship between the hedged item and the hedging instrument
- Identification and description of the hedging instrument
- Details of the hedged item or transaction
- Nature of the risk being hedged
- Description of how the entity will assess the instrument's effectiveness

Financial Reporting Points

Hedge Accounting

IFRS 9 applies an objective-based test that focuses on the economic relationship between the hedged item and the hedging instrument and the effect of credit risk on that economic relationship

IFRS 9 allows treatment as either a fair value or cash flow hedge

IFRS 9 has an objective-based assessment for hedge effectiveness, under which the following criteria must be met

(1) there is an economic relationship between the hedged item and the hedging instrument i.e. the hedging instrument and the hedged item have values that generally move in the opposite direction because of the same risk, which is the hedged risk

(2) the effect of credit risk does not dominate the value changes that result from that economic relationship i.e. the gain or loss from credit risk does not frustrate the effect of changes in the underlying on the value of the hedging instrument or the hedged item, even if those changes were significant

(3) the hedge ratio of the hedging relationship (quantity of hedging instrument vs quantity of hedged item) is the same as that resulting from the quantity of the hedged item that the entity actually hedges and the quantity of the hedging instrument that the entity actually uses to hedge that quantity of hedged item

Example model answer content on hedging criteria

Example of past paper model answer text which provided sufficient detail on the IFRS 9 conditions being met (taken from Corporate Reporting July 2019 past paper Q1)

"IFRS 9 conditions are met because there is:

an economic relationship between the hedged item and the hedging instrument

credit risk does not dominate

the same hedge ratio"

Please note that this example model answer text is significantly shorter than the related text contained in the Corporate Reporting Study Manual so please be careful not to write too much!

Cash flow hedge – movements **stored up in Equity (and through OCI, not P&L)** and released later

Fair value hedge – movements **straight into P&L**

Disclosures under IFRS 7 will be needed

Matching assets and liabilities

Minimal impact prior to a loan being drawn down (costs likely to be rolled up into the borrowings (assuming that we are matching against a liability)) – if are matching against a liability by taking on an asset/investment then may be some interest earned as income

Consider commenting on whether the hedged item is monetary or non-monetary and therefore whether there are year end implications when updating for a new exchange rate

Money market hedge

Requires accounting entries at inception as the relevant loan is taken out

This creates a monetary asset which will be translated at spot value on inception and then retranslated

See also Hedging – Choices, Methods and Risks 224
Overseas Operations topics

Hedging – Choices, Methods and Risks

For advice on derivatives calculations, see our various topics starting on **page 150** of these Exam Room Notes.

Exam warning for this topic – do not just list out hedging strategies – the examiners have stated they are tired of this – ensure you select appropriate strategies only and look out for any examiner "twists" which mean that the technique will not work as it normally would in the Financial Management examination (e.g. company is paid in advance of delivery of goods or has large costs in the foreign currency and may therefore not need any hedging)

Methods

Forward contracts

Futures

Money market hedge

Forward Rate Agreement (FRA)

Currency swaps – explanation

A currency swap is an interest rate swap with cash flows in different currencies – the entity first takes out a domestic currency loan and immediately swaps this into foreign currency to set up the project – the entity then takes out a currency swap with a bank: this involves the entity taking out a foreign currency loan and paying interest on this amount and the bank taking out a loan in the domestic currency of the client, paying interest to the entity on this amount

The entity pays interest on the foreign currency amount and receives interest on an amount in its domestic currency: at the end of the term, the entity pays the foreign currency loan back and receives payment from the bank to cancel the domestic currency loan extended by the entity to the bank – the interest received during the loan on its domestic currency loan to the bank could be used to pay interest on the initial domestic currency loan taken out at the start of the project to fund the project (after being instantly swapped into foreign currency) – the swap interest in a foreign currency that the entity needs to pay could be repaid from cash flows from the foreign investment, **without the need for any currency exchange**

At the end of the project, the repayment of the foreign currency leg of the swap could be made from proceeds realised on disposal of project assets – the domestic currency amount received from the swap bank could be used to make an instant repayment of the underlying domestic currency loan.

(See SBM November 2016 Mock 2 Q1 for an example of a currency swap.)

FX swap – spot transaction with agreement to reverse at a pre-set date by an offsetting forward transaction

Example of currency swap
Parent and subsidiary in different countries but need each other's currency

Example of FX swap
Overseas investment to set up a factory but borrowing done in domestic currency – spot swap to get the forex needed now and loan in domestic currency starts; use the forex to set up production and then convert back into domestic when the domestic currency loan needs repaying

*Do not forget to take into account the interest accruing on the domestic currency loan between the date of the spot deal and the date of reversal at a later time

Points to make

Can be expensive and unnecessary

Removes upside risk

Look at macro hedging – i.e. hedging total amounts rather than looking at each contract individually
If the transaction is uncertain and does not happen then actually hedging worsens the risk

The 3 currency risks

Mnemonic	**TET**
Transaction risk	adverse short term movements during ordinary progress of business
Economic risk	effect of exchange rates over the longer term on international competitiveness of a company
Translation risk	risk of exchange losses when translating foreign branches/subsidiaries into home currency

Managing economic risk

Diversification of operations worldwide

Market and promotional management to promote the diversification

Product management

Pricing

Production management – set up production in countries with lower relative production costs

Reasons not to hedge

Costs may be too high

May not be a material amount

Company may want to leave opportunity for upside risk

Portfolio effect – company may have products/shareholdings which reduce risk

If shareholders are already fully diversified then no need to hedge

Key risk identified in SBM Question Bank questions – removes upside risk and ability to benefit from improvements

Risks of using derivatives

- Legal
- Market
- Currency
- Credit
- Settlement
- Solvency
- Interest rate
- Accounting – complexity of the accounting, impact on financial statements (if not a hedging instrument, accounted for in the income statement at FV so introduces volatility)
- Business may lack necessary expertise

Forwards versus futures versus options

Forwards

- Fix amount due in advance
- Binding contract – trade must take place even if foreign currency is no longer received/needed
- Customised to user's needs
- Bank may default (if using an OTC contract)
- Administrative convenience – agreed with the bank and nothing required until the settlement date

Futures

- Binding contract
- Standardised amounts which may not match requirements precisely
- Lower transaction costs due to standardisation
- Deposit is smaller than a forward or option
- Ready market – not a contract which a specific counterparty (bank) which could default
- Basis risk
- Only a limited number of currencies are available
- Administrative complexity – system of regular margin payments to cover potential and actual losses on futures positions
- Can be closed at any time (unlike forwards)

Options

- Not binding – can be left to lapse if no longer desirable outcome
- Can be tailor made or bought on market
- Cost generally 5% of total foreign currency covered

- Not available for all currencies

Using interest rate options – considerations

Premium may be high

If using OTC options:

- Can be tailored
- Used over a long period
- May only be exercisable at a particular time
- Not transferrable

If using traded options:

- Exercisable at any time
- Straightforward to use
- Could be sold on if an early exit is needed

Reasons to use an interest rate swap

- Gain lower interest rate for preferred type by exploiting quality spread difference
- Better match of assets and liabilities
- Access to market rates that may not be possible otherwise
- Swap from floating to fixed or vice versa
- Restructure debts without incurring new loans/fees
- Speculate on future course of interest rates
- Available for longer period than other methods

Risks of interest rate swaps

Mnemonic DUT

- Default – other party may default and not pay its side
- Unfavourable movements – one side will lose out when things change
- Transparency – may undermine the clarity and transparency of financial statements

Hedging without use of derivatives

Change invoice currency

Use money market hedging

Matching payments and receipts

Matching assets and liabilities

Leading and lagging

Netting

Hedge the net investment in a foreign subsidiary by borrowing in a foreign currency

Note that most hedging methods are relatively short term in nature and unlikely to protect against economic exposure of long-term shifts in exchange rates

See also

Derivatives Calculations topics	
Hedging – Audit and Financial Reporting Points	222
Interest Rate Calculations	254
Overseas Operations topics	

IFRS 9 – classification and measurement

The **IAS 39** classification of financial assets has been criticised as a **complex** and **inflexible rule-based** approach so the IAS 39 approach will be replaced by a **principles-based** approach under **IFRS 9**

IFRS 9 is **mandatory** for accounting periods beginning **on or after 1 January 2018**

Impact of IFRS 9 on financial statements

IFRS 9 classification-based measurement categories may lead to **different accounting treatment** compared with IAS 39.

On transition to IFRS 9, some instruments **may no longer be eligible** for **amortised cost** classification.

Other instruments, like those that are not held within the business model to collect contractual cash flows or hybrid contracts with a financial host, will have to be measured **at fair value** under IFRS 9.

If a financial liability is classified at FVtPL, **fair value movements due to changes in credit risk** are recognised in **OCI** under IFRS 9 – this will reduce the **volatility** arising in profit or loss as a result of the "**own credit**" problem (see below) in IAS 39.

Aspects with no significant changes under IFRS 9

The basic **scope** of IFRS 9 is the same as that of IAS 39

Recognition and derecognition criteria are unchanged from IAS 39 – however, improved **disclosure requirements have been added to IFRS 7**, *Financial Instruments: Disclosures* in relation to transfers of financial assets

New rules under IFRS 9

Classifications of financial assets on initial recognition

On initial recognition, financial assets will have to be classified as at **amortised cost**, fair value through other comprehensive income (**FVtOCI**) or fair value through profit or loss (**FVtPL**)

Subsequent measurement of financial assets

Subsequent measurement is based on the entity's **business model** for managing the financial assets and the **contractual cash flow characteristics** of the financial assets

Assets held at **amortised cost** are **not revalued** to fair value at each year end – **interest** measured at the effective interest rate (**EIR**) is recognised in **profit or loss** – **gains and losses** on disposals are recognised in **profit or loss**

Assets held at **FVtOCI are remeasured** to fair value at each reporting date – gains or losses are recognised in **OCI** and are **reclassified** to profit or loss on disposal – **interest** measured at the **EIR** is recognised in profit or loss – **foreign exchange gains or losses** and **impairment** are recognised in profit or loss

Assets held at **FVtPL are remeasured** to fair value at each reporting date – **gains or losses** (whether at a year-end remeasurement or on disposal) are recognised in **profit or loss** – interest measured at the **EIR** is recognised in **profit or loss**

Reclassification of financial assets

If an entity **changes** its business model for managing financial assets, it should **reclassify** all **affected** financial assets – however, this is expected to be a **rare** event which would only occur when an entity **begins** or **ceases to perform** an **activity** that is **significant** to its operations such as **acquiring**, **disposing of**, or **terminating** a business line

The following are **not** changes in business model: a change in **intention** related to particular financial assets even in circumstances of significant changes in market conditions, the **temporary disappearance** of a particular market for the financial assets or a **transfer** of financial assets between **parts** of the **entity with different business models**

Any **reclassification** is applied **prospectively** from the reclassification date – a **reclassification** requires **disclosures** under **IFRS 7**

If an asset at **amortised cost** or at **FVtOCI** is reclassified, the **recognition** of **interest revenue** will **not** change and the **same EIR** applies in future

If an asset at **FVtPL** is reclassified, the EIR is determined on the basis of the **fair value** of the asset at the **reclassification date**

Classifications of financial liabilities on initial recognition

The classification rules are **unchanged** from those previously contained within IAS 39.

Initial recognition should always be at **fair value**, which is normally the transaction price.

Financial liabilities can be measured either at **FVtPL** or at **amortised cost** – **transaction costs are deducted** from the amount of any financial liability classified at amortised cost.

Subsequent measurement

Measurement at FVtPL or amortised cost continues

Derivatives are **always** measured at **FVtPL except** for **effective hedging instruments** in certain types of hedge

"Own credit" liabilities (liabilities for instruments issued by the entity itself)

IFRS 9 **improves** on IAS 39 rules here – under IAS 39, **all gains or losses on financial liabilities held at FVtPL are recognised in profit or loss** – this is **counterintuitive** because a **gain** would be recognised in profit or loss when the **creditworthiness** of the issuer (the issuer's "own credit") **deteriorates** – in other words, if an entity **issues** a bond and so has a financial liability, under IAS 39 it would record a **gain** in profit or loss if its **own creditworthiness suffers** and the bond loses fair value, meaning that the entity **records a profit when its performance is weak**

To **correct** for this problem, **IFRS 9** requires a gain or loss in the period on a FVtPL financial liability to be **split** into (1) the gain or loss resulting from **credit risk** and (2) any **other** gain or loss

The gain or loss as a result of **credit risk** is recognised in **OCI** unless it creates or enlarges an accounting mismatch, in which case it is recognised in profit or loss

The **other** element of any gain or loss is recognised in **profit or loss**

On **derecognition**, any gains or losses recognised in OCI are **not** transferred to **profit or loss**, although the cumulative gain or loss **may** be transferred within **equity**

Reclassification of financial liabilities

Reclassification of financial liabilities is **not** permitted under IFRS 9

Fair value designation for credit exposures

Many banks use credit derivatives to manage credit risk exposures arising from their lending activities – the hedges of credit risk exposure allow banks to transfer the risk of credit loss to a third party – this may also reduce regulatory capital requirements

IFRS 9 allows credit exposure or part of the credit exposure to be **measured** at fair value through profit or loss if an entity uses a credit derivative **measured** at fair value through profit or loss to manage the credit risk of all, or part of, the credit exposure

In addition, an entity may make the designation at initial recognition or subsequently, or while the financial instrument is unrecognised

FVtOCI category – expectation of nil gain/loss on derecognition

While the gain/loss on derecognition of an equity instrument at FVtOCI is recognised in profit or loss, in practice this should normally be a nil amount (assuming that the disposal is at fair value) because the asset's carrying amount should be remeasured to fair value at the date of derecognition immediately prior to the disposal – any change resulting from such a remeasurement is recognised in OCI so all of the adjustment up to fair value will pass through OCI immediately prior to derecognition and then if the asset is sold at fair value, there can be no profit/loss to include in profit or loss as the asset has just been remeasured to that same fair value

Impact of classification as a financial liability

If a financial instrument is classified as a financial liability, it will be reported within current or non-current liabilities

Non-current liabilities are relevant to determining an entity's gearing i.e. the proportion of debt finance versus equity finance of the business

The amount of gearing helps to identify the risk to ordinary equity holders – additionally, companies with high gearing may also find it harder to get financing or financing may be at a higher interest rate – high gearing is particularly unpopular in the current economic climate and there have been high-profile cases of companies that have been pressed to sell off parts of their business to reduce their "debt mountains"

Distributions relating to instruments classified as financial liabilities are categorised as finance costs, having an impact on reported profitability

Classification can have a financial implication for a business – for example, debt covenants on loans from financial institutions often contain clauses that reported gearing cannot exceed a stated figure, with penalties or call-in clauses if it does

Impact of classification as equity

If a financial instrument is classified as equity, reported gearing will be lower than if it were classified as a financial liability

However, classification as equity is sometimes viewed negatively as it can be seen as a dilution of existing equity interests

Distributions on instruments classified as equity are charged to equity and therefore do not affect reported profit

If a company elects for changes in the value of an equity instrument to be recorded in OCI, rather than profit or loss, this will affect key profitability ratios – the requirement for such an election to be irrevocable prevents manipulation by booking gains to the P&L one year and losses to OCI in the following year

Financial assets – summary of treatment under IFRS 9

		Initial measurement	Subsequent measurement
1	**Investments in debt instruments** Business model approach: (a) Held to collect contractual cash flows and cash flows are solely principal and interest	Fair value plus transaction costs	Amortised cost
	(b) Held to collect contractual cash flows and to sell – cash flows are solely principal and interest	Fair value plus transaction costs	Fair value through OCI (with reclassification to profit or loss on derecognition) **Note** – interest revenue calculated on amortised cost basis recognised in profit or loss
2	**Investments in equity instruments not "held for trading"** (Optional irrevocable election on initial recognition)	Fair value plus transaction costs	Fair value through profit or loss by default If irrevocable election made on initial recognition, fair value through OCI (no reclassification to profit or loss on derecognition) **Note** – dividend income recognised in profit or loss
3	**All other financial assets** (and any financial asset if this would eliminate or significantly reduce an "accounting mismatch")	Fair value with transaction costs expensed in profit or loss	Fair value through profit or loss

Financial liabilities – summary of treatment under IFRS 9

		Initial measurement	Subsequent measurement
1	**Most financial liabilities** e.g. trade payables, loans, preference shares classified as a liability	Fair value less transaction costs	Amortised cost
2	**Financial liabilities at fair value through profit or loss** – "Held for trading" (short-term profit making) – Derivatives that are liabilities – Designated on initial recognition at "fair value through profit or loss" to eliminate/significantly reduce an "accounting mismatch" – A group of financial liabilities (or financial assets and financial liabilities) managed and performance evaluated on a fair value basis in accordance with a documented risk management or investment strategy	Fair value with transaction costs expensed in profit or loss	Fair value through profit or loss

IFRS 9 – embedded derivatives

Identification of an embedded derivative

An embedded derivative may be identified when a contract contains:

- rights or obligations to exchange at some time in the future
- rights or obligations to buy or sell
- provisions for adjusting the cash flows according to some interest rate, price index or specific time period
- options which permit either party to do something not closely related to the contract
- unusual pricing terms such as a bond which pays interest at rates linked to the FTSE 100 yield

Examples of host contracts

An investment in a debt instrument that is convertible into ordinary shares of the issuer – the debt instrument is the host contract and the conversion option is the embedded derivative

A debt instrument with an extension option with the interest rate in the extension period reset to 1.2 times the market rate – the debt instrument is the host contract with the extension option involving an embedded derivative

A lease contract which has a rent adjustment clause based on changes in the local inflation rate – the lease is the host contract with inflation-related rentals being the embedded derivative

Examples of embedded derivatives

A bond which is redeemable in 5 years' time with part of the redemption price being based on the increase in the FTSE 100 Index

A construction contract priced in a foreign currency – the construction contract is a non-derivative contract but the changes in the foreign exchange rate involve an embedded derivative

Accounting treatment of embedded derivatives under IFRS 9

IFRS 9 requires embedded derivatives that would meet the definition of a separate derivative instrument to be separated from the host contract unless:

- the economic characteristics and risks of the embedded derivative are closely related to those of the host contract, or
- the hybrid (combined) instrument is measured at fair value through profit or loss, or
- the host contract is a financial asset within the scope of IFRS 9, or
- the embedded derivative significantly modifies the cash flows of the contract

IFRS 9 – hedge accounting

Note – although IFRS 9 is now the main examinable standard on financial instruments (replacing IAS 39), entities retain the option to apply the previous IAS 39 rules in relation to **hedge accounting only** – we have therefore retained some notes and references to IAS 39 in this section of notes and also the next section on comparisons between IFRS 9 and IAS 39 hedge accounting rules (see **page 241** of these Exam Room Notes): this retention of content on IAS 39 in relation to **hedge accounting only** does not represent an error.

Candidates should assume that IFRS 9 is the default standard for the SBM (and CR) examination – however, in practice, the IAS 39 rules for hedging are still permitted.

Problems with IAS 39 hedge accounting rules

Considered to be **complex** and not reflective of the way in which an entity normally **manages** its risks

Often **prevents entities applying hedge accounting** to transactions which have **genuinely** been entered into for hedging purposes and which do involve a **hedging effect in practice**

IFRS 9 – impact on the entity and auditors

IFRS 9 is effective for reporting periods commencing on or after **1 January 2018**

Adoption of IFRS 9 rules on hedge accounting will require the **entity** to have appropriate processes in place to identify **new hedging opportunities** and to ensure that the extensive new disclosure requirements of IFRS 9 are met

Auditors will need to test management's judgements with regard to the hedge effectiveness criteria (the "**economic relationship**" test – see below) and will also need to obtain comfort over the fair value measurement of the components of non-financial hedged items, purchased options, forward contracts and cross currency swaps

IFRS 9 approach – basics

Applies a **principles-based** approach (compared to the **rules-based** approach of IAS 39)

Use of a principles-based approach will require **judgement** in relation to the determination of whether a hedging relationship meets the **hedge effectiveness criteria** (the "**economic relationship**" test – see below) and the determination of when "**rebalancing**" will be required (see below)

Aims at **better alignment** with the risk management practices actually used by **management**, allowing transactions which are **genuinely intended to be hedges** to **apply hedge accounting** in situations where **IAS 39 rules may preclude this**

Allows **both** derivatives and non-derivative financial assets or liabilities to be hedging instruments, provided that they are measured at Fair Value through Profit or Loss – IAS 39 requires hedging instruments to be **derivatives** except for the hedge of foreign currency

Replaces the **IAS 39 "bright line" 80% - 125% test** with an "**objective-based assessment**", designed to create an assessment more closely aligned with the actual practices of companies in managing their risks

Requires an "**economic relationship**" between the hedged item and hedging instrument – in other words, the hedging instrument and the hedged item must have values that generally move in opposite directions because of the same risk (which is the hedged risk)

Allows **changes to the hedging relationship** if the risk management objective for that designated hedging relationship remains the same – this is known as "**rebalancing**" – IAS 39 generally requires discontinuation of hedge accounting if there is a change in the hedging relationship

Conditions for hedge accounting under IFRS 9

All the following conditions must be met:

- the hedging relationship must consist only of eligible hedging instruments and eligible hedged items
- at the inception of the hedge, there must be formal designation and documentation of the hedging relationship and the entity's risk management objective and strategy for undertaking the hedge – documentation must include identification of the hedged item, the hedging instrument, the nature of the hedged risk and how the entity will assess whether the hedging relationship meets the hedge effectiveness requirements (including its analysis of the sources of hedging effectiveness and how it determines the hedge ratio)
- the hedging relationship meets all of the hedge effectiveness requirements:
  - an economic relationship exists between the hedged item and the hedging instrument i.e. the hedging instrument and the hedged item are expected to have offsetting changes in fair value
  - the effect of credit risk does not dominate the fair value changes i.e. the fair value changes due to credit risk are not a significant driver of the fair value changes of either the hedging instrument or the hedged item, and
  - the hedge ratio of the hedging relationship (quantity of hedging instrument versus quantity of hedged item) is the same as that resulting from the quantity of the hedged item that the entity actually hedges and the quantity of the hedging instrument that the entity actually uses to hedge that quantity of hedged item

Example model answer content on hedging criteria

Example of past paper model answer text which provided sufficient detail on the IFRS 9 conditions being met (taken from Corporate Reporting July 2019 past paper Q1)

"IFRS 9 conditions are met because there is:

- an economic relationship between the hedged item and the hedging instrument
- credit risk does not dominate

the same hedge ratio"

Please note that this example model answer text is significantly shorter than the related text contained in the Corporate Reporting Study Manual so please be careful not to write too much!

Non-financial items as hedged items

IFRS 9 allows separately identifiable and reliably measurable risk components of non-financial items to be designated as hedged items

Designation of a group of assets as hedged items

IFRS 9 permits the designation of a group of assets as a hedged item provided that the following conditions are met:

the group consists of items which would individually be eligible to be hedged items

the items in the group are managed together on a group basis for risk management purposes, and

in the case of a cash flow hedge of a group of items, if the variability in cash flows is not expected to be approximately proportional to the overall variability in cash flows of the group, the net position is eligible as a hedged item only if it is a hedge of foreign currency risk and the designation of that net position specifies the reporting period in which the forecast transactions are expected to affect profit or loss, as well as their nature and volume

For a hedge of the net position whose hedged risk affects different line items in the statement of profit or loss and OCI, any hedging gains or losses in that statement are presented in a separate line from those affected by the hedged items

IFRS 9 approach – discontinuation of hedge accounting

Voluntary discontinuation of hedge accounting is **not permitted** when the risk management objective for the hedging relationship has not changed

This is a notable **contrast** with IAS 39 rules which allow an entity to **revoke hedge accounting at any time**

As such, **discontinuation** of hedge accounting is a **rare instance** where the **IFRS 9** rules are **less flexible** than the **IAS 39** rules

IFRS 9 and IAS 39 – shared rules

The following 4 points have not changed under the IFRS 9 approach

the **terminology** of the standards is generally the same

the **3 types** of hedge (fair value hedge, cash flow hedge and hedge of a net investment) are the same

hedge **ineffectiveness** is recognised in **profit or loss** (except for the Other Comprehensive Income option for equity investments, which is a category only available under IFRS 9)

hedge accounting with **written options is prohibited**

Summary of hedge accounting under IFRS 9

	Fair value hedge	Cash flow hedge
Gain or loss on hedging instrument	Profit or loss (or OCI if the hedged item is an equity instrument for which an entity has elected to present changes in fair value in OCI)	OCI
Adjustment to hedged item	Profit or loss (or OCI if an equity instrument and OCI election made)	N/A
Hedge ineffectiveness is recorded in profit or loss?	Yes	Yes
Gains or losses reclassified to profit or loss later?	N/A	Yes

Types of hedge and their treatment

	Firm commitment	Forecast transaction (highly probable)
Foreign currency	Either fair value hedge or cash flow hedge	Cash flow hedge
Other	Fair value hedge	Cash flow hedge

IFRS 9 approach – more complex points

Allows the **time value** of purchased options and the **forward element** of forward contracts and foreign currency basis spreads to be **excluded** from the hedging relationship, which should decrease volatility in profit or loss – under IFRS 9 the time component of an option is a cost of hedging presented through **OCI** (rather than in the P&L) and the forward element of forward contracts may also be presented in **OCI** (rather than in the P&L)

Allows **more items** to be designated as **hedged items** than under IAS 39 – examples include risk components of non-financial items, groups of items and net positions even if the change in value attributable to the hedged risk is not proportional to that of the designated items within the group (unlike under IAS 39) and equity investments at Fair Value through Other Comprehensive Income (this category does not exist under IAS 39)

May be beneficial to **banks** – under IAS 39, banks do not often achieve hedge accounting on the **credit risk of exposures** due to certain complications with the rules – IFRS 9 will make it easier to achieve hedge accounting on this type of risk

Does **not permit** hedge accounting to apply when **credit risk dominates the value changes** that result from an otherwise qualifying "economic relationship"

IFRS 9 – hedge accounting – IFRS 9 versus IAS 39

	IAS 39	IFRS 9
Eligibility of hedging instruments	Derivatives may be designated as hedging instruments Nonderivatives may be designated as hedging instruments only for hedges of foreign currency risk	Any financial instrument may be a hedging instrument if it is measured at fair value through profit or loss

Therefore, under IAS 39, non-derivative items are less widely used as hedging instruments than under IFRS 9

	IAS 39	IFRS 9
Eligibility of hedged items	Recognised assets, liabilities, firm commitments, highly probable forecast transactions and net investments in foreign operations may be designated as hedged items In some circumstances, risk components of the financial asset or liability may be designated as a hedged item	In addition to IAS 39 eligible hedged items, IFRS 9 allows a risk component of a non-financial asset or liability to be designated as a hedged item in some circumstances

Therefore, fewer items can be designated as hedged items under IAS 39

	IAS 39	IFRS 9
Qualifying criteria for applying hedge accounting	A hedging relationship only qualifies for hedge accounting if certain criteria are met, including a quantitative hedge effectiveness test under which hedge effectiveness must fall in the range 80% to 125%	Hedge effectiveness criteria are principles-based and aligned with risk management activities

Therefore, genuine hedging relationships captured by IFRS 9 may be missed when applying IAS 39 rules

	IAS 39	IFRS 9
Rebalancing	The concept of rebalancing does not exist within IAS 39	Rebalancing is permitted by IFRS 9 in some circumstances

Lack of guidance on rebalancing means that hedge accounting needs to be discontinued under IAS 39 while it could continue under IFRS 9

	IAS 39	IFRS 9
Discontinuation of hedging relationships	Hedge accounting may be discontinued at any time	Hedge accounting may not be discontinued where the hedging relationship continues to meet qualifying criteria – can only discontinue when qualifying criteria are no longer met

	IAS 39	IFRS 9
Accounting for the time value component of options and forward contracts	The part of an option that reflects time value and the forward element of a forward contract are treated as derivatives held for trading purposes	The time value component of an option is a cost of hedging presented in OCI The forward element of a forward contract may also be presented in OCI

Therefore, IAS 39 leads to greater volatility in profit or loss than IFRS 9

IFRS 9 – impairment

IAS 39 used an "**incurred loss**" model for the impairment of financial assets – impairment only occurred once a specific **event actually happens** (even if, earlier in time, it was almost certain that this event would occur)

IFRS 9 instead uses an "**expected losses**" model in which the financial statements reflect the general pattern of deterioration or improvement in the credit quality of financial instruments – there is **no need to wait for a specific event** to **actually happen** before impairment is recognised

Impairment on initial recognition under IFRS 9

The entity creates a credit loss allowance/provision equal to 12 months' expected credit losses

This amount is calculated by multiplying the probability of a default occurring in the next 12 months by the total lifetime expected credit losses that would result from such a default (which is not the same thing as the expected cash shortfalls over the next 12 months)

Subsequent years under IFRS 9

If credit risk increases significantly after initial recognition, the 12 months' expected credit losses figure per the above is replaced by lifetime expected credit losses – this is calculated as the present value of expected credit shortfalls over the remaining life of the asset

If credit quality subsequently improves and the lifetime expected credit losses criterion is no longer met, the 12 months' expected credit loss basis can be reinstated

Amount of impairment under IFRS 9

The amount of impairment to be recognised depends on the IFRS 9 Stage of impairment:

Stage 1 – financial instruments whose credit quality has **not significantly deteriorated** since their initial recognition

In this case, the **12 months' expected credit losses** figure is used and **interest revenue** continues to be recognised based on the **gross** value of the assets (i.e. **before** deducting expected credit losses from the carrying amount)

Stage 2 – financial instruments whose credit quality **has significantly deteriorated** since their initial recognition

In this case, the **lifetime expected credit losses** figure is used and **interest revenue** continues to be recognised based on the **gross** value of the assets (i.e. **before** deducting expected credit losses from the carrying amount)

Stage 3 – financial instruments for which there is **objective evidence of impairment** as at the reporting date

This case is the same as Stage 2 except that **interest revenue** would be recognised based on the **net** value of the assets (i.e. after deducting expected credit losses from the carrying amount)

In both Stage 2 and Stage 3, entities are required to reduce the gross carrying amount of financial assets in the period in which they no longer have a reasonable expectation of recovery.

IFRS 13 and Valuation of Intangibles

Valuation under IFRS 13

Some intangibles such as brands are not recognised separately in the SFP but there may be a need to value before an acquisition or disposal

IFRS 13, paragraph 9: fair value is "the price that would be received to sell an asset or paid to transfer a liability in an orderly transaction between market participants at the measurement date"

IFRS 13 requires us to determine FV based on "highest and best use" from a market participant's perspective – acquirer permitted to assume that current use is highest and best use without searching for alternatives unless market or other factors suggest otherwise

Level 1 inputs – quoted prices in an active market – not normally relevant as a brand is unique

Level 2 inputs – other observable prices e.g. in non-active markets such as a recent bid

Level 3 inputs – unobservable inputs, including internal company data

Methods set out in IFRS 13:

Market basis – market price and other market transactions – difficult if intangible is unique

Income basis – present value of **incremental** income generated by the intangible, considering value including any possible price premium effect and additional sales

Cost basis – current replacement cost of the intangible, which might be estimated as the present value of the expenditure needed to set up an equivalent intangible, including an allowance for risk and how expenditure could replicate the intangible in varying market conditions (this requires a large amount of judgement and estimation, hence apply **professional scepticism** – see **page 347** of these Exam Room Notes)

Revaluation – highest and best use of an asset

A revaluation in accordance with IFRS 13 should be based on the highest and best use of an asset

For example, assume that a plot of land had a carrying amount of £3m based on the market value in its current use as an industrial site but that residential development in the area near the site means that, if the land were to be made available for residential purposes, it would have value of £3.75m

In this case, the highest and best use is for residential purposes so it does not matter how the land is currently used – therefore, under IFRS 13, the appropriate value to use would be £3.75m

See also Branding and Rebranding (IFRS 13) 87
Valuations topics

Impairment (IAS 36)

Impairment testing is designed to ensure that assets and cash-generated units (CGUs) are stated at no more than their **recoverable amount**

Recoverable amount is the **higher** of

FV less costs to sell, and

Value in use (the present value of net cash inflows relating to the asset)

Recoverable amount therefore effectively measures the best return the entity could generate (either by selling or continuing to use the asset)

IAS 36 requires an entity to discount future cash flows at a rate that reflects the current market assessments of (a) the time value of money, and (b) the risks specific to the asset for which future cash flow estimates have not been adjusted

The discount rate should also be a before tax interest rate

Tax and interest should be excluded from cash flows from the asset or cash generating unit

The FV less costs to sell should be estimated following IFRS 13 – this should represent the market value of the assets at a point in time

If the asset is impaired, remember to mention that this will reduce the asset value on the SFP but would also reduce the future amortisation charge in profit or loss

Goodwill

Remember that goodwill is not amortised under IFRS but is tested annually for impairment

See also IFRS 13 and Valuation of Intangibles 244

Initial Public Offerings (IPOs)

(Based on SBM November 2019 past paper Q1)

An IPO is a stock market launch, taking the form of a public offering of shares on a public market

New shares might be issued by the company but existing shares will have a market and become more liquid

There are some costs to an issue which would include an underwriter, such as an investment bank – these costs will reduce the net proceeds obtained

There will be uncertainty regarding the IPO – whilst the company may wish to obtain a given price, this may not be a reasonable price for a successful float if the market does not value the company's shares at this pricing level

There is a risk that the shares may not be fully subscribed – the underwriter might take on this risk but if the risk is high it may not be possible to find an underwriter to act for the company

Comparison to private equity route

Make sure you first use the question Exhibit material to perform some basic calculations such as the different number of shares or different price per share that would be involved in an IPO versus private equity route

An advantage of a private equity route is that the funds are more certain than an IPO

A downside of a private equity issue is that the existing shares would not be listed

Remember to come to a brief, reasoned Recommendation on which option should be prepared and why, drawing as much as possible on the question Exhibit material

Corporate Governance consequences: comparison of IPO and private equity route

Make sure you work through the question Exhibit material to create a table showing the number of shares and therefore percentage shareholding taken by key Board members and possibly other corporate investors under the different financing routes – this is more likely to apply to a private equity route than an IPO because the point of an IPO is that the shares are sold to the public in general

You should then comment on whether particular directors would no longer control or would now control Board meetings or shareholder votes – make sure you analyse which shareholders could potentially work together to outvote the previous controlling shareholders or at least perform some kind of analysis regarding how "factions" might develop within the Board based on the shareholding involved

Remember to briefly discuss the difference between a 50% and 75% shareholding under UK company law – a 75% shareholding is required to adopt special resolutions and therefore undertake significant company activities, such as altering the company's Articles of Association (giving complete control of the company)

Under an IPO it is likely that the shares would be dispersed amongst many shareholders so voting may not be active or concentrated – such shareholders would also not require a seat on the Board

Issues in the market and IPOs – Study Manual points

Issues in the market account for around 10% of new equity finance

When issues in the market occur, they are often large in terms of the amount raised

Issues in the market are often used at the time the company obtains a listing and quotation on the stock exchange known as an Initial Public Offering (IPO)

An IPO is an offer to sell shares in the company to the public for the first time – the shares may be existing shares owned by the founders of the business who wish to realise profits from their investment or new shares issued to raise additional capital to support growth, or a combination of both

The company is normally advised on its IPO by an investment bank

Issues in the market are also popular when a firm wants to raise a very large amount and therefore needs a high-profile issue

See also

Insurance

Arguments in favour of using insurance

- Scale of risk
- May be a higher incidence of unfavourable events than expected
- Potential going concern issues in some cases
- Shows that the company has taken financially reasonable steps
- Ensures that can pay third parties following impact – beneficial from a public interest perspective
- Demonstrates corporate responsibility

Arguments against using insurance

- Cost – may exceed cost of the negative event
- Liquidity – needs to be paid upfront whereas the events may occur sometime in the future
- Does not offset all costs such as reputational damage
- May lead to higher claims – the claimant may know that the insurance company has a lot of money available to make the payment

Integrated Reporting

Integrated Reporting (IR) aims to combine the different strands of reporting (financial, management commentary, governance and remuneration and sustainability reporting) into a coherent whole

Looks at the short, medium and long term – highlights the importance of long-term business sustainability

Helps to make decisions more sustainable and allocate scarce resources effectively

Entity will report on financial and operational performance as normal but also social and environmental aspects

This may include controls over environmental risks, for example

"What gets measured, gets done" – should force more attention onto key issues

6 different types of capital: (1) financial, (2) manufactured, (3) intellectual, (4) human, (5) social and relationship, and (6) natural – this gives a much broader framework for analysis than just financial performance

"Integrated" means highlighting the **interrelatedness and dependencies** between various factors – helping to understand how to generate value

Greater focus on future strategy and outlook than traditional reporting which is backward-looking – IR emphasises the importance of planning and looking forward, considering strategy, governance and performance

Performance measurement – (1) to what extent has a company achieved its strategic objectives? (2) what are the outcomes of its performance in terms of the 6 capitals? Assumed that you need all 6 types of capital (but obviously with varying significance)

So performance measures needed for all 6 capitals with related targets

Probably the case that existing targets will be financial in nature so will need to look at the other capitals – important to consider properly how these will really add to long-term value and then measure accordingly

Social capital – includes company reputation, brand reputation and relationships with stakeholders – reputation for fair dealing and compliance with regulations – hard to have KPIs for this aspect

Benefits of Integrated Reporting

Streamlined performance reporting with efficiencies found within the organisation

Reduction in duplication of information and consistency of messaging

Aligns and simplifies internal and external reporting for consistency and efficiency

Greater focus on what is material to the organisation and helps identify what is not material

Less time and effort is wasted on reporting unimportant issues

IFAC support for Integrated Reporting

IFAC has already published its strong support for Integrated Reporting as a way of "creating long-term value and promoting longer term behaviour in capital markets" – IFAC states that Integrated Reporting "can bring about a more coherent corporate reporting system, which is currently largely fragmented, complex and compliance driven"

The 6 Capitals

There has been increasing interest in Integrated Reporting (IR) due to a belief that traditional corporate reporting does not "tell the whole story".

The International Integrated Reporting Council (IIRC) introduced the integrated reporting framework in 2013. This framework is based around the concept of 6 different "types of capital":

Financial capital – funds available and obtained from operations, debt, equity or grants

Manufacturing capital – manufactured physical objectives available for use

Intellectual capital – knowledge-based intangibles developed by the organisation

Human capital – competencies, capabilities and experience

Natural capital – environmental resources and processes

Social and relationship capital – relationships with stakeholders and networks

These types of capital will interact in positive and negative ways.

Integrated reporting should look at the long-term impact and value creation, where value creation is not understood simply in monetary terms.

Some implications of introducing integrated reporting into an entity include:

- IT costs
- Time and staff costs
- Consultancy costs

- Disclosure risk – the entity may disclose more information about its operational performance than intended

The Corporate Reporting Study Manual provides ICAEW's own integrated report as an example of integrated reporting: the following sections were included:

- Organisational overview of aims, people, relationships and thinking.

- Performance: student and membership numbers, year on year changes and commentary

Guiding Principles of Integrated Reporting

Strategic focus and future orientation – insight into strategy

Connectivity – holistic and relates to the connections between different elements

Stakeholder relationships

Materiality

Reliability and completeness

Conciseness

Consistency and comparability

Elements of an integrated report

Organisational overview and external environment

Governance

Business model

Risks and opportunities

Strategy and resource allocation

Performance

Future outlook

Implications of an integrated report

Need to be careful what forward-looking information is disclosed – do we want to reveal our strategy?

Should force the business to take a long-term perspective and think about the 6 capitals

Increased use of non-financial information

Report must give insight into strategy

Significantly increased information requirements: need to consider whether systems can provide this, whether non-financial issues can be embedded and any necessary improvements to reporting

Auditing Integrated Reports

Performance will depend on a variety of factors rather than separate independent variables. Therefore, the auditor may have to adjust for background factors that have changed in the meantime to assess performance correctly. However, this will require substantial professional judgement.

Additionally, look out for any incentive to manipulate the figures, particularly if there is any performance-related element.

The auditor should also look out for any dysfunctional behaviour where motivations are not appropriate for the organisation as a whole: if the performance metric for a call centre is "number of calls answered", will this result in good quality responses from operators or will it just result in a lot of short and unhelpful calls, just to meet targets?

Note that the Management Commentary is not audited

However, as investors are increasingly paying more attention to the information in the Management Commentary, there are calls for this to be separately evaluated by auditors in order to determine whether the story presented in the Management Commentary is balanced and reasonable in the opinion of the auditors

Conducting an audit of performance information

- Identify the objectives against which the organisation is to be evaluated
- Plan procedures to determine whether objectives are being achieved: these procedures could include social-scientific research methods as well as more traditional audit-type approaches.
- Express a conclusion in the form of a report, either separately or within another document. Ideally, both the performance statistics and the auditor's view will be presented alongside each other within the same document

South Africa study by ACCA

Integrated reporting is mandatory for listed entities in South Africa

The main finding of ACCA research carried out in South Africa was that although there is an appetite for third-party assurance to be provided on integrated reports, the skills required, coupled with the associated costs and the limited areas on which assurance could actually be placed, do not suggest that this will be easy to implement

See also	Balanced Scorecard	60
	Critical Success Factors	140
	Key Performance Indicators	284

Interest Rate Calculations

Importance of Annuity Factors

Most calculations will be "rough and ready" or simple calculations – the easiest way for the examiner to set this style of question is to use an Annuity Factor approach (so that you do not need to do separate calculations for each year of the analysis). So ensure that you are comfortable with using Annuity Tables!

Zero Coupon Bond with a Premium – Effective Interest Rate

Example: a £1m bond is redeemable at a premium of 15% in 4 years

Find a rate which fairly allocates the 15% (or £150,000) over each of the 4 years, but which also takes into account the effect of compound interest

The correct formula to use is to apply the nth root (where n is the number of years) to a fraction of 100 + interest rate/100, and then deducting 1 to find the interest rate.

So for the example bond above the calculation would be $[(115/100)^{0.25 \text{ or } ¼}] - 1$ or **3.6%**

Exam Tip – this is an excellent opportunity to comment on cash versus accounting principles – no cash flow until the final year (with a large outflow) but finance charges each year under accounting rules

Exam Tip – check whether the loan is in a foreign currency – this further increases risk due to uncertainty regarding the future exchange rate

Standard Bond with Transaction Fees – Effective Interest Rate

Example: issue of a £20m bond with fees of 2% and a 5% coupon payment for 4 years

Exam tip – the EIR should be just slightly higher than 5% because we are going to set up a liability just below £20m as transaction fees are always a debit entry

Coupon will be £1m or £20m x 5% and final cash flow can be done in one go as £20m plus £1m

$(£20m \times 0.98) = £1m/(1 + i) + £1m/(1 + i)^2 + £1m/(1 + i)^3 + £21m/(1 + i)^4$

Implicit Interest Rate on a Sale and Leaseback

Example

The business sells an asset for £150,000 receivable immediately and in return has to pay rentals of £70,000 for 3 years

The entity thus gains £150,000 now in return for paying £70,000 for 3 years.

Solution

The internal rate of return of the transaction is given by finding the Annuity Factor A such that

150,000 – (70,000 x A) = 0

Therefore **A = 2.1429.** Using Annuity Tables, this implies an interest rate of around **19%** (quite a high rate)

Bond transaction fees – always a Debit entry

Since the cash paid on the intermediary or lawyer's fee must result in a Credit entry to cash then it follows that the Debit must be to the financial instrument.

In the case of an issued bond (liability), this will **reduce** the first liability entry in the bond working.

In the case of a purchased bond (asset), this will **increase** the first asset entry in the bond working.

See also		
	Acquisitions – Financing	38
	Bank Loans	61
	Bonds (Loan Notes) v Bank Loans – Comparisons	85
	Option valuation	320

Internal Audit – cyber security

Note – the following points are taken from SBM July 2018 past paper Q1 which contained a useful question on Internal audit (the only example of the testing of this area in the SBM past papers to date) which accounted for 9 marks on the markscheme

The context was that the candidate was required to "explain the issues that should be considered with respect to the possible causes and consequences of the cyber security incident reported by the internal audit department": the incident related to malware unintentionally sent by a third-party supplier – the candidate was also required to "recommend actions that should be taken to provide the board with greater assurance over cyber security"

Although the question apparently focused on internal audit, please note how few of the remarks in the model answer relate to technical points on internal audit procedures and standards – in fact, most of the marks relate to more commonsense points on IT deficiencies and improvements (including cyber security risk management strategies) rather than to internal audit as such

As a first step, the board needs to establish that:

- there has been full data cleansing and systems cleansing such that there is no continued contamination from the breach
- similar files from third-party service providers must be checked in future and tested for malware with a more robust firewall (the same as from non-trusted external communications)
- there has been a review of the security systems of third-party providers on a regular basis as part of any agreement

The fact that a cyber security incident has occurred in relation to one supplier highlights the risk of other types of cyber attack from other sources

Internal audit work should not treat the matter simply as a technical risk but rather as a wider business risk where responsibility lies throughout the organisation and not just within the sphere of the IT department

External partners who could intentionally or unintentionally cause cyber risks include:

- the supply chain
- customers
- business partners
- IT service providers
- subcontractors

All of these external relationships should be part of a wider internal audit assurance engagement

It may be unproductive and unrealistic to try to gain assurance over **all** third-party service providers and so a degree of prioritisation is required in any cyber security risk management strategy

It will be important to target efforts on the greatest risk providers, which may not be the same as the highest value providers

At a minimum, the company should at least require third parties to confirm their security measures and procedures in their terms and conditions documents

Third parties with IT systems which are integrated with those of the company represent one of the greatest risks

Small companies which do not have a significant IT security budget may also be a significant risk

Customers may not have well-developed IT security systems as these may not be important to their business

It will be important to make cyber assurance part of an ongoing process rather than being simply a one-off exercise – this is likely to require regularly reviewing processes and procedures over the entire life-cycle of a third-party service provider's contract

To the extent that common platforms, programs and processes are used, the assurance engagement should review for cross contamination into the company's systems in general

Recommendations

Consider the nature of any critical business relationships alongside IT security in relation to selected third-party service providers which have been identified as a significant cyber risk

This may require building a culture of a common approach to risk and a common risk vocabulary, rather than imposing conditions

There may be a requirement to share data security across the supply chain, including tier 2 and tier 3 suppliers (i.e. suppliers of suppliers)

ISO 27000 could provide a benchmark for required standards and related Due Diligence

If full co-operation is not forthcoming, the business consequences of losing the relevant third-party service provider may need to be weighed up against cyber risks

Service level agreements with third-party service providers may need to include transparency and access conditions relating to files and systems in order to obtain assurance as a condition of doing business with the relevant provider – this will facilitate ongoing IT Due Diligence procedures throughout the life-cycle of the supply contract

Service level agreements may also include penalty clauses for cyber breaches in order to provide incentives for suppliers to comply with conditions and install IT security systems

Internal Audit – Objectives, Contribution and Comparison to Statutory Audit

Objectives of Internal Audit

The objectives of internal audit include:

- review of accounting and internal control systems
- examination of financial and operating information
- review of the economy, efficiency and effectiveness of operations
- review of the safeguarding of assets
- review of the implementation of corporate objectives
- identification of significant business and financial risks
- special investigations such as fraud investigations

Relationship between Internal Auditors and External Auditors

Internal Audit can help the board by liaising with external auditors, particularly where external auditors can use Internal Audit work and reduce the time and therefore cost of the external audit

> However, note that using internal auditors for "direct assistance" on the external audit is prohibited in the UK under ISA 610.5-1

Internal Audit can also check that external auditors are reporting back to the board everything they are required to under auditing standards

Differences to Statutory Audit

The following table provides some useful reminders of the key differences on which you may be tested:

	Internal audit	External audit
Purpose	Add value to operations	Express an opinion on the financial statements
Reporting to	Board of Directors or Audit Committee	Shareholders
Relating to	Operations of the organisation	Financial statements
Relationship with the company	Often employees of the entity – can be outsourced	Independent of the company and its management

Therefore, internal audit has a much wider scope than statutory audit as internal audit considers all the operations and objectives of the entity and is not limited just to the financial statements.

Does an Entity Need an Internal Audit Function?

Per the Study Manual, several factors should be considered:

- scale, diversity and complexity of the company's activities
- number of employees
- cost-benefit considerations
- changes in organisational structure
- changes in key risks
- problems with internal control systems
- an increased number of unexplained or unacceptable events

These factors could be relevant if you have a particularly small client in your scenario and the company does not yet have an internal audit function: it may perhaps be too early for the smaller client to implement internal auditing formally.

How Does the Internal Audit Function Assist the Board?

The internal audit department can act as auditors for Board reports which are not audited by the external auditors.

Internal auditors may be experts in fields such as auditing and accounting standards and can assist in implementing new standards.

Internal auditors can liaise with external auditors to reduce the time and therefore cost of the external audit.

Internal auditors can check that external auditors are performing their job properly and reporting all relevant facts back to the Board.

Internal auditors also have a two-fold role in relation to risk management:

- Monitoring the overall risk management policy to ensure that it operates effectively
- Monitoring the strategies implemented to ensure that they continue to operate effectively

See also Internal Audit topics

Internal Audit – Types of Assignment

Value for Money (VFM) Audits

A VFM audit tests for the 3 Es: **economy**, **efficiency** and **effectiveness** where these concepts are defined as follows:

Economy – obtaining the appropriate quantity and quality of resources at minimum cost

Efficiency – maximising the output from a given set of inputs or minimising the inputs used to produce a given output

Effectiveness – how well an activity achieves its policy objectives or other intended effects

We strongly recommend you to learn the difference between the 3 Es above. Remember to relate them to the scenario by quoting back information in the extracts.

Information Technology Audits

An IT Audit tests the computer systems of a business. Effective IT systems are vital to the functioning of most modern businesses. The internal auditors would look at issues such as:

- the operating system
- e-business
- the database management system
- system development processes
- problem management
- change management
- asset management
- desktop audits
- capacity management
- access controls

Financial Audits

A financial audit involves reviewing all the available evidence (usually the company's records) to substantiate information in management and financial reporting. As such, this role is quite like that of external or statutory audit and therefore the Study Manual indicates that it is a minor part of the function of internal audit and one which does not add huge value to the business.

Operational (or Management and Efficiency) Audits

This type of audit involves examination of the operational processes of the organisation. The primary objective is to monitor management performance to ensure that company policy is adhered to.

The internal auditor will ensure that the policies in place are adequate for the purpose and will then also ensure that the policy works effectively in practice.

Examples of operational audits given in the Study Manual include:

Procurement – checks to ensure that the process of purchasing for the business achieves its key objectives and that it operates per company guidelines

Marketing – checks to ensure that the process of assessing and enhancing demand for the company's products is managed effectively. This will require that information is freely available to manage demand and to ensure that risks are being managed correctly.

Treasury – checks to ensure that the risks involved (such as interest rate and foreign exchange risk) are managed effectively and in accordance with company procedures. As with marketing, this will require that information is freely available to the treasury department so that they can ensure funds are available when required.

Human resources – checks to ensure that processes are in place to ensure that people are available to work for the business and that there is appropriate planning and control of the business. Once again, this will involve ensuring that company polices are maintained and that information is freely available on key risk factors.

Example model answer points from a scenario where the candidate is required to comment on the findings of a company's Internal Audit department (based on SBM November 2019 past paper Q2 (model answer pages 25 and 26) (worth 8 marks)

Here the client company owned and managed purpose-built student accommodation (PBSA) for UK university students – **important note**: the points described below are (in line with best practice for SBM answers) tailored to the scenario-specific information provided in the question Exhibit content so please only use them as an **approximate guide** as to the types of point you could consider in your own response)

Issue 1 – rooms found to be occupied when the accounting records showed no occupancy

The concern here is the completeness of reported rental incomes with the risk of understatement of revenue – there may be misappropriation of assets which would be fraudulent behaviour

Management may have rented out apartments during less busy periods and taken money directly for their own personal use – however, this may only have been possible through collusion as it would be difficult for one person to achieve such an outcome on their own

Actions and procedures in relation to Issue 1

Review the booking system to establish whether the local manager had any ability to enter or alter booking records

Obtain a full explanation of why the "delay" in recording occurred and investigate treatment of cash and other means of payment

Discuss the matter with other local staff not involved in the finance function such as housekeeping and clerical staff to establish if they knew anything about the matter

Speak to "guests" to establish the facts surrounding booking and payment

Examine housekeeping records of occupancy and cleaning for other cases of understatement of income

Review other bookings for similar omissions

If there is evidence of fraud, then suspend the manager and contact the police

Issue 2 – Internal Audit's estimate of the fair value of 3 properties was 10% lower than that recognised in the financial statements

The concern here is that the fair value of properties could be overstated in the SFP – profit for the period may also be overstated if the fair values are overstated relative to last year

The matter is material as the claimed overstatement is a significant proportion of the fair value movement for the year and 10% of the fair value of the assets concerned

Additionally, the issue has only been identified in relation to 3 properties at present so there could be further issues relating to the fair value of other properties

Actions and procedures in relation to Issue 2

Undertake an independent review of the methods used by the Internal Audit team to determine their fair values including assumptions, estimates and other evidence – IFRS 13 Level 3 criteria should have been applied by Internal Audit (Level 1 and Level 2 seem unlikely in relation to investment property as there is no market for quoted investment properties (so Level 1 is not possible) and it is relatively difficult to find observable inputs of a Level 2 type)

Review compliance with IAS 40 which does not require an external valuer

The external valuer is a management expert and should be reviewed for independence and competence – his or her methods need to be independently reviewed including assumptions, estimates and other evidence

If there is no agreement on the method after reviewing both sets of estimates, then a further independent valuer may be used, appointed by the Board

If these 3 properties have been the only sampled items then there may be an issue of overstatement of fair value for the company's other properties – a wider review should be considered

Inform the external auditor, who may wish to use an auditor's expert – it may well be that the audit is currently taking place

Recent loans have been taken out but if these have been based on false valuations then the bank should be informed

Additional point – involvement of the Finance Director

In the scenario, the Finance Director had asked the candidate to respond to some concerns raised by the Audit Committee chairman – the Finance Director had stated that she was not happy that the matters had been raised by the Audit Committee chairman for the attention of the Board and also that she thought the Internal Audit team had overstepped its responsibilities as they did not have the expert knowledge of the external valuers which the Finance Director had appointed

The model answer includes credit if the candidate observed that the Finance Director was their line manager and therefore an **implied intimidation threat** had arisen as there was some suspicion, based on the Finance Director's comments, that she was in some way at fault or involved in the matters of concern to the Internal Audit function

See also Internal Audit topics

Internal Audit – Process and Reporting

The standard steps in an Internal Audit assignment are:

- setting the process objective
- determining the audit terms of reference
- reviewing current processes and controls
- analysing risks
- testing and results
- reporting
- management actions and monitoring

The Standard Internal Audit Report

There are no formal requirements for internal audit reports (unlike with statutory audit): the document can be adapted to suit the relevant purposes. A suggested outline would include:

- Executive Summary – objectives, outcomes, key action points and further work to complete
- audit tests carried out and their findings
- list of action points
- future time-scale and costs
- summary of existing culture of control
- overall opinion on the managers' willingness to address risks and improve
- implications of outstanding risks
- results of control evaluations
- causes of basic problems detected

The Qualities of Good Internal Audit Recommendations

Internal audit recommendations should consider:

- the available options, emphasising the internal auditor's preferred solution

- the removal of obstacles to control such as poor communication or lack of management willingness to enforce controls

- resource issues: how much will recommendations cost and what are the costs of poor control?

- the terms of reference of the internal audit report, the work performed and the results

See also Internal Audit topics

Internal Controls

Responsibilities

Duty of management to implement and monitor the effectiveness of risk management procedures to manage the risk for investors and other stakeholders – therefore the responsibility of the Board – if a listed company then needs to comply with the disclosure requirements of the UK Corporate Governance Code

Assurance assignments

ISAE 3410 identifies varied procedures depending on the nature and purposes of the assurance to be provided

This assignment should review the assertions about risk management made by the Board if an annual report is produced

Important to have clarity over the desired purpose of the assurance report: is the scope the design of risk management procedures and internal controls and/or the operation of those controls? The nature and scope of each of these engagements would be different and therefore the benefits would also differ

Sufficient appropriate evidence that internal controls have operated as designed

Judgement needed to assess the likelihood and potential impact of risk

Impossible to determine whether all significant risks have been identified and properly evaluated and managed

Limited assurance in the form of a negatively expressed conclusion

Benefits of assurance on internal controls

If carried out by a professional accountant with the relevant experience applying the highest standards to examine data, processes or information and expressing an assurance conclusion which provides a strong signal of reliability and offers attestation to stakeholders

Identifying deficiencies in internal control and risk management procedures helps LL's management to enhance the quality of its internal systems and controls

Assurance conclusion and any related recommendations resulting from the work of the assurance provider can be used by management to improve the quality of systems and controls and the information derived from them

See also Internal Audit topics

Investment Appraisal Methods

Use round thousands in your calculations to save time – you do not have to be exact

General Narrative Points

State the highest outcome, the next highest and so on – not hard but needs to be done

Examine the project with the best result very carefully – is there some kind of downside?

Consider operational and strategic issues, thinking of scenario-specific points

Pros and Cons of Different Standard Methods

	Positive	**Negative**	**Overall rank**
Payback period	-simple -quick -considers risk to certain extent	-too simple -does not consider time value of money -ignores flows after payback achieved (i.e. total returns)	Useful for initial filtering
ARR	-uses profit, so consistent with ROCE -uses balance sheet values -easy to understand	-does not consider time value of money -does not maximise wealth -profits can be manipulated -higher % ARR is not necessarily best in absolute terms	Not very useful
NPV	-considers time value of money -absolute measure -considers all cash flows	-hard to estimate discount rate -difficult to be accurate about all costs/benefits -assumes flows occur at year ends	Technically strong technique
IRR	-considers time value of money -not dependent on discount rate chosen -considers all cash flows	-may conflict with NPV -assumes cash reinvested at IRR – is this possible?	Easier to use and communicate practically

Also consider our notes on the **APV**, **EVA®** and **Free Cash Flow** models.

Exam tips

Flex some of the figures and retest the results – what difference is made? How likely is this in practice? (There are no right answers here, just try to make some suggestions.)

If a foreign currency is involved, try to do as much as possible in that currency and then only do one translation into sterling at the end

Standard scepticism points for any model

Length of model time horizon – too long or too short

How have revenue and cost figures been arrived at

Query the exchange rate assumptions

What happens after the end of the time horizon?

Query the discount rate applied

Calculating the breakeven exchange rate (sensitivity analysis)

We need to find how much the present value of a particular flow can change before the project realises an NPV of 0.

Example

PV of revenues	\$100,000
NPV of project	\$7,000
Current exchange rate	\$2:£1
Breakeven exchange rate	100,000/(100,000 – 7,000) x 2 = 2.15

Provided that the dollar does not depreciate to \$2.15:£1 then the project will continue to break even This would be a change in the rate of 0.15/2 or 7.5%

See the model answer to the July 2015 past paper Q1 for further explanation.

Investment Appraisal Methods – APV

Adjusted Present Value approach

Based in NPV methodology but adding in the present value of the tax shield (i.e. interest savings from using loans as a financing method)

Cash flows are discounted at the ungeared cost of equity

Tax savings (tax shield) are discounted at the interest rate of the debt used to finance the activity

Therefore you must use 2 different discount rates and allocate these to the correct parts

Step 1 **Calculate free cash flows and discount at an ungeared cost of equity**

Calculate cash flows after CAPEX and discount using a cost of equity which does not take into account any loan financing (loan financing and its tax impact are considered in Step 2 below)

To obtain the ungeared cost of equity you may need to use the CAPM formula

$\mathbf{k_{eu} = r_f + \beta_a (r_m - r_f)}$

where

r_f risk free interest rate
r_m expected market return
β_a asset beta

Do not forget to value the terminal value (i.e. cash flows into perpetuity from the final year of detailed data: see question and reference to flows for the "foreseeable future") and then discount this terminal value and note that the discount factor should be the same as the final year for which non-perpetuity figures are given – see **page 272** of these Exam Room Notes on this principle.

Step 2 **Calculate interest tax savings and discount at the (risk-free) cost of debt**

Find the annual tax savings (interest x tax rate) and discount at the same interest rate as the debt

This should be at a lower discount rate than in step 2

If the tax saving is to **perpetuity** rather than for a fixed number of years, then simply find (tax rate x debt principal) – due to interest rates cancelling, this will quickly find the present value.

Step 3 **Add up the present value of step 1 and 2**

This will give the total present value of the undertaking/acquisition so compare this to the cost to find the APV

If the APV is positive, **proceed**

See also Investment Appraisal Methods 268
Investment Appraisal Methods – Free Cash Flow Model 271

Cash flows vs after tax profit.
Q8

Investment Appraisal Methods – Free Cash Flow Model

Exam tip – do not forget to **knock off the value of debt** at the final stage of the calculation to obtain the **equity value of shares only** (students always seem to forget to do this!).

For some important narrative points, see next page.

Step 1 **Find Free Cash Flows (based on precise estimates given)**

Earnings before interest and tax (EBIT)

Less	tax
Plus	non-cash charges such as depreciation
Less	CAPEX
Plus/Less	net change in working capital
Plus	sales proceeds from PPE sales

Step 2 **Find Terminal Value (TV) (to cover the period after the end of the estimates)**

Find value of perpetuity flows using formulae below:

If no growth TV = annual flow / discount rate

If growth of g assumed $TV = \frac{cash\ flow\ x\ (1+g)}{(discount\ rate-\ )}$

Do not forget to discount the TV using the same discount factor as for the final specific Free Cash Flow figure estimated above (see below) – e.g. if you have 3 years of specific figures and the TV applies from year 4 onwards, then discount the TV using the **year 3 discount rate**

Step 3 **Discount at the WACC**

Find the discounted value of the cash flows, using WACC as the discount factor.

You may have to calculate the WACC, given the cost of equity, cost of debt and market values of equity and debt:

$$WACC = k_e \ x\ (E / E + D) + k_d\ x\ (D / E + D)$$

Step 4 **Remember to deduct the market value of debt**

This transforms the cash flows into an equity value (the value of the shares of the company)

Future Flows into Perpetuity – Same Discount Factor in Final 2 Columns

It will be common to be given 3 years (for example) of specific figures and then a statement that "from year 4 into the foreseeable future" cash flows will be at a particular level

Use the formula cash flow / discount factor to find this terminal value

e.g. £1m into perpetuity at a discount factor of 10% is £1m / 0.10 = £10m terminal value

Note that this terminal value should be discounted at **the same discount factor as the previous year of figures for which a specific estimate is possible** (year 3 in our example) – this is because (for mathematical reasons) the formula provides the PV of the perpetuity **one year before the perpetuity flows start**

	Year 1	**Year 2**	**Year 3**	**Year 4+**
	Precise estimate	Precise estimate	Precise estimate	***Perpetuity formula***
Discount factor at 10%	0.909	0.826	**0.751**	**0.751**
			Identical discount factors for final 2 columns	

In this example, the perpetuity formula applied for Year 4+ gives the PV of Year 4+ flows but **in terms of Year 3 values**. Therefore discount at the Year 3 discount rate.

Use of current WACC

The current WACC partly reflects the average risk of the company rather than the risk of a new particular project

The current WACC is determined at a point in time and may not be applicable over a long future time horizon

Advantages of the FCF approach

Model is flexible to allow for specific data and details, including a period of temporary growth followed by a perpetuity (with or without growth)

Depreciation and CAPEX

Add back depreciation and deduct CAPEX

If no data given, perhaps the best you can do is assume that these are approximately equal but make sure you state this and then criticise this assumption (as it is not realistic)

Perpetuity cash flows – the correct discount factor

Example: exam paper gives detailed specific cash flows for years 1 to 4 followed by a perpetuity from year 5 onwards

Remember that the correct discount factor to apply to the perpetuity is the **year 4** value (not the year 5 value) – this is because the perpetuity formula provides the present value of flows starting with **1**

year of delay – so applying the formula to the flows from **year 5** onwards gives the present value in **year 4** and therefore needs to be discounted by the **year 4 discount factor**

Professional scepticism points

Perpetuity assumption may be simplistic and unsustainable – requires forecasts to be reliable and the discount rate to be correct – future cash flows are just estimates

Query whether there is enough information on capital cash flows, CAPEX outlays and taxation

Determine whether depreciation assumptions/add backs are reasonable

Query validity of the discount rate (risk, changes in business, size, nature of business (private?))

Possible adjustments

Consider all incremental costs and revenues that may result

Will director salaries and remuneration change if the Board of Directors is changed?

Eliminate one off items

Adjustments for inflation and other similar changes?

Deduct earnings from opportunities now foregone?

CAPEX

See also Investment Appraisal Methods 268
Investment Appraisal Methods – APV 270

ISAE 3402 – example answer points

Note – ISAE 3402 is potentially more relevant than ever as **cloud computing** and other technological services grow – organisations will increasingly be relying on **third parties for the provision of services** and may therefore require **assurance** over those services – ISAE 3402 may then apply

[Useful points taken from SBM November 2017 Mock 1 Q2]

ISAE 3402 may be applicable when the assurance provider needs to review the controls of a "service organisation" – example from SBM November 2017 Mock 1: the adviser's client was a manufacturer of paints which offered an online system for its regular customers to place orders – a new customer was interested in a contract but required assurance over the online ordering system as a pre-condition of signing the contract: the paint manufacturer would be acting as a "service organisation" for the new customer

Benefits of assurance under ISAE 3402

Provides an **independent**, **expert** opinion on the effectiveness of controls at a third-party organisation

The assurance conclusion and any related recommendations resulting from the assurance provider's work can be used by the client to provide assurance over the **integrity** and **quality** of systems which ensure the complete, accurate and timely processing of transactions – assurance could also be provided that the systems are **available for use as required**, **protected** from unauthorised access and that **confidential information is protected**

If the system has an online element, there could be concerns about **cyber-security** – assurance could be provided regarding firewalls and also virus and ransomware protection

The assurance conclusion and any related recommendations resulting from the assurance provider's work can be used by the **service organisation's management to improve the quality of systems** and controls if this is deemed necessary

Exam tip – ensure that you develop the above benefits by referring to scenario-specific details

Requirements for an ISAE 3402 report to be possible

Disclosure regarding the system of controls and processes must be **sufficiently detailed**

Sufficient appropriate evidence must be gathered by the assurance provider

Type of assurance offered under ISAE 3402

Limited assurance in the form of a **negatively expressed** conclusion may be all that can be offered based on the information available – this was the point made in SBM November 2017 Mock 1

Judgement is needed and it is likely to be impossible for the assurance provider to be able to determine, with any degree of certainty, that all risks have been identified and properly evaluated

Objectives of the service auditor under ISAE 3402

To obtain assurance whether, in all material respects, and based on suitable criteria:

- the service organisation's **description** of its systems fairly presents the systems as designed and implemented (assurance provided by both Type 1 and Type 2 reports)
- the controls related to the control objectives stated in the service organisation's description of its system are **suitably designed** (assurance provided by both Type 1 and Type 2 reports)
- the controls **operated effectively** to provide reasonable assurance that the control objectives stated in the service organisation's description of the system are achieved (assurance provided by a Type 2 report only)

Types of report under ISAE 3402

Type 1 report – provides an opinion on the **design** and **existence** of the control measures in place

Type 2 report – provides an opinion on the same matters as a Type 1 report but also on the **operating effectiveness of the controls in practice**

Ethical implications if the ISAE 3402 assurance provider is also an auditor

If the auditor's client implements **new** procedures **based on assurance work carried out by the auditor** then it would be more difficult to be **critical** of the client's systems during the audit

Safeguards would be required:

- **separate staff** on the audit engagement and the assurance engagement
- **Inform the client** that internal controls remain the **responsibility of its management**
- consider **not accepting** the assurance work, if the above safeguards are deemed insufficient

See also Assurance Reports on Controls at a Service Organisation 56

IT Due Diligence

Assesses the suitability and risks arising from IT factors in the target company – for example, any issues surrounding IT security or integrating IT systems post-acquisition

Given the increasing importance of IT systems to modern businesses and increased cyber-risks, IT Due Diligence has become more important

The ICAEW (2014) publication Cyber-Security in Corporate Finance provides an example of a larger company purchasing a smaller company and therefore inheriting the weaknesses of the smaller company's security – a cyberattack on the smaller company then allowed access to the whole network, resulting in theft of data relating to a new technology used by the larger company

Key questions to ask on cyber-security as part of a Due Diligence exercise:

When did the board last consider cyber-security? Who is responsible for managing cyber-security?

Has the company audited its cyber-security?

Is the company confident that its most valuable information is properly managed and protected from cyber-threats?

Has the company experienced a cyber- or information-security breach? What steps were taken to mitigate the impact of the breach?

See also

Acquisitions – Due Diligence	33
Big Data topics	
Cloud computing and cloud accounting	104
Cyber security	145
Digital Strategies	176
Digital Transformation	184

IT – Strategic Information Systems

Benefits

Facilities improved decision-making – summarises key information whilst also allowing drill down into operational records

Amount of information available – increases the amount of information that will be available to managers and the speed with which it becomes available to them – may provide real time information

Consistency – collates information into a single database and should use the same principles and processes – less time required to reconcile and convert

Tactical information – provides access to tactical information such as budgets and comparisons to budget

External information – allows access to external sources as well as internal information

Problems and issues

Information overload – could lead to too much time reviewing and studying data, particularly detailed data, rather than looking at strategic issues and overall performance against KPIs

Training – managers will need to be trained to get the best use from the system – this will take time and money

Extent of data captured – may not be clear how much non-financial information the system will collect or provide to management – if important information is not recorded, then it will still not be possible to monitor performance in some of the key areas of the business

Specific Types

Do not discuss these in too much detail unless the question appears to need it

Executive Information Systems

A system that pools data from internal and external sources and makes information available to senior managers in an easy to use form. Assists in the making of strategic, unstructured decisions.

Management Information Systems

A system that that converts data from mainly internal sources into information such as summary reports and exception reports. Allows managers to make timely and effective decisions for planning, directing and controlling the activities for which they are responsible.

Decision Support Systems

A system that combines data and analytical models or data analysis tools to support semi-structured and unstructured decision-making.

Value added networks (VANs)

Networks that facilitate the adding of value to products and particularly to services by the strategic use of information – often the VAN will link separate organisations together through electronic data interchanges (EDIs), contributing to the development of business networks

See also	Balanced Scorecard	60
	Big Data topics	
	Cloud computing and cloud accounting	104
	Critical Success Factors	140
	Cyber security	145
	Digital Strategies	176
	Digital Transformation	184
	Key Performance Indicators	284

Joint Arrangements – Assurance

Benefits of Assurance

If profits are to be shared equally between 2 parties, it could be valuable for both of the parties to have assurance that those profits have been calculated correctly in accordance with the terms of their agreement

Although the percentage split of profits in the joint arrangement may be clear, the profit allocation/determination may still need clarification between the 2 parties – both parties will benefit from assurance that the profit allocation has been calculated properly and that full disclosures have been made

This is likely to require initial Due Diligence and ongoing monitoring of the arrangement to sustain assurance

Nature of the Assurance work

Determine the scope of the engagement by establishing the rights and access to information noted in the contract

Level of assurance needs to be determined (reasonable or limited)

Procedures prior to commencement of operations

Review the agreement in combination with legal advisers for onerous, ambiguous or omitted clauses

Ensure that the purpose of the arrangement is clear and that the respective rights of the parties are established in the initial contractual arrangements

Ensure that there is clear separation from the other operations of each company which is a party to the joint arrangements

Review the tax status of the joint arrangement entity (if applicable)

Review the governance procedures involved in the arrangement including shared management, control, rights over assets, key decision-making processes

Establish that any initial capital has been contributed in accordance with the agreement and that legal rights over assets have been established

Establish the creditworthiness, going concern and reputation of the other party based on local enquiries from stakeholders and a review of internal documentation as well as that in the public domain

Ensure that the terms of disengagement and residual rights at the end of the arrangement are clear so that there is a transparent and legitimate exit route

Establish the fair value of any assets to be transferred into the joint arrangement

Clarify the revenue sharing agreement with respect to existing sales in progress or orders contracted for but not yet commenced

Investigate health and safety responsibility and establish how liability will be shared

Procedures – ongoing assurance

Determine rights and access to information as this will affect the scope of the assurance work

Level of assurance needs to be determined (reasonable or limited)

Ensure that operations are within the terms of the joint arrangement agreement and that there have been no violations of the contractual agreement

Ensure that internal controls and accounting systems are being applied and are effective

Ensure that the accounting systems for any joint arrangement entity are capable of recording time accurately and completely

If permitted within the terms of the contract, access to the accounting records of the other party would provide additional assurance – this could mean, however, that a reciprocal arrangement may need to be made available so that information can be transferred to (and not just from) the other party

Consider the additional assurance problems relating to the eventual dissolution of the agreements – terms of disengagement, return/sale of assets, intellectual property rights, rights to future customer access

Audit-specific points

If a separate joint arrangement entity is established then this may mean that our firm is a component auditor and will need to report to the principal auditors – question over independence of advisory work being done?

May be a requirement for a separate audit/assurance for a joint arrangement entity

Joint Arrangements – Strategy and Financial Reporting

Strategy – benefits

Likely to lead to **diversification** (geographical, product)

May involve **less financial risk** than setting up a new subsidiary if a **lower level of borrowing** is required

Costs are **shared** – particularly beneficial for **risk-averse** firms or where **expensive new technologies** are being established

Lower setup costs **reduce exit costs** if the venture fails

Could allow **economies of scale** and **economies of scope**, subject to what the other party offers

Shares the **risk** of the project if it fails but the **benefits** must also be **shared**

Allows the party to capitalise on **reputational enhancement** by making use of **existing** brand recognition and/or experience (making the most of the more recognised/more experienced party in the arrangement)

Synergies – one firm's production expertise can be **supplemented** by the other's marketing and distribution expertise, for example

Joint arrangement partner may have **better local knowledge** of foreign markets allowing a quicker expansion

Joint arrangement partner may have an **existing supply chain** in operation

Strategy – disadvantages

Shares the **risk** of the project if it fails but the **benefits** must also be **shared**

May be **conflicts of interest** between the parties in terms of prioritisation of the short-term use of resources as well as longer-term objectives (one party may be looking for short-term profits whilst the other wants to invest over the longer term)

Disagreements may arise over profit shares, amounts invested, the management of the joint arrangement and marketing strategy, amongst other areas

Requires a degree of **business trust** between the parties to promote openness and access to information

Project could be **cut short** if one of the parties decides to **terminate** the arrangement earlier than the other party would wish – a **wholly-owned subsidiary** would prevent this possibility

Financial Reporting – Joint Ventures versus Joint Arrangements

The terms of the contractual arrangement between the parties to a joint arrangement are key to determining whether the arrangement is a "joint venture" or a "joint operation" – if the parties have **rights to the net assets** of the arrangement, then a "joint venture" occurs whereas if the parties have **rights to the assets, and obligations for the liabilities, of the arrangement**, then a "joint operation" occurs

An arrangement **not** structured through a **separate** entity is always a **joint** operation

Financial Reporting – Joint Operation

A joint operation should be recognised **line by line** in each of the party's own financial statements in relation to its interest in the joint operation's:

- **assets**, including a share of any jointly-held assets
- **liabilities**, including a share of any jointly-incurred liabilities
- **revenue** from the sale of its share of the output arising from the joint operation
- **expenses**, including a share of any expenses incurred jointly

Where the operations are in a foreign currency, each of the amounts relating to items in the statement of profit or loss will be translated into the functional currency of the entity, normally using the average exchange rate.

Where the operations are in a foreign currency, in respect of assets and liabilities, **monetary items should be translated** and then reported using the **closing rate** – **non-monetary** items carried at historical cost are translated using the exchange rate **at the date of the transaction** when the asset or liability arose

Investment to joint operation

An entity may have a previously held interest in a joint operation, held as an investment

A 2017 amendment to IFRS 11 clarified that when an entity obtains joint control of a joint operation it does not re-measure any previously-held interest

Financial Reporting – Joint Venture

Joint control of an entity is split between different parties – **usually** there will be a **separate entity** set up (but activity involving a separate entity could also potentially be a **joint operation**)

There is a **contractual arrangement** to share profits and losses and the parties have rights to the **net assets** of the arrangement

Apply the **equity method** – recognise the investment at cost and then add the **share of the joint venture's post-acquisition change in net assets** (**generally** the change in net assets will be equivalent to the **profits and losses** of the venture) – look out for time apportionment here

The **share** of the joint venture's post-acquisition change in net assets will be recognised in the **P&L**

The investment will be shown as a **non-current asset** in the SFP

An **investor** in a joint venture is a party to the joint venture which does not have **joint control** over the joint venture – if there is **significant influence** then an Associate exists: if there is no **significant influence** then the accounting should be as for a financial asset

Investment to joint venture

In the case of a joint venture previously held as an investment, IFRS 11 requires that a joint venture recognises its interest in a joint venture as an investment in its consolidated financial statements and accounts for that investment using the equity method in accordance with IAS 28

Note that in its separate financial statements, a joint venturer should account for its interest in a joint venture in accordance with IAS 27 *Separate financial statements* i.e. at cost or in accordance with IFRS 9 *Financial instruments* or using the equity method specified in IAS 28

Financial Reporting – comparison to the establishment of a separate foreign subsidiary

If the subsidiary operates in a foreign currency, it would have a **different functional currency to the parent** – the subsidiary's financial statements would therefore be **consolidated in accordance with IAS 21** into the consolidated financial statements of the parent, translated into the parent's presentation currency

Translate all **assets and liabilities** (both monetary and non-monetary) in the SFP using the **closing rate** at the reporting date

Translate **income** and **expenditure** in the current statement of profit or loss and OCI using exchange rates applicable at the transaction dates (in practice, an **average rate** for the year may be used)

Report the exchange differences which arise on translation as **Other Comprehensive Income**

Any loan from the parent to the subsidiary would be a "**net investment in a foreign operation**" – exchange differences will be recognised in profit or loss for the company which has a different functional currency to the currency of the loan itself (for example, if the **parent** has loaned money in the **parent's** functional currency to the subsidiary, then any exchange differences will be recognised in the **subsidiary's** profit or loss)

Key Performance Indicators

Quantifiable measures that can be used for setting strategic targets and monitoring actual performance by comparing performance against targets

Does depend on having an appropriate strategy first before designing the KPIs

Need an indicator and then also a way of measuring this easily and objectively

Some examples (SBM Question Bank question on a travel company: ensure that you amend these to your scenario!)

Strategic aim – Develop an online business

KPIs

Increase in volume of online bookings (percentage annual revenue growth) – target relating to volume

Increase in online sales as a percentage of total annual sales revenue – target relating to diversification

Strategic aim – Sell a tailored product

KPIs

Percentage annual growth in sales revenue from the tailored product

Average operating profit margin on tailored holidays

Strategic aim – Develop a new brand and ensure good awareness

KPIs

Percentage annual growth in sales of the brand

Operating profit margin

Annual market survey responses to the brand

Strategic aim – Exploit technology and Big Data

KPIs

Growth in the number of visits to the website

Average time for visitors to remain on the web site (length of time browsing)

Strategic aim – Geographical expansion

KPIs

Growth in annual sales in the specific geographical area

Total sales growth in geographical areas where the company has established new operations within the previous 3 to 5 years

Strategic aim – Developing the company's people

KPIs

Minimum retention rates for employees including strategically important employees

Training provided to employees measured by average training days or expenditure per employee

Other examples – retail example

Customer satisfaction rating per outlet

% of staff who have been trained

Employee satisfaction scores

Staff retention rates per outlet

See also	Balanced Scorecard	60
	Critical Success Factors	140
	IT – Strategic Information Systems	277

Key Risk Indicators

KRIs are derived from specific events or root causes that can prevent performance goals from being achieved

Examples include the introduction of a new product by a competitor, a strike at a supplier's plant, proposed changes in the regulatory environment and input price changes

Importantly though, KRIs are measures designed to **identify changes to existing risks** – therefore, it is important to distinguish risk indicators from performance measures, which are typically **retrospective** in nature

See also

Lease or buy?

Use an after-tax cost of borrowing as the cost of capital

Lease

Set up a normal NPV calculation – remember that tax benefits will arise from interest payments on the lease – if the lease is for an intangible asset then there may also be a tax benefit from amortisation (if the item is a tangible asset then it is possible that depreciation will not be allowable for tax purposes: you may have to raise a scepticism point here if the information is not available)

Make the point that a lease approach is more flexible, especially in a market where technologies are changing quickly – rather than purchasing the item outright, a lease means that the company only has to pay for the asset for a certain period of time and can make a decision at the end of that period whether to continue using the same asset or upgrade to a better option

Buy

Set up a normal NPV calculation – look out for an opportunity to apply an annuity formula approach to save time i.e. if the annual flows are the same the several years (this is quite likely in SBM)

Remember to consider whether tax savings on capital allowances are possible

Consider the company's existing overall borrowing position (or raise a scepticism point if there is no information) – consider how additional borrowing could affect earnings and gearing as well as the ability to raise debt for other purposes

Consider whether there are other better uses of the substantial upfront cash requirement under a "buy" decision

A "buy" decision means more of a commitment to a particular asset/technology (unless this can be re-sold easily at a future date) – on the other hand, a lease is only for a certain period of time and there is less risk of being stuck with an obsolete technology (which is then hard to sell in future)

Decision

Consider a comparison in relation to

Lease term and useful life

Results of NPV but also other factors

Liquidity – buying requires an initial payment which could use up cash – company may be near its debt capacity

Risk and flexibility – what happens if the business/project does not succeed as well as planned? A lease might include a break-clause (or you could recommend to include one) whereas buying the asset might involve more risk unless it can be sold off easily

Tax implications would need to be known

Interest rate assumed in the PV calculation is a key variable that would need to be confirmed

Do not forget to conclude and recommend on the best option – easy to forget to do!

Do not make a decision based only on the different NPV – look at some other issues surrounding the decision

Consider a mixed recommendation – lease some assets, buy other assets?

See also

Leases – IFRS 16 – definitions and exemptions

IFRS 16 was published in January 2016

IFRS 16 is effective for annual reporting periods beginning on or after 1 January 2019

IFRS 16 takes the approach of measuring the "right-of-use" of an asset and recognises the asset on the SFP

Definitions under IFRS 16

Lease – a contract, or part of a contract, that conveys the right to use an asset (the underlying asset) for a period of time in exchange for consideration

A contract contains a lease under IFRS 16 if the contract conveys the right to control the use of an identified asset for a period of time, in return for consideration

The right to control the use of an identified asset depends on a lessee having:

- the right to obtain substantially all of the economic benefits from use of the identified asset and
- the right to direct the use of the identified asset – this right arises if either:
    - the customer has the right to direct how and for what purpose the asset is used during the whole of its period of use, or
    - the relevant decisions about use are predetermined and the customer can operate the asset without the supplier having the right to change those operating instructions or the customer designing the asset in a way that pre-determines how and for what purpose the asset will be used throughout the period of use

A lessee does not control the use of an identified asset if the lessor can substitute the underlying asset for another asset during the lease term and would benefit economically from doing so

Underlying asset – an asset that is the subject of a lease, for which the right to use that asset has been provided by a lessor to a lessee

Right of use asset – an asset that represents a lessee's right to use an underlying asset for the lease term

Lease payments – payments made by a lessee to a lessor in order to use an underlying asset during the lease term, less any lease incentives (IFRS 16 requires lease payments to also include the exercise price of the purchase option if the lessee is reasonably certain to exercise that option, and any penalty payments for terminating the lease)

Non-lease components – some contracts may contain elements that are not leases such as service contracts – these must be separated out from the lease and accounted for separately

The **lessor** is the owner and supplier of the underlying asset – the lessor retains legal ownership but transfers to the **lessee** the right to use the asset for an agreed period of time in return for specified payments

The "identified asset" concept

The asset must be specified in the lease

The asset may be part of another asset such as part of an office facility

If the supplier has the practical ability to substitute the asset for an equivalent asset during the lease and would benefit economically from doing so then there is no identified asset and the contract is **not** a lease

IFRS 16 – illustration of concept of substitution and economic benefit to the lessor

User Ltd has entered into an arrangement with Provider Ltd regarding the use of certain machinery which will be used to produce car engine parts. Provider Ltd has agreed to provide User Ltd with any one of a selection of 10 similar machines on a weekly basis and has also agreed that the relevant machine must be able to produce 5,000 car parts per day. Provider Ltd can provide User Ltd with any of its 10 similar machines as required at its absolute discretion

A lease **does not arise** because there is **no identifiable asset** and Provider Ltd (**the lessor**) can **substitute** the machine as it wishes, deriving **economic benefits** from doing so in terms of **convenience**

User Ltd should account for the rental payments as **a normal expense** in the P&L rather than applying IFRS 16

Definition of "period of time"

IFRS 16 offers the following methods of defining the term "period of time":

- a period of time such as years
- the amount of use, based upon the production of the asset, such as the number of units produced

Right to obtain substantially all of the economic benefits

This right can be achieved through holding, using or sub-leasing the asset

This right can be assessed only within the parameters of the contract – for example, a lease contract for a car may restrict its use to within a single country, in which case only economic benefits within that country are considered

Right to direct the use of the asset (control)

If such a right is held then the lessee can direct how and for what purpose the asset is used throughout the period of use

The assessment is unaffected by protective rights within the terms of the contract that are designed to protect the asset – for example, prohibiting a truck from being used to carry explosives

Election to adopt simplified accounting under IFRS 16

If this election is made, the lessee simply recognises lease payments on a straight-line basis over the lease term

Short-term leases – these are leases for less than 12 months that do not contain a purchase option – the election to use this exemption must be made by asset class

Leases for low value assets – these are assets with a low value when used such as laptop computers, mobile phones or small items of office furniture – the election to use this exemption may be made on a lease-by-lease basis

Leases of low value assets are leases of assets with a value, when new, of $5,000 or less

(Note that the monetary value is stated in US dollars and no equivalent pound sterling figure is given in the Corporate Reporting Study Manual)

In addition, to be a low value lease, it must be the case that:

- the lessee can benefit from using the underlying asset on its own or with other available resources
- the underlying asset is not highly dependent on, or interrelated with, other assets – the Study Manual gives the example of a circuit board costing £200 but which is required to operate an item of plant worth £40,000 as an example of an apparently low value item which is highly interrelated with another higher value asset and which is therefore not an item which can qualify for treatment as "low value" for the purposes of IFRS 16 even though it has a low monetary value

Meaning of the lease "term"

The lease term comprises the period for which the lessee has contracted to lease the asset and any further terms for which there is reasonable certainty at the inception of the lease that the lessee will exercise the option

Leases – IFRS 16 – disclosure requirements

Under IFRS 16, the SFP should disclose the right-of-use asset and the lease liability

Right-of-use assets may be presented as a separate line item in the SFP under the heading of non-current assets

Alternatively, they may be included in the total of the relevant class of assets – in this case the carrying amount of right-of-use assets is disclosed in the notes to the financial statements

Unlike IAS 17, IFRS 16 has no specific requirement to split lease liabilities between non-current and current liabilities

However, in accordance with the *Conceptual Framework*'s fundamental principle of faithful representation, a split of lease liabilities between non-current and current liabilities should be presented anyway as best practice so that users of the financial statements can understand the impact of the lease liability in future years

Leased assets and lease liabilities may not be netted off against each other for disclosure purposes

Disclosures in relation to the non-current assets part of the SFP include:

- the carrying amount of right-of-use assets, by class of underlying assets, either on the face of the SFP or in a note
- depreciation charge for right-of-use assets
- additions to right-of-use assets
- carrying amount of right-of-use assets at the end of the reporting period by class of underlying assets
- gains/losses resulting from any sale and leaseback transactions

In the liabilities part of the SFP, there should be disclosure of the interest expense on lease liabilities

In the case of most entities, the IAS 1 requirement to disclose significant accounting policies would result in the disclosure of the policy in respect of leases

There should also be disclosure of:

- expenses relating to short-term and low-value leases
- total cash outflow for leases

Leases – IFRS 16 – Ethics

IFRS 16 has removed the differentiation between operating and finance leases from the lessee's point of view, although it remains for lessors

However, the incentive to keep liabilities off the SFP remains, and preparers of financial statements who wish to do this may argue that a transaction is not a lease when in fact it is and therefore should appear on the SFP

An exam question could present an ethical dilemma where the auditor or junior accounting staff member is under pressure to accept an incorrect financial reporting treatment i.e. an argument that a transaction is not a lease when in fact it is in order to keep the item off the SFP

Leases – IFRS 16 – impact of adopting IFRS 16

IFRS 16 will have an impact on the SFP, P&L and Statement of Cash Flows

Impact on SFP

Companies will be required to report larger amounts of assets and liabilities on their SFPs – this will particularly affect companies that currently have much of their leasing commitments off balance sheet in the form of operating leases

For example, many airlines lease their planes and showed no assets or liabilities for their future commitments under the previous leasing standard (IAS 17) – under IFRS 16, an airline entering into a lease for an aircraft will show an asset for the "right to use" the aircraft and an equal liability based on the present value of the lease payments it has promised to make – possibly, as a result, loan covenants may be breached and have to be renegotiated

Impact on P&L

For companies that previously held material operating leases, the pattern of expenses will change – specifically, the lease expense will be "front-loaded" because IFRS 16 has replaced the previous straight line operating lease expense used under IAS 17 with a depreciation charge for leased assets, (included within operating costs) and an interest expense on lease liabilities (included within financing costs)

While the depreciation charge is usually even, the interest expense is higher in the early years of the lease but reduces over the life of the asset

The total expense will generally be the same but there will be a difference in expense profile between IFRS 16 and IAS 17 with a consequent effect on EBITDA and operating profit:

> under IAS 17 a single operating lease expense would be entered within operating costs, which will feature within EBITDA and then flow through into operating profit
>
> under IFRS 16 there will be a split between depreciation (which would be deducted from EBITDA since EBITDA is by definition a statement of earnings **before** depreciation is deducted) and finance costs which will be deducted after operating profit has been calculated and will therefore only affect PBT

Impact on Statement of Cash Flows

While IFRS 16 does not change the amount of cash paid by the lessee to the lessor or the total amount of cash flows reported, it will generally change the presentation of cash flows in respect of leases previously accounted for as operating leases

Operating cash flows, which is where operating lease payments were reported under IAS 17, will reduce – however, there will be a corresponding increase in financing cash outflows because repayments of the capital component of the lease liability are included within financing activities

Incentives for management under IFRS 16 – points for the examination (from 2020 edition of SBM Study Manual)

Under the previous standard on leases (IAS 17), there was a distinction between an operating lease and a finance lease – a classification of the type of lease was essential to how the lessee and lessor would account for the transaction in their financial statements

Examination questions were therefore set on this distinction because accounting for an item as an operating lease removed it from the lessee's SFP so companies who wished to create a favourable gearing ratio, for example, were incentivised to account for leases as operating leases

IFRS 16 has removed the differentiation between operating and finance leases from the lessee's point of view (although it remains for lessors)

However, the incentive to keep liabilities off the SFP remains and preparers of financial statements who wish to do this may argue that a transaction is not a lease when in fact it is, and therefore should appear on the SFP

An exam question could present an ethical dilemma where the auditor or junior accounting staff member is under pressure to accept this incorrect financial reporting treatment

Irrelevance of distinction between operating leases and finance leases for lessees

A useful advisory point which would apply to **any** client that has been leasing assets in recent years (i.e. is a lessee) will be to point out that under IFRS 16 the distinction between operating leases and finance leases ceases to apply for lessees

With the exception of leases for less than 12 months or leases of low value assets, all leases must be recognised in the SFP – this means that there will definitely have to be an SFP entry (for both the asset and liability side) of some kind for all lessees once IFRS 16 is adopted

Continuing importance of distinction between operating leases and finance leases for lessors

A useful advisory point regarding future accounting periods which would apply to **any** client that currently leases out an asset (i.e. is a lessor) under an operating lease or finance lease will be to point out that under IFRS 16 the distinction between operating leases and finance leases ceases to apply for lessees **but remains applicable to lessors**

Impact of a potential fall in rental income under a lease – interaction with onerous contract rules

In a question which appears to be primarily about an onerous contract (i.e. a situation where the client company no longer needs to lease a property but faces a high penalty charge if the lease is terminated early), look out for a situation where the client can potentially sublet the property but at a reduced rent – as well as having an impact under the onerous lease rules, this could also have implications under IFRS 16

Under IFRS 16, the potential fall in rental income indicates that the right-of-use asset is impaired because it is underperforming – an impairment test must be carried out and an impairment loss recognised for the right-of-use asset

Impact on auditors of moving from IAS 17 to IFRS 16

Clients may not understand how IFRS 16 should be adopted so may ask for assistance from their auditor

Financial statements may be deliberately misstated to present short term or low value assets inappropriately to avoid the need to show lease liabilities

Clients with assets previously classified as operating leases may misstate the new lease asset and liability, either deliberately or by mistake

Sale and leaseback arrangements will now require accounting treatment that supports IFRS 15 and auditors will need to ensure their clients have followed this treatment in such cases

General implications of the move to IFRS 16 (based on Corporate Reporting July 2018 past paper Q2)

IFRS 16 replaces IAS 17

The new standard adopts a single accounting model applicable to all leases for lessees – there is no requirement to distinguish between operating and finance leases for lessees

Under IFRS 16, a lease is defined as a contract or a part of a contract that conveys the right to use an asset for a period of time in exchange for consideration

A lessee will need to recognise on its SFP for each lease a right-of-use asset and a corresponding lease liability – this change in treatment could potentially lead to large increases in both the assets and liabilities shown in the SFP

In most cases, the initial amount to be recognised as an asset will be equal to the obligation to make future lease payments (discounted as appropriate) but the asset value will also be adjusted for payments in advance, lease incentives and costs

After initial recognition, the asset will be depreciated over the shorter of its useful life and the lease term – it is this depreciation charge, rather than the operating lease rentals, which will be the cost reflected in the P&L

There may also be impairment charges where a leased asset is impaired

An entity may select 1 of 2 accounting alternatives when first adopting IFRS 16 – it may apply IFRS 16 with full retrospective effect – alternatively, it, as the lessee, is permitted not to restate comparative information but to recognise instead the cumulative effect of initially applying IFRS 16 as an adjustment to opening equity at the date of initial application

Leases – IFRS 16 – lessor lease accounting

Definitions

Finance lease – a lease to transfer substantially all the risks and rewards incidental to ownership of an underlying asset

Operating lease – a lease that does not transfer substantially all the risks and rewards incidental to ownership of an underlying asset

Unguaranteed residual value – that portion of the residual value of the underlying asset, the realisation of which by the lessor is not assured or is guaranteed solely by a party related to the lessor

Gross investment in the lease – the sum of (a) the lease payments receivable by the lessor under a finance lease and (b) any unguaranteed residual value accruing to the lessor

Net investment in the lease – the gross investment in the lease discounted at the interest rate implicit in the lease

Unearned finance income – the difference between (a) the gross investment in the lease and (b) the net investment in the lease

Lessor lease accounting – principles (concept, risks and rewards)

Under lessor lease accounting, the classification of a lease is based on the extent to which the risks and rewards incidental to ownership of a leased asset lie with the lessee or the lessor

The relevant risks are the risks of ownership, not other types of risk – examples would include the possibility of losses from idle capacity or technological obsolescence and variations in return due to changing economic conditions

Examples of the rewards of ownership would include the expectation of profitable operation over the asset's economic life and any gain from appreciation in value or realisation of a residual value

Lessor accounting is largely unchanged under IFRS 16 as IFRS 16 retains the IAS 17 distinction between finance leases and operating leases for lessors (but not for lessees)

Indicators that a lease is a finance lease

The lessee receives ownership of the asset at the end of the lease term

The lessee is expected to exercise the option to purchase the item at the end of the lease term

The lease term forms the majority of the asset's economic life

The asset is substantially loaned whereby the present value of lease payments is almost all of the fair value of the asset

The asset is specialised for use by the lessee or entities authorised by the lessee

Lessor accounting of a lease which includes both land and building elements

When a lease includes both land and building elements, the classification of each element as an operating or finance lease should be made separately

In determining whether the land element is an operating or finance lease, an important consideration is that land normally has an indefinite economic life

Lessor lease accounting – treatment by the lessor of an operating lease

The lessor continues to recognise an asset that is leased out by way of an operating lease and charges depreciation over the useful life of the asset

Lease income from the operating lease is recognised on a straight-line basis over the lease term unless another systematic and rational basis is more representative of the time pattern in which the benefit from the leased asset is receivable

The cost of incentives provided to the lessee is recognised as a reduction of the rental income over the lease term, generally on a straight-line basis

If the lessor incurs costs to negotiate and arrange an operating lease, these costs are capitalised within the carrying amount of the underlying asset that is the subject of the lease and they are amortised over the lease term on the same basis as lease income

Lessor lease accounting – treatment by the lessor of a finance lease

The lessor derecognises the asset and instead recognises a receivable equal to the net investment in the lease – although a lessor is the legal owner of an asset leased to another party, it has passed the risks and rewards of ownership to the lessee in return for a cash flow stream so derecognition occurs

The net investment in the lease is the present value of the aggregate of (a) the lease payments receivable by the lessor and (b) any unguaranteed residual amount accruing to the lessor

Initial direct costs incurred in negotiating and arranging the lease are added to the receivable

The amount received in cash is allocated between the repayment of principal and finance income

The finance income should be recognised so as to generate a constant periodic rate of return on the outstanding net investment

Summary of rules for lessor accounting

Finance lease	Operating lease
Substance – risks and rewards with the lessee (or other third parties)	– risks and rewards with the lessor
Accounting treatment – recognise a receivable equal to the "net investment in the lease" – this is the gross investment (minimum lease payments plus any unguaranteed residual value accruing to the lessor) discounted at the interest rate implicit in the lease – initial direct costs incurred by the lessor are not added separately to the net investment as they are already included in the discounted figures since they are included in the calculation of the interest rate implicit in the lease (reducing the return) – finance income is recognised reflecting the constant periodic rate of return on the lessor's net investment outstanding	– asset retained in the books of the lessor and is depreciated over its useful life – rentals are credited to profit or loss on a straight line basis over the lease term unless another systematic basis is more representative

Leases – IFRS 16 – recognition and subsequent measurement

Separating the components of a contract

A contract may contain both a lease component and a non-lease component – in other words, it may include an amount payable by the lessee for activities and costs that do not transfer goods or services to the lessee (these activities and costs might, for example, include maintenance, repairs or cleaning)

In this case, there should be a separation of components

IFRS 16 requires entities to account for the lease component of the contract separately from the non-lease component

The entity must split the rental or lease payments and:

account for the lease component under IFRS 16, and

account for the service element separately, generally as an expense in profit or loss

Consideration in the contract is allocated on the basis of the stand-alone prices of the lease component(s) and non-lease component(s)

Initial recognition under IFRS 16

A right-of-use asset and a lease liability are recognised – recognition occurs at the commencement date

The right-of-use asset is then measured at cost less accumulated depreciation and impairment losses in line with IAS 16

The lease liability is measured at the present value of future lease payments, including any payments expected at the end of the lease

The lease liability is amortised – interest will accrue on the outstanding lease at the rate stated in the lease contract and payments made in respect of the lease by the lessee will reduce the outstanding liability

There should be a Debit to a Right-of-use asset account and a Credit to Payables: Lease liabilities

The amount to be recorded in this way is the lower of (1) the fair value and (2) the present value of the minimum lease payments at the inception of the lease

IFRS 16 requires the accounting in the lessee's books to reflect the substance of the transaction

An investment property held by a lessee as a right-of-use asset must be recognised in accordance with IFRS 16

An entity may select 1 of 2 accounting alternatives when first adopting IFRS 16 – it may apply IFRS 16 with full retrospective effect – alternatively, it, as the lessee, is permitted not to restate comparative information but to recognise instead the cumulative effect of initially applying IFRS 16 as an adjustment to opening equity at the date of initial application

Amounts to include in the cost of the right-of-use asset

The amount of the initial measurement of the lease liability

Any lease payments made before the commencement date, less any lease incentives received

Any initial direct costs incurred by the lessee related to the asset

An estimate of any costs or penalties to be incurred by the lessee at the end of the lease term, such as dismantling costs or removal costs

Note that marketing costs for a new product to be made by the leased asset are not included as these costs are not directly attributable to the lease – this is consistent with IAS 16 where marketing costs cannot be capitalised as part of the non-current asset

The initial deposit, if any, counts as one of the lease payments and hence is included in the cost of the asset

Initial direct costs can be treated as part of the cost of the asset, provided that they are directly attributable to activities performed by the lessee to obtain the lease

Amounts to include in the lease liability

The lease is measured at the present value of future lease payments, including any payments expected at the end of the lease

The lease liability will include

fixed payments less any lease incentives receivable

variable lease payments that depend on an index such as the consumer price index or rate such as market rental rates

amounts expected to be payable by the lessee under residual value guarantees

purchase options if reasonably certain to be exercised

penalties for early termination if expected to be paid

The discount rate used to determine present value is the interest rate implicit in the lease or, if this is not available, the lessee's incremental borrowing rate

Subsequent measurement of the lease liability

In future periods, the lease liability is amortised

Interest will accrue on the outstanding lease at the rate stated in the lease contract

Payments made in respect of the lease by the lessee will reduce the outstanding liability

Lease payments should include

the exercise price of a purchase option if the lessee is reasonably certain to exercise that option

any penalty payments for terminating the lease

The initial payment in advance (and/or any deposit) is not included in the calculation of the lease liability – it is added to the right-of-use asset

The discount rate applied should be the interest rate implicit in the lease or, if this is not available, the lessee's incremental borrowing rate

Depreciation of the right-of-use asset

The asset should be measured at cost less accumulated depreciation and impairment losses unless the right-of-use asset is

a class of PPE that is measured using the revaluation model, or

an investment property and the lessee applies the fair value model

Depreciation should begin at the commencement date and should then cease at the earlier of (1) the end of its useful life or (2) the end of the lease term, unless the asset is expected to be transferred to the lessee at the end of the lease term – in such a case, the asset will be depreciated over the useful life of the asset

Depreciation of the asset

DR Depreciation expense

CR Accumulated depreciation

Depreciation policies adopted under IFRS 16 should be consistent with other non-current assets of the same class

If any impairment reviews are required, these must be conducted in accordance with IAS 36

If there is reasonable certainty that the lessee will eventually own the asset, then it should be depreciated over its estimated useful life

The lease term comprises the period for which the lessee has contracted to lease the asset and any further terms for which there is reasonable certainty at the inception of the lease that the lessee will exercise the option

Entries following initial recognition

To record the payment made in each relevant period, the lessee records a Debit to Payables: lease liabilities and a Credit to Cash

To record the finance charge in each relevant period, a Debit to Profit or loss: finance cost and a Credit to Payables: lease liabilities should be entered

The amount recognised in this way should be the interest which has accrued over the period

Impact of the lease on the SFP

IFRS 16 requires that, when an asset is leased, the accounting treatment should reflect the substance of the transaction

Therefore, in the lessee's books:

DR Right-of-use asset account

CR Payables: Lease liabilities

The amount to be recorded in this way is the present value of the future lease payments

The initial deposit, if any, counts as one of the lease payments and hence is included in the cost of the asset

The entries are made at the commencement of the lease term, with the values determined at the start of the lease

The present value of the future lease payments is derived by discounting them at the interest rate implicit in the lease – if it is not practicable to determine the interest rate implied in the lease, then the lessee's incremental borrowing rate can be used

Initial direct costs can be treated as part of the cost of the asset provided they are directly attributable to activities performed by the lessee to obtain the lease

Although interest is payable under the lease, this is accrued over time – a justification is that the capital could, in theory, be paid off at any time, with cancellation charges – these charges could be avoided so they are not a "true" long-term liability – interest is therefore recognised as it accrues

Making the payment

DR Payables: Lease liabilities

CR Cash

Each lease payment is comprised partly of a repayment of capital and partly of an interest charge for the period

Finance charge

DR Finance cost (profit or loss)

CR Payables: Lease liabilities

The amount recorded here is the interest accrued over the period

IFRS 16 requires the total finance charge to be allocated to each period during the lease term so as to produce a constant periodic rate of interest on the outstanding lease obligation

As the lessee pays off the capital sum, the total capital owed falls from period to period – one would therefore also expect a reduction in the total interest payable on the outstanding balance

Therefore, in the earlier years, the finance charge (interest) is a higher proportion of the annual lease payments – towards the end of the lease, the finance charge will be smaller as the outstanding lease liability is smaller

Example lease liability tables

The following figures are simply for illustration and are not exact calculations

Payments in arrears – 4 columns

b/f	interest	payment	c/f
10	2	(3)	9
9	1.5	(3)	7.5*

Payments in advance – 5 columns, with one extra column for the first payment

b/f	payment	capital after payment	Interest	c/f
10	(2)	8	1.5	9.5
9.5	(2)	7.5*	1.5	9

Figures marked * should be used when calculating the current/non-current split of the liability

The rule here is always look to the **right** of next year's payment to find the relevant * figure

Note that where instalment payments are made in advance, the first instalment repays capital only as no time has yet elapsed for interest to accrue – this will therefore reduce the initial amount on which you need to charge interest as compared to a calculation where instalments are paid in arrears

In the case of instalments in advance, at the end of each accounting period, the year-end liability will include capital and interest that has accrued to date which has not been paid

The initial payment in advance (and/or any deposit) is not included in the calculation of the lease liability – it is added to the right-of-use asset

Splitting the year-end liability into current and non-current components

Always look to the **right** of next year's payment. This will give you the non-current liability because it is the total liability remaining after next year's payment (i.e. the current liability) has been cleared. This rule works regardless of whether you are looking at payments in arrears or in advance

The difference between this "to the right" amount and the c/f amount at the end of the current year is the current liability. The balance is the non-current liability

Example

b/f	interest	payment	c/f
10	2	(3)	9
9	1.5	(3)	**7.5***

Bold * figure is the "to the right" figure. The total liability at the year-end is 9 but 7.5 of that is non-current. Therefore 9 - 7.5 = 1.5 is the current liability.

Leases – IFRS 16 – sale and leaseback transactions

Purpose of a sale and leaseback transaction

The original owner of the asset sells the asset (typically to a finance house or bank) and immediately leases it back

This process raises cash whilst retaining use of the asset so such arrangements provide entities with the opportunity to release capital caught up in the business for investment in other opportunities or to return it to shareholders

Effectively, an entity acquires cash in exchange for a commitment to make regular lease payments without losing use of the asset

Genuine sale?

The key initial assessment is whether or not the transfer of the asset constitutes a genuine sale – for this to be the case, there must be a fulfilment of the requirements of IFRS 15 (revenue recognition) for determining when a performance obligation is satisfied

The transfer qualifies as a sale under IFRS 15 if the customer obtains control of the asset – the following 5 factors should be considered:

whether the selling entity has a present right to payment for the asset

whether the selling entity has transferred legal title to the asset

whether the selling entity has transferred physical possession of the asset

whether the selling entity has transferred the risks and rewards of ownership of the asset to the customer

whether the purchaser has accepted the asset

According to the Corporate Reporting Study Manual, criterion 4 relating to the risks and rewards of ownership is likely to be the most important in considering whether control passes to the customer

Sale and leaseback transaction – the 3 stages of the calculation

Stage 1 – the seller/lessee measures the "right-of-use asset" arising from the leaseback

Stage 2 – the seller/lessee only recognises the amount of any gain or loss on the sale that relates to the rights **transferred** to the buyer so in Stage 2 the gain that relates to the rights **retained** is calculated

Stage 3 – the gain relating to the rights transferred is calculated as a balancing figure

Stage 1 – measure the "right-of-use asset" arising from the leaseback

The right-of-use asset arising from the leaseback is calculated as the proportion of the previous carrying amount of the asset that relates to the right-of-use retained by the seller/lessee – this should be calculated using the following formula:

carrying amount x (PV of future lease payments at transfer date / FV of asset at transfer date)

Please be careful to get the fraction the right way round – you need to have PV on the top and FV on the bottom – you may wish to remember this as **P**V on to**p** and then **F**V **f**ollows (meaning on the bottom)

Stage 2 – calculate and apportion the gain or loss on sale to determine the gain on rights retained

Within this stage, a pro-forma is used to calculate the gain or loss on sale:

Fair value	X
less: carrying amount	(X)
Total gain/loss on sale	X/(X)

A second pro-forma is used to determine the gain which relates to the rights retained:

gain x (PV of future lease payments at transfer date / FV of asset at transfer date)

Notice how the bracketed fraction element of the second pro-forma is similar to that used in Stage 1 so use the same mnemonic: **P**V on to**p** and then **F**V **f**ollows (meaning on the bottom) – this is correct because we are again assessing how much of the total fair value relates to what has been retained rather than sold

Stage 3 – calculate the gain or loss on rights transferred

The gain relating to the rights transferred is calculated as the balancing figure involved in the 2 pro-forma calculations used in Stage 2 (see previous question) – it can be calculated as:

gain on rights transferred = total gain - gain on rights retained (from Stage 2 apportionment)

IFRS 16 sale and leaseback numerical example – calculation of gain

First Ltd owned a machine with a carrying amount of £5,040,000 on 1 July 2020. On this date, First Ltd sold the machine to Second Ltd for £7,920,000, which was the fair value of the machine. First Ltd then undertook to lease back the machine under a 20-year lease. Annual lease payments were £240,000 in arrears and the present value of future lease payments at the 6% interest rate implicit in the lease were £2,752,800 at 1 July 2020.

Solution

Stage 1 – measure the "right-of-use asset" arising from the leaseback

Right-of-use asset	5,040,000 x (2,752,800 / 7,920,000) = 1,751,782

The remaining carrying amount of £3,288,218 (5,040,000 - 1,751,782) represents the transferred asset

Stage 2 – calculate and apportion the gain or loss on sale to determine the gain on rights retained

Overall gain 7,920,000 - 5,040,000 = 2,880,000

Gain relating to retained rights 2,880,000 x (2,752,800 / 7,920,000) = 1,001,018

Stage 3 – calculate the gain or loss on rights transferred

Gain relating to transferred rights 2,880,000 - 1,001,018 = 1,878,982

Depreciation

The right-of-use asset continues to be depreciated as normal but there may be a revision of the useful life required

If the transfer is not a genuine sale

Where the transfer is not determined to be a sale (using the revenue recognition rules of IFRS 15 which are applied in the usual way under IFRS 16), the performance obligation is not satisfied and so the seller/lessee will continue to recognise a transferred asset and also recognises a financial liability equal to the transfer proceeds, accounting for it using IFRS 9

The treatment is then the opposite in the books of the buyer/lessor so no physical asset is recognised and instead a financial asset measured at the value of the transfer proceeds is recognised, accounting for it in line with IFRS 9

	Seller/Lessee	**Buyer/Lessor**
Treatment of asset	Continue to recognise the transferred asset	No physical asset recognised
What to recognise	Recognise a financial liability measured at transfer proceeds	Recognise a financial asset measured at transfer proceeds

Sale and leaseback where the fair value of consideration does not equal the fair value of the asset or the lease payments are not at market rates

In these cases, an adjustment should be made as such a structure would be deemed to be a method of additional financing

Sale and leaseback transaction at below market rates

Treat as a prepayment of lease payments

Adjust the PV of future lease payments by the excess of consideration over the fair value of the asset

Sale and leaseback transaction at better than market rates

Treat as additional financing by the lessor/buyer

Sale and leaseback transactions – strategic considerations

Leasing is a commonly used source of finance, especially for small and medium-sized entities

Leasing is a form of debt finance that can be very useful where capital is rationed

Rather than buying an asset outright (which would require use of either available cash resources or borrowed funds) a business may lease an asset

Sale and leaseback arrangements are particularly appropriate for highly specialised assets that may have a low realisable value and therefore would be poor security for a more traditional loan

Liquidation

In a liquidation, the main stakeholders to comment on are likely to be:

- A bank or provider of funds (which probably holds a charge over property)
- Shareholders
- Suppliers and other creditors

Try to find some different points to say under 3 specific headings for these groups.

The funds generated should be based on a pro forma, probably involving PPE, inventories and trade receivables. The liquidator's fee should then be deducted, together with any **fixed** charge due.

Once this amount ("Remaining funds") is calculated we know what we can potentially repay to any creditors with a **floating** charge – this is found by dividing the Remaining funds by the floating charges due to find how much per £1 of floating charge will actually be repaid (it will probably be less than £1 due to the difficulties the company is facing).

(A fixed charge is a charge over a specified asset of the entity: the entity loses the freedom to dispose of this asset without the permission of the owner – a floating charge is a charge over the assets in general of the entity: the entity retains the freedom to dispose of assets unless a default has occurred as the charge is not in connection with any specified asset.)

Financial Reconstruction – possible calculation pro-forma

The funds generated may need to be calculated based on the following pro forma, probably involving PPE, inventories and trade receivables. The liquidator's fee should then be deducted, together with any **fixed** charge due.

Once the remaining net amount after the liquidator's fee and fixed charge(s) ("Remaining funds") is known then we can estimate what we can potentially repay to any creditors with a **floating** charge – this is found by dividing the Remaining funds by the floating charges due to find how much per £1 of floating charge will actually be repaid (it will probably be less than £1 due to the difficulties the company is facing).

(A fixed charge is a charge over a specified asset of the entity: the entity loses the freedom to dispose of this asset without the permission of the owner – a floating charge is a charge over the assets in general of the entity: the entity retains the freedom to dispose of assets unless a default has occurred as the charge is not in connection with any specified asset.)

Overall the proforma might look like that below:

Funds generated

PPE
Inventories
Trade receivables
Total proceeds

Less liquidator's fee
Less paid to holder's of a fixed charge
Remaining funds R

Floating charges

Loans
Overdraft

F

Amount paid to holders of a floating charge (per £1 of floating charge) = R/F

For example, if the company has been lent amounts subject to floating charges of £10m but the R figure is only £5m then holders of floating charges will only receive back 50% (5/10) of their original investment.

After this, you should make some standard narrative points (see below).

Note that if the result of the fraction R/F is less than 1, then this means that floating chargeholders will not receive back the full amount of their investment – it follows that unsecured creditors and shareholders (neither of whom have any charges at all) will not receive anything back at all.

The calculation steps to follow again are:

Step 1	Calculate proceeds received based on assets
Step 2	Deduct liquidator's fee and fixed charges
Step 3	Arrive at Remaining funds (R)
Step 4	Calculate Floating charges (F)
Step 5	Find amount repayable per £1 of Floating charge (R/F) (probably to a bank)
Step 6	Make standard narrative points (see below)

Based on SBM November 2014 past paper Q1, you can ignore the "prescribed part" in your calculation but should comment that this would be reserved for unsecured creditors by law: effectively, this preserves a small amount for the unsecured creditors.

Financial reconstruction and liquidation: Narrative points

Unsecured creditors and shareholders will receive nothing if the ratio of R/F is less than 1 – if the ratio is less than one, then we are saying that floating chargeholders are not receiving all of their money back so there is clearly nothing further available to those without any charges recorded at all (unsecured creditors and shareholders).

In some cases, it may be that you need to **compare a liquidation against an alternative option** (such as keeping the business going, but on revised terms – this would be a financial reconstruction). Again, try to consider the matter from the perspective of different **stakeholders** such as the funding bank, shareholders and creditors.

Bank

The bank receives **certain cash back under a liquidation** but could be subject to **further risk if the money is left invested under a financial reconstruction**.

Consider the **interest rates** under the financial reconstruction – these will probably be higher than before in order to give the bank an incentive to continue to invest.

Consider **whether other stakeholders would invest** under the financial reconstruction or **will the bank remain the main funder** and therefore subject to the most risk?

Consider the **potential return** under the financial reconstruction – is this probable and/or attractive to the bank?

Shareholders

The shareholders **may get nothing back under a liquidation** but at least have some **voting power** to determine what happens.

You may wish to comment on what **shareholders are being asked to do** under the financial reconstruction option.

The amount invested in the original shares could be considered to be a sunk cost if liquidation is an active option: in other words, if the financial reconstruction does not happen then that money is lost anyway so the cost of the original investment is not a relevant or incremental cost – only the new capital injected under the financial reconstruction is a relevant cost.

Use the **forecast returns** for calculation purposes but **apply professional scepticism** as the projections may be optimistic in order to keep the company going (look at the position of the Board of Directors here).

Suppliers

Suppliers **may get nothing back under a liquidation** and, unlike shareholders, have no **voting power** to determine what happens.

Unsecured creditors would only get a small "**prescribed part**" back in a liquidation whereas if a financial reconstruction works then, over time, they may receive the **full** amount back.

As **suppliers are in a weak position**, it may be possible for the client company to negotiate hard and improve its position.

Resorting to court action would be a waste of time if there are other creditors which rank ahead of the suppliers (fixed and floating charge holders).

Financial reporting points

Although it remains outside the scope of this book to discuss financial reporting issues in detail, any discussion of liquidation and financial reconstruction is likely to be paired up with some financial reporting marks for points such as:

- IAS 1 and going concern presentation (valuation and also classification of liabilities and assets as current or non-current)
- ISA 570 *Going Concern* issues and the position of the auditor
- IAS 10 *Events after the reporting period*

See also	Cash Flow Forecasts – Evaluation	100
	Change – Definition & Models	101
	Change – Management & Implementation	103
	Disposals and Assets Held for Sale (IFRS 5)	186
	Financial Reconstruction	203

Loan Decision by a Bank

The bank will consider 3 main areas:

- creditworthiness of the borrower
- term and structure of the loan
- return for the bank

Creditworthiness of the borrower

The bank will consider the financial stability of the borrower, its existing capital structure and the track record of management (including past credit behaviour and credit histories)

The bank will examine published financial statements, financial forecasts of future periods and key ratios in the areas of performance, efficiency and gearing.

Financial forecasts should cover the term of the loan.

The terms and structure of the loan

Is the loan amount appropriate for what the funds will be used for?

Is the length of time before repayment appropriate? A longer term loan will generate more interest but could present a greater risk of default for the bank.

How will the repayments be structured? Will there be gradual repayment of capital throughout the life of the loan will alone be interest only with a final "bullet" repayment of capital at the end of the term?

What security will be offered in terms of legal charges such as fixed or floating charges over assets?

The bank is likely to attach covenants which impose conditions and obligations on the borrower – these can be financial, such as meeting a specified ratio, or non-financial, such as requiring disclosure of significant events

The return for the bank

The bank will consider

- The rate of interest on the loan, and the term over which interest will be paid
- Other remuneration from the loan such as arrangement, underwriting or facility fees
- The value of other relationships within the bank – the potential borrower may have lucrative relationships with other banking operations

Marketing Strategies

The 4 Ps for a physical product

Price

Product

Place

Promotion

The additional 3 Ps for a service

People

Physical evidence

Process

See also		
	Branding and Rebranding (IFRS 13)	87
	Organic Growth	322

Modified Internal Rate of Return (MIRR)

This is similar to an IRR calculation but assuming that amounts are invested at the cost of capital

Therefore if we have a 4 year project then cash generated in year 1 will have 3 further years of growth at the cost of capital, cash generated in year 2 will have 2 years of growth at the cost of capital, and so on

We adjust the cash flows upwards by these relevant multiples to find the total amount generated after allowing for reinvestment

We then compare this to the initial investment and use this as the basis of finding the MIRR by using a compound growth formula

Worked example

Assumes a discount rate of 10%

	Year 0	Year 1	Year 2	Year 3
Cash outflows	-5,000	0	0	0
Cash inflows	0	2,000	5,000	6,000

Answer

Interest rate multipliers

Year 1 1.1 x 1.1 = 1.21 (cash received at the end of year 1 has 2 further periods to grow)

Year 2 1.1

Year 3 no multiplier for the final year

	Year 0	Year 1	Year 2	Year 3
Cash outflows	-5,000	0	0	0
Cash inflows	0	2,000	5,000	6,000
Multiplier		1.21	1.1	no multiplier
Reinvested value		2,420	5,500	6,000

Total reinvested value is 13,920

Present value of the outflows is 5,000

MIRR is $(13,920/5,000)^{1/3} - 1$ or 40.7%

Advantages of MIRR

Avoids the problem of multiple IRRs

Avoids the weakness of traditional IRR of assuming that profits are reinvested at the IRR itself (which is often not possible)

Disadvantages of MIRR

May lead an investor to reject a project which has a lower rate of return but which, in terms of size, is a very good project – this is because it is based on a rate

Does not look at project life – a high return project with a short life may be preferred over a lower-return project with a longer life

See also Investment Appraisal Methods topics

Natural capital

Natural capital can be defined as natural assets (e.g., air, water, land, habitats) that provide everyday resources including timber, agricultural land, fisheries and clean water as well as services such as air and water filtration, flood protection and pollination for crops (otherwise known as 'ecosystem services')

The focus on natural capital has increased dramatically in recent years as organisations consider how their actions impact on the natural world

If organisations take more out of the natural environment than they put back, they are essentially running up a debt which needs to be paid back or the organisation risks causing a permanent collapse in the natural environment and hence the end of its activities

Poorly managed natural capital therefore becomes not only an ecological liability but a social and economic liability too

This perspective has changed the way in which organisations report on their activities with many now attempting to place financial values on the natural assets they use to enable them to make more informed business decisions

The impact of business activities on natural resources which are not typically accounted for or allowed for ("externalities") could result in business risks (legal action, consumer boycotts or brand damage)

Incorporating natural capital into business cases and decision-making requires an ability to measure and value natural capital – this is complicated and will likely involve contributions from environmental economists, scientists, ecologists and data analysts

"Natural capital valuation" prices environmental resources so that companies can see their true value to the business

As resources become depleted due to population growth, companies are likely to have to pay more for their natural capital as a result of increased regulation, resource scarcity, pollution or extreme weather events that reduce supplies

The PwC document "Valuing corporate environmental impacts" highlights 3 key steps in the valuation process:

- Quantify resource use or environmental emissions in biophysical units such as kilograms, litres etc

- Understand how the resource use or environmental emissions cause changes in the natural environment (for example, through water pollution or changes in air quality)

- Value the impacts on people associated with these changes in the natural environment e.g. impacts on health, or on agriculture or fisheries

When trying to value and manage natural capital, organisations need to apply a consistent methodology to be able to make meaningful comparisons between different projects or in comparing performance over time

The Natural Capital Protocol (developed by the Natural Capital Coalition) is an example of a general framework which aims at the consistent measurement and valuing of natural capital

Managing natural capital

Various methodologies have been proposed for managing the value of natural capital elements:

Shadow pricing – shadow pricing adds a hypothetical surcharge to the market prices for goods or services that involve significant carbon emissions in their supply chain – a growing number of companies are putting a shadow price on carbon to reduce their carbon footprint and inform business decisions

Procurement and supply chain management – practical ways to apply natural capital accounting could be through the use of supply chain risk assessments, supplier relationship management and implementation of sustainable procurement strategies – this could involve requesting data on the carbon emissions or water use of suppliers and rejecting those suppliers who do not comply with standards – companies could switch to certified sustainable supplies for commodities such as timber or cotton

Product design – Life Cycle Analysis (LCA) can quantify and reduce impacts associated with sourcing, manufacturing, using and disposing of products

Scenario planning – companies can use natural capital valuations to help with decisions on where to grow and invest capital (or alternatively withdraw from a market or project) or, for example, when considering online retailing versus investing in bricks and mortar stores

See also Sustainability Reporting and Social Reporting 399

Online Sales Strategies

Data required to determine whether a worthwhile investment

Generally seems reasonable to develop a strategy as most modern companies have an online presence

Without a presence, may be a competitive disadvantage

Requires careful planning and efficient implementation

Plans needed for web site design, marketing and advertising the online service, online payment arrangements and arrangements for distributing goods/services to customers (globally)

Clear timetable needs to be designed

Clear target date set for "going live"

Exam tip

The points made here definitely not rocket science! There will be nothing wrong with making simple and obvious points

See also		
	Big Data topics	
	Cloud computing and cloud accounting	104
	Cyber security	145
	Digital Strategies	176
	Digital Transformation	184
	Marketing Strategies	314

Option Valuation

Possible models

Black-Scholes-Merton – standard model based on formula which looks at volatity and other factors

Binomial Lattice – probability based model which looks at different alternative outcomes

Monte Carlo simulation – based on running thousands of scenarios to determine likely outcome

Exam tip – you are not expected to include detailed information here so no need to go beyond the points identified here

Model inputs

Underlying price of the instrument (e.g. share price)

Exercise price – high value for a call option if the exercise price is well below today's price (much larger chance of making a profit on exercise)

Time to exercise – longer time period adds more value as more chance for things to move favourably for the option holder

Volatility – more volatility adds to option value as more chance of a favourable move

Interest rates – rise in interest rates increases the value of a call option (the alternative to an option would be to buy the instrument right now but then the entity will have an opportunity cost of lost interest on that cash whereas using an option it can generate interest whilst "waiting" to buy the instrument)

Income generated from the instrument (e.g. dividends)

Assurance aspects

Is the model designed for the purpose it is applied?

Review of all inputs for reasonableness

Consult with expert in valuations?

The main 2 assurance issues/risks relate to

The fair value of any options issued

Estimate of the number of options that will be exercisable based on the vesting conditions and conditions at the reporting date

Requirement to check

Share price	easy if a listed company but not if unlisted
Exercise price	should be specified in the option contract
Time to expiry	should be specified in the option contract
Volatility of the underlying share	easy if a listed company but not if unlisted
Interest rates	information easily available
Dividend yields	should be possible to check based on the accounts

Vesting conditions check

Check what the conditions are
Check how many options may be exercised under any given circumstances
Check the likelihood of those conditions being satisfied given the current circumstances

See also Investment Appraisal Methods topics
Real Options 360
Valuation topics

Organic Growth

Reasons for

May be cheaper than an acquisition

Much more control than in an acquisition – able to continue existing trends and initiatives

Make use of existing resources fully (employees, supply chain)

Less disruptive for staff and customers

Considerations

Management structure

Overseas issues

Information strategies

Quality maintenance

Company legislation

Tax position

Methods

Investment in marketing

Could be expensive with limited impact

May be more urgent or significant issues to address

Investment in product development

Need to keep up with competitors

Product diversification

Reduces risks but can be expensive

Could increase the level of profits achieved

If penetration to date is limited then it may make sense to focus on developing existing products

Focuses on existing core competencies in the same activity

Ansoff Matrix Ideas

Market development – same product in a different market sector

Uses existing resources and increases their utilisation ("making the assets sweat")

Operational side of the business is identical to the existing business – near complete overlap with existing core competencies in operational activities

Limitations of a market development strategy

Loss of sales in the existing market if too much effort in the new market

Reputational risk

Investment and reorganisation costs likely to be largely sunk if the venture fails

Cash inflows in early years likely to be low and so payback slow if market conditions change

Need reliable market research when entering a less well known market

Related diversification – both the product and market have changed but in neither case is the change substantial

Accesses a new market where there is currently no presence

Margins may be greater

No loss of sales to existing customers

Limitations of related diversification

No current market knowledge

Product is slightly different from the existing product so some departures from existing core competencies

May be significant initial costs which are likely to be sunk costs

Level of synergy may be questionable

See also		
	Change – Definition & Models	101
	Change – Management & Implementation	103
	Overseas Operations topics	

Organisational Structures

Challenges that inform organisational structure

Johnson, Scholes and Whittington identify 3 major groups of challenges for modern organisational structures:

1. flexibility of organisational design – the rapid pace of environmental change and increased levels of environmental uncertainty demand flexibility of organisational design

2. effective systems – the capture, organisation and exploitation of knowledge requires effective systems to link the people who have knowledge with the applications that are needed

3. internationalisation – internationalisation creates new types (and a new scale of) technological complexity in communication and Information Systems – at the same time, diversity of culture, practices and approaches to personal relationships bring their own new problems of organisational form

Of these 3 sets of issues, the need to capture, organise and exploit knowledge is probably the most pressing for most organisations

Types of basic organisational structure

Johnson, Scholes and Whittington review 7 basic structural types:

1. functional
2. multi-divisional
3. holding company
4. matrix
5. transnational
6. team
7. project

Detailed summary notes on the above 7 organisational structures are provided below (please note that we have followed the SBM Study Manual in discussing the multidivisional and holding company structures within the same subsection)

You may also need notes on the meaning of the term "network structure" as this is discussed in the SBM Study Manual – see the end of this section for relevant notes on this more general concept which potentially applies regardless of which of the above 7 basic structural types is the best specific formal description of the organisation's structure

Choosing a structure

An organisational structure must provide a means of exercising appropriate control

It must also respond to the challenges of rapid change, knowledge management and globalisation

In many cases, it is likely that there will not be a single model of organisational structure suitable for all purposes – managers must make choices as to which challenges they regard as most pressing

Goold and Campbell proposed 9 tests that may be used to assess proposed structures:

Tests relating to the organisation's objectives

Market advantage – where processes must be closely coordinated in order to achieve market advantage, they should be in the same structural element

Parenting advantage – the structure should support the parenting role played by the corporate centre – for example, a "portfolio manager" would need only a small, low-cost corporate centre

People test – the structure must be suited to the skills and experience of the people that have to function within it – for example, skilled professionals used to a team-working approach might be frustrated by a move to functional hierarchy

Feasibility test – this test sweeps up all other constraints, such as those imposed by law, stakeholder opinion and resource availability

Tests relating to matters of design principle

Specialised cultures – specialists should be able to collaborate closely

Difficult links – it is highly likely that some interdepartmental links will be subject to friction and strain e.g. the link between sales and production when there are frequent problems over quality and delivery – a sound structure will embody measures to strengthen communication and cooperation in such cases

Redundant hierarchy – the structure should be as flat as is reasonably attainable

Accountability – effective control requires clear lines of accountability

Flexibility – the structure must allow for requirements to change in the future so that unexpected opportunities can be seized

1. The functional structure

People are organised according to the type of work that they do

Departments are defined by their functions, based on the work that they do e.g. production department, sales department, finance department and so on

The functional structure is a traditional, common sense approach and many organisations are structured in this way

Advantages of a functional structure

Based on work specialism and therefore logical

The organisation can benefit from economies of scale

Offers a career structure

Disadvantages of a functional structure

Does not reflect the actual business processes by which value is created

Hard to identify where profits and losses are made on individual products

People do not have an understanding of how the whole business works

There are problems of coordinating the work of different specialisms

Hampers cross functional creativity and innovation i.e. sharing of knowledge between functions

2. and 3. The multidivisional and holding company structures

A multidivisional structure divides the organisation into semiautonomous divisions that may be differentiated by territory, product or market – each division will then have separate functions within it

A holding company structure is an extreme form of multidivisional structure in which the divisions are separate legal entities (subsidiaries) – the holding company can be a company with a permanent investment or one that buys and sells businesses or interests in businesses – the subsidiaries may have other shareholders

Each division has its own revenues, expenditures and profits

Communications between divisions and head offices are restricted, formal and related to performance standards – influence is maintained by headquarters' power to hire and fire the managers who are supposed to run each division

Divisionalisation is a function of organisation size, in numbers and in product-market activities

Advantages of a divisional structure

Focuses attention of subordinate management on business performance and results

Management by objectives is the natural control default

Gives more authority to junior managers and therefore provides them with work that grooms them for more senior positions in the future

Provides an organisational structure which reduces the number of levels of management – the top executives in each division should be able to report direct to the Chief Executive of the holding company

Disadvantages of a divisional structure

Each division is partly insulated by the holding company from shareholders and capital markets, which ultimately reward performance

The economic advantages it offers over independent organisations reflect fundamental inefficiencies in capital markets – in other words, different product-market divisions might function better as independent companies

The divisions are more bureaucratic than they would be as independent corporations, owing to the performance measures imposed by the strategic apex

Headquarters management have a tendency to usurp divisional profits by management charges, cross subsidies, head office bureaucracies and unfair transfer pricing systems

In some businesses it is impossible to identify completely independent products or markets for which divisions would be appropriate – one particular problem for divisional structures is that they struggle to cope with large customers who span the divisions

4. The matrix structure

A matrix structure attempts to ensure coordination across functional lines by the embodiment of dual authority in the organisational structure

Matrix structures provide for the formalisation of management control between different functions while at the same time maintaining functional departmentation

Matrix structures can be a mixture of a functional, product and territorial organisation

Matrix and project organisation may possibly be thought of as a reaction against the golden rule of classical management theory of unity of command: i.e. the principle that an individual should have only one boss – a matrix approach has a project management structure superimposed on top of the functional departmental structure

Under a matrix structure, an individual may be responsible to both a product manager and a manager in the finance department, for example

				Boss 1		
		Production Department	**Sales Department**	**Finance Department**	**Distribution Department**	**Marketing Department**
	Product Manager A					
Boss 2	**Product Manager B**					
	Product Manager C					

The key issue in a matrix structure is the need for the division of authority between product managers and functional managers to be carefully defined

A subordinate cannot easily take orders from 2 or more bosses and so an arrangement has to be established, perhaps on the following lines:

> a subordinate takes orders from one boss (the functional department manager) and the second boss (the project manager) has to ask the first boss to give certain instructions to the subordinate, or
>
> a subordinate takes orders from one boss about some specified matters and orders from the other boss about different specified matters – this would require the authority of each boss to have been carefully defined and good cooperation between the bosses would be necessary

Advantages of a matrix structure

Offers greater flexibility in relation both to people and to the task and structure itself as the matrix may be short-term (as with project teams) but with a longer term functional structure underneath

Should improve communication within the organisation

Dual authority gives the organisation multiple orientation so that functional specialists do not get wrapped up in their own concerns

Provides a structure for allocating responsibility to managers for end results – a product manager is responsible for product profitability and the project leader is responsible for ensuring that the task is completed

Provides for interdisciplinary cooperation and the mixing of skills and expertise

Disadvantages of a matrix organisation

Dual authority threatens a conflict between managers – subordinates must know to which boss they are responsible for each aspect of their duties

One individual with 2 or more bosses is more likely to suffer role stress at work

It is sometimes more costly – for example, product managers are additional jobs which would not be required in a simple structure of functional departmentation

It may be difficult for management to accept a matrix structure – it is possible that a manager may feel threatened that another manager will usurp his or her authority

Requires consensus and agreement which may slow down decision-making

Suitability of a matrix organisation

A matrix organisation is most suitable in the following situations:

> there is a fairly large number of different functions, each of great importance
>
> there could be communications problems between functional management of different functions at the present time so a matrix structure could improve matters here

work is supposed to flow smoothly between functions but such communications problems might stop or hinder the workflow so a matrix structure could improve work flows

there is a need to carry out uncertain, interdependent tasks – work can be structured so as to be task centred with a task manager who is appointed to look after each task and provide the communications (and cooperation) between different functions

there is a need to achieve common functional tasks so as to achieve savings in the use of resources i.e. product divisions would be too wasteful because they would duplicate costly functional tasks

5. The transnational structure

A transnational structure attempts to reconcile global scope and scale with local responsiveness: some markets may require high volumes of a single low-cost product whilst others require a range of low-volume and therefore high cost products

The **global approach** leads to global divisions, each responsible for the worldwide production and marketing of a related group of standardised products

The **multi-domestic** approach leads to the setting up or acquisition of local subsidiaries, each with a great deal of autonomy in design, production and marketing

A transnational approach tends to have a high proportion of fixed responsibilities in the horizontal lines of management and has 3 specific operational characteristics:

national units are independent operating entities but also provide capabilities (such as R&D) that are used by the rest of the organisation

such shared capabilities allow national units to achieve global, or at least regional, economies of scale

the global corporate parent adds value by establishing the basic role of each national unit and then supporting the systems, relationships and culture that enable them to work together as an effective network

To work effectively, the transnational structure must have very clearly defined managerial roles, relationships and boundaries:

managers of global products or businesses should have responsibilities for strategies, innovation, resources and transactions that transcend both national and functional boundaries

country managers must feed back local requirements and build unique local competencies

functional managers nurture innovation and spread best practice

managers at the corporate parent lead, facilitate and integrate all other managerial activities – they must also be talent spotters within the organisation

Disadvantages of the transnational structure

Makes great demands on its managers, both in their immediate responsibilities and in the complexity of their relationships within the organisation

Complexity of the organisation can lead to difficulties of control and complications introduced by internal political activity

(Please note that the SBM Study Manual does not provide a specific sub heading on the advantages of the transnational structure.)

6. The team-based structure

Although the transnational and matrix structures use project teams, projects naturally come to an end so project teams disperse at this point under those organisational structures

A team-based structure therefore extends the matrix structures use of both vertical functional links and horizontal, activity-based ones by using cross functional teams

Business processes are often used as the basis of organisation with each team being responsible for the processes relating to an aspect of the business – a purchasing team might contain procurement specialists, design and production engineers and marketing specialists, for example

(Please note that the SBM Study Manual does not provide a specific sub heading on either the advantages or the disadvantages of the team-based structure.)

7. The project-based structure

A project-based structure involves employees from different departments working together on a temporary basis to achieve a specific objective or to address a specific issue – employees within the team perform specific job functions

A project-based structure is similar to a team-based structure except that projects, by definition have a finite life and so, therefore, do the project teams dealing with them under the project-based structure approach

Advantages of a project-based structure

This structure is very flexible and easy-to-use as an adjunct to more traditional organisational forms

Management of projects is a well-established discipline with its own techniques

Disadvantages of the project-based structure

Requires clear project definition if control is to be effective and comprehensive project review if longer term learning is to take place

The network structure

The network structure is a very modern idea, applied both within and between organisations

Within an organisation, the term is used to mean something that resembles both the organic organisation and structure of informal relationships that exists in most organisations alongside the formal structure

Such a loose, fluid approach is often used to achieve innovative responses to changing circumstances

The network approach is visible in the growing use of outsourcing as a strategic method

Some writers such as Ghoshal and Bartlett point to the likelihood of network organisations becoming the corporations of the future, replacing formal organisational structures with innovations such as virtual teams

Virtual teams are interconnected groups of people who may not be in the same office (or even the same organisation) but who share information and tasks, make joint decisions and fulfil the collaborative function of a team

Organisations are now able to structure their activities very differently, allowing increased flexibility:

Staffing – certain areas of organisational activity can be undertaken by freelance or contract workers such as in Charles Handy's "shamrock organisation" which is gaining recognition as a workable model for a leaner and more flexible workforce, within the control framework – the key question is: how can the necessary control be achieved?

Leasing of facilities such as machinery, IT and accommodation is becoming more common

Production itself might be outsourced, even to offshore countries where labour is cheaper

Interdependence of organisations is emphasised by the sharing of functions and services – databases and communication create genuine interactive sharing of, and access to, common data

Examples of network organisational structures

Johnson, Scholes and Whittington give 4 examples of network organisational structures:

Teleworking – this combines independent work with connection to corporate resources

Federations of experts who combine voluntarily – this is common in the entertainment industry

One-stop shops for professional services in which a package of services is made available by a coordinating entity – a point of access to such conglomerates may be a website

Service networks such as the various chains of franchised hotels that cooperate to provide centralised booking facilities

Cooperation on non-core competence matters can lead to several benefits such as cost reduction, increase market penetration and an experience curve effect

Typical areas for cooperation between competitors include R&D and distribution chains – for example, the spread of the Toyota system of manufacturing, with its emphasis on just-in-time, quality and the elimination of waste has led to a high degree of integration between the operations of industrial customers and their suppliers

Outsourcing

General considerations

- Fees
- Cost of the business doing the task itself
- Redundancies
- Time and cost in arranging and monitoring agreement
- Previous experience with outsourcing

Requirements for successful outsourcing

- Ability to specify with precision what is supplied
- Ability to measure what is actually supplied
- Ability to make adjustments elsewhere if specification is not achieved

Deciding what to outsource

- Strategic importance of the system – does outsourcer company have the required information? Can it be provided without creating risks?
- Functions with limited interfaces are most easily outsourced
- Can we manage the arrangement easily?
- Do we know enough about our own systems to make a sensible decision?
- Will our needs change? Can the outsourcer company adapt?

Possible benefits

- Access to cheaper inputs including labour
- Improves competitive advantage
- Reduces fixed costs and operating gearing
- Reduces risk exposure
- Allows the business to concentrate on its core competence
- Allows specialist to do the work
- Outsourcer business may be better able to deal with high demand
- Legal recourse including compensation if something goes wrong
- Positive impact on other divisions

Possible negative impact

- Redundancies and closure costs
- Data protection issues
- Co-ordination with rest of supply chain
- Time, effort and expense of monitoring
- Harder to guarantee and control supply
- Delays
- Quality control
- Hidden costs such as disruption or unexpected charges

Recently, some UK companies have begun bringing customer service jobs back to the UK in response to customer complaints about their dealings with offshore call centres

Outsourcing

[Useful points from SBM November 2017 Mock 2 Q1]

Selecting an outsourcing partner

This will be a very important decision as the partner could be a **key element** of operations – problems could cause **significant disruption** to the business – factors to consider include:

- **capability and capacity** – experience and ability to meet service requirements – capacity will also be important to provide the opportunity to expand the volume of business
- **cultural compatibility** – a good working relationship is essential – this will be easier to achieve with an organisation that shares a similar culture and values because this will help **communication**, particularly when dealing with **problems** – consideration of the customer base could be relevant here: if one partner works with small organisations but the other works with larger multinationals then there may be **different assumptions** and **working styles**
- **location** – this could be very important to manufacturing operations but also to service organisations – costs of transportation/travel could be very **significant** and **outweigh** costs saved in other respects
- **financial considerations** – using the **cheapest** option may not necessarily be best (skills and capabilities also matter) but costs are obviously important – **a comparison with the costs of performing the work internally should be made** to determine if outsourcing is worthwhile

Managing the outsourced relationship

Managing the relationship **once operations have started** is just as important as **choosing** the right partner in the first place

If performance is not as expected this could affect the company's **sales** and **reputation**

The company should consider a **Service Level Agreement** (SLA) with its outsourcing partner to identify the standards expected by both parties

The company must then ensure that the **terms of the SLA are being adhered to** – if not, this should be **discussed** and **corrective action** should be taken to improve performance

The company must ensure it is not **transferring across overall responsibility** that the work is performed well – in other words, the outsourcing partner must be **monitored** and **held accountable** for any problems which occur

Issues to include in a Service Level Agreement with an outsourcer company

- Service level — minimum standards required and penalties
- Exit route — arrangements to exit or transfer to another supplier
- Timescale
- Ownership of tangible and intangible assets
- Dependencies
- Employment issues

Types of outsourcing arrangement (example of IT services)

	Arrangement		
Features	**Timeshare**	**Service**	**Facilities Management (FM)**
What is it?	Time-based access to external processing system	Focus on specific function	Outside agency manages organisation's IS/IT facilities. Client retains equipment but all services provided by the FM company
Management responsibility	Mostly retained	Some retained	Very little retained
Focus	Operational	A function	Strategic
Timescale	Short-term	Medium-term	Long-term
Justification	Cost savings	More efficient	Access to expertise, better service, management can focus on core business activities

Overseas Operations – Exporting

Considerations

- Tax
- Exchange risk
- Political risk
- Business risk
- Pre-export financing – period in which export is produced and prepared for delivery
- Post-export financing – period in which export has been sent and payment is being awaited

Pre-export financing sources

- Bank lending – structured lending where the bank funds the exporter but funding is tied to production and export activities
- Export credit agencies – government departments – provide insurance against political and commercial risks and UK Export Credits Guarantees Department (ECGD)

Invoicing in the buyer's currency

Competitive advantage – means that purchasers do not need to concern themselves with the administrative necessity of buying sterling and do not have risks from adverse exchange rate movements

Disadvantage for the seller – exposed to risks of adverse exchange rate movements – may require hedging if there is a long enough period between invoicing and receipt and if the amounts are material

Working Capital Management for Exporters

Factoring – passing debts to an external party who will take on the responsibility for collecting the money due: the factor advances a proportion of the money it is due to collect so the exporter now has funds to pay suppliers and finance growth

If the factoring is "non-recourse" then the factor will not have any claim on the exporter even if the end customer does not pay – this removes the risk for the exporter but at a cost

Documentary credits or letter of credit – fixed assurance from the customer's bank in the customer's own country which states that payment will be made provided that the exporter complies with all terms and conditions – given this assurance, the exporter's own bank may advance some credit before the goods are shipped

Forfaiting – for larger projects and involving a bank purchasing 100% of the value of the invoice at a discount – this allows the exporter to in turn offer financing to the customer, making products and services more attractive. The bank deal will include a discount rate, a number of grace days added to the period to allow for transactions to go through and a commitment fee.

Credit insurance – assigns credit-insured invoices to bank who will offer up to 100% of the insured debt as a loan. These instruments may carry a guarantee from the government of the customer's home country

See also	Finance – Sources for SMEs	199
	Other Overseas Operations topics	

Overseas Operations – Financing

Background considerations

- Local finance costs and subsidies
- Taxation
- Restrictions on dividend remittances
- Possibility of flexibility in repayments
- Access to capital – may be easier in local markets to optimise gearing

Methods and considerations

Takeover/merger – quick, can choose established/experienced partner, access to information, market share and distribution channels, disadvantage: premium may have to be paid

Overseas subsidiary – must remit profit back in order for parent to have access, choices over equity share, subsidiary's borrowings and currency

Branches – better than losing withholding tax on dividends from a subsidiary, lower level of formalities, greater profile for sales and marketing

Additional agency costs in setting up, running and monitoring the local subsidiaries

Using local sources of finance – issues

- Local finance costs
- Availability of subsidies
- Tax systems
- Tax structuring
- Restrictions on dividend remittances
- Possibility of flexibility in repayments from parent sub relationship
- Different covenants and options – subsidiary may be able to gear more than parent

See also Finance – Sources for SMEs 199
Other Overseas Operations topics

QB: 47// Set up warehouse vs Distribute from UK://

QB -> risks of new subsidiary//

Overseas Operations – Operational Aspects

- Management structure – could become more complex
- Choice whether to recruit local management or whether senior management will move abroad
- Decision on the amount of autonomy to give the subsidiary management – determine how much central management should be involved in determining strategy
- Determines performance targets and how much emphasis is placed on achieving financial targets

Overseas operations and human resources

Key questions

Use expatriate staff to control local operations or employ local managers with more knowledge but risking loss of control?

Are expatriate staff skilled and comfortable with local culture?

Exporting – considerations

- Often requires financing – pre-export financing and post-export working capital
- Length of time to receive payment
- Costs
- Risks

Exporting – risks

- Loss or damage in transit – use insurance, risk assessment, transfer obligations to delivery agent
- Faults with products
- Non-payment by customers – use references or credit scoring, use export credit insurance, consider stage payments
- Liquidity
- Exchange rate movements – impact on forecasts/NPV
- Discount factor used should be higher due to additional risks
- Inflation
- Higher delivery costs – sensitivity analysis, sourcing low cost transport, breaking large deliveries up
- Price risk – confidentiality, link to order size

Mitigation export risks

- Hedging
- Due Diligence on customer and contract terms
- Insurance against default
- Sensitivity analysis

Calculating the breakeven exchange rate (sensitivity analysis)

We need to find how much the present value of a particular flow can change before the project realises an NPV of 0.

Example

PV of revenues	$100,000
NPV of project	$7,000
Current exchange rate	$2:£1
Breakeven exchange rate	100,000/(100,000 – 7,000) x 2 = 2.15

Provided that the dollar does not depreciate to $2.15:£1 then the project will continue to break even. This would be a change in the rate of 0.15/2 or 7.5%

See the model answer to the July 2015 past paper Q1 for further explanation.

Foreign currency transactions

IAS 21 considerations – transactions will be denominated in a currency other than the functional currency of the entity – the entity must translate these items into its own functional currency according to the rules in IAS 21 in its individual company financial statements – sales made in the overseas country and any receivables outstanding will need to be translated at the closing rate, as these are monetary items – these may then need to be translated again into the group presentation currency (if different)

See also

Change – Definition & Models	101
Change – Management & Implementation	103
Globalisation	221
Other Overseas Operations topics	

Overseas Operations – Risks

- Currency risks*
- Physical risks – risk of goods being lost or stolen in transit or documents being lost
- Credit risks – risk that the customer will default
- Trade risks – risk that customer will cancel or refuse to accept the goods
- Liquidity risks – risk that company cannot finance the credit terms given to customers

*Note – do not focus on currency risks too much unless specifically asked to do so

Institutions which can help to reduce risks of overseas operations

- Banks
- Insurance companies
- Credit reference agencies
- Government agencies – UK Export Credits Guarantee Department (ECGD)
- Transfer risks via contractual rules (e.g. courier shares part or all of the losses)

Transactions in a foreign currency – risks

Revenue risks – fixed contract price, credit/default risk, order cancellation

Cost side risks – commodity price volatility, movement in exchange rate

Opportunity cost – if at full capacity and decide to undertake a transaction in a foreign currency which does not materialise then wasted an opportunity to earn income

Liquidity risk – delays in receipt

Note – revenue risks and cost side risks can become benefits if the exchange rate moves favourably

Exchange controls

Note: exchange controls are controls on transfers of funds – the related risks are different to risks relating to movements in exchange rates

Impact is to ration the supply of foreign currency and restrict certain types of transaction

Strategies: transfer pricing, royalty payments, loans, management charges

Legal risks

- Export and import controls for political, environmental or health and safety reasons
- Favourable trade status for some countries
- International trademark, copyright and patent conventions (some countries do not recognise these)
- Restrictions on promotional message and methods

Mitigation of legal risks

- Keep up to date with changes
- Good citizenship – compliance with best practice and going beyond the minimum required
- Ensure staff are fully informed of changes
- Local versus central management

Reputational risks

- Bad press in host and domestic country
- Companies with high standards may be accused of hypocrisy if practices are not as good elsewhere
- May be low quality standards due to need to save costs

Due Diligence and auditing of overseas financial risk

- Has management taken legal, taxation and accounting advice
- Has hedging been used?
- Has management considered the cultural and political implications of an overseas investment?
- Other discussions with management – other issues that have arisen
- Examine terms of loan capital
- Examine contractual liabilities
- Check remittance records to bank and cash records
- Review movement of exchange and interest rates
- Obtain details of hedging if used
- Examine financial statements for accurate disclosure of accounting policy and treatment
- Have directors satisfied themselves as to going concern?

See also	Change – Definition & Models	101
	Change – Management & Implementation	103
	Globalisation	221
	Other Overseas Operations topics	

Overseas Operations – Strategic Considerations

Reasons to develop overseas operations

- Earn contribution
- Establish a reputation abroad
- Diversification to reduce risks
- Extend scale of operations – economies of scale, meet targets
- Government incentives
- May be less competition than in mature/home markets
- Changes in tastes
- Changes in regulations
- First mover advantage – be the first into a market
- Follow competitors if not first into a market
- Product life cycle
- Home market image may be a selling point (e.g. fashionable US brands)
- Defeat seasonality – having sales in the other hemisphere can be helpful (e.g. summer clothing)
- Growth rates in foreign market
- Vent for surplus – sell excess production/capacity
- Low cost production

International investment appraisal – further considerations

- Interest rates
- Tax rates and incentives – Corporation Tax in the foreign country, investment allowances in the foreign country, withholding taxes, double tax relief in home country
- Inflation
- Exchange rates – if sterling falls in value, NPV in sterling rises because each unit of foreign currency translates back into a higher amount of sterling
- Reduction in exports (as direct production in the foreign country will account for the sales instead)
- Subsidies
- Exchange restrictions
- Transaction costs

Risks to consider

Transaction risk – future transaction in a foreign currency

Translation risk – impact on translation of foreign subsidiary's accounts

Economic risk – longer term exchange rate movements and impact on sales and present value.

Economic risk can affect the company even if it does not trade via foreign currency transactions by affecting competitiveness of imports and other costs

Political risk – quotes, tariffs, legal, safety, expropriation

Cultural risk – unfamiliar language, customs and laws – ignorance of how business transactions take place, media

Pensions – Strategic Impact, Accounting and Auditing

Strategic Impact

May retain loyalty of staff if based on years served and rewards more highly weighted to employees with a long employment record

Accounting

Impact on financial statements

Acquisition of a company with a defined benefits scheme

In an exam scenario, more likely to be a net liability (deficit) assumed

Business risk – company will need to consider how to fund this deficit – this will affect reported profits

Business risk – uncertainty as to the contributions needed in future (unlike a defined contribution scheme)

Financial risk – value of assets affected by market factors such as share price movements and interest rate changes – higher market interest rates will reduce the value of the bonds held

Need to report under IAS 19 Employee Benefits: report net obligation (asset or liability) and annual cost of the scheme (depending on the contributions of the employer into the fund, changes in asset values and changes in the FV of the present value of future obligations) – this element is not predictable and is likely to vary

Then consider materiality – is the pension issue a big issue?

Changes in the terms of membership of a defined benefit plan may give rise to a plan amendment, curtailment or settlement – if this occurs, the current service cost and the net interest for the period after the re-measurement must be determined using the assumptions used for the remeasurement rather than the assumptions determined at the beginning of the period

Auditing

Obtain client permission to liaise with the actuary and review the actuary's professional qualification

Agree the validity and accuracy of the actuarial valuation

Agree that the actuarial valuation method satisfies the accounting objectives of IAS 19

Review the assumptions made by the actuary e.g. on the expected return on assets

Agree the completeness of the actuarial valuation

Identify major events that should have been taken into account

Scrutinise relevant correspondence

Review minutes of board meetings

Agree opening balances to last year's working papers

Reconcile closing balance provision to the opening SFP

Agree contributions to the cash book and to the funding rate recommended by the actuary in the most recent actuarial valuation

Check that disclosures comply with the requirements of IAS 19

Pricing Strategies

Price penetration

Gain **market share** by setting a low price **initially** to enter the market and get the brand name known amongst as many consumers as possible

Can also help gain **economies of scale**

A **temporary** policy – prices need to be **increased** later to generate profit if sales are being made at full cost price – may be **difficult to increase the price** once this lower price has been established

Low initial prices could **damage** the **brand name**

Price skimming

The initial price is set **high** for **new** products launched into a market and a **smaller** market share is normally gained but at a **greater** margin

Company charges **higher prices** when a product is **first** launched – then spends **heavily** on **advertising and sales promotion** to win customers

Company then **lowers** its prices later to attract more **price-elastic** segments of the market – these price **reductions** are **gradual**

Should generate a **higher** sales volume at a **higher** price

Price could be taken as a **signal of quality** and **image** of the product – therefore a **high price** is **not** necessarily a **bad** thing

Choosing a pricing strategy

The **choice** of strategy should be based on **market research** – a **trial** or A/B testing (using one strategy in one location/market and another strategy elsewhere) could also be used

Professional Scepticism

Forecasts are inherently unreliable and may change

Missing variables and information

Seasonality

Are assumptions in line with **trend**?

Query the weak points of the **methodology** (accounting profit-based, NPV, payback)

Forecast period too long or too short

Source of information – just one view, press report, any reason for the information to be **biased**?

Initial discussions only? Nothing confirmed

Capacity – is this **practical** and **possible** for the business?

How has the **cost of capital** been arrived at? **How** has the estimate of **g** been arrived at? Absolutely key variables

Need for **independent assurance on key figures** before making a decision

Ability and **knowledge** of **staff** who prepared forecasts

Unrecognised assets and liabilities

Perpetuity assumption (including assumption of continual growth) is unrealistic

> For example, sustaining a particular % increase in incremental cash flows over a long period of time is unlikely

Proposal is **too much of a change** for the company e.g. merging companies in 2 completely different markets

Contract negotiations – a customer may request lower **prices** but promise that this will be compensated for by greater **volumes** – the lower price will be built into the contract (and so will definitely happen) whereas the volume response may be unknown if not built into the contract – the customer may be making unrealistic promises simply to obtain a better price

See also Q1 – Technique Reminders 354

Project Management

Aspects to monitor

1. Targets
2. Timing
3. Cost and keeping within budget
4. Risks and risk management

1. Targets

Should achieve performance targets

Should relate to procedures, systems and outcomes

Design, test and implement operating procedures that achieve certain performance standards

Draw up a list of key targets when the project is initiated

Progress towards each of the targets should be monitored

2. Timing

Complete the project in the planned time

Break down the overall project into activities with estimated times

Critical path chart can be used to monitor progress and ensure that time-critical activities are given the most attention

Consider allocating more resources to critical activities if needed

Identify possible delays in advance

3. Cost and keeping within budget

Break down the budget into time periods, comparing actual costs with budgeted costs

4. Risk and risk management

Consider operational risks with the project work

Create a system to identify and assess risk

Suitable and effective internal controls

Ask internal auditors or an external firm to review the effectiveness of the planned internal controls

See also		
	Change – Definition & Models	101
	Change – Management & Implementation	103
	Organisational Structures	324

Prospective Information (ISAE 3400)

Exam examples

Skeleton Outline of ISAE 3400 Points to Include

The available model answers always include the following points:

Statement that reporting on prospective information is covered by ISAE 3400 *The Examination of Prospective Financial Information*

Statement that ISAE 3400 highlights that prospective information is based on assumptions about the future and is therefore highly subjective – judgement is required in its preparation

Definition of a "forecast" and of a "projection"

Procedures must be used to obtain sufficient appropriate evidence that

> management's best-estimate assumptions are not unreasonable and that any hypothetical assumptions are consistent with the purpose of the information. Then apply these points by referring to the scenario.
>
> the information has been properly prepared on the basis of the assumptions. Then apply these points by referring to the scenario.
>
> the information is properly presented and all material assumptions are adequately disclosed, including a clear indication as to whether they are best-estimate assumptions or hypothetical assumptions. Then apply these points by referring to the scenario.
>
> the information is prepared on a consistent basis with historical financial statements, using appropriate accounting principles. Then apply these points by referring to the scenario.

Statement that as prospective financial information is subjective, it is impossible to give the same level of assurance regarding forecasts as can be provided regarding historical information e.g. may be over a significant future time horizon, which creates uncertainty

Procedures are used to support limited assurance in the form of a negatively expressed opinion in relation to whether

> the assumptions provide a reasonable basis for the prospective financial information
>
> the information is properly prepared on the basis of the assumptions and relevant reporting framework

Appropriate caveats should be given as to the achievability of any forecasts, together with examples from the scenario as to why they may not be achieved.

General notes

A **forecast** is prospective financial information based on assumptions as to future events which management expects to take place and the actions which management expects to take: it is a best-estimate

A **projection** is based on hypothetical assumptions and scenarios, rather than events which management necessarily expects to happen

ISAE 3400 governs the reporting of prospective financial information. Under this standard, there should be agreement with the directors regarding the intended use of the information, whether the information will be distributed generally, the types of assumptions used, the elements to be included in the information and the period covered by the information

The opinion expressed should be in the form of a **negative and limited assurance opinion** that nothing has come to the practitioner's attention to doubt the assumptions and proper preparation of the information – caveats should be indicated – assurance given is not to the same standard as for historical statements – as with any forecast, it is important to recognise that assumptions may subsequently prove incorrect even if they were completely reasonable at the time of formulation

The practitioner/auditor must have sufficient knowledge of the business. The assurance provided is **limited** and **negative** in nature.

The options of a **qualified**, **adverse** or **disclaimer of opinion** are available

The procedures for reporting on prospective information noted in the Corporate Reporting Study Manual can be split into 2 types: general and specific

General procedures involve obtaining sufficient appropriate evidence regarding whether management's best-estimate assumptions are not unreasonable and consistent with the purpose of the information. It should also be determined whether the prospective financial information is properly prepared and presented and whether the information is consistent with the historical financial statements

Specific procedures are provided for the areas of profits, capital expenditure and cash flows.

Review of profit forecasts: procedures

- verify projected income figures to suitable evidence, including comparison of the basis of projected income to similar existing projects in the firm

- reviewing competitor prices for the relevant product or service to determine whether projected information is reasonable

- verify projected expenditure figures to suitable evidence, such as quotations or estimates, current bills, interest rate assumptions or costs such as depreciation

- check assumptions about annual revenues based on market prices and estimates of costs and how these have been divided into fixed and variable elements

Review of capital expenditure forecasts: procedures

- check capital expenditure for reasonableness by ensuring that all relevant costs are included and that costs estimated are reasonable
- verify projected costs to estimates and quotations
- review projections for reasonableness by examining the prevailing market rates
- verify that there is evidence that the required capital assets can be located and purchased

Review of cashflow forecasts: procedures

- review cash forecasts to determine whether the timings involved are reasonable
- check the cash forecast for consistency with profit forecasts, looking at both the expenditure and income side or undertake some other method of verification if there is no relevant or comparable profit forecast

Testing of Prospective Information (past paper review from *Smashing SBM*™)

- is there a **lack of information from the client** on exactly what level of detail will be published (and therefore on the subject matter of the assurance engagement) – scepticism and risk issue
- the **terms of the engagement should be agreed in advance** – the terms would probably involve an arrangement to test the assumptions that management has used in making the forecasts
- **ISAE 3400 provides the guidelines** for this sort of assurance engagement
- **forecasts will be based on assumptions**, generally including historical information
- the practitioner needs to satisfy itself about the **reliability of any historical information** that has been used as the basis of the forecasts
- the practitioner should consider the **reasonableness of the assumptions** that have been used to prepare the forecast **and that the forecast has in fact been prepared on the basis of those assumptions** (and correctly so)
- the **assumptions must be stated as part of the published forecast**
- **predicting the future is a speculative matter** and can lead to errors if events turn out differently
- therefore the assurance provider's task cannot be to say whether the results will be "correct" or turn out as planned – rather **the practitioner's role is instead to consider whether the assumptions are free from any material misstatement or weakness**

- if the **assumptions appear to be unrealistic**, then the assurance provider **should not accept or continue with the assurance engagement**
- if historical information has been used as the basis for making the forecast then it would be necessary to **check whether the information has been audited** or to obtain other evidence of its reliability
- the report provided at the end of the engagement should include a **statement of negative assurance** as to whether the assumptions used provide a reasonable basis for making the forecast
- the report should **contain an opinion as to whether the forecast has been properly prepared** based on these assumptions
- **caveats should be included regarding the prospective nature of the results** and therefore the fact that the figures included may not necessarily be achievable

See also Professional Scepticism 347

Provisions and Reorganisations

IAS 37 conditions:

Legal or constructive obligation as a result of a past event, and

Probable that an outflow of economic benefits will occur

Exam tip

Look carefully at the dates involved and exactly what the Board has done or (not done) to communicate reorganisation plans to stakeholders

Note that it is possible for there to be some uncertainty as to whether a provision exists – this may need to be discussed

See also Liquidation 309

Q1 – Technique Reminders

Since we know that Q1 will always be at least 60% of the marks available, this is a very important question so we provide some specific reminders here*

In Q1 DO:

Use a table of data at the start of the answer

Use the scenario-specific indicators/performance measures thoroughly – do not just look at standard points such as gross profit margin or revenue growth

Calculate additional scenario-specific metrics

Look for cause and effect relationships and describe these

Try to separate out different divisions/revenue streams and find something different to say on each one

Look for interconnections between parts of the business

Use appropriate headings – consider a separate section for each set of affected stakeholders

Provide a reasonable and clear discussion of the actions to be taken

Exercise professional scepticism over figures, especially forceasts

Separately and clearly identify your answer to each Task and sub-Task

Start each Task on a new page with a clear heading

Use the estimated mark allocation in Q1 to inform your estimate in Q2 – the marks will balance across the standard allocation*, being

Topic	Standard weighting
Strategy	35-45%
Finance, valuations & investment appraisal	30-40%
Financial reporting[8]	15-20%
Assurance	10%
Ethics	5-10%

In Q1 DO NOT:

Forget to use the data thoroughly – everything needs to be driven by the data given

[8] The examiners generally use the term "corporate reporting" to refer to this angle or perspective but because we think this may lead to confusion with the separate Corporate Reporting ACA paper, we have adopted the term "financial reporting" to refer to this perspective. By "financial reporting" we do **not** just mean the lessons that you learned in the Financial Accounting and Reporting paper but also the new IFRS corporate reporting rules that you learn at the Advanced Level.

Forget to explain why things have changed

Waste time on trivial issues – look at the important issues and changes

Start copying out lists of standard points (including from this book!) – ensure you are **applying** everything to the question set – to ensure that you are applying the point, try to quote the data (numbers, narrative, people, products) back to the examiner in your sentences to show that you have read and used the data

Mix your calculations randomly into the discussion – have a separate table of figures at the start

Forget to look out for the examiner "twists" – can you just list out the standard points on hedging or is there a twist here? Is it a net asset valuation where fair value has already been taken into account (defeating this standard point)?

Forget to look for all Tasks – these are not necessarily just listed at the end of the section (e.g. SBM November 2014 past paper)

* See our book *Smashing SBM*™ for further explanation of our strategy to Q1 and for justification of our statement that Q2 will provide a "balancing" of the marks across the SBM topic areas within the table of syllabus weightings indicated above

See also	Financial Performance Review in SBM – Some Advice	200
	Ratios – Calculations	356

Ratios – Calculations

Important notice: we are including these for reference only – do not spend too long on the numbers – **choose only the most relevant ratios** – at the same time, in SBM do not expect the question wording to remind you to use ratios.

Always start by first using the scenario-specific indicators given in the question (e.g. the client's own internal performance metrics) and only move onto these more "generic" analysis points after the scenario-specific indicators have been thoroughly used.

Performance

$$gross\ profit\ margin = \frac{gross\ profit}{revenue}\ x\ 100\%$$

Replace gross profit with **operating profit to arrive at operating profit margin**. This allows you to see whether cost of sales (gross profit) or admin costs (net profit) are more significant as a constraint on returns

$$return\ on\ capital\ employed\ [ROCE] =$$

$$\frac{PBIT + associate's\ post\ tax\ earnings}{equity + net\ debt}$$

Net debt = interest-bearing debt (current and non-current) less cash and cash equivalents

Equity = exclude redeemable preference shares, in line with general treatment as a loan, not equity

$$return\ on\ equity\ [ROE] = \frac{profit\ before\ tax}{equity\ or\ net\ assets}\ x\ 100\%$$

Note that ROE is quicker to calculate than ROCE and with less chance of error – ROE was used in the model answer to the November 2015 past paper

$$return\ on\ shareholders'funds\ [ROSF]$$

$$= \frac{profit\ attributable\ to\ owners\ of\ parent}{equity\ less\ NCI}$$

Profit attributable to owners of parent will usually be profit after tax

Note the difference: ROCE uses profit *before* tax; ROSF uses profit *after* tax

You can remember this by thinking of ROSF as measure of what the shareholders get i.e. after tax, whereas ROCE is more of a measure of the capacity of the business to generate a return, and tax is then a subsequent cost to be considered later

Exam tip ROSF is usually quicker and easier to calculate; you can then comment that ROSF only looks at equity as a source of resources

Liquidity

$$current\ ratio = \frac{current\ assets}{current\ liabilities}$$

Usually expressed as a multiple e.g. 3x (equivalent to 6/2)

$$quick\ ratio = \frac{current\ assets\ less\ inventories}{current\ liabilities}$$

Basically, the current ratio adjusted for inventories as these cannot be turned into cash very **quickly**.

Long-term solvency

$$gearing = \frac{net\ debt\ as\ per\ ROCE}{equity\ as\ per\ ROCE}\ x\ 100\%$$

$$interest\ cover = \frac{PBIT\ plus\ investment\ income}{interest\ payable}$$

Efficiency

$$net\ asset\ turnover = \frac{revenue}{capital\ employed}$$

$$receivables\ period = \frac{trade\ receivables}{revenue}\ x\ 365\ days$$

$$payables\ period = \frac{trade\ payables}{cost\ of\ sales}\ x\ 365\ days$$

Strictly, use credit purchases but usually you will have to use cost of sales

Investor ratios

$$dividend\ cover = \frac{earnings\ per\ share}{dividend\ per\ share}$$

$$price\ earnings\ ratio = \frac{market\ price\ per\ share}{earnings\ per\ share}$$

Other ratios

$$CAPEX\ to\ depreciation = \frac{capital\ expenditure\ (CAPEX)}{depreciation}$$

Measures whether new expenditure compensates for depreciation.

$$non - current\ asset\ ageing = \frac{accumulated\ depreciation}{non - current\ assets\ at\ cost}$$

Allows an estimate of how far non-current assets are through their working lives. e.g. if depreciation is £2m and the assets cost £4m, then we are 2/4 = 50% through its working life.

Note: the above two ratios require data on depreciation. Hence they are subject to the depreciation method/charge decided upon by management (i.e. subjective).

$$dividend\ yield = \frac{dividend\ per\ share}{current\ market\ price\ per\ share}\ x\ 100\%$$

Cash flow ratios

Least likely to be possible to calculate in SBM but included for completeness

Note: the concept of “cash return” is important here and is used in several ratios

cash return = cash generated from ops + interest received + dividends received

$$cash\ ROCE = \frac{cash\ return}{capital\ employed}x\ 100\%$$

$$cash\ from\ operations\ as\ \%\ of\ profit\ from\ operations = \frac{cash\ return}{profit\ from\ operations}x100\%$$

$$cash\ interest\ cover = \frac{cash\ return}{interest\ paid}$$

$$cash\ flow\ per\ share = \frac{cash\ return - int\ paid - tax\ paid}{number\ of\ ordinary\ shares}$$

$$cash\ dividend\ cover = \frac{cash\ return - int\ paid - tax\ paid}{equity\ dividends\ paid}$$

Only look at equity dividends.

The result of (cash return – int paid – tax paid) is also known as “cash flow for ordinary shareholders”.

Impact of classification as a financial liability

If a financial instrument is classified as a financial liability, it will be reported within current or non-current liabilities

Non-current liabilities are relevant to determining an entity's gearing i.e. the proportion of debt finance versus equity finance of the business

The amount of gearing helps to identify the risk to ordinary equity holders – additionally, companies with high gearing may also find it harder to get financing or financing may be at a higher interest rate – high gearing is particularly unpopular in the current economic climate and there have been high-profile cases of companies that have been pressed to sell off parts of their business to reduce their "debt mountains"

Distributions relating to instruments classified as financial liabilities are categorised as finance costs, having an impact on reported profitability

Classification can have a financial implication for a business – for example, debt covenants on loans from financial institutions often contain clauses that reported gearing cannot exceed a stated figure, with penalties or call-in clauses if it does

Impact of classification as equity

If a financial instrument is classified as equity, reported gearing will be lower than if it were classified as a financial liability

However, classification as equity is sometimes viewed negatively as it can be seen as a dilution of existing equity interests

Distributions on instruments classified as equity are charged to equity and therefore do not affect reported profit

If a company elects for changes in the value of an equity instrument to be recorded in OCI, rather than profit or loss, this will affect key profitability ratios – the requirement for such an election to be irrevocable prevents manipulation by booking gains to the P&L one year and losses to OCI in the following year

See also Financial Performance Review in SBM – Some Advice 200
Q1 – Technique Reminders 354

Real Options

These options are traditionally not considered with traditional investment appraisal analysis but they are important

Option to delay

Option to expand

Option to abandon

Option to redeploy

Product options (patents, copyrights and natural resource ownership)

See also Investment Appraisal Methods topics
Valuation topics

Recommendations – Keeping It Practical

Follow the 8 areas applied in the ACA Case Study – these points should often work in both SBM and Case Study so you can "kill 2 birds with 1 stone" through learning the list below well:

1. Pricing
2. Cost reduction
3. Timing
4. Impact on staff
5. Capacity
6. Further information
7. Discuss and negotiate
8. Consider alternatives

Remuneration Strategies

Retention of talent – policy needs to ensure sufficient incentives for talented managers and staff to remain at the company

Rolling nature – a rolling set of incentives (with increases and new incentives issued each year) should help as a staff member may lose options or opportunities if he or she leaves the company

Goal congruence – the package should ensure that there is alignment of the interests of managers and shareholders so that what benefits the manager will also benefit the company

Value of share options – must be set in such a way that the exercise price should be below the market price at the end of the vesting period: otherwise there is no benefit to the employee

Controllability – the employee/manager must have some control over the variable which is the basis of the incentive or the employee/manager will not have a reason to improve performance

Cash savings – some incentives such as share options or bonuses payable in several years' time will preserve cash in the short run whilst still improving performance and therefore generating cash

Impact on EPS – this will need to be considered – for example, share options need to be included in the calculation of diluted EPS

Elements

Basic pay

Performance-related bonuses

Shares

Share options – align stakeholder and employee interests

Benefits in kind

Pensions

Behavioural Objectives

Support recruitment and retention

Motivate employees to high levels of performance

Should promote compliance with business rules and strategy

Always consider the impact on motivation and commitment of employees

Director remuneration – use of options

You should first use the question Exhibit material to assess whether the monetary value involved in the share options suggests that the options could be significant enough to impact upon the incentives of directors in making decisions (we would expect that in most exam scenarios, the options would have such a material impact as otherwise there would not be anything worthwhile to say in the rest of your answer! Even so, make reference to the monetary figures involved, including via a quick calculation if required, in order to pick up skills marks)

Share options can be used to align management and shareholder interests, particularly in the case of options held for a long time when value is dependent on long-term performance

The UK Corporate Governance Code states that shares granted (or other forms of remuneration) should not vest or be exercisable in fewer than 3 years in order to ensure that incentives are given not just for short-term performance – you could then look at the vesting period involved in the question Exhibit material and make an appropriate statement here

If directors or employees are granted a number of options in one package, these options should not all be able to be first exercised at the same date – this could promote short-termist behaviour around the exercise date to manipulate the share price (including financial statement disclosures and measurements) if a large number of options are due to be exercised

Share options may give an incentive to align the risk preferences of directors and shareholders but in some cases directors may reject an opportunity which could benefit shareholders because directors are exposed to the risks of an investment failing – additionally, where options are in the money, directors may become more risk averse as they could become afraid of losing key related past gains, particularly given the volatility of option prices

On the other hand, if the options are out of the money, directors may be incentivised to make risky decisions as there is then upside potential if they increase the share price and limited downside potential because the options will expire worthless under the current position i.e. directors have nothing to lose in relation to the options

If the options become significantly out of the money then they may need to be renegotiated or else they would fail to provide any relevant incentives for decision-making – here you could refer to the dates involved in the question Exhibit material and comment on how long is left to expiry (for example, in SBM July 2019 past paper Q2, the model answer states that the company's options (which were out of the money) were not yet at the stage where renegotiation was required because there were nearly 2 more years remaining before expiry)

More generally, an increase in volatility according to the Black-Scholes-Merton model will increase the value of options so directors are incentivised to take risky business decisions

See also

Bonuses – Audit Procedures	84
Change – Definition & Models	101
Change – Management & Implementation	103

Reporting on Information Contained in a Prospectus

Regulated by ISAE 3420, a project undertaken in the context of the increasing globalisation of capital markets which makes it important for financial information to be understandable across borders and for related assurance to be provided

“Pro forma financial information” is defined as financial information shown together with adjustments to illustrate the impact of an event or transaction on unadjusted financial information

The practitioner’s sole responsibility is to report on whether the pro forma financial information has been compiled in all material respects by the responsible party on the basis of applicable criteria – the practitioner has no responsibility to compile pro forma information

The practitioner must perform procedures to assess when the applicable criteria used in the compilation of the pro forma information provide a reasonable basis for presenting the significant effects directly attributable to the potential event or transaction – this work must also involve an evaluation of the overall presentation of the pro forma financial information

Under ISAE 3420 the following opinion wording is permitted (2 alternatives are allowed):

"The pro forma financial information has been compiled, in all material respects, on the basis of the (applicable criteria)"

"The pro forma financial information has been properly compiled on the basis stated"

The FRC has also issued guidance in this area in Standard for Investment Reporting (SIR) 1000 *Investment Reporting Standards Applicable to Engagements in Connection with an Investment Circular*

An investment circular is defined as any document issued by an entity pursuant to statutory or regulatory requirements relating to securities on which it is intended that the third party should make an investment decision, including a prospectus, listing particulars, a circular to shareholders or similar document

The approach which the practitioner is required to take under SIR 1000 is similar to that of a statutory audit:

- agree the terms
- comply with ethical requirements and quality control standards
- plan the work and consider materiality
- obtain sufficient appropriate evidence
- document significant matters

adopt an attitude of professional scepticism

express an opinion (modified if required)

Revenue accounting (IFRS 15)

IFRS 15 – replacing IAS 18

Important note – for **exam purposes**, as IFRS 15 has now replaced IAS 18, you should only refer to IAS 18 **if you are asked to do so specifically in the question** (for example, as a current issue with regard to how future accounting periods may be affected by a switch in standards)

Weaknesses of IAS 18 and IAS 11 include:

- **timing of revenue recognition** – there is a lack of clear guidance in the current standards particularly regarding combined packages of goods and services because goods are sold at a point in time whereas services may be provided over time
- **distinguishing between goods and services** – IFRS accounting does not clearly distinguish between goods and services so some companies may not be sure whether to apply IAS 18 or IAS 11 but these standards are very different
- **multielement arrangements** – these transactions involve the delivery of more than 1 good or service – IFRS does not give sufficient guidance on dealing with such transactions

IFRS 15 will therefore **replace** IAS 18, IAS 11 and IFRIC 13

Significance of IFRS 15 to examination candidates (comments from the 2020 edition of the Corporate Reporting Study Manual)

IFRS 15 is a recent, topical standard and could be tested in a number of ways

It was first examined in CR July 2019 Question 3 when it formed a large part of the content of this audit and financial reporting question

The question focused mainly on performance obligations satisfied (or not satisfied) over time and was set in the context of financial reporting (comment on recognition policy), risk of misstatement and a potential ethical issue (breach of contract)

Reference was also made to data analytics, which could be a focus of future questions on revenue

The IFRS 15 five step model

1. identify the **contract** with the customer
2. identify the **separate performance obligations** in the contract
3. determine the **transaction price** – this is the amount to which the entity expects to be "entitled" – for variable consideration, the probability weighted expected amount is used – the effect of any credit losses is shown as a separate line item (just below revenue)
4. **allocate** the transaction price to the **separate performance obligations** in the contract

5. **recognise revenue** when (or as) the entity **satisfies a performance obligation** – this is when the entity transfers a promised good or service to a customer – the good or service is only considered to be transferred when the customer obtains control of it

Example of IFRS 15 recognition of a combined contract

A company offers a software package to customers.

The company can supply and install the software for £2,000 and offers a separate 2-year technical support service for £1,000. The company offers a combined contract which includes both of these elements for £2,400. Payment for the combined contract is due 1 month after the installation.

When a combined contract is sold, revenue in respect of the supply and installation should be recognised at the time of installation. Revenue for the technical support should be recognised over 2 years. This is because the performance obligation for the installation is satisfied when the package is supplied but the performance obligation for the support service is satisfied over time.

The company should recognise £1,600 at the time of installation, calculated based on the proportion of value relating to the installation within the total package, applying the normal stand-alone pricing. In this case, the installation is worth a proportion of 2,000/(2,000+1,000) or 2/3 of the normal stand-alone pricing: 2/3 of £2,400 (the price of the combined contract) is £1,600.

Impact of the IFRS 15 approach

By far the most significant change is to the **pattern** of revenue reporting – even if the total revenue reported does not change, the **timing will change** in many cases

Separate performance obligations will be recognised for distinct goods or services – this will mean some revenue being attributed to goods or services that are currently considered incidental to the contract.

For example, under IFRS 15 revenue may be allocated to mobile phones that are provided free of charge with airtime contracts and to some post delivery services such as maintenance and installation

The **transaction price will be allocated in proportion to the stand-alone selling price** – this will affect some practices, particularly in the software sector, that currently result in the deferral of revenue if a company does not have objective evidence of the selling price of the good or service to be provided

Revenue recognition and fraud

Some of the most high-profile accounting scandals have involved manipulation of revenue – some companies have adopted questionable practices concerning the reporting of revenue as part of aggressive earnings management policies

IFRS 15 is therefore designed to be an effective and credible accounting standard on revenue

Timing of revenue recognition

IFRS 15 states that revenue is recognised to depict the transfer of promised goods and services to customers

Revenue is therefore generally recognised as being earned at the point of sale for goods – in the case of services, revenue is, in general, recognised over the period that the service is delivered

The recognition criteria in IFRS 15 are usually applied separately to each transaction

However, in some circumstances it is necessary to apply the recognition criteria to the separately identifiable components of a single transaction in order to reflect the substance of the transaction – IFRS 15 refers to the separately identifiable components as "separate performance obligations"

Discounts

IFRS 15 requires that the transaction price should take into account the amount of any trade discounts and volume rebates allowed by the entity – the discount should be allocated proportionately to the performance obligations in the contract

Accounting for customer loyalty programmes

IFRS 15 requires that separately identifiable performance obligations are accounted for separately – this suggests that when a loyalty card customer buys a product or service, the proceeds of the sale should be split into 2 components: an amount reflecting the value of the goods or services delivered in the sale and an amount which reflects the value of the loyalty award credits

Example of accounting for customer loyalty programmes

The allocation should also take into account the likelihood of customers actually claiming the loyalty points – for example, if there are total reward points with a face value of £5 million at the year-end but only 2 in 5 customers are expected to actually redeem their points then the value of the points should be calculated as £2 million (i.e. £5m x 2 / 5)

Once the correct value of the reward points (taking into account the probability of actual claim) has been calculated, this should be added to the revenue on the underlying sales for apportionment purposes – for example, if there is total underlying revenue of £100 million on equipment sales plus £2m of loyalty point value (after taking into account the probability of actual claim) then the allocation would be as follows:

Equipment sales	100 / 102 x 100	98.04
Loyalty points	2 / 102 x 100	1.96
		100.00

In substance, customers are implicitly paying for the reward points they receive when they buy other goods and services and hence some of the total revenue should be allocated to the points as a separate performance obligation

In the above example, £98.04 million would be recognised as revenue for the year and the balance of £1.96 million would be recognised as a contract liability (deferred revenue) in the SFP until the reward points are actually redeemed

Revenue auditing (IFRS 15)

[Following the replacement of IAS 18 by IFRS 15 with effect from the 2019 Advanced Level syllabus and therefore in the absence of many available model answers on IFRS 15, the following set of audit procedures has been created by summarising the new Audit focus section found at the end of chapter 10 of the 2019 Corporate Reporting Study Manual]

Step 1 – identify the contract(s) with a customer

- obtain copies of contracts between entities and customers
- inspect contracts to confirm they are legally binding and effective for the year of audit
- for implied contracts such as retail contracts, clarify the likely contractual terms to establish rights and responsibilities in each case

Step 2 – identify separate performance obligations

- confirm the goods or services to be transferred, either individually or as part of a series, by reference to the contracts in place
- confirm whether any of the goods or services are not distinct by reference to the contracts in place and if separate bundles

Step 3 – determine the transaction price

- identify the amount of consideration by reference to the contract
- where appropriate, confirm the split between variable and fixed elements and recalculate any variable amounts by reference to the contract terms
- test the hypothesis that variable consideration is highly probable by reviewing the reasonableness of the underlying assumptions used in the entity's calculations

Step 4 – allocate transaction price to performance obligations

- confirm stand-alone prices to individual elements of the contract as performance obligations are settled
- in the case of estimated stand-alone prices, test the assumptions underpinning the calculations used by the entity for reasonableness

Step 5 – recognise revenue as or when each performance obligation is satisfied

For performance obligations satisfied at a point in time (such as retail sales) confirm the occurrence of the event required (such as the sale itself) by reference to supporting documentation

In the case of performance obligations satisfied over time:

- confirm contract price to contract agreed between client and customer
- determine any amounts of conditional revenue/cost including the associated conditions
- confirm the progress to date of the work completed, including any potential delays or problems
- confirm costs incurred to date (inputs) by reference to management accounts, invoices, budgets and other relevant documentation
- identify any expenditure not supporting fulfilment of the contract by inspecting board minutes, management accounts or other documentation (such as legal correspondence)
- confirm total costs estimated for contract to ensure no planned overspends have been identified (again, budgets, board minutes or management accounts can be inspected)

- confirm the amount of contract work certified as complete (outputs) at the year end by reference to relevant documentation such as surveyors reports or client estimates

Other tests

For deferred consideration, confirm the proportion split between the value of the goods on the date of sale and financing income by reference to the contract and test the reasonableness of the entity's calculations for recognising revenue (such as interest rates for estimating fair value)

Consignment arrangements

Consider the existence of any indicators of consignment arrangements such as confirming who controls the product and what (if any) conditions need to have occurred for control to be passed on and by clarifying who can require the return of a product or transfer it to a third party

Bill and hold arrangements

Consider the existence of such arrangements and if present, review the conditions required by IFRS 15 have been met by confirming that the customer owns the products stored by the seller by reference to the contract terms, and obtain confirmation from the customer that they are happy for the seller to hold them

Inspect the agreement between the seller and customer to confirm that the products can be accessed at any time and not transferred to another customer

Review Engagements (ISRE 2400)

Gives a reduced degree of assurance based on a **negative assurance** statement that **nothing has come to the attention of the auditor which causes the auditor to believe that the statements have not been prepared in accordance with the relevant financial reporting framework**.

Often relates to review of **interim financial information**

ISRE 2400 provides the rules and relevant guidance for this type of review. Note that this standard has not been adopted in the UK.

Materiality should be applied in the same way as for a statutory audit.

Specific inquiries could include:

- how management makes significant accounting estimates
- identification of related parties and related party transactions
- consideration of significant, unusual or complex transactions
- actual or suspected fraud
- whether management has identified and addressed events after the reporting period
- the basis of management's assessment of going concern
- material commitments, contractual obligations or contingencies
- material non-monetary transactions or transactions for no consideration in the reporting period

Analytical procedures should be used to help the practitioner to:

- obtain or update an understanding of the entity and its environment
- identify inconsistencies or variances from expected trends, values or norms
- provide corroborative evidence in relation to inquiry or other analytical procedures
- serve as additional procedures when the practitioner becomes aware of matters that indicate that the financial statements may be materially misstated

The practitioner should also determine whether the data available is adequate for the above purposes.

A typical practitioner's review report should contain the following headings/report sections:

- **report on the financial statements** – statement regarding which set of statements has been reviewed
- **management's responsibility for the financial statements**
- **practitioner's responsibility**
- **conclusion**

The conclusion can be **qualified**, **adverse** or a **disclaimer** of a conclusion based on the usual rules applicable to a statutory audit and considering whether the matter is pervasive or not.

Suspected non-compliance with laws and regulations

Under ISRE 2400, the practitioner should follow 5 steps if there is a suspicion of non-compliance with laws and regulations:

Communicate the matter to the appropriate level of management/those charged with governance

Request management's assessment of the effects, if any, on the financial statements

Consider the implications for the practitioner's report

Determine whether law, regulation or ethical requirements require that the matter should be reported to a third party outside the entity

Determine whether law, regulation or ethical requirements establish responsibilities under which reporting to an authority outside the entity may be appropriate

The practitioner should always consult internally, obtain legal advice and consult with the regulator or professional body in order to understand the implications of different courses of action

Review of interim financial information (common focus of a review engagement) – procedures

- reading last year's audit file and considering any significant risks identified
- reading the most recent and comparable interim financial information
- considering materiality
- considering the nature of any corrected or uncorrected misstatements in last year's financial statements

- considering significant financial accounting and reporting matters of ongoing importance
- considering the results of any interim audit work for this year's audit
- considering the work of internal audit
- reading management accounts and commentaries for the period
- considering any findings from prior periods
- asking management what their assessment of the risk of fraud in the interim financial statements may be
- asking management whether there have been any significant changes in internal controls or business activity
- reading the minutes of meetings of shareholders, those charged with governance or other appropriate committees
- considering the effect of matters giving rise to a modification of the audit or review report and accounting adjustments
- communicating with other auditors that audit different components of the business
- performing analytical procedures designed to identify relationships and unusual items that may reflect a material misstatement
- reading the interim financial information and considering whether anything has come to the auditors' attention indicating that it has not been prepared in accordance with the applicable financial reporting framework
- agreeing the interim financial information to the underlying accounting records
- reviewing consolidation adjustments for consistency and reviewing relevant correspondence with regulators
- inquire with the members of management responsible for financial and accounting matters regarding issues such as the applicable reporting framework, changes in accounting policies, significant misstatements, fair value assumptions, compliance with debt covenants and fraud issues, amongst others

Comparative information should be considered to determine whether this is consistent with that presented in the interim financial statements.

Written representations should be obtained from management in which management recognises its responsibility for the design and implementation of internal controls and that significant facts relating to frauds or non-compliance with law and regulations have been disclosed to the auditor and that all significant subsequent events have been disclosed to the auditor.

The format of the report should be very similar to the above noted format for review engagements: relevant sections to include in the report would be:

- Introduction
- Directors' Responsibilities
- Practitioner's Responsibilities
- Scope of the Review
- Conclusion

See also Cash Flow Forecasts – Evaluation 100

Risks – Governance

Aspects to consider

The governance structure must be reviewed as the business grows and changes

Governance structures between a single person or entrepreneurial structure and a larger corporate structure are very different

Consider implications of listing, if appropriate – the UK Corporate Governance Code may be applicable although there is an exemption for AIM-listed companies and more limited exemptions for non-FTSE 350 companies

Consider the size of the board and the skills

Are there any independent directors who are not shareholders?

Are there any NEDs (Non-Executive Directors)? A complete lack of NEDs would be unusual for a large company

Is there any remuneration committee, and nomination committee or an audit committee, if the company is a large? These committees give shareholders more control and insights into the actions of the directors

Is the remuneration policy transparent, certain and one that ensures **goal congruence** between different stakeholders? (are directors rewarded more if shareholder wealth is promoted, for example?)

Are there any rotation periods? Do these appear reasonable?

Are powers and voting rights clear and transparent?

Is there any risk of a split board and therefore an inability to get anything done?

If the question relates to an acquisition, always consider shareholdings and voting percentages before and after the business change?

Risk assurance

Changes in the external environment such as new regulations or development of new technologies mean that organisations face a changing, and increasingly complex, risk environment

A challenge which this presents for Boards is to ensure that they identify the key risks facing their business and have those risks under control

This could be particularly important in the context of cyber risks, hacking and data breaches where, in line with GDPR requirements, businesses need to be able to demonstrate that they have appropriate safeguards in place if a data breach should occur

The Board should therefore ensure that it adequately assesses the risks that the company faces – potentially, an additional "risk" could be that a Board's assumptions about the risks the company faces do not accurately reflect the risk realities

In this respect, independent assessment – either by specialist internal auditors or external advisers – could be very valuable in providing comfort that the Board has a complete view of the risks relevant to its business – having this complete view of the risks helps to ensure that the Board is then in a good position to develop appropriate risk mitigation strategies

See also Risks topics
FRC Risk Guidance 215

Risks – Horizontal Acquisition

Strategic

Overpayment if synergies do not emerge

Significantly different market

May be little or no common customer base

Customers may not continue to be loyal to the new organisation – continuance of relationships is not guaranteed

Contract renewal risk if major suppliers change their views?

Relatively low risk of understanding the market and processes as similar?

Operational

Post-acquisition integration may not deliver the synergies and operational activity that was planned – this could mean a real risk of overpayment

May be unforeseen merging costs such as compatibility of process, employee resistance, skills gaps

May be unforeseen problems in merging information systems and support processes such as accounting, HRM, IT, internal controls, supply chain management, deliveries and marketing

Sale of surplus assets may be uncertain

May be hidden contractual or other legal obligations

Hidden financial liabilities such as tax

If debt financed, then adds to the financial gearing of the group

Management skills and available time may not be as appropriate for the new group

May be issues with covenants and providers of finance with a change of use or disposal of assets

See also Risks topics

Risks – Types and Examples

Background considerations

- Risk appetite
- Culture
- Response
- Reporting
- Monitoring

TARA Framework

Transfer – transfer the risk, wholly or partly, to someone else – risk transfer is possible by means of arrangements such as insurance, credit default swaps, franchising arrangements and joint ventures

Avoid – avoid the risk entirely, usually by withdrawing from the business – businesses must accept some risks in order to make profit

Reduce – reduce the risk to an acceptable level by means of arrangements such as diversification of operations or investments, internal control over financial, operational and compliance risks and hedging with derivative instruments

Accept – accept the risk and do nothing – if the risk is not considered significant, or if future price movements are more likely to be favourable than at first, it may be appropriate to accept the risk and remain exposed to it

Diagram for TARA Framework

		Severity	
		Low	**High**
Frequency	**Low**	**Accept** Risks are not significant. Keep under review but costs of dealing with risks unlikely to be worth the benefits	**Transfer** Insure risk or implement contingency plans. Reduction of severity of risk will minimise insurance premiums
	High	**Control or reduce** Take some action e.g. enhanced control systems to detect problems or contingency plans to reduce impact	**Abandon or avoid** Take immediate action e.g. change major suppliers or abandon activities

Q46/1

Levels of risks

- Strategic
- Operating
- Financing risks

Exam tip – the above represents a very useful framework that you may wish to use

Strategic risks

- Becoming involved in an unfamiliar market
- Overpaying for an acquisition
- Failing to understand demand and supply
- Reliance on others for knowledge and skills
- Lack of strategic fit or direction
- Reputational damage
- Focusing on the wrong product/service with poor margin
- Failing to consider the opportunity cost of a project

Operating risks

- Post-integration problems in an acquisition
- Synergies failing to emerge
- Administrative integration
- Problems in integrating cultures, accounting, HRM, IT, internal controls, supply chain management, deliveries and marketing
- Hidden contractual and other legal obligations (assuming that there are no indemnities)
- Hidden financial liabilities (assuming that there are no indemnities)
- Financing methods such as debt
- Dependence on key suppliers or individuals
- Limited amount of assets against which to raise future debts
- Uncertain sales of surplus assets
- Overuse of fixed assets, causing damage due to a lack of downtime for repairs

Key general risks

- Customers
- Currency – revenue, raw material
- Economic/Market
- Transportation
- Financial
- Liquidity
- Operating

Revenue risks

Note – in SBM, may well interact with currency risks

Risk of a fall in revenue

Currency risks

Note that these risks may have offsetting effects (if revenue falls due to a high value of the domestic currency then costs of imports will fall)

Note that there is also **upside** risk – the exchange rate may move in a **more favourable** direction

Currency revenue risks

- Fixed prices but changing exchange rates
- Credit or default risk – the purchaser may fail to pay
- Order cancellation risk – can the materials/WIP be used on another project?

Currency raw material risks

- Some raw materials have very volatile and fluctuating market prices
- Changes in currency value can change import costs

Cultural risks

- Cultures and practices of customers and consumers to individual markets
- Media and distribution systems in overseas markets
- Different ways of doing business in overseas markets
- National cultural differences

Governance risks

- Structure – weak? Control methods?
- Style – entrepreneurial v corporate
- Individual management style
- Listed company – Corporate Governance Code may apply (AIM exempt; non FTSE 350 limited exemptions)
- Size of company
- Non-Executive Directors (NEDs) – independent? quality?
- Committees for remuneration, nomination and audit – exist? transparency?
- Correct balance between performance and pay
- Rotation of control/power (but not so often that lose skills)
- Changes in voting rights and power

Information technology risks

Strategic IT risks

- Loss of competitive advantage by not staying up to date
- Dependence on IT – breakdown could threaten the business
- Cost of updates etc

Operational IT risks

- Theft of information/hacking
- Penalties for non-compliance with laws e.g. Data Protection Act
- Loss of information – human error, virus

Political risks

- Government stability
- Economic stability
- Inflation
- Degree of international indebtedness
- Financial infrastructure
- Level of import restrictions
- Remittance restrictions
- Evidence of expropriation
- Special taxes or investment incentives

Dealing with political risks

- Negotiations with the host government
- Insurance such as export credit guarantees
- Production strategies such as outsourcing or producing locally
- Management structure – consider JVs, giving control to local investors to keep government happy

Operating risks

- Capacity – hitting full capacity has an opportunity cost: will have to reject new orders – also may have impact on costs and staff morale/working hours
- Transportation risks

Liquidity risks

- Timing – difference between outlays on a contract and the cash returns generated – may leave the entity short of liquid cash resources at just the wrong time

Supply chain risks

- Short-term disruption to supply
- Inadequate quality of goods
- Increases in purchase costs
- Reputation risk
- Delays in delivery
- Lack of capacity to cater for demand

See also		
	Enterprise Risk Management (ERM) and the COSO Framework	188
	IT Due Diligence	276
	Key Risk Indicators	286
	Risks topics	

Risks – Risk Reviews

Considerations in creating a risk review

Objective setting	consider the objectives of the business, in the light of risks faced
Risk appetite	consider how much risk is acceptable
Risk culture	consider attitudes and examples of senior management, documentation, training and emphasis placed on risk in performance appraisal
Risk consolidation	consider systems in place for identifying and assessing risk
Risk response	consider how risks are managed and the priorities for action
Risk reporting	consider if risks are reported frequently enough and to the right level of management and that external reporting is appropriate
Risk monitoring	consider whether risk management is considered at all board meetings and whether any applicable governance codes are being followed

See also Risks topics

Segmental Reporting (IFRS 8)

Applies to entities with equity and/or debt which is listed on a public market (so check that the question relates to a listed entity) – **if so, any business change could potentially affect this aspect**

Examples could include a large diversification into a new geographical area or product

An operating segment is a component of an entity:

- That engages in business activities from which it may earn revenues and incur expenses (including revenues and expenses relating to transactions with other components of the same entity)

- Whose operating results are regularly reviewed by the entity's Chief Operating Decision Maker to make decisions about resources to be allocated to the segment and assess its performance

- For which discrete financial information is available

Consider whether discrete financial information about different revenue streams is provided and whether this is reported to the Chief Operation Decision Maker to assess performance and/or allocate resources

Consider whether different activities/products are similar enough to be aggregated (similarity of products, similar production processes, customers, regulation and distribution methods)

If represents 10% of revenue, profits or assets then needs to be disclosed as a separate segment

Must also meet the 75% external revenue test – if insufficient segments have been added then need to keep disclosing segments until 75% of external revenue has been analysed

Information which must be given includes information regarding the determination of the operating segments, the products and services they provide, profit or loss, significant income and expense items and segment assets and liabilities

See also Acquisitions topics
Change topics
Organic Growth 322

Sensitivity Analysis

Assesses how responsive the project's NPV is to changes in the variables used to calculate the NPV

Could vary depending on changes in selling price, sales volume, cost of capital, initial cost, operating costs, benefits, cost savings and residual value

Sensitivity = NPV / PV of project variable %

Weaknesses of a sensitivity analysis

Requires variables to be changed one at a time which is not realistic

Looks at factors in isolation which is not realistic as variables are interdependent

Sensitivity does not examine the probability that any particular variation in costs or revenues might occur

The critical factors may not be under the control of managers

Does not provide a decision rule itself – managers must still interpret the results to reach a decision

See also Investment Appraisal Methods topics

Share Options – Strategic Impact, Accounting and Auditing

Strategic Impact

Incentivise strong performance from Directors and managers – ensure goal congruence with other stakeholders such as shareholders

No **immediate cash flow outflow** – no cash outflow on maturity either if equity settled (but will be cash outflow if cash settled) – therefore can boost cash flows immediately at limited short term risk

Fair value scheme has **constant** impact on earnings but **cash settled** scheme is more **variable** as the expense is based on amounts **remeasured** at each year end

Volatility introduced into the financial statements due to staff leaving and joining each year

Cash settled schemes can lead to perverse outcomes – a **rising share price** will increase the FV used to determine the P&L expense and therefore depress **profits/earnings**

Accounting (IFRS 2)

See also your Corporate Reporting notes

Equity settled

Find FV at inception and then leave this alone over time – constant yearly charge

(However, if the share price is rising and there are new issues of options then the yearly charge will be higher in later years as the FV at inception will be higher)

Cash settled

Use the latest available FV when determining the expense for the year – in other words, introduce a variable P&L charge as FV fluctuates

As the share price increases, then the P&L expense will increase – possible tension for the Directors and shareholders?

Market-based vesting condition – connected to the share price in some way

Non-marked-based vesting condition – all other conditions

Modifications – continue to recognise the original FV of the instrument in the normal way, recognise any increase in FV at the date of modification spread over the period between modification date and vesting date (if the modification occurs after the vesting date then recognise the additional expense immediately unless there is an additional service period, in which case spread the increase)

Cancellations and settlements – immediately charge any remaining FV (accelerate the charge rather than avoiding it) and recognise any amount paid to the employees on settlement as a buy back, treated as a deduction from equity (if this amount exceeds FV then recognise the excess immediately in the IS)

Auditing

Number of employees/leavers – examine HR records for historic and forecast patterns, check whether new joiners are eligible, examiner HR budgets and plans, consider whether level of recruitment is sensible in the light of the stated aim to expand the business

Note: dependence on future forecasts does not matter for audit purposes because these will be confirmed in future years (and these would be irrelevant to an equity-settled scheme anyway as the FV already reflects the probability of settlement)

See also Option Valuation 320
Remuneration Strategies 362

Shareholding Percentages – Narrative Comments

Why acquire less than 100%?

Cost reasons
Existing shareholders may be unwilling to sell their shares
A controlling shareholding of 50% may be considered enough

Shareholding of 75%+

75% is enough to give full control – Articles of Association can be altered

Shareholding of 50%-74%

Should have a control premium attached and therefore a value above a simple pro-rata valuation

Articles of Association

Worth checking these to see if there are any special rules e.g. on acquisitions or appointment of directors – there may also be specific rules on valuation principles e.g. if a founding shareholder is leaving the business – there may be restrictions on the percentage shareholding which can be required for control or specific decisions and sometimes control is even possible with less than 50%

Largest single holding but below 50%

Gives power but look at the other shareholdings: if these are concentrated amongst a few groups/individuals, those other groups/individuals may have effective control

Discount Rules of Thumb

Always explain that these are suggested discounts, not precise figures, and an element of judgement is involved

To gain extra credit, mention 1-2 judgemental areas briefly

Other Factors to Consider Regarding Discounts

Where the shareholders are likely to vote together to obtain a 50% or 75% vote – for example, are there any related parties such as brothers and sisters or very close friends who are likely to work together?

Will dividends be paid in future?

Consider the concentration of other shareholdings – are there other groups that are likely to work together to have a high percentage of votes?

75% share – with this share of votes or more, the Articles of Association can be changed so any protections within those articles would not be applicable

What role will the shareholder have, if any – will he or she be a director, for example? This would give them additional power

See also Valuations topics

Stakeholders and Stakeholder Management

Very important SBM topic – always look for different stakeholders and even consider using them as headings in your answer

Managers and employees

Shareholders

Lenders

Suppliers

Customers

Government and regulatory agencies

Environmental and social bodies and other non-governmental organisations

Industry associations and trade unions

Local communities

Focus of the stakeholders can be **economic or social**, **local or national**

Mendelow's Matrix

		Level of interest	
		Low	*High*
Power	*Low*	Not significant "Minimal effort"	Passive, but may change "Keep satisfied"
	High	Could influence others "keep informed"	Key players "make strategy acceptable to them"

Strategic Analysis Tools & Models

Note: use your judgement but in SBM you are very unlikely to be rewarded just for drawing out any of the following models – what matters is the **application of the concepts within the models**, which may be rewarded in your narrative analysis (e.g. reference to a "cash cow" or using PESTEL to create your report headings)

The key elements of strategy are:

Long term – strategies are measured over years (in some cases a decade or more)

Direction – strategies must follow some kind of long-term direction based on the organisation's objectives

Organisation – there must be an organisation with a variety of internal and external relationships and stakeholders who could influence strategy

Suitability, Acceptability and Feasibility (SAF) Framework

According to the Study Manual, evaluation in SBM means assessing strategic options or situations in a balanced way, considering potential advantages and disadvantages, and future consequences, as a basis for sound decision-making – although the SAF framework **can** be used **to help identify** aspects of a proposal which could be advantageous or disadvantageous, **the assessment of the advantages and disadvantages (rather than use of SAF as such) is ultimately the most important aspect of an evaluation**

PESTEL

- Political
- Economic
- Socio-cultural
- Technological
- Environmental protections
- Legal

Porter's Five Forces

- Threat of new entrants
- Threat of substitute products or services
- Bargaining power of customers
- Bargaining power of suppliers
- Rivalry amongst current competitors in the industry

Porter has now added a sixth force to his 5 Forces model – this force is "complementors" or companies that produce closely-related products or services

Product life cycle

- Introduction
- Development and growth
- Maturity
- Decline

Boston matrix

		Market share	
		High	*Low*
% rate of market growth	*High*	Star	Problem child/ Question mark
	Low	Cash cow	Dog

SWOT analysis

Strengths
Weaknesses
Opportunities
Threats

(Hopefully you did not need reminding of these elements but just in case …)

Market positioning

Price	**High**		Cowboy brands		Premium brands	
	Low		Economy brands		Bargain brands	
		Very poor	**Poor**	**Reasonable**	**Good**	**Very good**
				Perceived quality		

Porter's 2 generic competitive strategies

Low cost
Differentiation

Ansoff matrix

		Product	
		Existing	New
Market	Existing	Market penetration	Product development
	New	Market development	Diversification

Resource audit

Identify the resources available to an organisation:

- Financial
- Human
- Intangible
- Physical

Recency-Frequency-Monetary (RFM) Analysis

RFM analysis can be a useful way of extracting insights from Big Data (see SBM November 2018 past paper Q2 for an example)

Recency of the latest purchase – useful for evaluating whether the customer is a "live" target

Frequency of purchases – useful for distinguishing regular customers from one off purchasers

Monetary value of purchases – useful in targeting efforts upon customers who appear likely to spend the most

Value chain analysis

Activities of the organisation that add value to purchased inputs

Used to identify critical success factors and opportunities to use information strategically

Primary activities	those involved in the production of goods and services
Support activities	provide necessary assistance
Linkages activities	relationships between activities

Benchmarking

Internal – versus company's own historical performance, or perhaps against branches

Competitive – compare against other firms in the same industry or sector*

Activity/best in class – best practice in any industry

Generic benchmarking – conceptually similar procedure

* problem here is that whole sector might be performing badly, hence the third or "activity/best in class" alternative

GE Business Screen

	Strong	Invest for growth	Invest selectively for growth	Develop for income
Business strength	**Average**	Invest selectively and build	Develop selectively for income	Harvest or divest
	Weak	Develop selectively Build on strengths	Harvest	Divest
		Weak	**Average**	**Unattractive**
			Market attractiveness	

Business process analysis

Helps organisation to improve how it conducts functions and activities

Reduce costs
Improve efficient use of resources
Better support for customers

Balanced scorecard

- Customer
- Internal business
- Innovation and learning
- Financial

Industry analysis

- Degree of rivalry – growth rate, number and relative size of firms, product differentiation, scale economies, degree of operating leverage, capital specificity
- Barriers to entrance – minimum size of operation, early entry advantage, distribution channels, regulation and legal constraints
- Product substitutability
- Price elasticity
- Structure of input markets

See also	Balanced Scorecard	60
	Key Performance Indicators	284

Strategic Case Study – Tips from the Study Manual

Based on the SBM Study Manual, here are some key questions to consider:

Company's main line of business

Current strategy and long-term objectives

Conflicts in objectives

External issues and stakeholders

Financial performance

Areas for obvious improvement

Particular company strengths it could exploit

Limitations on resources

What are competitors doing?

Is the company generating value for its shareholders?

Ruth Bender's 4 Factors (Impact on Shareholder Value)

Product

Business – activity

Company – management of that activity

Investment

See also

See also	Financial Performance Review in SBM – Some Advice	200
	Q1 – Technique Reminders	354

Supply Chain Improvements

Supply chain management – definition

The planning and management of all activities involved in sourcing and procurement, conversion, and all associated logistics and distribution activities.

Activities include procurement, inventory management, production, warehousing, transportation, customer service, order management, logistics and distribution.

Try to distinguish between goods and services as these will require different types of supply chain management.

Principles of effective supply chain management

For services, the process should be "pull" driven – for goods, the process should be "push" driven

Services – "pull" approach responding to demands

Ensure that all activities are undertaken with the needs of customers in mind

Be aware of the needs of customers and keep in communication

Use flexible manufacturing systems to commence manufacture as soon as possible in the case of bespoke orders

Implement effective transportation methods

Ensure a local presence with associated expertise in the case of supply of maintenance services

Goods – "push" approach with the entity taking action in advance

Hold inventories in response to uncertainty in customer orders -- should reduce lead time and improve customer service

Produce goods according to schedules based on historical sales patterns – may be hard in a new market

Ensure all staff employed are appropriately skilled

Improvements possible

Economies of scale leading to increased margins

Reducing the number of suppliers to reduce administrative time and ensure economies of scale

Reduce pressure on logistics

Consider using generic inputs rather than specialised to create purchasing economies of scale and reduce wastage

Reduce the range of products offered whilst maintaining choice and quality

Establish clear and effective criteria for selecting suppliers – develop these in advance and apply them carefully

Ensure reliability by offering incentives and discussing with suppliers at all times

Revising the terms of supply chain contracts – considerations

Will take time whilst a period of notice is given or the contract is fulfilled until its natural end date (e.g. a time limited contract)

Otherwise there may be breach of contract resulting in significant legal costs

Use a suitably qualified member of the legal team before finalising any changes

Consider the time frame of the new contract and any minimum order guarantees

Carefully consider bonuses and incentives – could these lead to unethical behaviour?

Consider the new balance of power between the different companies

See also

	Risks – Types and Examples	379
	Working Capital	446

Sustainability Reporting and Social Reporting

Examination example points

For a good example, see **SBM July 2016 past paper Q2** (model answer pages 24 and 25) (worth **7 marks**)

Sustainability is about ensuring that development meets the needs of the present without compromising the ability of future generations to meet their own needs.

Recycling is an aspect of sustainability as an organisation should only use resources at a rate that allows them to be replenished. However, sustainability is about much more than simply just recycling. Wider social, environmental and economic issues also need to be addressed to demonstrate genuine corporate responsibility.

Sustainability reporting is considered in the ICAEW publication *Outside Insights: Beyond Accounting* which indicates that sustainability policy in an annual report should include information such as:

- who the report is for
- links to corporate/business strategy
- materiality of issues reported
- validity of indicators
- reliability of indicators
- objectivity of reporting
- transparency of information
- comparability of information
- balance of information
- understandability of the report
- audit/assurance of the report and corporate performance
- external stakeholder engagement
- integration with financial reporting
- addressing true sustainability

(The model answer states that only some of the examples from this list would need to be mentioned by candidates to score the marks relating to the type of disclosures needed for sustainability reporting.)

Integrated report should explain how the organisation creates value, using both quantitative and qualitative information.

Natural capital includes the impact of the company's activities on air, land, water, minerals and forests – recycling could be one element of addressing this area.

The benefit of sustainability disclosures for the company is that such disclosures communicate the company's attempts to demonstrate corporate responsibility by explaining what the proposed sustainability policy is.

Including environmental issues within integrated reporting makes environmental assurance more feasible as it provides a statement of policies which have been implemented – the effectiveness of implementation can then be confirmed as part of the assurance purpose.

Why apply assurance to social responsibility reports?

Entities are increasingly supplying more information of this type to stakeholders so stakeholders need reassurance that the information is correct – however, the information is not part of the financial statements and so will not be audited as part of a statutory audit engagement

An independent, external party can verify the data and information – this will increase credibility – the stakeholders can have more confidence the information is drawn from reliable sources and that it has been calculated accurately using a consistent methodology over time

The assurance engagement should provide assurance as to compliance with certain fundamental standards promised but also more detailed assurance as to whether performance indicators are accurately and consistently recorded

Difficulties

Often performance will relate mainly to non-financial indicators – these may not be part of standardised information flows and may involve judgement – it is also not possible to apply certain types of assurance procedures to information which is not financial e.g. analytical procedures, ratio analysis or computer analytics

Sometimes questionnaires are issued to the entity or its staff or interviews are conducted – a problem here is knowing whether the information is truthful

The Triple Bottom Line

According to the Study Manual, the triple bottom line in reporting should be to consider the **economic**, **environmental** and **social** impacts of the operations of an entity. You may therefore wish to use this framework in your answer.

Reporting Frameworks

There is currently no single consensus framework on social and environmental reporting so you need to be aware of the following frameworks:

Global Reporting Initiative (GRI)

The GRI is a reporting framework that aims to develop transparency, accountability, reporting and sustainable development

Its vision is that reporting on economic, environmental and social impact should become as routine and comparable as financial reporting

It also seeks to achieve as much standardisation as is possible in sustainability reporting by organisations

The GRI's G4 Sustainability Reporting Standards, published in 2016, emphasise the need for organisations to disclose their most critical impact on the environment, society and the economy

The GRI Standards also highlight the importance of generating reliable, relevant and standardised information, with which to assess opportunities and risks and enable more informed decision-making both within the business and among its stakeholders

Under GRI, a sustainability report should have 5 sections:

1. Strategy and analysis
2. Organisational profile
3. Report parameters
4. Governance, commitments and engagement structure and management systems
5. Performance indicators

GRI is based on the following principles:

- stakeholder inclusiveness
- sustainability context
- materiality
- completeness
- balance
- comparability
- accuracy
- timeliness
- clarity
- reliability

New Sustainability Reporting Standards replace the previous G4 Guidelines but the new Standards are based on the previous Guidelines – the new "universal standards" should be used by every organisation that prepares a sustainability report under GRI – the "universal standards" are:

GRI 101: Foundation – this sets out the Reporting Principles

GRI 102: General Disclosures – contextual information about an organisation and its sustainability reporting practices, including information about an organisation's profile, strategy, ethics and integrity, governance stakeholder engagement practices and reporting processes

GRI 103: Management approach – information about how an organisation manages a material topic

Companies Act 2006

Requires the business review in the Directors' Report for quoted companies to include information on environmental, social and community issues. The information should include both financial and non-financial key performance indicators.

From 1 October 2013, Companies Act 2006 requires all UK quoted companies to report on their greenhouse gas emissions within the annual Directors' Report. Other companies are encouraged to report this information but it remains a voluntary process for unquoted companies.

DEFRA Guidelines

Originally published in 2006 and updated in June 2013

The guidelines help companies to understand what to report in various situations such as when preparing a Business Review, making mandatory greenhouse gas emissions statements and for SMEs who are part of a larger supply chain and who need suppliers to behave responsibly

Accounting for Sustainability (A4S) Connected Reporting Framework

Aims to help ensure that sustainability is embedded in the DNA of an organisation – 3 core aims of A4S:

To inspire finance leaders to adopt sustainable and resilient business models

To transform financial decision-making to enable an integrated approach, reflective of the opportunities and risks posed by environmental and social issues

To scale up actions across the global finance and accounting community

Requires sustainability to be clearly linked to the organisation's overall strategy and requires consistency in presentation to aid comparability between years and organisations

Contains 5 key elements:

- explanation of how sustainability is connected to the overall operational strategy of an organisation
- five key environmental indicators to be considered in all reporting: greenhouse gas emissions, energy usage, water use, waste and significant use of other finite resources
- other key sustainability information should be given where the business or operation has material impacts
- use of industry benchmark key performance indicators when available
- upstream and downstream impact of the organisation's products and services

Advantages of sustainability reporting

- employee satisfaction with working for a company that behaves appropriately
- improved stakeholder satisfaction
- investors may want to see a company adopt sustainable practices
- abuses of social and environmental issues can damage reputation
- using resources effectively can save money

Disadvantages of sustainability reporting

- moves focus away from financial returns which could be argued to be the main point of the business
- shareholder value may be reduced if profits are lost
- costs incurred to become more green

Impact of environmental and social issues on statutory audit

- impairment of assets after introduction of new laws and regulations
- accruals for remediation, compensation or legal costs
- constructive obligations
- contingent liabilities and provisions
- development cost expenditure for new products
- going concern issues
- impact on understanding the entity and assessing risks
- need for the auditor to ask environmental questions such as what laws and regulations are applicable or any history of legal penalties or proceedings

Social Audits

A social audit involves:

- establishing whether the entity has a reason for engaging in social activities

- identifying that all current environmental programmes are congruent with the mission of the company
- assessing the objectives and priorities related to these programmes
- evaluating company involvement in such programmes past, present and future

United Nations Global Goals

The UN Global Goals for Sustainable Development aim to transform our world by 2030

The UN has set 17 Global Goals illustrating what the UN perceives to be the most important issues:

- no poverty
- zero hunger
- good health and well-being
- quality education
- gender equality
- clean water and sanitation
- affordable and clean energy
- decent work and economic growth
- industry, innovation and infrastructure
- reduced inequalities
- sustainable cities and communities
- responsible consumption and production
- climate action
- life below water
- life on land
- peace and justice
- partnerships for the goals

ICAEW believes it has a vital role to play regarding the UN Global Goals because the actions businesses take will be critical to translating this vision into a new reality – the accountancy profession will have a major role in aligning measurement systems in different countries

Additionally, the accountancy profession has a proven record of building strong local institutions which could be essential for achieving the goals

AA1000 (AccountAbility)

In 2018, AccountAbility revised its reporting standard AA1000 so that this now refers to 4 principles for sustainability reporting (the Impact principle has been newly-added to the 2018 edition of AA1000):

Inclusivity	The participation of stakeholders in developing and achieving an accountable and strategic response to sustainability

Materiality	Determination of the relevance and significance of an issue to an organisation and its stakeholders – an issue is material if it will influence the decisions, actions and performance of an organisation or its stakeholders
Responsiveness	The ability of an organisation to respond to stakeholder issues that affect its sustainability performance – responsiveness stems from decisions, actions and performance, as well as communication with stakeholders
Impact	The effect of behaviour, performance and/or outcomes on the part of individuals or an organisation, on the economy, the environment, society, stakeholders or the organisation itself Material topics have potential direct and indirect impacts which may be positive or negative, intended or unintended, expected or realised, and short, medium or long-term

See also Integrated Reporting 249
Natural capital 317

Tendering and cost-plus methods

In determining a tender price, there are 2 issues:

maximising expected probability of winning the contract

maximising the profit on contracts won

There will always be uncertainty as to the price tendered by rival companies as this is unknown at the time of the bid – however, prior experience of successes and failures in tenders against rivals and exposed information on winning tenders would build managerial experience to help determine what a winning tender bid price is likely to be

Cost-plus pricing

Cost-plus pricing is particularly weak in a competitive market as it is rigid and therefore rivals may become able to predict the company's tender bids and undercut them

This method also fails to consider the varying competitive conditions from contract to contract

Cost-plus pricing also does not guarantee a profit, despite expectations that profits are guaranteed as pricing will always exceed (i.e. use of a "plus" methodology) costs – excessive pricing means failure to win bids and so standardised development costs and other indirect costs cannot be recovered

It would be easy to say that only incremental costs should be covered but in an industry where a large majority of costs are fixed (such as in the case where there are significant development costs) then covering only incremental costs will not be sustainable in the long-term

Example of problems with a cost-plus formula used by an SBM client company

(Based on SBM July 2019 past paper Q1)

The method used does not distinguish between incremental costs for the contract and non-incremental costs which are not affected by the contract

The manner in which the standardised development costs are allocated to the contract can distort the contract price – for example, there were some programming problems in developing the standardised software and costs therefore exceeded expectations

While fixed standardised development costs are allocated, there is no attempt to recover other indirect costs such as administrative costs – unless part of these costs increase due to the contract then it is legitimate to exclude these but they need to be covered in the long run

It may be that quality and service delivery are also factors in determining who wins the contract and rigid application of cost-plus pricing may not consider these

The costs included are pure financial costs but if the business is at full capacity then the acceptance of the tender may mean that there is an opportunity cost of a more profitable contract being rejected – this should be built into considerations for the tender price

The learning costs expected to be incurred are a direct cost and legitimately should be recovered unless such learning can be used on other contracts but it is unjustified to magnify extra learning costs fivefold by the allocation of standardised development costs

Treasury Operations

Role of the Treasury team

Corporate financial objectives – policies, aims and strategies and systems

Liquidity management

Funding management – managing investments, policies and rates

Currency management

Corporate finance – raising share capital, dividend policies and obtaining a stock exchange listing

Advantages of having a separate treasury department

Centralised liquidity management avoids mixing cash surpluses and overdrafts

Bulk cash flows allow lower bank charges to be negotiated

Larger volumes of cash can be invested, giving better short-term investment opportunities

Borrowing can be agreed in bulk, probably at lower interest rates than smaller borrowings

Better currency risk management

Specialist department can employ staff with a greater level of expertise than would be possible in a local, more broadly based finance department

Company will be able to benefit from the use of specialised cash management software

Access to treasury expertise should improve the quality of strategic planning and decision-making

Hedging

Consider time scale needed for the hedge: are the instruments dated too far into the future?

Treasury department's task involves measuring as accurately as possible the company's net exposures in each currency and its exposure to cost and revenue changes

Complete accuracy is not possible and 100% hedging accuracy is not possible

Treasury department should have some discretion as to whether it should hedge or not, based on the amounts involved and its estimation of the probability that spot prices will move in a particular way

Not hedging is a valid choice in many situations

Example of risk assurance over Treasury controls

(Based on SBM July 2019 past paper Q2)

If there is suspicion of inappropriate transactions authorised by the Head of Treasury, it will be necessary to introduce controls **on** Treasury, rather than **within** Treasury

Controls could include:

changing the incentives of Treasury – if the Treasury department is a profit centre then it could end up undertaking speculative transactions to make currency gains rather than hedging transactions to reduce the current level of risk – making Treasury a cost centre would be a radical move to control transactions that would enable more Board control (see below) and would significantly affect the control environment

require Board authorisation – the key control would be to require Board authorisation of large individual transactions – authorisation would be a preventative control

require Board monitoring – there should also be Board monitoring of monthly performance and Treasury activity overall – monitoring would be a detective control

improved documentation to leave a better audit trail – this would assist monitoring and control particularly if the current level of notes and information appears to be very thin for a transaction of the relevant size and type – there should be a review of documentation including the rationale for the transaction, risk analysis, sensitivity analysis for a range of outcomes, evidence of authorisation and approval at all levels, segregation of duties where the final implementation of this type of transaction is always outside Treasury to prevent controls being circumvented by Treasury staff

use of a procedures manual – such a manual should have constraints on the nature and size of transactions to be undertaken by Treasury – limits imposed should not be too small as Treasury needs to carry out day-to-day functions without every transaction requiring high-level approval but for large transactions over a particular size, constraints should be in place so that the transaction does not take place entirely within Treasury in future

Treasury Operations and IT

Inefficiencies in the Treasury function

Inefficiencies and weaknesses that may expose the Treasury function to risk include:

- duplication of effort such as the re-input of information
- tasks which take too long to complete or are frequently delayed
- poorly functioning links with older ("legacy") systems or those of other departments
- management reports which are incomplete, inaccurate, late or in the wrong format
- inaccurate cash flow forecasts
- credit risk not properly identified
- difficulty in complying with accounting standards

Benefits of IT to the Treasury function

A variety of technological tools to improve the efficiency of treasury operations in areas such as cash management, investment and debt management and foreign exchange capabilities now exist

Many systems are now integrated with trading platforms and bank portals and include customised reporting tools

Technology can bring benefits in many areas of treasury management such as:

- cash and liquidity management – with improved visibility of cash flows around the business, a greater understanding of pooled cash positions and improved cash flow forecasts could be achieved
- virtual accounts – companies can minimise bank account fees and improve accounts receivable processes by maintaining a single account with many associated virtual accounts – virtual accounts make it easier for a company to establish automated reconciliation processes
- transactions – speedier settlements, confirmation of deals and timely reporting will result from improved interfaces between trading systems
- debt management – understanding of the company's debt position in terms of its outstanding loans, mortgages and lease finance
- greater control over financial risk management – foreign exchange risk, interest rate risk and the management of specific instruments for associated hedging strategies can be more tightly controlled
- automated foreign exchange conversions – companies can make payments in a foreign supplier's local currency by using a bank's automated forex conversion service – an automated forex service enables a company to pay in multiple currencies from a single account, eliminating the expense of maintaining multiple foreign currency accounts – this tool

helps corporations avoid maintaining idle balances on a range of currencies while accessing competitive forex rates

general risk management – understanding of exposure limits, credit limits, authorisation levels and the undertaking of scenario and sensitivity analysis should help to reduce risk exposure and ensure compliance with company procedures

access controls – resulting in improved security, clear audit trails and tracking of transactions

Benefits of software as a service (SaaS) to the Treasury function

SaaS solutions employ internet technology and remote servers, enabling users to access software online from anywhere, using a device with an internet connection

The software does not need to be installed on hardware in the company's offices

Advantages include:

SaaS could remove the need for an internal IT capability

the supplier is responsible for all updates and maintenance so the user gets access to these as part of its subscription fee

costs can be adjusted according to the company's own requirements (for example, number of transactions or number of licensed users)

Cyber security and the Treasury function

Cyber threats can include:

stealing confidential data/information

fraudulent payments

denial of service attacks – flooding a server with information requests so that it crashes

ransomware – malware that blocks system access or disrupts it until a ransom fee is paid

It is important to identify the most critical company information, data and processes in the Treasury function that may come under attack

Companies need to ensure that the Treasury processes which attract cybercrime (such as payment processing) are reviewed and controls embedded, including segregation of duties, enforcement of approval limits and daily reconciliations

Companies should undertake appropriate technical measures such as encryption and use of antivirus software

Cyber security policy should also take account of human factors:

directors must understand the effects that a cyber security breach could have – strong corporate governance and clear policies must be in place the board should be aware of the guidance issued by government agencies and all employees should be trained in cyber and information security

there should be appropriate restrictions around sensitive data and the company should have clear computer use policies

insurance policies should cover the effects of a cyber breach

an incident response plan should be in place and should be well rehearsed and understood by staff

Cyber security and fraud mitigation

Whilst investment in Treasury Management Systems (TMSs) has increased, many companies still maintain a significant proportion of their work using spreadsheets, leaving them open to both operational and fraud risks

There has also been an increasing trend for vendors of TMSs to move to “cloud-only” offerings, which could increase fraud risks

To mitigate fraud risks, organisations need to consider:

governance – strong corporate governance, in the form of a global policies culture – corporations need to create a culture that recognises shared responsibility for preventing cybercrime

technology – technology must include the latest encryption/security features

training – ongoing training for all employees, coupled with job-specific training for certain teams

process – companies need to ensure that the processes that attract cybercrime (such as payment processing) are reviewed regularly and that controls are embedded in new processes including segregation of duties, multiple levels of approval and daily reconciliation of all transactions

United Nations Sustainable Development Goals

The United Nations 2030 Agenda for Sustainable Development is a 15-year plan, adopted by the UN in September 2015, which includes 17 global goals:

1. No poverty
2. Zero hunger
3. Good health and well-being
4. Quality education
5. Gender equality
6. Clean water and sanitation
7. Affordable and clean energy
8. Decent work and economic growth
9. Industry, innovation and infrastructure
10. Reduced inequality
11. Sustainable cities and communities
12. Responsible consumption and production
13. Climate action
14. Life below water
15. Life on land
16. Peace, justice and strong institutions
17. Partnerships for the goals

These overall goals are supported by a range of associated targets (169 in total)

ICAEW and the UN Sustainable Development Goals

ICAEW has championed the relevance of the UN's goals to business and to the accounting profession

The **actions** that **businesses** will take will be **critical to translating the UN's vision into reality** – businesses have a duty to act in the **public interest** and the UN Sustainable Development goals provide a **definition** of what "public interest" means

The accounting profession will have a **major role** in **aligning measurement systems** across countries to **help monitor progress** in achieving the Sustainable Development Goals

There is a **role** for the **accountancy profession** in providing **high quality reporting**, **audit** and **assurance** of organisations' performance – **timely**, **reliable** and **relevant** information will be central

Additionally, the **accountancy profession** has a proven record of **building strong local institutions** which could be **essential** for achieving the goals

SDG Compass

The **SDG Compass** has been developed by various organisations to provide companies with guidance about how to align their strategies towards realisation of the Sustainable Development Goals

The **Compass** identifies 5 steps for companies to take:

1. **Understanding the SDGs** – companies need to familiarise themselves with the SDGs
2. **Defining priorities** – companies should define priorities based on an assessment of their impact (positive and negative) on the SDGs across their value chain – companies should consider both current and potential future impact
3. **Setting goals** – setting goals will help to foster shared priorities and better performance across the organisation – by aligning company goals with the SDGs, leadership can demonstrate its commitment to sustainable development
4. **Integrating** – the integration of sustainability into the core business and governance is key
5. **Reporting and communicating** – the SDGs enable companies to report information on sustainable development performance using **common indicators** and shared sets of priorities – the SDG Compass encourages companies to incorporate the SDGs into their communication and reporting with stakeholders

Benefits of the SDGs

Identifying future business opportunities – the SDGs aim to redirect public and private investment flows towards the **challenges** highlighted in the goals – the SDGs therefore **define markets** that could grow in future for companies that can deliver innovative solutions and transformative change

Enhancing the value of corporate sustainability – the SDGs could strengthen **economic incentives** for companies to use resources **more efficiently** as sustainability indicators are increasingly **quantified** and **measured**

Strengthening stakeholder relations – by aligning their priorities with the SDGs, companies can strengthen **engagement** with their customers, employees and other stakeholders – companies whose **strategies** are **not aligned** with the SDGs could be exposed to **growing legal and reputational risks**

Stabilising societies and markets – the SDGs look to support and develop the infrastructure necessary for business success including transparent financial systems and non-corrupt and well-governed institutions

Using a common language and shared purpose – the SDGs define a common **framework** of action that will help companies **communicate more consistently and effectively with stakeholders** about their impact on performance

Encourages businesses to think about the wider, longer term implications of business decisions rather than focusing on just internal, financial ones

As an example of the last benefit, 2 of the indicators raised in relation to Global Goal 8 (promoting decent work and sustainable economic growth) involve consideration of (1) whether the company's buying practices impact the price volatility of key commodities, materials, crops and/or inputs that suppliers rely on in local or national markets and (2) what type of business model the company plans to invest in, a matter which will help to assess security of income for suppliers and workers in the longer term

Navigating the SDGs

As PwC have noted in their report *Navigating the SDGs*, data will be crucial to determine what to measure and how, as well as to the processes of actually measuring, monitoring and reporting it

These will be significant challenges themselves – the demands for a more granular understanding of business impact could drive a data revolution in itself

Valuations – Standard Points

The biggest risk in a valuation is **overpaying** for the target

Exercise professional scepticism over the figures given (including distortions caused by accounting principles)

Always consider the **percentage shareholding** on offer – always marks on this

75% shareholding gives almost complete control (can amend Articles of Association)

50% shareholding gives substantial power over ordinary resolutions

Valuations are subjective and only a starting point for negotiations – **final value to a specific purchaser** determined by:

Cost of acquiring a similar company

Cost of purchasing assets and setting up a similar company

Value of the brand name

Future earnings potential

Value of key personnel

Strategic fit

Nature of the consideration required

Bargaining power

Results of a risk analysis

Valuations based on accounting figures may be subject to distortion due to accounting principles (not cash-based)

Is there a perpetuity calculation involved? If so, then this is obviously a simplification

Is the assumed growth rate (if any) reasonable?

Query the discount rate and query any synergistic savings

In an acquisition we should also always consider

Synergies

Risk

Real options

Financing

Opening Bid

If the valuation is for a first suggested opening bid to buy a target, it makes sense to estimate everything very conservatively

Of course, if we are the seller facing an opening bid then we want the opposite to occur!

Exceptionals and adjustments to revenue and costs

Particularly for cash flow and earnings based models, it is important to know whether there are any exceptional one-off items which have distorted (decreased or increased) profits and whether these are anticipated

Lost revenue opportunities as a result of the acquisition should be allowed for (e.g. a customer may not be willing to continue to deal with the merged entity or the acquirer may have to give up a revenue stream to preserve the cash needed for the acquisition)

Changes in the cost basis as a result of the acquisition should be allowed for (e.g. will more or fewer Directors be needed in the new business? Will we now have to allow for salaries of a management team for a smaller company which was previously owner-managed?)

IFRS 13 Levels for discussion

Level 1 inputs – quoted prices in an active market – not normally relevant as a brand is unique

Level 2 inputs – other observable prices e.g. in non-active markets such as a recent bid

Level 3 inputs – unobservable inputs, including internal company data

Methods set out in IFRS 13:

Market basis – market price and other market transactions – difficult if intangible is unique

Income basis – present value of **incremental** income generated by the intangible, considering value including any possible price premium effect and additional sales

Cost basis – current replacement cost of the intangible, which might be estimated as the present value of the expenditure needed to set up an equivalent intangible, including an allowance for risk and how expenditure could replicate the intangible in varying market conditions (this requires a large amount of judgement and estimation, hence apply **professional scepticism**)

Valuation of synergies

State first that this is a subjective area and synergies may often not occur as expected – likewise there may be other possible synergies not considered (try to give some specific examples)

Consider a quick perpetuity valuation of the synergies – you may have to assume a cost of capital to do this (give a reason for your assumption, based on the scenario) – simply divide the annual synergy value by the cost of capital to gain some quick skills marks for the value of the synergies e.g. synergies will contribute £5m per year for the foreseeable future and estimated cost of capital is 10% so value of the synergies is £5m/0.1 = £50m – this amount should be added to the valuation but with various caveats on the subjective and uncertain nature of the estimate

Discounts to apply

Discount the valuation if the company is a private limited company (less marketable, higher risk, smaller size, lower expectations of a cash return from dividends)

Discount if the shareholding is small (below 25% of the shares)

Discount if another single party holds a substantial amount such as 50% – easy for that party to assert itself

Note that it may be necessary to **apply 2 discounts** if the company is a limited company – one discount for the fact that its shares are not as easily marketable and another for the specific shareholding being discussed

Discounts Rules of Thumb

Discounts for shareholding %

Shareholding	**Discount**
75%+	0-5%
50% to 74%	10-15%
50%	20-30%

Discounts for the status of the company

Status	**Discount**
Plc	Nil
AIM	20-30%
Limited company	40-50%

Consider Natural capital?

The increasing focus on natural capital is starting to change the way in which organisations report on their activities, with many now attempting to place financial values on the natural assets that they use, to enable them to make more informed business decisions

The use of natural capital valuation is likely to be increasingly significant in assessing a company's value although at the moment methodologies and approaches in this area are still evolving

Valuations – Asset-Based Model

Often used for companies whose value can be accurately reflected by the value of assets held

Examples: property development companies, companies which invest in capital assets with long lives

For other companies, likely to be an undervalue (see below) so used to establish a minimum value or lower floor

Can be considered to show a measure of the security of the share value (i.e. asset backing for the shares)

May also be used in a merger or business combination – if one company has a low asset backing compared to the other company then the shareholders of the company with the higher asset backing may want some compensation for the risk they are taking on

Criticisms

For many companies, there are sources of value which are not reflected in the SFP such as brands and staff expertise so this method would result in a significant **undervaluation** (common exam position)

A business with lots of future opportunities to generate cash flows might have an approximate **balance of assets and liabilities** simply from normal trading but this would give an incorrectly low valuation

Update to fair value (see also IFRS 13 notes)

The examiners seem to like the point **that carrying value (book value) is not necessarily an indication of market value (and is not intended to be)** – mention this as a theory point but then apply to the scenario

Look out for any indications that fair value may vary from book value and suggest adjustments

Establishing FV can be difficult, costly or time-consuming – FV may fluctuate between the valuation date and the acquisition date

FV is subjective and could lead to disagreement

Determining FV requires an active market and a large number of similar items but in practice many assets are unique

Add brand value and unrecognised assets/liabilities

In addition to updating recognised assets/liabilities to fair value (see above), look out for any assets or liabilities which cannot be recognised for accounting purpose but which affect the practical business value/cash flows of the target

Additions

Brands

Staff quality

Technologies

Unrealised gains on financial instruments and/or pension schemes

Deductions

Legal or tax disputes

Deduct goodwill shown on the SFP

Goodwill already on the SFP indicates goodwill from a previous purchase by the target company.

This simply records a previous transaction and does not mean that the same amount still remains (since under IFRS goodwill is an historic balance and is not adjusted for any increases in value (but may have been reduced for impairment))

Therefore deduct goodwill from the net asset value used

Preference shares: possible discussion point

If preference shares are presented on the SFP within liabilities rather than equity, these shares are a type of loan and should be excluded from the equity value of the company.

See also		
	IFRS 13 and Valuation of Intangibles	244
	Valuation topics	

Valuations – Administration Scenario

Key questions

What is the company worth to the potential acquirer?

What will the administrator be willing to sell the company for?

Company cannot remain in administration indefinitely as the Enterprise Act 2002 puts a one year time limit on administration

Methods of acquisition

Acquire share capital – this would mean acquiring the liabilities

Acquire business assets, leaving the liabilities in the insolvent company

Acquire assets on an individual or piecemeal basis

Position of the administrator

Must save the company as a going concern as the first priority

Must act in the best interests of the creditors

Company cannot remain in administration indefinitely as the Enterprise Act 2002 puts a one year time limit on administration

Probably should not break up the business if possible as the return will then be lower – the Enterprise Act 2002 requires the administrator to attempt to save the business as a going concern

Establishing asset values – possible methods

Historic costs

Historic replacement costs

Current replacement costs

Net realisable values

Value in use

Assets to consider

Goodwill, PPE, Inventories, Receivables

Brand value may be an off-SFP asset to be valued – could have been damaged by going into administration

Liabilities to consider

Under the Transfer of Undertakings (Protection of Employment) Regulations 2006, even if the acquirer only purchases business assets, then that acquirer assumes obligations with respect to employees and potentially also some subcontractors – however, there will be no obligations regarding directors' service contracts unless shares were being acquired

Other off balance sheet contractual rights

Rights or charges over assets held by third parties – this could reduce their value or prevent individual sale

There may be a discount for sale of business assets – the cost of liquidating assets individually on a piecemeal basis may be greater than selling all the assets in one transaction so the administrator may offer a discount for the latter

Need for re-evaluation

In this scenario, things will change quickly over time so there may need to be another valuation at the date of acquisition rather than based on historic reporting date figures

Enterprise Act 2002

Permits the administrator to continue to trade for a while if he or she cannot sell the company as a going concern immediately – this is to give time to enable a sale on a going concern basis in the near future if possible

If the company is making losses there is greater urgency for disposal in order to prevent losses accruing to the creditors

Exit risks

If the acquisition of a struggling company does not result in the realisation of strategic and financial benefits then exit may be necessary

If the acquirer only pays the fair value of the assets, then the exit routes should not result in a significant loss and could even be a gain

Issues relating to obligations and penalties under contracts insofar as these relate to disengagement

Obligations to employees which will incur costs

Errors or uncertainties in the fair value estimates e.g. the cash flows and discount rate used

Closure costs

Delays in closing down the trading may alter the commercial viability of the company – the longer the time period, the more risk there is of a fall in the fair value of assets

Issues relating to inventories unsold – these will increase over time

See also IFRS 13 and Valuation of Intangibles 244
Valuation topics

Valuations – Dividend Valuation Model (DVM)

Value of a share estimated as the present value of all future expected dividends on the shares, discounted at the shareholders' cost of capital

Dividend Valuation Model – no growth assumed

Apply the formula **D_0 / discount rate**

where

D_0 = most recent dividend

Dividend Valuation Model – growth assumed

Apply the formula **D_0 (1 + g) / (discount rate - g)**

where

D_0 = most recent dividend

g = expected growth rate

Estimating g

Use a compound growth formula

(end value / start value)$^{1/n}$) -1

where n is the number of growth periods

For example, with 3 growth periods use the third root of the bracketed value

Remember to look at the **number of growth periods** possible – **this is always one less than the number of years analysed**:

2008	2009	2010	2011
50	75	98	110

There are **4** years of figures but only **3** years of growth as the 2008 figure is the end of 2008.

Therefore growth can occur in 2008 to 2009, 2009 to 2010 and 2010 to 2011 so therefore calculation would be

$$[(110 / 50)^{1/3}] - 1$$

As an alternative, we can use the Gordon growth formula where **g = rb** and r is the rate of return on capital employed and b is the proportion of earnings (after tax profits) that are retained in the business

r can also be calculated as profits/equity

DVM Criticisms

Assumed that investors have perfect information and are motived by dividends – may not be correct

Assumes that figure used for D_0 is not divergent from trend and so is a reasonable indication (rather than an exceptional figure)

Cost of capital (discount rate) may be hard to establish with confidence – **the acquisition process may change the risk profile and make this rate out of date**

Assumes a constant growth rate, which is unlikely to be the case in practice

There are many other factors that will influence share price such as acquisitions, analyst estimates, earnings performance and these are not considered in DVM

Dividends may not be a fair reflection of the strength of the company

DVM and Professional Scepticism

Always review all variables for reasonableness – D_0, g and the cost of capital are all very important variables and slight changes

If g is greater than the discount rate, then the model does not work as the bottom of the fraction is negative

Dividend growth cannot exceed the growth in earnings forever or there will be no earnings available to pay those dividends

If you feel you have time, perhaps re-estimate the outcome with slightly changed g and/or cost of capital and comment on the sensitivity – you should find major changes in the valuation with minor changes in the variables because you are estimating flows into perpetuity so a very long time for changes to have an impact on the outcomes!

Due Diligence involving DVM should therefore definitely undertake a lot of work on these variables

We may need information on the entity's cash position to evaluate if a dividend is even possible

Dividend yield

As well as being used to calculate the value of the company, the dividend yield % shows the income that can be generated from holding the shares of the target – this provides a useful income stream

See also	IFRS 13 and Valuation of Intangibles Valuation topics	244

Valuations – Earnings-Based

Start with maintainable earnings but should also consider forecasts if reasonable and company is clearly growing

Apply a multiple – this choice of multiple is very important

Examiners seem to like the point that this method should only be used if a cash flow based model is not possible

Apply a net assets-based model as well as a lower benchmark

Possible equation – perpetuity flows with growth

earnings x (1 + g) / (discount rate - g)

Fixed costs

May need to deduct the present value of fixed costs

Tax

Difficult to estimate – depends on profit flows and tax rule changes in the future – unpredictable

May need to allow for capital allowances as well

Appropriateness of using earnings/accounting profit as an indicator of value

Problems

Not appropriate for a loss-making business

Accounting profits are a financial reporting-based measure so may not reflect the cash flows of the operation

Does not consider the incremental, relevant cash flows of the operation or any savings made

Does not weight results based on the level of risk involved

No allowance made for the costs of financing the expansion

Might only consider a limited number of years of results rather than future possibilities (assuming that the appraisal does not look into perpetuity – if it does look at a perpetuity, use the criticism of a perpetuity that it is a simplification and flows cannot continue forever: similarly growth cannot continue at the same rate forever)

Might not take account of improvements over time

Include interest in sustainable earnings?

Arguably interest should not be included for these purposes as there is no guarantee that it will be received in perpetuity

Possible adjustments

Consider all incremental costs and revenues that may result

Will Director salaries and remuneration change if the Board of Directors is changed?

Eliminate one off items

Adjustments for inflation and other similar changes?

Deduct earnings from opportunities now foregone?

See also

	IFRS 13 and Valuation of Intangibles	244
	Investment Appraisal Methods – APV	270
	Valuations topics	

Valuations – EBITDA Model

EBITDA = approximation to operating cash flows (earnings before interest and taxation and also before non-cash flows such as depreciation and amortisation)

Earnings before interest, tax, depreciation and amortisation

Commonly used figure which is considered to be a good (although not perfect) proxy for operating cash flows

Strips out depreciation, amortisation and usually any separately disclosed items such as exceptionals

Concerns with EBITDA as a valuation method

Does not exclude all subjective accounting practices such as revenue recognition

There may be unusual accounting aspects which are not disclosed separately and therefore not added back or deducted to arrive at a cash position

The presentation of items as exceptional can be subjective

EBITDA is not a sustainable figure as there is no charge for capital replacement such as depreciation or CAPEX

Does not create a separate valuation for equity only – this is because it does not represent the flow of earnings to equity holders only as interest is not taken into account – the method values debt and equity jointly at the same time as both shareholders and debt holders need to be paid from the EBITDA figure

Excludes taxation which may be a significant, relevant cost

Usually based on a current year only – ignores growth and the current year may be exceptionally high or low

Sometimes based on an estimate of the current year which is a forecast and unaudited – the actual figure may be different

EBITDA – Professional Scepticism

Like the PE Model, the choice of multiple is absolutely fundamental to the EBITDA calculation

Always query the multiple!

Model is very sensitive to what is put into the IS – for every £1 change there will be a multiplied effect

Look for any disputed figures

Look for exceptionals

Ignores importance of CAPEX

Ignores expectations of future growth (although sometimes based on a prospective multiple: check what data you are using)

Remember to discount a listed company/industry multiple if this is used as a benchmark

Look out for any inappropriate accounting adjustments or policies – unlike the Free Cash Flow approach, accounting adjustments/policies will continue to affect EBITDA

You may wish to suggest some adjustments before applying the multiple

Reasons to favour an EBITDA valuation

A significant element of PPE cost in accruals terms is depreciation which is excluded from EBITDA – conversely, all the cost of purchasing components and raw materials is included in EBITDA

Using a Multiple to Estimate the Cost of Capital

Assume a multiple of 5 and no growth – value of a company with EBITDA of £1m is £5m. This is the same thing as 1/0.20, so **cost of capital is 1/multiple** (since 1/5 = 0.20 or 20% as needed)

Assuming a multiple of 5 and growth of 2% – we can use the following formula based on the dividend valuation model and replacing the future dividend D_1 with future earnings E_1 (which is today's earnings x 1.02 to represent growth to earnings in 1 year):

$$\textbf{cost of capital} = (E_1 / P_0) + g$$

We know that for every £1 of earnings then the valuation or price (P_0) must be 5 times that figure. Therefore applying the formula:

$$\textbf{cost of capital} = [(1 \times 1.02) / 5] + 0.02 = 22.4\%$$

See also IFRS 13 and Valuation of Intangibles 244
Valuations topics

Valuations – Economic Value Added (EVA®)

Find the extent to which earnings exceed the minimum rate of return that shareholders require

In other words, how much better are we doing than the minimum to keep shareholders happy and invested into our company?

Assume that the WACC represents the minimum that the shareholders require.

EVA® works using NOPAT (net operating profit after tax)

Advantages of EVA®

Emphasises the importance of the cost of capital to managers and sets them a target to beat the minimum acceptable return – takes into account the **financing** aspect of a project/valuation

Disadvantages of EVA®

Based on historical figures which could be distorted by accounting conventions (a disadvantage shared with other techniques of course)

Method

1. Find the Return on Invested Capital (ROIC)

Divide **this year's** NOPAT by **last year's** invested capital

This generates a percentage figure, representing the return on last year's invested capital (ROIC).

2. Compare ROIC to the WACC to find EVA® percentage

Perform the calculation EVA® = ROIC – WACC

This will indicate the extent to which our returns exceed the minimum required by the shareholders/debtholders.

(Note that it is possible for EVA® to be negative if the WACC exceeds ROIC)

This again generates a percentage figure, representing an EVA® percentage.

3. Apply EVA® percentage to last year's capital invested

This will find the absolute EVA® for that particular year

4. Discount absolute EVA® figures at the WACC

Apply discounting as normal to the absolute EVA® figures and then total these as normal to find the present value of the EVA®

Note – nothing really needs to be completed in the Year 0 column for NOPAT, ROIC etc.

EVA® – Worked Example

Assumes a WACC of 10%

		Year 0	Year 1	Year 2
	Invested capital	2,000	1,600	800
	NOPAT		88	400
Step 1	ROIC (NOPAT/PY invested capital)	-	4.4%	25%
Step 2	EVA® % = ROIC less WACC assumed of 10%	-	(5.6%)	15%
Step 3	Apply EVA® % to PY investment capital		(112)	240
Step 4	Discount factors	n/a	0.91	0.83
	Discounted EVA	n/a	(102)	199

Then complete as per an NPV calculation but do not apply any discounting to the Invested capital – EVA® simply evaluates the flows that occur from year 1 onwards and does not treat the initial capital investment as an outflow – the EVA® only occurs once we compare ROIC to the WACC to analyse flows in subsequent years. Therefore the figures of 2,000, 1,600 and 800 are used to calculate the ROIC but are not themselves discounted.

See also IFRS 13 and Valuation of Intangibles 244
Valuations topics

Valuations – Free Cash Flow Model

Exam tip – do not forget to **knock off the value of debt** at the final stage of the calculation to obtain the **equity value of shares only** (students always seem to forget to do this!).

Advantages of the FCF approach

Model is flexible to allow for specific data and details, including a period of temporary growth followed by a perpetuity (with or without growth)

Depreciation and CAPEX

Add back depreciation and deduct CAPEX

deduct. working capital.

If no data given, perhaps the best you can do is assume that these are approximately equal but make sure you state this and then criticise this assumption (as it is not realistic)

Perpetuity cash flows – the correct discount factor

Example: exam paper gives detailed specific cash flows for years 1 to 4 followed by a perpetuity from year 5 onwards

Remember that the correct discount factor to apply to the perpetuity is the **year 4** value (not the year 5 value) – this is because the perpetuity formula provides the present value of flows starting with **1 year of delay** – so applying the formula to the flows from **year 5** onwards gives the present value in **year 4** and therefore needs to be discounted by the **year 4 discount factor**

Professional scepticism points

Perpetuity assumption may be simplistic and unsustainable – requires forecasts to be reliable and the discount rate to be correct – future cash flows are just estimates

Query whether there is enough information on capital cash flows, CAPEX outlays and taxation

Determine whether depreciation assumptions/add backs are reasonable

Query validity of the discount rate (risk, changes in business, size, nature of business (private?))

Use of current WACC

The current WACC partly reflects the average risk of the company rather than the risk of a new particular project

The current WACC is determined at a point in time and may not be applicable over a long future time horizon

Possible adjustments

Consider all incremental costs and revenues that may result

Will director salaries and remuneration change if the Board of Directors is changed?

Eliminate one off items

Adjustments for inflation and other similar changes?

Deduct earnings from opportunities now foregone?

CAPEX

See also IFRS 13 and Valuation of Intangibles 244
Valuations topics

Valuations – High Growth Startup

Challenges in valuing a high growth startup company (often undervalued)

No track record so hard to estimate

Might have historical losses but bright prospects

Few revenue streams and products/services are untested

Unknown level of market acceptance and demand

Unknown levels of competition

Unknown cost structures

High development or infrastructure costs

Inexperienced management

Which valuation method to use?

Free Cash Flow model is probably the most sensible …

Net assets method – not appropriate because probably has low amount of tangible assets (value of the startup is from its people, marketing and intellectual property)

PE method and EBITDA multiple method – difficulty of finding a quoted comparator in the same stage of development – lack of disclosed information

EVA® method – very short investment period so not enough years to consider and may not have an established WACC

Consider whether there have been acquisitions by the company (goodwill on SFP) – can indicate improved earnings and may be possible to value the acquisitions based on historic information (assuming that the targets have existed longer than the company)

Entry cost valuation – consider the cost that would be involved in entering the market and establishing a new business of the same type: costs of raising finance, costs of assets acquired, cost of product development, cost of recruiting and training employees and costs of building up the customer base

First Chicago method – produce best case, worst case and base case scenario and discount these figures – use an expected value approach by weighting each calculation by the probability of each type

Limitations with using the Free Cash Flow model

Very sensitive to small changes in variables such as the growth rate

May not adequately reflect growth potential and flexibilities of a company in an early stage of development

May not adequately reflect the options to expand, delay, abandon or switch investments at various decision points

See also IFRS 13 and Valuation of Intangibles 244
Valuations topics

Valuations – PE Model

Value of a company is given by

PE ratio x maintainable earnings x discount for shareholding % (x discount for not being a plc)

Used to value the shares of a quoted company where it is recognised that the offer price for the shares must be higher than the current market price in order to gain acceptance of the offer from the target company's shareholders

Shares of an unquoted company where the PE ratio is derived from the PE for similar quoted companies

Discounts Rules of Thumb

Discounts for the shareholding % acquired

Shareholding	**Discount**
75%+	0-5%
50% to 74%	10-15%
50%	20-30%

Note – the discount may need to consider the position of the other shareholders: is there another single shareholder with a 50%+ holding (powerful) or is the shareholding dispersed over many shareholders (less powerful as will need united co-ordination to achieve 50%+)

Narrative points

Discuss the difference between a 75% and 50% shareholding (special versus ordinary resolutions)

Discounts for the status of the company

Status	**Discount**
Plc	Nil
AIM	20-30%
Limited company	40-50%

Professional scepticism

All 3 elements (PE ratio, maintainable earnings and the discount percentage) are uncertain and so can be queried

It can be difficult to find comparable companies as every company is different in some way

Should be based on future maintainable earnings – how do we know what is maintainable (we need to adjust for exceptionals but this requires judgement) and how to we estimate future possibilities?

What Might a High PE Ratio Reflect?

Optimistic expectations – if future growth is expected, a high price will be paid now

Security of earnings – a well-established, low-risk company may be worth more than a new startup

Status – quoted companies should not have any discount applied

Low level of earnings without a reduction in share price – note that a high PE is achieved if earnings drop but the share price stays the same or falls by a proportionately smaller amount – hence a high PE ratio is not always a good thing

Calculating an Implied PE Ratio from the Cost of Equity

See SBM July 2015 past paper Q2 for an example calculation and related discussion.

If the cost of equity is known, the implied PE Ratio can be calculated as **1/cost of equity**.

For example, if the cost of equity is 10% then the implied PE Ratio is 10.

This is because if earnings are £2m valued on a perpetuity basis then the value of the company using the cost of equity will be £2m/0.10 or £20m. This is the same thing as applying a PE Ratio of 10 to the earnings as £2m x 10 is £20m.

Note that the standard scepticism points regarding use of perpetuities would also apply here i.e. a perpetuity approach assumes that earnings/cash flow will be earned for ever and that the relevant growth rate (if used) is constant.

See also IFRS 13 and Valuation of Intangibles 244
Valuations topics

Valuations – Shareholder Value Analysis (SVA)

Based on the idea that shareholder value comes from 7 main sources:

1. Sales growth
2. Operating profit margin
3. Tax rate
4. Changes in working capital
5. Fixed capital investment
6. Cost of capital
7. Competitive advantage period

Steps in the SVA Approach

1. Calculate the present value of the estimated future annual free cash flows

2. Add the value of non-operational assets held by the business, such as short-term investments and cash

3. Subtract the value of the company's debt to obtain a valuation of the company's equity

See also IFRS 13 and Valuation of Intangibles 244
Valuations topics

Value-Based Management

A management process which links strategy, management and operational processes with the aim of creating shareholder value

Elements

Strategic planning

Capital allocation

Operating budgets

Performance measurements

Management remuneration

Internal communication

External communication

See also Key Performance Indicators 284

Withdrawal from a Business

General methods

- Flotation of the company onto a stock market
- Sale of shares to a private investor or institution (followed by flotation)
- Sale of the business to a competitor or customer
- Sale of shares to fellow directors or employees
- Maintaining existing shareholders but obtaining a cash withdrawal from the company (methods: bonus, dividend, share buy back)

Flotation – advantages

- May obtain a better price because shares are more easily marketable than as a private limited company
- Increased access to third party capital
- Increased marketability of shares
- Increased public profile, resulting in greater shareholder confidence
- Possibility of future share for share exchange if company wishes to expand in future

Flotation – disadvantages

- Costs of obtaining a flotation
- Management time involved
- Increased regulation by the stock exchange (possible need for interim financial statements)
- UK Corporate Governance Code may now apply, reducing the powers of directors
- If selling individual retains control, this may reduce the sales price – others will have less power

Sale of shares to a third party – advantages

- May increase value of shares since more easily realisable into cash
- Sale of at least 50% of shares could attract a control premium

Sale of shares to a third party – disadvantages

- Discount may need to apply for lack of marketability

Sale of the business to a competitor or customer – advantages

- Diversifies risk for both parties if share for share exchange
- Increase liquidity and marketability
- Avoids costs of a flotation
- Possibility of horizontal/vertical integration

Sale of shares to fellow directors and/or employees – advantages

- Likely to obtain a fair price as worked together for some time
- Could be a way to reward staff and fellow directors for their loyalty

Sale of shares to fellow directors and/or employees – disadvantages

- Relies on fellow directors having the cash available to purchase the shares
- May not generate as much cash as the other options

How to withdraw cash from the business

Bonus

- If a controlling shareholder then could elect to pay a large bonus (but could be considered to breach fiduciary duties if excessive: could lead to an action for unfair prejudice against the non-controlling (minority) shareholders)
- Corporation tax for the company but taxable as earnings for the directors/shareholder

Dividend payment

- Not deductible for corporation tax and taxable as earnings for the director

Share buy-back

- Governed by Companies Act – permanent capital of the company must be maintained
- Any premium on repayment would need to be covered by distributable reserves
- May be necessary to transfer amounts to a non-distributable capital redemption reserve to cover the reduction in share capital (exam tip: can you quantify this amount?)
- Company's Articles of Association must provide for this method
- Likely that off-market purchase of shares would need approval by Special Resolution

Sell to a competitor or customer

- Could be done by share for share exchange to maintain some control/influence and for tax reasons
- Vertical/horizontal integration possibilities for purchaser
- May offer diversification for seller and purchaser

Stock market flotation

Advantages

- Makes shares marketable – easier to withdraw fully or partially later
- Increased access to capital
- Increased public profile and public confidence for company
- Future share for share exchanges easier

Disadvantages

- High costs
- Uses management time
- High level of regulation e.g. London Stock Exchange listing rules
- UK Corporate Governance Code procedures required
- May have to offer a discount on shares if maintaining control via retained shares

Cash withdrawal

Advantages

- Dividends – may be tax efficient if structured correctly
- Bonuses – tax deductible for the company (dividends are not)
- Appropriate use of cash if no better investment alternatives

Disadvantages

- Impact on cash available for working capital
- Limits ability to replace assets
- Limits ability to have later acquisitions

Share buy back

Benefits of a share buyback for stakeholders

Provides a use for surplus cash which may otherwise be an unproductive asset if there are no other suitable project proposals

Gives the opportunity for some shareholders to have their investment returned to reinvest elsewhere, with low transaction costs

Increase in EPS through a reduction in the number of shares in issue – this could lead to a higher share price than may otherwise be the case – this might benefit executive directors if their bonuses are aligned to this figure

The company may be able to increase dividend payments per share on the remaining shares in issue – this is particularly the case if a policy of maintaining the overall dividend payment is carried out

May facilitate a company withdrawing from a main public market and becoming a private company again

Drawbacks of a share buyback for stakeholders

Increase in gearing through a change in the relative proportion of debt to equity – this increases the risks for shareholders and any bank which is acting as a lender to the company

It can be difficult to determine a price per share that will be fair both to vendors and also to shareholders who are not selling shares to the company

A repurchase of shares could be seen as an admission that the company cannot make better use of the funds than shareholders

Some shareholders may suffer from being taxed on a capital gain following the purchase of their shares rather than receiving dividend income, as they may have expected

There may not be 75% of eligible shareholders willing to vote to approve the scheme so it may not be feasible

If the company is listed on a public market then the share price may have changed by the time the scheme can be approved and implemented

Sale of shares to Directors

- Simple solution
- Should be a fair price for everyone – all parties have knowledge
- Does the company have enough cash available?

Partial withdrawal/sale/disposal by existing owners

Is the offer attractive and suitable? Considerations

Control retained?

Cash received up front – amount and will this help the business (e.g. unable to obtain otherwise)?

Non-cash advantages such as technology received?

Exam tip – **always** consider the percentage shareholdings involved and then consider any agreement on director appointments

Note that if the shareholding is below 50% but close to that figure (e.g. 48% or 49%) then you could argue that if this is held by a single company/individual then it is a very powerful position particularly if the other 51% is spread across a large number of shareholders (since these may not all agree and work together)

Note that with a 49% shareholding but an ability to appoint several directors, it can be argued that the shareholder has considerable power

Withdrawal from a Business – Director Considerations

This topic considers some matters that Directors leaving a business may want to consider when negotiating the best deal for their future

Control

Will the Directors retain shares and therefore some element of control?

How many Directors are leaving and therefore how will control be shared?

Is the entire Board being replaced or just a few Directors? What will be the impact on management quality in future?

Can the Directors act together if they are retaining shares?

Financial Impact

Consider how the departure will be financed – termination payment? Bonus? Receiving or giving up share options?

Will new shares be issued as part of the departure and how will this affect the control aspects?

Shares versus Termination Payment

Will the Directors receive shares? Are these marketable (quoted) or not?

Sale of shares could offer a convenient exit route and may allow for tax-planning

Can the shares be sold easily or will the Directors have such a large amount that they have to "drip-feed" into the market?

Current value of a shareholding – affected by:

Role within the company – does the director earn a return through a salary? This may be above market rates due to the control connected with ownership of shares (but if it is below market rates it could actually be considered a cost to the director of holding the shares and being involved)

Dividends received

Whether a forced sale is required to realise cash urgently

Considerations for new shareholders

Dividends

Price paid

Percentage acquired and percentage of voting rights – ordinary resolution, special resolution and so on

Control

Ability to earn a salary if appointed as a director

Requirement to borrow personally?

Change in level of diversification, depending on the shareholders' other holdings

Consider any bonuses or share options and future potential benefit

Working Capital

Working capital is the excess of current assets over current liabilities – it represents the resources required to run the daily operations of a business

Why does effective working capital management matter?

Source of competitive advantage and therefore corporate and shareholder value – ensures that the right inventory is on hand when needed

Key element of the value chain – management of inventories, supplier relationships and customer relationships are important for operations, the supply chain and logistics management

Significant source of customer satisfaction

Concepts to consider

Working capital ratios (trade, payables and inventory days)

Cash operating cycle

Overtrading

Methods of managing inventory

Economic Order Quantity (EOQ) model – see below

Using trade credit

Credit control finance and management

Cash management

Cash budgets

Strategic Management of Working Capital

The 2 main objectives of working capital management are (1) to ensure that a company has sufficient liquid resources to meet its short and long-term requirements and (2) to increase its profitability.

This involves achieving a balance between the requirement to minimise the risk of insolvency (liquidity) and the requirement to maximise the return on assets (profitability).

The differences between businesses regarding working capital characteristics are generally of 3 main types:

- inventory holding period
- time taken to pay suppliers and other accounts payable
- time allowed to customers to make payments

Generally, a service business will have a low requirement for working capital whereas a manufacturing business will have a high requirement for working capital. This is because many service businesses do not require large inventories.

Organisations such as supermarkets and retailers will receive much of their sales in cash, via credit card or debit card – however, they will buy from their suppliers on credit so they have the advantage of significant cash holdings, which they could invest.

At the other end of the scale, a company that supplies other companies is likely to be selling and buying mainly on credit – coordinating the flow of cash can then be a problem – such a company may make use of short-term borrowing such as an overdraft to manage its cash but smaller companies with a limited trading record may face particular problems, such as difficulties in getting credit from suppliers – at the same time, the customers of a small company are likely to expect to receive the length of credit that is normal for that particular business activity and they will not allow any alternative terms just because the business is smaller.

The effective management of inventory, customer accounts, cash resources and supplier accounts can therefore be a source of competitive advantage.

Effective working capital management can also comprise a key element of the value chain. The management of inventories, supplier relationships and customer relationships are closely related to operations, supply chain and logistics management.

The working capital requirement

Determining the working capital requirement is a matter of calculating the value of current assets less current liabilities, perhaps by taking averages over a one-year period.

Over-capitalisation

Indicators of over-capitalisation (investing in excessive inventories and having a large amount of accounts receivable and cash) include:

- sales/working capital ratio reduced compared with previous years, or less than in similar companies
- high level of liquidity, indicated by a high current ratio of more than 2 and a high quick ratio of more than 1
- long turnover periods for inventory and accounts receivable

Conservative approach

Financing net current assets with medium-term loans – only an occasional need for short term financing when net current assets exceed the amount of medium-term borrowing

Net current assets fluctuate in amount but using a medium-term loan (which has a longer time period than the fluctuations) means that the loan is financing not just permanent net current assets but also temporary net current assets too

Often leads to surplus cash – interest earned on this is likely to be less than the interest paid on borrowings – so having surplus cash has a net cost from over-borrowing

Aggressive approach

Financing net current assets entirely with short-term finance such as a bank overdraft

Cost of this is likely to be lower than a medium term loan because overdraft interest accrues only when the overdraft is being used (rather than all the time under a loan) and the interest rate on an overdraft may be lower

But risky as overdraft can be called in at any time

Influences on working capital style

Industry norms – especially for receivables: will be hard to match shorter payment periods

Products – length of the production cycle will differ in different industries

Management issues – quality of management and degree of control and monitoring

Managing the Operating Cycle

Companies that are **more efficient at generating cash** are **better able to implement strategic plans** so effective management of the operating cycle can be a source of **competitive advantage**

Good control over **inventory** can be important in ensuring that there are items **on hand** when customers want them and that items are in **good condition**

Good management of **supplier accounts** enhances **supply chain management** and ensures that **costs** and **delivery times are minimised**

A **significant** part of working capital management affects the **interaction** with **customers** and can be a significant source of customer **satisfaction** (or **dissatisfaction**) – customers have grown accustomed to the time between order and delivery being **very short** so companies which **focus upon shortening** the **period** between order and invoice (and related eventual collection of cash) are **better placed to meet customer expectations**

Short-term actions to improve cash generation include delaying payments to suppliers or reducing inventory – however, this will **not create sustained competitive advantage** which instead requires a **longer-term** approach and engagement from departments across the business involved in procurement, sales, inventory management and finance

Effective working capital management can also comprise a **key element of the value chain** – enterprise resource planning (ERP) systems can integrate an entity's systems and facilitate the flow of information between all business functions within an organisation and can also be used to manage connections to outside stakeholders such as suppliers

Integration of the operating cycle could include:

- initial recording of the sales order
- procurement of necessary parts or components
- production planning and resource utilisation
- work-flow automation
- real-time order status updates including delivery and billing information
- electronic invoicing
- electronic payment interfaces with customers and suppliers
- credit management

Management of inventory

Modern systems of **inventory** management such as just-in-time techniques aim to **minimise** the level of inventory held

However, one of the **concerns** with **reducing** inventory to **minimal** levels is the potential **impact** on **customers** and their orders – if there are **problems**, it could lead to cancelled **orders** and lower sales

Developing **relationships** with **customers** to better **understand the likely demand levels** will improve service, ensuring that **sufficient** inventory is available whilst at the same time making sure that inventory levels are **not excessive**

Management of accounts receivable

Offering credit **incurs an interest cost** charged on an overdraft to fund the period of credit or the interest lost on the cash not received and deposited in the bank – it is also likely to lead to an **increase in bad debts**

If offering credit generates **extra sales**, then those extra sales will have **additional repercussions** on the amount of **inventory** maintained in the warehouse, to ensure that the extra demand can be satisfied – the amount of money the company owes to its **accounts payable** will also be affected as it will be increasing its supply of raw materials

Early settlement discounts may be employed to shorten average credit periods and reduce investment in accounts receivable and therefore interest costs – the **benefits and interest costs saved should exceed the cost of the discounts allowed**

Businesses can enter into arrangements with a **factor** or **invoice discounter** to improve cash flow and shorten the cash cycle

Management of accounts payable

Taking credit from suppliers is a **normal** feature of business and **paying suppliers as late as possible** is a **common working capital management technique** – **trade credit** is usually a **cheap** source of finance as **suppliers rarely charge interest** – this form of financing is **particularly important to small and fast-growing firms**

However, it is **important** that such a technique is **managed** in a way that **does not damage relationships** with the supplier – **doing so** could **adversely affect the smooth functioning** of the **supply chain**

If a supplier offers a discount for the early payment of debt, a company must consider whether the benefits of accepting the discount outweigh the finance costs of having to pay earlier (as the company may now require a greater overdraft or, alternatively, will have lost the opportunity

Economic Order Quantity Model (EOQ)

$$EOQ = \sqrt{2cd/h}$$

where

c = cost of placing one order

d = estimated usage of the inventory item over a particular period

h = cost of holding one unit of inventory for that period

Limitations of the EOQ Model

Not simple to apply

Unjustified assumptions about usage and constant purchase price that may be unjustified

Ignores the potential benefit of taking advantage of bulk discounts

Can be very difficult in practice to estimate holding costs and the cost of placing each order

See also Supply Chain Improvements 397

Appendix 1a

Detailed review of changes in 2020 CR Study Manual

This Appendix reviews the changes made in the 2020 edition of the Study Manual. References to "old page" are references to the related page in the 2019 edition of the Study Manual – in most cases, this reference relates to a very similar section in the 2019 edition but in cases where the 2020 edition has added completely new material, the reference to the "old page" indicates where within the relevant chapter the new 2020 content has been added. Similarly, in cases where the 2020 edition has deleted content, the reference to "new page" indicates where within the relevant chapter the 2020 edition would have contained the content if it had not been deleted from the equivalent place (indicated by our "old page" reference) in the 2019 edition.

Please note that we are providing these page numbers from the 2019 edition of the Study Manual for reference purposes only and primarily for the use of students who have already studied this paper using the 2019 syllabus – if you do not already have access to the 2019 edition of the Study Manual, we are in no way suggesting that you must purchase a 2019 edition to access the old content as this is not necessary and the references are being provided purely for the use of students who may already have access to the prior year edition. We have fully described all changes in the text below and you are not expected to use any prior year edition of the Study Manual to understand the points made in this Appendix.

There have been no changes in the number of chapters or the titles of the chapters.

Please note that our review below does not attempt to track all changes in the in-chapter Self-test questions and Interactive questions between the 2019 and 2020 editions. As we do not think that any of these changes are particularly material to your studies, we have not listed these out separately in our analysis but any changes to the main technical text in connection with such changes have been noted in full in our review below.

Chapter 1 Introduction

Page 10 (old page 10)

Section 3.1 is shorter in the 2020 edition: there has been a deletion of text which stated that audits serve the purpose of enforcing accountability and promoting confidence, as well as deletion of text on the stewardship role of Directors. The remaining text is identical to the equivalent text in the 2019 edition.

Page 11 (old page 11)

The discussion of the "expectation gap" is longer in the 2020 edition. The 2019 edition also contained the words "3.4 The audit opinion" as a sub-section heading just before the paragraph which starts "The key judgement made by the auditor" but these 3 words have been removed from the 2020 edition: otherwise, the subsequent text on this page is unchanged in the 2020 edition.

Page 12 (old page 12)

The 2020 edition deletes a reference to the requirements of ISA 260 which used to be included after the flowchart diagram.

Page 12 (old page 13)

The 2020 edition deletes some historical information on changes in the audit thresholds in the early 1990s and 2012: the 2020 edition only mentions the latest set of thresholds.

The 2020 edition also deletes a complicated diagram and discussion across several pages on situations in which an audit exemption cannot be claimed: the 2020 edition only contains a single sentence on this point so is much simpler.

Page 13 (old page 16)

The Section overview box is new for the 2020 edition.

The 2020 edition has a shorter discussion of the enlightened shareholder duty and duty of skill and care concepts.

Page 17 (old page 20)

The 2020 edition removes a Point to note which stated that the FRC is now responsible for Auditing Standards, which were previously issued by the APB.

Page 18 (old page 21)

The discussion of the Conduct Committee in the middle of the page is slightly longer in the 2020 edition.

Section 5.1.4 on "Current issues" is new for the 2020 edition. Several sections on the Audit and Assurance Council, Corporate Reporting Council, Actuarial Council and the Audit Quality Review Committee have been deleted from the 2020 edition. Further deletions on the Case Management Committee and Corporate Reporting Review Committee are made on the following page.

Page 19 (old page 22)

The first 2 paragraphs of Section 5.2 on "Interaction between FRC and IAASB Standards" are new for the 2020 edition.

Section 5.3 on "International Auditing and Assurance Standards Board" has been deleted from the 2020 edition.

Page 19 (old page 23)

Section 5.3 on "IAASB Projects" has been rewritten compared to the equivalent Section 5.4 in the 2019 edition.

Page 20 (old page 25)

Sections 5.5.2 on “Relationship between ISAs and UK standards” and 5.5.3 on “Harmonisation – Clarity standards for UK and Ireland” have been deleted from the 2020 edition.

Section 5.4.1 on “Implementation of EU Audit Regulation and Directive” has been amended for the 2020 edition.

Page 21 (old page 26)

The 2020 edition deletes a Point to note which states that the June 2016 revised ISAs are termed “ISA (UK)”.

The 2020 edition deletes Section 5.6 on “Brexit” and replaces it with Section 5.5 on “The global outlook” (which is Section 5.5 in the 2020 edition, given that Section 5.3 in the old edition has been deleted, as indicated above).

Page 22 (old page 27)

Section 6.2 on “Quality control at a firm level” has been rewritten for the 2020 edition which now contains a significantly condensed version of content previously in the 2019 edition: the 2020 version of this discussion is just over a page in length compared to 5 pages of discussion in the 2019 edition.

Page 26 (old page 34)

The paragraphs starting “This was followed in May 2018” and “While many might seem sceptical” (together with the 5 bullet points associated with the second paragraph noted here) are new for the 2020 edition.

Page 27 (old page 35)

The paragraph starting “Review of audit working papers is important” is new for the 2020 edition and replaces a longer discussion at the end of Section 6.5 on “Audit documentation” in the 2019 edition and also replaces content from Section 6.6 on “Review of working papers” which has been deleted from the 2020 edition.

Chapter 2 Principles of corporate reporting

Page 49 (old page 61)

The 2020 edition deletes a reference to leases as an example of accounting for substance: the only example given in the 2020 edition is that of the group financial statements.

Page 58 (old page 70)

The first set of bullet points in Section 2.10 on “Revised *Conceptual Framework* (March 2018)” is longer in the 2020 edition: the points in bold are the same as in the 2019 edition but the 2020 edition further elaborates on each point.

The wording "and affects many areas of financial reporting" has been added to the paragraph starting "The revised *Conceptual Framework* comes into force" in the 2020 edition.

The flowchart diagram at the bottom of the page is new for the 2020 edition.

Page 59 (old page 70)

Section 2.10.2 on "Qualitative characteristics of useful financial information" has been slightly re-worded for the 2020 edition.

Section 2.10.3 on "Financial statements and the reporting entity" is significantly longer in the 2020 edition.

Section 2.10.4 on "Recognition and derecognition" is significantly longer in the 2020 edition.

Page 61 (old page 71)

The flowchart diagram at the top of the page is new for the 2020 edition.

Page 61 (old page 72)

Section 2.10.6 on "Presentation and disclosure" is significantly longer in the 2020 edition.

Page 65 (old page 75)

The 2020 edition deletes reference to Defined benefit plans in the lettered list of Principal recognition and measurement simplifications within the IFRSs for SMEs.

Page 71 (old page 82)

The 2020 edition deletes a reference to Practice Note 26 (revised) which provides guidance on how the ISA requirements can be applied to smaller entities.

Page 77 (old page 88)

The 2020 edition deletes Section 4.9 on "Was the fair value project necessary?".

Page 77 (old page 89)

The 2020 edition deletes Section 4.9.1 on "Advantages and disadvantages of fair value (versus historical cost)" which also contained a flowchart diagram comparing fair value and historical cost as methodologies.

Page 83 (old page 95)

The list of "Expected dates" within the current IASB Work Plan has been updated compared to the same table provided in the 2019 edition.

Chapter 3 Ethics

Page 95 (old page 115)

The 2020 edition adds a statement that ICAEW proposes to amend its Code of Ethics to take effect from 1 January 2020. No further examinable details are provided in the 2020 edition.

Chapter 4 Corporate governance

Page 135 (old page 167)

The 2020 edition slightly condenses item (b) within Section 1.1 on "Introduction" and also now refers under the same item to the most recent update to the UK Corporate Governance Code in July 2018.

Page 136 (old page 168)

The 2020 edition contains a detailed OECD definition of "Corporate governance" which replaces a simple single line definition, which was not attributed to any specific source, used in the 2019 edition. However, note that the text starting "An alternative definition is" is identical to the 2019 edition so it is only the OECD definition material above this alternative definition which is new for the 2020 edition.

Page 141 (old page 173)

Section 3.1 on "Overview" has been extensively rewritten for the 2020 edition so that it now refers to the July 2018 edition of the UK Corporate Governance Code ("the Code"), including 4 specific bullet points on the main changes implemented by the new version of the Code.

Page 142 (old page 174)

The set of 5 bullet points on issues mentioned in the introduction to the Code is mostly different from a similar listing in the 2019 edition.

Page 143 (old page 174)

The 5 main categories of the Code are different in the 2020 edition compared to the 2019 edition, reflecting the fact that the 2020 edition uses the 2018 edition of the Code.

The 2020 edition states that the 5 main categories of the Code are supported by 18 core principles and a further 41 more detailed provisions.

The various tabular summaries of the elements of the 5 main categories which start on page 143 in the new edition are different to the 2019 edition.

Page 144 (old page 179)

The 2020 edition deletes 2 Points to note which were contained at the end of the tabular summaries of the elements of the 5 main categories of the Code in the 2019 edition.

Section 3.3 on "Disclosure requirements of the Code" has been completely rewritten for the 2020 edition.

Page 146 (old page 181)

Section 3.4 on "Additional requirements of the Code" is new for the 2020 edition.

Page 147 (old page 181)

The Section overview box at the start of Section 4 on "Role of the board" has been rewritten and condensed for the 2020 edition.

Page 147 (old page 182)

Section 4.1 on "Scope of role" now refers to the 2018 edition of the FRC publication *Guidance on Board Effectiveness* but otherwise the text in the relevant paragraph appears to be unchanged from the 2019 edition.

Page 148 (old page 182)

Section 4.2.1 on "Nomination committee" has been dropped from the 2020 edition.

Page 148 (old page 183)

Section 4.2.2 on "Commitment" has been dropped from the 2020 edition.

The 2020 edition refers to the "chair" rather than to the "chairman" in Section 4.3 on "Possession of necessary information".

Page 148 (old page 183)

The statement that there should be separate appraisal of the Chairman and Chief Executive (with links to the remuneration process) has been deleted from Section 4.4 on "Performance of board" in the 2020 edition.

The statement that the Code states that the Chief Executive should only become chairman in exceptional circumstances (together with related required consultation with major shareholders in advance) has been deleted from Section 4.5 on "Board membership and division of responsibilities" in the 2020 edition.

Page 151 (old page 186)

Section 4.6.5 on "Current developments and further reading" has been deleted from the 2020 edition.

Section 5.1 on "The UK Stewardship Code" has been rewritten and significantly condensed for the 2020 edition.

Page 152 (old page 188)

The 2020 edition deletes a statement in Section 5.2 on "The FRC's *Guidance on Risk Management, Internal Control and Related Financial and Business Reporting*" which stated that the Turnbull Report predates the Code but remains relevant.

Page 163 (old page 199)

The statement at the top of the page that the Listing Rules have not been updated for the 2018 edition of the Code is new for 2020 edition. This means that the discussion on the rest of the page is the same as in the 2019 edition.

Chapter 5 The statutory audit: planning and risk assessment

Page 175 (old page 219)

Section 13 is entitled "Data analytics, robotic process automation (RPA) and artificial intelligence (AI)" in the 2020 edition which is a slight change to the title "Data analytics and artificial intelligence (AI)" used in the 2019 edition.

Page 176 (old page 220)

The first and fifth bullet points have been very slightly expanded to give more detail on the specific technologies referred to in each bullet point.

Page 179 (old page 224)

The 2020 edition deletes Section 3.3 on "Briefing paper" which provided 4.5 pages of discussion of an APB briefing paper in the 2019 edition.

Page 180 (old page 229)

The bracketed phrase right at the bottom of the page is new for the 2020 edition.

Page 215 (old page 263)

The third paragraph at the end of Section 11.1 on "The use of information technology" is new for the 2020 edition.

Page 218 (old page 266)

Section 11.5 on "Cryptocurrencies and blockchain" is new for the 2020 edition.

Page 221 (old page 268)

Section 13 has been retitled to include the words "robotic process automation (RPA)".

Page 225 (old page 272)

The paragraph headed as "Auditing data analytics" is new for the 2020 edition.

Page 228 (old page 276)

Section 13.5.3 on "Robotic process automation (RPA)" is new for the 2020 edition.

Page 229 (old page 276)

The definition of "Artificial intelligence (AI)" is slightly longer as the final sentence is new for the 2020 edition.

The final sentence in the paragraph starting "Current examples of AI include" is new for the 2020 edition.

The final sentence in the paragraph starting "There is an increasing role of AI" is new for the 2020 edition.

Chapter 6 The statutory audit: audit evidence

Page 265 (old page 319)

The 2020 edition refers to the December 2018 revised version of ISA (UK) 540 rather than to the June 2016 revised version.

The definition of "Estimation uncertainty" is new for the 2020 edition.

All content below the "Estimation uncertainty" definition and before the start of Section 6.1 represents a slightly redrafted version of the 2019 edition content to allow for use of the December 2018 revised version of ISA (UK) 540 in the 2020 edition.

Page 265 (old page 320)

Section 6.1 on "Audit procedures" has been significantly rewritten to allow for use of the December 2018 revised version of ISA (UK) 540 in the 2020 edition.

Page 266 (old page 321)

Section 6.2 on "Evaluation of results of audit procedures" and Section 6.3 on "Key audit matter" have been rewritten to allow for use of the December 2018 revised version of ISA (UK) 540 in the 2020 edition.

Page 274 (old page 329)

Section 9.1 on "Direction" is significantly shorter in the 2020 edition. Note that Section 9.2, 9.3 and 9.4 on the same page and following page are also significantly shorter in the 2020 edition.

Chapter 7 The statutory audit: evaluating and testing internal controls

Page 311 (old page 385)

Steps 1 and 2 are shorter in the 2020 edition. Step 4 deletes a long tabular summary of internal controls issues which was contained in the 2019 edition.

Page 329 (old page 405)

The 2020 edition deletes a statement at the very end of the chapter that stated that the auditor's responsibilities with regards to communicating deficiencies in internal controls to those charged with governance and management are discussed in chapter 4 of the Study Manual.

Chapter 8 The statutory audit: finalisation, review and reporting

Page 341 (old page 427)

The words "robotic process automation (RPA)" have been added to the title of Section 1.4 and have also been added into the first sentence of the single paragraph which constitutes Section 1.4 but otherwise the text appears to be unchanged.

Page 342 (old page 428)

The sentence starting "In summary, these procedures consist" within Section 2.2 on "Events occurring up to the date of the auditor's report" is new for the 2020 edition.

The 2020 edition deletes a tabular summary of procedures testing in relation to subsequent events.

Page 345 (old page 431)

The reference to the headings of "financial, operating and other" is new for the 2020 edition. Section 3.2 on "Financial risk" then deletes a page of content.

Page 345 (old page 432)

A bullet point list of 4 major changes in relation to ISA 570 has been deleted from the start of Section 3.3 on "ISA (UK) 570, *Going Concern*" in the 2020 edition.

The content on "Management's responsibility" is shorter in the 2020 edition.

Page 348 (old page 435)

The 2020 edition deletes a reference to how the previous version of ISA 570 required the use of an Emphasis of Matter paragraph to highlight the disclosure of material uncertainties relating to going concern.

Page 348 (old page 436)

Section 3.4 on "Going concern issues during adverse economic conditions" is significantly shorter in the 2020 edition as the final paragraph condenses longer content on procedures and possible reasons for a bank's reluctance to provide positive confirmations. There has also been a deletion of content which used to be contained on page 437 in the old edition.

Page 357 (old page 445)

The 2020 edition removes a set of bullet points on the main changes in ISA (UK) 700.

Page 369 (old page 458)

The final paragraph on the page in relation to the "Basis for opinion paragraph" of an audit report is slightly shorter in the 2020 edition.

Page 373 (old page 462)

The 2020 edition deletes a set of bullet points on the main changes in ISA (UK) 720.

The discussion at the bottom of the page underneath the 3 definitions is shorter in the 2020 edition.

Page 375 (old page 464)

Section 6.5.6 on "Current issues" is new for the 2020 edition.

Chapter 9 Reporting financial performance

Page 400 (old page 496)

The 2020 edition removes a statement that the Disclosure Initiative (Amendments to IAS 1) is effective for annual periods beginning on or after 1 January 2016 (with earlier application permitted).

Chapter 10 Reporting revenue

Page 450 (old page 556)

Section 1.2.1 on "Significance for your exam" is new for the 2020 edition and explains that IFRS 15 is a recent, topical standard that could be tested in a number of ways – it is also noted that IFRS 15 was examined for the first time in July 2019 when it formed a large part of Question 3. The examiners also note that reference was made to data analytics "which could be a focus of future questions on revenue".

Page 472 (old page 578)

Section 3.12 on "Key effects of IFRS 15" has been deleted from the 2020 edition.

Page 472 (old page 579)

Section 3.13 on "Timing of revenue" has been deleted from the 2020 edition.

Page 473 (old page 581)

The content on Returns, Warranties, Revenue collected on behalf of third parties and Bundled services, licences, royalties and repurchase agreements is new for the 2020 edition.

Chapter 11 Earnings per share

Page 486 (old page 604)

Section 1.4.1 on "Auditing issues" is new for the 2020 edition.

Chapter 12 Reporting of assets

Page 523 (old page 646)

The table within Section 1.2 on "Inventories" is new for the 2020 edition but the content of the table simply reorganises identical language which was previously written in a single column of bullet points in the 2019 edition. Therefore, there has been no change in the related technical content for the 2020 edition.

Page 524 (old page 648)

Section 1.4 on "IAS 36, *Impairment of Assets*" has been almost entirely rewritten for the 2020 edition. The 2020 edition significantly reduces the length of the discussion and no longer contains reference to the fair value less costs to sell, value in use or discount rate concepts.

Page 527 (old page 651)

The "Leases" row in the table in Section 2.2 on "Initial measurement and further aspects of recognition" has been amended so that it now refers to IFRS 16.

Page 528 (old page 654)

The "Entity occupies part of property and leases out balance" row in the table no longer refers to the finance lease concept but otherwise the content is unchanged.

Page 543 (old page 670)

The Section overview box at the start of Section 6 on "Audit focus points" now contains a statement at the bottom of the box that "Other areas will have been tested at the Professional Level in Audit and Assurance but may still require some key questions to be answered by auditors in the Corporate Reporting exam".

Page 544 (old page 671)

The set of 3 bullet points at the top of the page which relates to the auditing of assets is new for the 2020 edition.

Chapter 13 Reporting of non-financial liabilities

Page 569 (old page 715)

The second bullet point within Section 2.1.2 on “Onerous contracts” regarding lease agreements is new for the 2020 edition.

Chapter 14 Leases, government grants and borrowing costs

Page 583 (old page 737)

Sections 1 to 4 of this chapter have been completely rewritten (and in some cases now refer to completely different areas of technical content) to allow for the transition from IAS 17 in the 2019 edition to IFRS 16 in the 2020 edition as the main examinable standard on leases.

Given the very extensive nature of the changes in these sections, we have not attempted to track the changes in Sections 1 to 4 of this chapter on a line by line basis (unlike in relation to all other changes noted in this review). We would recommend that if you have taken the examination in 2019 or an earlier year, you should simply start again from scratch in relation to your reading of the content on leases rather than attempting to track all the individual changes as this is likely to be a poor use of your time.

Page 584 (old page 738)

The 2020 edition deletes a Learning outcome which required candidates to identify and explain current and emerging issues in corporate reporting.

Page 614 (old page 762)

The Section overview box at the start of Section 8 on “Audit focus” has been rewritten for the 2020 edition.

Section 8.1 on “Auditing leases for lessees” has been completely rewritten for the 2020 edition.

Page 615 (old page 763)

Section 8.2 on “Auditing leases for lessors” is new for the 2020 edition.

Page 615 (old page 764)

The 2020 edition replaces the wording “Once IFRS 16 has replaced IAS 17” in the 2019 edition with the words “Now IFRS 16 has replaced IAS 17” at the start of Section 8.3 on “Issues following on from the adoption of IFRS 16” but otherwise the remainder of the text in this section appears to be unchanged in the 2020 edition.

Page 616 (old page 765)

The end of chapter Summary diagram has been extensively revised to allow for the move to IFRS 16. However, note that the diagrams on the following 2 pages in relation to technical areas other than leases appear to be completely unchanged in the 2020 edition.

Chapter 15 Financial instruments: presentation and disclosure

Page 631 (old page 789)

Section 1.1 on "Refresh your memory" is new for the 2020 edition.

Page 634 (old page 791)

The 2020 edition deletes a significant amount of content from Section 1.3.2 on "Practical implications" as the equivalent section in the 2019 edition was over a page in length whereas in the 2020 edition it is just 2.5 lines in length.

Chapter 16 Financial instruments: recognition and measurement

Page 655 (old page 815)

In the 2020 edition, the Section overview box no longer explains to candidates that IAS 39 was probably studied at the Professional Level.

Section 1.2 on "What are financial instruments?" is different to Section 1.2 in the 2019 edition which contained a review of material covered at the professional level.

Page 658 (old page 817)

Section 1.3 on "Practical implications for key ratios" is new for the 2020 edition.

Page 661 (old page 819)

The Section overview box at the start of Section 2 no longer refers to derecognition principles.

Page 662 (old page 820)

Section 2.2 on "IFRS 9 definitions" is new for the 2020 edition.

Page 663 (old page 822)

Sections 2.4, 2.5 and 2.6 (which start on page 663 and finish on page 669 of the 2020 edition) contain content that is identical to content contained later in the chapter in the 2019 edition. These sections therefore amount to a simple movement of existing content rather than new technical material. The only change within this moved content is the complete deletion of the decision tree (previously contained in Section 2.8.8 of the old edition) referred to in our next point.

Page 669 (old page 831)

The 2020 edition deletes Section 2.8.8 on "Decision tree" which provided a flow diagram to help with the classification of financial assets.

Page 675 (old page 820)

Section 2.11 on "Regular way transactions" contains content which was previously contained earlier in the same chapter in the 2019 edition. However, the Note which constitutes the first paragraph of this section has been added for the 2020 edition. Otherwise, the content appears to be unchanged.

Page 680 (old page 837)

The Note under the summary table in Section 3.6 on "Summary of measurement rules" is new for the 2020 edition.

Page 685 (old page 840)

The first paragraph of Section 4.2 on "Background and scope of IFRS 9 impairment model" is a shorter version of similar content in the 2019 edition. The 2020 edition removes references to IAS 39 and IAS 37 but otherwise the underlying technical points are unchanged.

Page 685 (old page 841)

The final bullet point in Section 4.2 on "Background and scope of IFRS 9 impairment model" has been slightly amended for the 2020 edition so that it no longer refers to IAS 17 and therefore now only refers to IFRS 16 in relation to leases.

Page 694 (old page 850)

Section 4.7 on "Possible effects" has been deleted from the 2020 edition. This contained 4 possible effects of the IFRS 9 impairment model in the 2019 edition.

Page 709 (old page 864)

The Section overview box has been amended so that it no longer refers to implementation issues following the introduction of IFRS 9 as stated in the 2019 edition.

The 2020 edition deletes Section 7.1 on "IFRS 9 implementation issues" which used to be contained within Section 7 on "Current developments" in the 2019 edition.

Page 709 (old page 865)

The 2020 edition deletes a detailed discussion of the "timing feature" and "amount feature" from Section 7.1.1 on "June 2018 Discussion Paper" which was contained in the 2019 edition. However, the 2020 edition retains brief reference to these 2 concepts.

Chapter 17 Financial instruments: hedge accounting

Page 749 (old page 913)

The 2020 edition deletes Section 9.1 on "Background" which was contained in the 2019 edition and explained that IFRS 9 became effective for accounting periods beginning on or after 1 January 2018, that an entity may choose its accounting policy in respect of hedge accounting when it first applies IFRS 9 and that the IASB planned to publish a Discussion Paper on dynamic risk management in 2019.

Page 749 (old page 914)

The 2020 edition places the sentence "Currently, IFRS 9 does not address macro hedging" in bold typeface: exactly the same wording was contained in the 2019 edition but it was not in bold typeface.

The 2020 edition deletes 2.5 pages of content on the different rules of IAS 39 in relation to hedge accounting.

Page 751 (old page 918)

Section 10.1 on "Audit issues around fair value" is significantly shorter in the 2020 edition at around half the length of the equivalent section in the 2019 edition.

Section 10.2 on "Auditing fair values" is a significantly shorter version of Section 10.2 on "Auditing fair value measurements and disclosures" as contained in the 2019 edition. Section 10.2 in the 2020 edition is just over half a page in length whereas it was over 2 pages in length in the 2019 edition.

Chapter 18 Employee benefits

Page 775 (old page 959)

The 2020 edition deletes a statement that IAS 19 was extensively revised in 2011.

Page 803 (old page 987)

The second sentence in the paragraph starting "Auditors need to ensure" which refers students back to the discussion in chapter 6 of ISA (UK) 540 (Revised) has been added for the 2020 edition. The additional sentence emphasises that complexity, subjectivity and estimation uncertainty are "extremely relevant" concepts.

Chapter 19 Share-based payment

There do not appear to have been any changes made to this chapter.

Chapter 20 Groups: types of investment and business combination

Page 903 (old page 1107)

The paragraph starting "as we saw in Chapter 16" in relation to the gain or loss on derecognition is new for the 2020 edition. Similarly, all paragraphs at the top of the following page (page 904) up to the start of the Worked example on "Control in stages - previous holding a simple investment" are new for the 2020 edition.

Page 941 (old page 1146)

The 2020 edition provides data on the 2019 inflation rate in Venezuela rather than the 2018 rate for the same country which was used in the 2019 edition of the Study Manual. However, the underlying technical point is unchanged.

Chapter 21 Foreign currency translation and hyperinflation

There do not appear to have been any changes made to this chapter.

Chapter 22 Income taxes

There do not appear to have been any changes made to this chapter.

Chapter 23 Financial statement analysis 1

Page 1088 (old page 1340)

The 2020 edition deletes some discussion in relation to finance leases and operating leases from Section 2.6.1 on "Capital expenditure to depreciation" towards the bottom of the page.

Page 1104 (old page 1356)

The 2020 edition deletes some text on operating leases and finance leases in the middle of the page just before the start of Section 7 on "Ethical issues".

Chapter 24 Financial statement analysis 2

Page 1120 (old page 1394)

The 2020 edition deletes a Learning outcome in relation to assurance issues in respect of social responsibility, sustainability and environmental matters. The 2020 edition also deletes a Learning outcome which required candidates to critically evaluate accounting policy choices and estimates, identifying issues of earnings manipulation and creative accounting.

Page 1131 (old page 1405)

Section 4.1.3 on "Leased assets" has been significantly redrafted for the 2020 edition to allow for IFRS 16 becoming the main examinable standard on leases.

Page 1132 (old page 1406)

Section 4.1.4 on "Sale and leaseback transactions" has been rewritten and extended so that it now refers to IFRS 16 and IFRS 15.

Page 1133 (old page 1407)

Section 4.1.6 on "Revenue recognition" has been slightly extended in the 2020 edition so that it now refers to IFRS 15.

Page 1136 (old page 1410)

The section with the sub-heading of "Leased assets" has been rewritten for the 2020 edition so that it now refers to IFRS 16.

Page 1166 (old page 1442)

The 2020 edition makes a very slight change to the final sentence in Section 9.1 on "Need for a management commentary" by stating that a Reporting Statement on the Operating and Financial Review was issued in 2006 – in the 2019 edition, it was stated that the Reporting Statement was issued in "January 2006" rather than simply "2006" as stated in the 2020 edition.

Page 1169 (old page 1445)

The 2020 edition adds a statement below the table in Section 9.7 on "Advantages and disadvantages of a compulsory management commentary" that the IASB is working to update and improve the Management Commentary.

Chapter 25 Assurance and related services

Page 1201 (old page 1489)

The 2020 edition deletes a short statement that in October 2013, the ICAEW issued technical guidance on ISRE 2400 (Revised).

Chapter 26 Environmental and social considerations

Page 1247 (old page 1541)

The final sentence on the page which starts "Guidance on the audit work required" is new for the 2020 edition.

Page 1252 (old page 1546)

The bracketed wording at the end of the first paragraph under Section 4.2 on "Environmental audits" is new for the 2020 edition.

At the end of Section 4.2, the bullet point list of steps which the auditor will carry out has been completely rewritten for the 2020 edition.

Page 1256 (old page 1550)

The length of Section 5.2 on “Due diligence and sustainability” is significantly shorter in the 2020 edition as only the single paragraph still contained in Section 5.2 has been retained from a section which was half a page in length in the 2019 edition.

Page 1263 (old page 1558)

The paragraph starting “Research carried out by ACCA” in Section 6.10 on “Concluding and reporting” has been added for the 2020 edition.

Chapter 27 Internal auditing

There do not appear to have been any changes made to this chapter.

Appendix 1b

Detailed review of changes in 2020 SBM Study Manual

This Appendix reviews the changes made in the 2020 edition of the Study Manual. References to "old page" are references to the related page in the 2019 edition of the Study Manual – in most cases, this reference relates to a very similar section in the 2019 edition but in cases where the 2020 edition has added completely new material, the reference to the "old page" indicates where within the relevant chapter the new 2020 content has been added. Similarly, in cases where the 2020 edition has deleted content, the reference to "new page" indicates where within the relevant chapter the 2020 edition would have contained the content if it had not been deleted from the equivalent place (indicated by our "old page" reference) in the 2019 edition.

Please note that we are providing these page numbers from the 2019 edition of the Study Manual for reference purposes only and primarily for the use of students who have already studied this paper using the 2019 syllabus – if you do not already have access to the 2019 edition of the Study Manual, we are in no way suggesting that you must purchase a 2019 edition to access the old content as this is not necessary and the references are being provided purely for the use of students who may already have access to the prior year edition. We have fully described all changes in the text below and you are not expected to use any prior year edition of the Study Manual to understand the points made in this Appendix.

There have been no changes in the number of chapters or the titles of the chapters.

Please note that our review below does not attempt to track all changes in the Self-test questions and Interactive questions between the 2019 and 2020 editions. As we do not think that any of these changes are particularly material to your studies, we have not listed these out separately in our analysis but any changes to the main technical text in connection with such changes have been noted in full in our review below.

Chapter 1 Strategic analysis

Page 7 (old page 6)

Section 1.4 on "Prescriptive vs emergent approaches to strategy" is shorter in the 2020 edition as specific discussion of the rational planning model developed by Ansoff and various points raised by Mintzberg have been deleted from the 2020 edition.

Page 38 (old page 38)

Section 5.3.3 on "Business ecosystems" is new for the 2020 edition.

Page 44 (old page 44)

The paragraph starting "Importantly, though, the Management Commentary is not audited" is new for the 2020 edition.

Page 53 (old page 52)

Section 7.3.1 on “Blockchain” has been deleted from the 2020 edition. Note, however, that the content from the 2019 edition has simply been moved into Section 7.6.1 on “Blockchain” on page 55 in the 2020 edition.

Page 54 (old page 55)

Section 7.6 on “Distributed ledger technology” is new for the 2020 edition. Note, however, that Section 7.6.1 on “Blockchain”, Section 7.6.2 on “Cryptocurrency” and Section 7.6.3 on “Accounting for cryptocurrencies” all retain unchanged content from equivalent sections in the 2019 edition. It is therefore only the 3 paragraphs at the start of Section 7.6 on page 54 which appear to be new for the 2020 edition.

Chapter 2 Strategic choice

Page 99 (old page 108)

The Definition of “Due diligence” and related set of bullet points at the top of the page have been inserted for the 2020 edition (note that identical content was previously contained on page 179 in the 2019 edition). An introductory statement which stated that there are several different forms of due diligence (some of which are carried out by accountants and financial consultants) which was contained in the 2019 edition has been deleted.

Page 133 (old page 142)

The text starting “The use of AI also raises some wider potential concerns” (including a set of related bullet points) towards the bottom of page 133 is new for the 2020 edition.

Page 134 (old page 142)

The text at the top of the page just before the “Chat bot” sub-section heading is new for the 2020 edition and continues the new content regarding Artificial Intelligence that starts towards the bottom of the previous page (see point above).

Page 137 (old page 146)

The sentence starting “Customers develop expectations about speed” in the first paragraph below the table is new for the 2020 edition.

Page 138 (old page 146)

The paragraph at the top of the page is new for the 2020 edition.

Section 6.5.1 on “From ‘products and services’ to ‘experiences’” is new for the 2020 edition.

Section 6.5.2 on “From ‘ownership’ to ‘access’” is new for the 2020 edition.

Page 139 (old page 146)

The final paragraph in Section 6.5.3 on "Platform-based business models" is new for the 2020 edition.

Page 139 (old page 147)

The 2020 edition contains a shorter definition of "cloud computing" from IBM, replacing a longer definition from the National Institute of Standards and Technology which was used in the 2019 edition.

Chapter 3 Strategic implementation

Page 178 (old page 198)

The paragraph starting "This does not, however, mean that implementing" is now longer in the 2020 edition as all content after the first sentence is new for the 2020 edition.

Chapter 4 Strategic performance management

Page 267 (old page 300)

The 2020 edition has deleted reference to a survey of budgeting practices in UK companies conducted by Lyne and Dugdale from the end of Section 1.4 on "Beyond Budgeting". The deleted content was only 2 short paragraphs in length.

Page 287 (old page 320)

The 2020 edition deletes a section entitled "Implementing the balanced scorecard" which was contained in the 2019 edition.

Page 311 (old page 344)

The paragraph headed up as "Decision making" is new for the 2020 edition.

Page 313 (old page 345)

The paragraph starting "'Natural capital valuation' prices these resources" is new for the 2020 edition.

Page 324 (old page 356)

The paragraph at the top of the page which starts "As PwC note in their report" is new for the 2020 edition.

Within Section 5.5.2 on "Sustainable Development Goals (SDG) Compass", the 2020 edition puts the phrase "by putting 'sustainability' at the centre of their strategies" in bold text: this same phrase was contained in non-bold text in the 2019 edition. Otherwise, the relevant paragraph is entirely unchanged in the 2020 edition.

Chapter 5 Strategic marketing and brand management

Page 347 (old page 390)

The 2020 edition deletes Section 1.3.2 on "Market sensing".

Page 374 (old page 417)

The paragraph starting "IFRS 15 refers to this as a contract" is a slightly revised and condensed version of 2 separate paragraphs that essentially made exactly the same points in the 2019 edition. This change does not therefore appear to represent any material technical change on IFRS 15 for the 2020 edition.

Page 377 (old page 420)

The 2020 edition deletes Section 4.1.2 on "The marketing mix and value to the customer" including a detailed table which used to be contained in the 2019 edition.

Chapter 6 Corporate governance

Page 446 (old page 502)

The 2020 edition adds the first Learning outcome on explaining the responsibility of those charged with governance in managing risk and assessing the role of assurance in risk mitigation.

Page 448 (old page 503)

The 2020 edition contains a longer definition of "Corporate Governance" which is taken from the OECD Principles document.

The 2020 edition adds a brief reference to the Wates Corporate Governance Principles at the bottom of the page.

Page 449 (old page 504)

The 2020 edition adds new content on Corporate Governance throughout page 449.

Page 451 (old page 505)

The 2020 edition rewrites Section 1.1 on "Principles of corporate governance" and changes the way in which the UK Corporate Governance Code 2018 is discussed.

Page 453 (old page 506)

The 2020 edition deletes the statement that companies with an AIM listing need to report on their application of a recognised corporate governance code "with effect from 28 September 2018". The remaining discussion in the relevant paragraphs is unchanged: it is only the specific reference to "28 September 2018" that has been deleted from the 2020 edition.

Page 455 (old page 508)

Section 1.5.2 on "Lack of independent scrutiny" is longer in the 2020 edition.

A reference to the Equitable Life scandal has been deleted from Section 1.5.3 in the 2020 edition.

Page 457 (old page 509)

The paragraph relating to the OECD under Section 2 on "Stakeholders" has been rewritten for the 2020 edition and now refers to the UK Corporate Governance Code. The following paragraph which starts "Stakeholders can be internal" is new for the 2020 edition.

Page 459 (old page 511)

Section 2.4.1 on "Workforce engagement" is new for the 2020 edition.

Page 462 (old page 514)

Section 2.9.2 on "Role of institutional investors" has been rewritten and condensed for the 2020 edition.

Page 463 (old page 515)

The Note in the middle of the page on an FRC consultation paper published in 2019 is new for the 2020 edition.

Page 465 (old page 517)

Section 3.1 on "Role of board" has been rewritten for the 2020 edition through the inclusion of more detail (including 3 bullet points) on the Principles of the UK Corporate Governance Code.

Page 467 (old page 518)

Section 3.3 on "Board effectiveness" has been rewritten for the 2020 edition and is now based on the *Guidance on Board Effectiveness* document which was published by the FRC in 2018, replacing reference to a similar FRC document published in 2011 and which was referred to in the 2019 edition.

Page 469 (old page 520)

Section 3.3.3 on "Diversity" is longer in the 2020 edition.

Page 473 (old page 523)

Section 3.5 on "Non-executive directors (NEDs)" has been rewritten for the 2020 edition.

Page 475 (old page 525)

The bracketed statement towards the top of the page that "although the chair of the board must not chair the committee if it is dealing with the appointment of their successor" is new for the 2020 edition.

Page 476 (old page 527)

The paragraph starting "The UK Corporate Governance Code highlights" towards the middle of the page is new for the 2020 edition.

Page 483 (old page 533)

The bracketed statement at the top of the page that "One of the board's key responsibilities is to measure a company's performance against its objectives" is new for the 2020 edition.

Page 484 (old page 535)

The bracketed statement in Section 4.1.1 on "Strategic perspective of corporate governance" that "For example, when setting remuneration, it is important to ensure that incentives and rewards are aligned with an organisation's culture" is new for the 2020 edition.

In the same section, the sentence starting "Importantly, however, these elements" is new for the 2020 edition and replaces a similar sentence ("This is a similar framework to that of Johnson and Scholes' cultural web, in that each element supports the others.") from the 2019 edition.

Page 498 (old page 550)

In the "Pay" row in the table at the bottom of the page, the 2020 edition refers to "regional locations" where living costs are lower than in London rather than specifically using the example location of "Aberystwyth" as in the 2019 edition. However, the underlying technical point is unchanged in the 2020 edition.

Page 500 (old page 552)

Section 5.1.12 on "Data protection" is new for the 2020 edition.

Chapter 7 Business risk management

Page 522 (old page 577)

The 2020 edition condenses the discussion in Section 1.9.1 on "The General Data Protection Regulations (GDPR)": in the 2020 edition the reader is referred to chapter 9 for a more detailed discussion of the GDPR.

Page 529 (old page 584)

Section 1.12.2 on "Risk assurance" is new for the 2020 edition.

The 2020 edition uses a different definition of "Enterprise risk management (ERM)" taken from a COSO document. The subsequent discussion in Section 2.1 on "Nature of enterprise risk management" has been significantly changed so that it now refers in detail to the COSO approach.

Page 530 (old page 585)

Section 2.2 on "COSO's ERM Framework" is new for the 2020 edition.

Page 532 (old page 585)

Section 2.3 on "Benefits of ERM" has been substantially rewritten to refer to the COSO approach in a different way to that used in the 2019 edition.

Page 533 (old page 586)

Section 2.4 on "Criticisms of ERM" has been deleted from the 2020 edition.

Page 534 (old page 587)

The first paragraph of Section 2.5 on "The Risk Guidance" has been slightly condensed in the 2020 edition as there is no longer any reference to the point that an FRC Risk Guidance document was published in September 2014. However, the relevant paragraph is otherwise unchanged in terms of content.

Page 535 (old page 585)

Section 2.5.3 on "Going concern: viability statement" now refers to the 2018 UK Corporate Governance Code rather than the 2014 version of the same Code. However, despite this reference to a different version of the Code, the text is almost entirely unchanged from the 2019 edition of the Study Manual.

Page 537 (old page 590)

The 2020 edition adds a statement that the UK Walker Report was published in 2009: the 2019 edition of the Study Manual referred to the same Report but did not state the year of publication. Otherwise, the discussion of the Walker Report is unchanged in the 2020 edition.

Page 547 (old page 601)

The 2020 edition removes reference to the COSO report *Enterprise Risk Management Framework* from Section 5.4.2 on "Event identification". However, other than this change, the text of Section 5.4.2 is unchanged in the 2020 edition.

Page 548 (old page 601)

The second paragraph of Section 5.4.3 on "Key risk indicators" has been rewritten for the 2020 edition as compared to similar content in the 2019 edition.

Chapter 8 Data analysis

There do not appear to have been any changes to this chapter.

Chapter 9 Information strategy

Page 624 (old page 700)

The 2020 edition adds the final Learning outcome to explain the impact of regulations relating to data security (such as GDPR) and including the issues incurred in complying with such regulation.

Page 630 (old page 705)

The phrase starting "by allowing customers to buy" at the end of the paragraph starting "The internet has also changed" is new for the 2020 edition.

Page 631 (old page 706)

The 2020 edition adds a statement right at the bottom of the page to alert readers to the fact that the concepts of digital disruption and digital transformation were introduced in chapter 2 of the Study Manual.

Page 676 (old page 751)

Section 3.6 on "Linking strategic and operational information" is significantly shorter in the 2020 edition. Discussion of the "performance pyramid" developed by Lynch and Cross has been deleted, meaning that a graphical presentation of the "performance pyramid" which was provided on page 752 in the 2019 edition has also been deleted. Similarly, a section on "Practical steps in developing a multi-dimensional performance management system" on page 752 in the 2019 edition has been deleted.

Page 693 (old page 770)

A short 2 paragraph discussion of the GDPR which used to be contained at the top of page 770 in the 2019 edition has been deleted from the 2020 edition. The relevant paragraphs explained that the GDPR was introduced in May 2018, that the GDPR requires appropriate security measures to be in place to protect personal data about customers, that security breaches must be reported within 72 hours and that organisations which do not comply with the regulations can be liable for fines of up to EUR20m or 4% of global turnover, whichever is higher.

Page 698 (old page 774)

The 2020 edition now refers to the 2018 ICAEW publication *Audit insights: cyber security* towards the top of the page and the bullet points which follow this reference on the remainder of the page amount to a substantial rewriting of equivalent content contained on page 775 in the 2019 edition.

Page 703 (old page 779)

Section 6.3 on "Security and data protection: GDPR" is new for the 2020 edition and includes almost 4 pages of discussion of various aspects of the GDPR.

Page 709 (old page 782)

Section 7.3 on "Learning organisations" has been dropped from the 2020 edition.

Chapter 10 Human resource management

Page 750 (old page 831)

Section 2.5.2 on "Automation" is new for the 2020 edition.

Page 763 (old page 844)

Section 3.3 on "Performance rating" has been deleted from the 2020 edition.

Page 797 (old page 879)

Section 5.4.2 on "Change roles" has been deleted from the 2020 edition.

Chapter 11 Finance awareness

Page 816 (old page 909)

Section 1.7 on "The finance function as a business partner" is new for the 2020 edition.

Page 824 (old page 917)

Section 1.11.4 on "Leasing" has been updated for IFRS 16 becoming the main examinable standard on leases, replacing IAS 17.

Page 828 (old page 920)

Section 3.2 on "Brexit" is significantly shorter in the 2020 edition as content in the 2019 edition regarding how much the UK will pay to leave the European Union and Section 3.2.1 on "The ICAEW response to Brexit" has been deleted from the 2020 edition.

Chapter 12 Business and securities valuation

There do not appear to have been any changes to this chapter.

Chapter 13 Financial instruments and financial markets

Page 963 (old page 1072)

Section 8.1 on "Leasing" is new for the 2020 edition to allow for the fact that IFRS 16 is now the main examinable standard on leases

Page 964 (old page 1074)

The 2020 edition deletes content on the attractions of operating leases specifically.

Page 991 (old page 1101)

The 2020 edition deletes Section 9.11.5 on "Accountancy and tax complications".

Page 997 (old page 1108)

The summary tables within Section 11.1.1 on "Summary of accounting treatments – financial assets and financial liabilities" have been significantly amended in the 2020 edition.

Page 1016 (old page 1126)

Section 11.7 on "Reporting on leasing arrangements" has been significantly amended for the 2020 edition to allow for the fact that IFRS 16 is now the main examinable standard on leases. As the new Section 11.7 is 12 pages in length, there are a significant number of amendments and new points made in the 2020 version of this section.

Chapter 14 Financial structure and financial reconstruction

There do not appear to have been any changes to this chapter.

Chapter 15 Financial risk management

Page 1166 (old page 1304)

The 2020 edition adds a statement to item (d) in Section 4.9.1 which states that the IAS 39 rules for hedging are still permitted.

The 2020 edition adds Section 4.9.3 on "Fair value designation for credit exposures" and then deletes a number of sections which provide detailed comparisons between IAS 39 and IFRS 9. However, both editions have the same Summary of key differences table on pages 1167 and 1307, respectively: there do not appear to have been any changes to this table.

Chapter 16 International financial management

There do not appear to have been any changes to this chapter.

Chapter 17 Investment appraisal

There do not appear to have been any changes to this chapter.

Chapter 18 Treasury and working capital management

There do not appear to have been any changes to this chapter.

Chapter 19 Ethics

Page 1293 (old page 1476)

The 2020 edition adds the Note which explains that whilst ICAEW intends to amend its Code of Ethics with effect from 1 January 2020 in order to respond to the 2018 revisions to the IESBA Code, the revised ICAEW Code will not be examinable in SBM until 2021.

Page 1314 (old page 1500)

Section 4.3 on "Ethics, data and artificial intelligence (AI)" is new for the 2020 edition.

Printed in Great Britain
by Amazon

47709869R00271